San Diego
day BY day

1st Edition

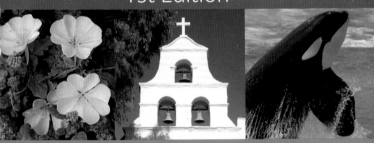

by Mark Hiss

WILEY

Wiley Publishing, Inc.

Contents

Published by:

Wiley Publishing, Inc.

111 River St.
Hoboken, NJ 07030-5774

ISBN: 978-0-470-20935-6
Editor: Maureen Clarke
Production Editor: Eric T. Schroeder
Photo Editor: Richard Fox
Cartographer: Andrew Dolan
Production by Wiley Indianapolis Composition Services

For information on our other products and services or to obtain technical
support, please contact our Customer Care Department within the U.S.
at 800/762-2974, outside the U.S. at 317/572-3993 or fax 317/572-4002.

Wiley also publishes its books in a variety of electronic formats. Some
content that appears in print may not be available in electronic formats.

Manufactured in China

5   4   3   2   1

A Note from the Publisher

Organizing your time. That's what this guide is all about.

Other guides give you long lists of things to see and do and then expect you to fit the pieces together. The Day by Day guides are different. These guides tell you the best of everything, and then they show you how to see it *in the smartest, most time-efficient way*. Our authors have designed detailed itineraries organized by time, neighborhood, or special interest. And each tour comes with a bulleted map that takes you from stop to stop.

Hoping to loll on a beach in San Diego's year-round perfect weather? Sample fish tacos or visit the giant pandas at one of the nation's finest zoos? How about strolling through Old Town, the cradle of modern California, or the Gaslamp Quarter, where San Diego's urban revival began? Whatever your interest or schedule, the Day by Days give you the smartest routes to follow. Not only do we take you to the top attractions, hotels, and restaurants, but we also help you access those special moments that locals get to experience—those "finds" that turn tourists into travelers.

The Day by Days are also your top choice if you're looking for one complete guide for all your travel needs. The best hotels and restaurants for every budget, the greatest shopping values, the wildest nightlife—it's all here.

Why should you trust our judgment? Because our authors personally visit each place they write about. They're an independent lot who say what they think and would never include places they wouldn't recommend to their friends. They're also open to suggestions from readers. If you'd like to contact them, please send your comments my way at mspring@wiley.com, and I'll pass them on.

Enjoy your Day by Day guide—the most helpful travel companion you can buy. And have the trip of a lifetime.

Warm regards,

Michael Spring, Publisher
Frommer's Travel Guides

About the Author

A third-generation Southern Californian, **Mark Hiss** is a writer and photographer who has lived in San Diego for more than 25 years. Founding editor of the visitor guide *Where San Diego* and *Performances,* he wrote *Frommer's San Diego 2008* and contributed to *Frommer's California 2008.*

An Additional Note

Please be advised that travel information is subject to change at any time—and this is especially true of prices. We therefore suggest that you write or call ahead for confirmation when making your travel plans. The authors, editors, and publisher cannot be held responsible for the experiences of readers while traveling. Your safety is important to us, however, so we encourage you to stay alert and be aware of your surroundings.

Star Ratings, Icons & Abbreviations

Every hotel, restaurant, and attraction listing in this guide has been ranked for quality, value, service, amenities, and special features using a **star-rating system.** Hotels, restaurants, attractions, shopping, and nightlife are rated on a scale of zero stars (recommended) to three stars (exceptional). In addition to the star-rating system, we also use a **kids icon** to point out the best bets for families. Within each tour, we recommend cafes, bars, or restaurants where you can take a break. Each of these stops appears in a shaded box marked with a coffee-cup-shaped bullet ☕.

The following **abbreviations** are used for credit cards:

AE	American Express	DISC	Discover	V	Visa
DC	Diners Club	MC	MasterCard		

Frommers.com

Now that you have this guidebook to help you plan a great trip, visit our website at **www.frommers.com** for additional travel information on more than 3,600 destinations. We update features regularly to give you instant access to the most current trip-planning information available. At Frommers. com, you'll find scoops on the best airfares, lodging rates, and car rental bargains. You can even book your travel online through our reliable travel booking partners. Other popular features include:

A Note on Prices

In the "Take a Break" and "Best Bets" sections of this book, we have used a system of dollar signs to show a range of costs for 1 night in a hotel (the price of a double-occupancy room) or the cost of an entree at a restaurant. Use the following table to decipher the dollar signs:

Cost	Hotels	Restaurants
$	under $100	under $10
$$	$100–$200	$10–$20
$$$	$200–$300	$20–$30
$$$$	$300–$400	$30–$40
$$$$$	over $400	over $40

An Invitation to the Reader

In researching this book, we discovered many wonderful places—hotels, restaurants, shops, and more. We're sure you'll find others. Please tell us about them, so we can share the information with your fellow travelers in upcoming editions. If you were disappointed with a recommendation, we'd love to know that, too. Please write to:

Frommer's San Diego Day by Day, 1st Edition
Wiley Publishing, Inc. • 111 River St. • Hoboken, NJ 07030-5774

18 Favorite **Moments**

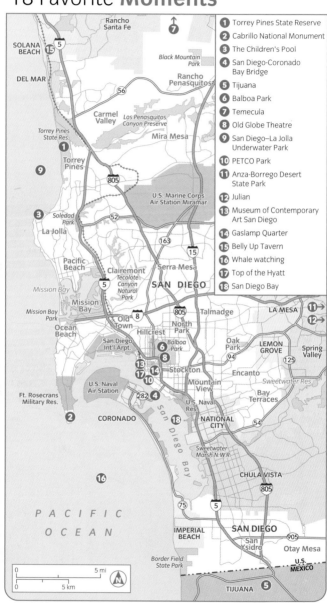

1 Torrey Pines State Reserve
2 Cabrillo National Monument
3 The Children's Pool
4 San Diego-Coronado Bay Bridge
5 Tijuana
6 Balboa Park
7 Temecula
8 Old Globe Theatre
9 San Diego–La Jolla Underwater Park
10 PETCO Park
11 Anza-Borrego Desert State Park
12 Julian
13 Museum of Contemporary Art San Diego
14 Gaslamp Quarter
15 Belly Up Tavern
16 Whale watching
17 Top of the Hyatt
18 San Diego Bay

A surfer in La Jolla.

If you think San Diego is just about wiggling your toes in the sand or cooing over panda bears, prepare yourself to be surprised by this seaside destination with big-city style and small-town heart. This place has it all. It's an embarrassment of riches, really, but they stack up undeniably—stunning natural beauty, high-octane nightlife, world-class cultural organizations, family-friendly attractions, and sophisticated dining. Oh, did I mention we have the country's best weather? We're also perched on the world's busiest international border—with the sights, sounds, and tastes of Mexico just a chihuahua's length away.

❶ Escaping to Torrey Pines State Reserve. Dramatically set atop 300-foot (91m) cliffs overlooking the Pacific, this reserve is home to the rarest pine tree in North America. Short trails crisscross the delicate landscape, which also encompasses one of San Diego's best beaches. *See p 87.*

❷ Taking in the city's best panorama. Cabrillo National Monument affords a whirlwind history tour, beginning with San Diego's European discovery in 1542, as well as unsurpassed 360-degree views of downtown and beyond. From its location at the tip of Point Loma—and at 422 feet (129m) above sea level—it's also a great vantage point from which to watch migrating Pacific gray whales in the winter. *See p 88.*

❸ Communing with seals and sea lions. The Children's Pool, a picturesque cove in La Jolla, was named for the toddlers who could safely frolic behind its protective, man-made seawall. A colony of

Torrey Pines State Reserve.

The lighthouse at Cabrillo National Monument.

pinnipeds came to like it equally, and now the beach is shared—sometimes a little uneasily—between humans and seals. *See p 60.*

4 **Zipping across the San Diego–Coronado Bay Bridge.** Roll down the windows, put the top down, and let the wind blow through your hair as you cruise along this graceful engineering marvel. It's always a bit of a rush, and the views are spectacular, so don't forget to keep your eyes on the road. *See p 66.*

5 **Making a run for the border.** What a difference a line makes. Once you cross it, you're instantly immersed in the chaotic vibrancy of Mexico's fourth-largest city. Just a 20-minute drive from downtown, Tijuana has a raucous tourist zone with plentiful shopping, as well as an array of cultural and culinary delights. *See p 155.*

6 **Spending an idyllic day in Balboa Park.** San Diego's crown jewel is one of the world's great urban cultural parks, home to more than a dozen of the city's top museums. There are dazzling gardens, glorious Spanish Golden Age buildings, and the world-famous San Diego Zoo as well. *See p 9.*

7 **Toasting the good life.** Just across the county line in Temecula, about 60 miles (97km) north of downtown San Diego, are some two-dozen wineries. They range

The Cabrillo National Monument.

Sea lions lolling on the beach at the Children's Pool in La Jolla.

from mom-and-pop operations with minimal amenities to slick commercial ventures with fancy tasting rooms, retail boutiques, and restaurants. Cheers! *See p 149.*

8 **Being a groundling.** You won't have to stand as they did in William Shakespeare's day, but you can see the Bard's works alfresco at the Old Globe Theatre's summer Shakespeare Festival. The Tony Award–winning Old Globe hosts performances of Shakespeare's work in repertory style, alternating three different productions at its open-air theater. *See p 22.*

9 **Paddling with the fishes.** The calm surfaces and clear waters of the San Diego–La Jolla Underwater Park are the ultimate local spot for a little kayaking. This ecological reserve features sea caves and vibrant marine life, including California's state fish, the electric-orange garibaldi. *See p 60.*

10 **Buying some peanuts and Cracker Jacks.** San Diego's Major League Baseball team, the Padres, plays at PETCO Park, a state-of-the-art ballpark that opened in 2004. Incorporating seven buildings that date as far back as 1909, PETCO's clever design and downtown location have made it a local favorite. *See p 129.*

11 **Witnessing the desert's spring fling.** For a period of several weeks—usually late February through March—Anza-Borrego Desert State Park magically comes alive with a carpet of blooming wildflowers. A brilliant palette of pink, lavender, red, orange, and yellow transforms the rugged landscape into a colorful oasis. *See p 98.*

12 **Getting in touch with your pioneer spirit.** The mountain hamlet of Julian was founded as a gold-mining town in the 1860s, but it gained fame as a mother lode for apples as well. Today, this rustic community has a distinctly Victorian, Old West charm, redolent of hot apple pies. *See p 150.*

13 **Challenging your perception.** The city's newest cultural icon is the downtown expansion of the Museum of Contemporary Art San Diego, which has grafted gorgeous

Balboa Park.

The Bitter End in the Gaslamp Quarter.

exquisitely restored Victorian commercial buildings in this 16½-block district. See p 11.

⑮ Rocking out in a Quonset hut. Since the mid-1970s, the Belly Up Tavern has been San Diego's best live-music venue. Ensconced in a World War II–era Quonset hut in a now-chic neighborhood, the BUT has a classic beach-bar vibe, great sound, and zero attitude. It presents international artists of all genres. See p 120.

⑯ Scouting for whales. Every year, from December through March, Pacific gray whales pass through San Diego waters, making their way to and from breeding lagoons in Mexico. There are ample opportunities to observe these gentle giants from both land and sea as they undertake one of the longest migrations of any mammal. See p 32.

⑰ Watching for the green flash. There's no better place to watch for the storied "green flash"—which occurs when the sun sinks beneath the horizon—than the Top of the Hyatt. This luxe lounge is located 40 stories above the Embarcadero in the West Coast's tallest waterfront building. See p 119.

galleries onto the historic Santa Fe Depot. There are permanent, commissioned works by blue-chip artists such as Richard Serra, as well as ongoing exhibitions of cutting-edge work. See p 57.

⑭ Strolling the Gaslamp Quarter. For dining, shopping, dancing, drinking, or just wandering around without a set plan, this is the place to be. People-watching opportunities are rampant here—if you can manage to take your eyes off the

⑱ Cruising the bay. Whether you take a weekend-brunch sightseeing tour, a chartered sailboat excursion, or a water-taxi ride to Coronado, don't miss an opportunity to spend some time on San Diego Bay. Spanish conquistador Sebastián Vizcaíno described it in 1602 as "a port which must be the best to be found in all the South Sea." Discover it for yourself. See the Embarcadero Neighborhood tour on p 54. ●

The Best **in One Day**

1 Old Town State Historic Park
2 Balboa Park
3 The Prado
4 Gaslamp Quarter
5 Altitude Skybar

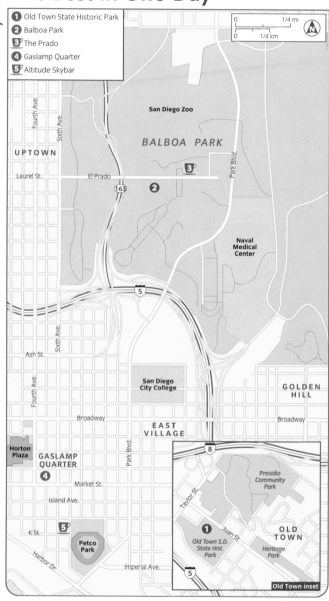

A peacock at the San Diego Zoo.

If you have only 24 hours in San Diego, you may be tempted to blow the whole day on the beach or at the zoo. While it's hard to challenge that approach, it would deprive you of experiencing San Diego's robust and unusual heritage as the birthplace of California, with deep ties to Spain, Mexico, Wild West history, and the U.S. military. Besides, you'll still get plenty of sun as you tour through Old Town, and you just might hear the animals squawk and roar from the zoo as you explore Balboa Park next door. START: **Blue or Green Line trolley to Old Town Transit Center.**

❶ ★ Old Town State Historic Park. Dedicated to re-creating the early life of the city from 1821 to 1872, this is where San Diego's Mexican heritage is best celebrated. It's California's most-visited state park, featuring 20 structures (some original, some re-constructed), including the home of a wealthy family, circa 1872, and the fledgling town's one-room schoolhouse. Memorabilia and exhibits are on view in some buildings; visitor-oriented shops and restaurants are incorporated into the rest. On Wednesdays, from 10am to 1pm, costumed park volunteers reenact life in the 1800s with cooking and crafts demonstrations, a

working blacksmith, and parlor singing. Free 1-hour walking tours leave daily at 11am and 2pm from the Robinson-Rose House. ⏱ *90 min. The park is bordered by Juan, Congress, Twiggs, and Wallace sts.* ☎ *619/220-5422. www.parks.ca. gov. Free admission. Museums daily 10am–5pm, most restaurants till 9pm. Trolley: Blue or Green Line to Old Town.*

❷ ★★★ kids Balboa Park. Like New York's Central Park and San Francisco's Golden Gate, Balboa Park is the emerald in San Diego's crown. This 1,174-acre (475 hectare) city-owned playground is the largest

A synagogue in Old Town's Heritage Park.

Balboa Park.

urban cultural park in the nation. The park's most distinctive features are its mature landscaping, the architectural beauty of the Spanish Golden Age–style buildings lining the pedestrian thoroughfare (byproducts of expositions in 1915 and 1935), and its 15 engaging and diverse museums. You'll also find eight different gardens, walkways, 4½ miles (7km) of hiking trails in Florida Canyon, an ornate pavilion with the world's largest outdoor organ, an old-fashioned carousel, an

Flamingos at the San Diego Zoo.

IMAX domed theater, the acclaimed Old Globe Theatre, and the San Diego Zoo. ⏱ *3 hr. (or more, depending on which museums pique your interest). Primary entrances are at Sixth Ave. and Laurel St. on the west side and Park Blvd. and Presidents Way on the east side.* ☎ *619/239-0512. www.balboapark.org. Museum prices vary, but several are free every Tues; free organ concerts are presented every Sun at 2pm and Mon–Thurs at 7:30pm in summer; free as well as paid, self-guided tours are available from the Visitor Center, open daily 9:30am–4:30pm (extended hours in summer). Attraction hours vary, but many are 10am–5pm. Bus: 7, 7A/B, 1, 3, and 120; a free tram operates within the park, daily 8:30am–6pm (extended hours in summer).*

3⃝ The Prado. For lunch, dinner, or drinks and appetizers, Balboa Park's sophisticated-but-casual Prado restaurant is a great place to catch your breath. This sprawling restaurant complex in the baroque House of Hospitality has lovely patio dining, a lounge with live entertainment, and special event spaces where wine tastings and cooking classes are held. *1549 El Prado.* ☎ *619/557-9441. www.cohnrestaurants.com. $$.*

④ ★★ Gaslamp Quarter.

Where others had seen only dismal mudflats melting into a shallow bay, businessman Alonzo Horton saw untapped potential. In 1867 he undertook an audacious plan to lure citizens away from Old Town with the founding of "New Town," several miles to the south. New Town is now known as the Gaslamp Quarter, and it has become more successful than anything Alonzo could have hoped for. It's comprised of 16½ blocks of restored historic buildings housing dozens of restaurants, bars, clubs, and boutiques—this is where you'll find San Diego's most vigorous nightlife, fabulous Victorian architecture, and excellent people-watching. You can begin your tour of the area at Horton Plaza shopping center, where you can not only shop and dine, but also catch a play or a movie. ⏱ *90 minutes (not including dining or entertainment options). The district is bounded by Broadway on the north, L St. and the waterfront to the south, Fourth Ave. to the west, and Sixth Ave. to the east. Gaslamp Quarter Association* ☎ *619/233-5227. www.gaslamp.org. Mall stores tend to stay open till 9pm,* *6pm on weekends; smaller stores are open till 5 or 6pm. Restaurants serve till 10pm, with longer hours on weekends. Bars and clubs are open till 2am. Crowds are thick Thurs–Sat and whenever there's a large convention in town or a baseball game at PETCO Park. Parking structures are available at Horton Plaza, Market St. and Sixth Ave., and Sixth Ave. and K St. Trolley: Orange Line. Bus: Any downtown route.*

⑤ Altitude Skybar.

Finish off your day by rising above it all for a nightcap at this open-air bar 22 floors above the Gaslamp commotion. This long, narrow space is located in the Gaslamp Quarter Marriott and looks down on PETCO Park and the Convention Center. It offers fire pits, lounges, and DJ-spun grooves, as well as appetizers from the first-floor restaurant. As with many Gaslamp Quarter venues, lines begin forming around 10pm on weekends (or when the Padres are playing). *660 K St. (between Sixth and Seventh aves.).* ☎ *619/696-0234. www.atltitudeskybar.com. Daily 5pm–1:30am. $–$$.*

The scene on the roof at Altitude Skybar.

The Best **in Two Days**

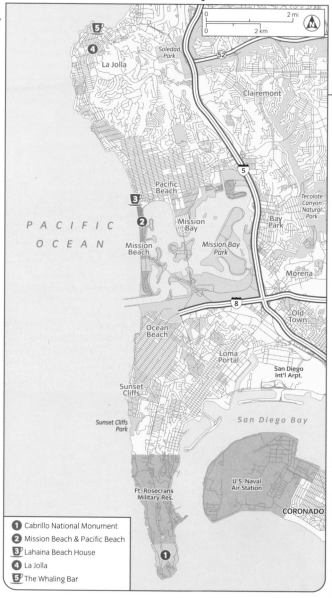

1 Cabrillo National Monument
2 Mission Beach & Pacific Beach
3 Lahaina Beach House
4 La Jolla
5 The Whaling Bar

You don't have to venture far for stunning natural settings in San Diego, which means it's easy to season your nature romps with a little history, great food, and even some shopping. This itinerary showcases the extremes of SoCal coastal living, from rollicking Pacific Beach to refined La Jolla. You'll really need your sunscreen today, though. A car is in order too. While it is possible to tackle this itinerary via public transportation, it's much more practical to have your own set of wheels. START: **Bus route 28C to Cabrillo National Monument.**

① ★★★ kids Cabrillo National Monument. Breathtaking views mingle with the early history of San Diego—specifically the arrival of Juan Rodríguez Cabrillo in 1542. His statue is prominently featured here, along with a historic lighthouse built in 1855, a small museum, the remnants of World War II artillery batteries, a visitor center with lots of books and souvenirs for sale, and a theater screening short videos about local natural history and the age of exploration. The park's setting, 422 feet (129m) above sea level at the tip of Point Loma, makes it a great vantage point for watching migrating Pacific gray whales December through March. National Park Service rangers also lead walks at the monument, and there are tide pools to explore at the base of the peninsula. The Bayside Trail is an easy hike (3.2-miles/5km round-trip) along an interpreted walkway that leads to a lookout over the bay. ⏱ *2 hr. There are great picnicking spots here, but no food facilities, so pack a lunch. 1800 Cabrillo Memorial Dr.* ☎ *619/557-5450. www.nps.gov/cabr. Admission $5 per vehicle, $3 for walk-ins. Daily 9am–5pm. Bus: Route 28C from Old Town Transit Center.*

② Mission Beach and Pacific Beach. This is it. Ground zero for the party hearty, freewheeling Southern California beach life. These two beaches form a 3-mile (5km) stretch of sand paralleled by a cement boardwalk that hosts a nonstop parade of surfers, skaters, bikers, joggers, and plain old beach lovers. South Mission Beach is where you'll find serious beach volleyball and a seaside basketball court. Farther north is Belmont Park, an amusement park whose star attraction is a 1925 wooden roller coaster. Another 1925 holdover is Crystal Pier at the foot of Garnet Ave. in Pacific Beach (or PB as it's known). This 400-foot- (122m-)

Cabrillo National Monument.

The boardwalk at Mission Beach.

Lahaina Beach House. This old beach bungalow transformed into a simple, unpretentious, utterly rocking eatery and bar, has been a PB institution for a generation. Its weathered wooden deck, just inches from the boardwalk, is standing-room-only on sunny weekends, and provides a sensory overload of sights and sounds. The food is basic—omelets, burgers, fish tacos; the atmosphere is pure beach party. Cash only. *710 Oliver Ave. (along the boardwalk between Reed Ave. and Pacific Beach Dr.).* ☎ *858/270-3888. 8am–9pm. $.*

long wooden pier now supports rental cottages, but is open daily to the public, offering great views of the local surfers. The streetside action in these beach zones takes place primarily on Mission Blvd. (heading north from Belmont Park) and Garnet Ave. (running east from Mission Blvd.), which are both overflowing with restaurants, clubs, and retailers. Rent a bike and join the parade. 🕐 *3 hr. (or more, depending on how much frolicking in the surf you want to do). Discover Pacific Beach:* ☎ *858/273-3303. www. pacificbeach.org. Bus: Route 8 from Old Town Transit Center.*

A surfer on Pacific Beach.

❹ ★★★ **La Jolla.** About the only thing La Jolla shares in common with the beach communities to the south is the Pacific Ocean. Locals refer to La Jolla's principal shopping and dining district as "the village," and it's one of the classiest villages you could imagine. High-end boutiques, antique stores, art galleries, and fine restaurants line the streets; while just steps away, a dramatic coastline of sandstone cliffs and picturesque coves with tropical-blue waters awaits. And this beauty has brains, too—La Jolla is a center for local arts and culture, providing a

Seaside inspiration in La Jolla.

home for the University of California, San Diego (where you'll find the Tony Award–winning La Jolla Playhouse and the Stuart Collection of site-specific art); the flagship space for the Museum of Contemporary Art San Diego; and the Athenaeum Music and Arts Library, which presents concerts and art exhibits. La Jolla is a Southern California Riviera. ⏱ *3 hr. (or more if you want to enjoy an exhibit or show). www.lajolla bythesea.com. ☎ 858/454-5718. Bus: Route 30 from Mission Blvd. and Grand Ave. in PB.*

⑤ ★ **The Whaling Bar.** La Valencia Hotel is the grande dame of La Jolla. The Pink Lady originally opened in 1926, and its Mediterranean style and killer location made it a favorite of Hollywood Golden Age celebs like Greta Garbo and Charlie Chaplin. The hotel's clubby watering hole, The Whaling Bar, became something of a West Coast Algonquin for literary types, as well as a popular spot for a second generation of movie stars

brought in by La Jolla native Gregory Peck, who also co-founded the La Jolla Playhouse. Stop in for a drink and listen closely—you just might hear those walls talking. *1132 Prospect St. (at Herschel Ave.). ☎ 800/451-0772 or 858/454-0772. www.lavalencia.com. 11:30am–10pm. $–$$.*

A kite runner on Pacific Beach.

The Best **in Three Days**

1. San Diego Zoo
2. Extraordinary Desserts
3. Embarcadero
4. Hotel del Coronado

MIDDLETOWN

UPTOWN

163

1
San Diego Zoo

Reynard Way

Kettner Blvd.

Laurel St.

El Prado

San Diego International Airport

BALBOA PARK

5

First Ave.

LITTLE ITALY

Sixth Ave.

2 Ash St.

San Diego City College

N Harbor Dr.

Pacific Hwy.

Kettner Blvd.

State St.

Fourth Ave.

Sixth Ave.

Park Blvd.

Broadway

3

EAST VILLAGE

Horton Plaza

GASLAMP QUARTER

Market St.

Orange Ave.

Harbor Dr.

CORONADO

Embarcadero Marina Park

Star Park

SAN DIEGO BAY

Orange Ave.

4

0   1/4 mi
0   1/4 km

N

Coronado inset

Now that you have an overview of the city—from its Spanish colonial and Mexican-American frontier roots to its super-charged nightlife and lively, lovely beach communities—it's time to go where the wild things are. Put on a pair of comfortable shoes and head out to San Diego's best-known attraction, the San Diego Zoo. Then cap your day with a visit to the area's most iconic structure: the Hotel Del Coronado. START: **Bus 7 or 7A/B to the San Diego Zoo.**

① ★★★ kids San Diego Zoo. "World famous" often precedes any mention of the San Diego Zoo, and for good reason. Established in 1916, the zoo was a pioneer in developing naturalistic, humane enclosures. It's also a global leader in endangered species preservation with its breeding programs. Highlights include **giant pandas** (this is one of only four zoos in the country with pandas in residence); **Monkey Trails and Forest Tales,** the zoo's largest, most elaborate habitat, re-creating a wooded forest filled with a variety of rare creatures; and **Gorilla Tropics,** housing two troops of lowland gorillas. Also notable are **Ituri Forest,** which simulates an African rainforest (complete with hippos viewed from underwater via a wall of glass), and the ever-popular **Children's Zoo,** featuring lots of pettable animals. ⏱ *At least 4 hr. 2920 Zoo Dr.* ☎ *619/234-3153 (recorded info), or 619/231-1515. www.sandiegozoo.org. Admission $23 adults, $16 children 3–11, free for military in uniform; "Best Value" package (admission, 35-min. guided bus tour, round-trip Skyfari aerial tram) $33 adults, $29 seniors, $22 children. Sept–mid-June daily 9am–4pm (grounds close at 5 or 6pm); mid-June–Aug daily 9am–8pm (grounds close at 9pm). Bus: 7 or 7A/B.*

Elephants at the San Diego Zoo.

2 ★★★ Extraordinary Desserts. You've earned this one. After all the walking you've done, even the most demanding diet plan will surely allow for a sinful creation from this local standout. Set in an architecturally striking space, Extraordinary Desserts also serves panini, salads, and artisan cheeses, as well as wine and beer. Chef/proprietor Karen Krasne sells her own line of jams, confections, and syrups, too, so you can take a taste of San Diego home. *Bus 7 or 7A/B to Broadway and Union St., walk 4 blocks north to 1430 Union St.* ☎ *619/294-7001. www.extraordinarydesserts. com. Mon–Thurs 8:30am–11pm; Fri 8:30am–midnight; Sat 10am–midnight; Sun 10am–11pm. $–$$.*

3 Embarcadero. Take a leisurely stroll down San Diego's waterfront, where the sights include the flotilla of historic vessels that make up the San Diego Maritime Museum. Most impressive is the **Star of India,** which originally put to sea in 1863, making it the world's oldest active ship. Continue to the Broadway Pier where you can catch the ferry to Coronado. ⏱ *20 min. Broadway Pier, 1050 N. Harbor Dr., at the intersection of Broadway.* ☎ *619/234-4111. Ferries run Sun–Thurs on the hour 9am–9pm; Fri–Sat until 10pm. They return from the Ferry Landing in Coronado to the Broadway Pier Sun–Thurs every hour on the half-hour 9:30am–9:30pm; Fri–Sat until 10:30pm. The ride takes 15 minutes. The fare is $3 each way. Buy tickets at the Harbor Excursion kiosk on Broadway Pier or at the Ferry Landing in Coronado.*

4 ★★★ Hotel Del Coronado. This is the last of California's stately old seaside hotels. In continuous operation since 1888, the Del is a monument to Victorian grandeur, with cupolas, turrets, and gingerbread trim, making it San Diego's most recognizable property. There is plenty here to engage a non-guest, including a gallery devoted to the hotel's history, a shopping arcade, and several wonderful options for drinks or dining. The hotel sits on one of San Diego's best beaches. ⏱ *1 hr. 1500 Orange Ave.* ☎ *800/468-3533 or 619/435-6611. www.hoteldel.com. Bus: 904 from the Ferry Landing.* ●

The Midway in the Embarcadero.

Balboa Park

1 Cabrillo Bridge
2 San Diego Museum of Man
3 Old Globe Theatre
4 Alcazar Garden
5 Mingei International Museum
6 San Diego Museum of Art
7 Timken Museum of Art
8 Visitors Center
9 Palm Canyon
10² Japanese Friendship Garden Tea Pavilion
11 Spreckels Organ Pavilion
12 House of Pacific Relations International Cottages
13 San Diego Automotive Museum
14 San Diego Air & Space Museum
15 San Diego Hall of Champions Sports Museum
16 Botanical Building & Lily Pond
17 Museum of Photographic Arts
18 San Diego Model Railroad Museum
19 Reuben H. Fleet Science Center
20 San Diego Natural History Museum
21 Spanish Village Art Center
22 San Diego Miniature Railroad & Carousel
23 Gardens

Mission Basilica San Diego de Alcalá.

Established in 1868, Balboa Park is the second oldest city park in the United States. Much of its striking architecture, which now houses a variety of museums, was the product of the 1915–16 Panama-California Exposition and the 1935–36 California Pacific International Exposition. What makes Balboa Park unique is its extensive and mature botanical collection, owing largely to the efforts of Kate Sessions, a horticulturist who devoted her life to transforming the desolate mesas and scrub-filled canyons into the oases they are today (*see p 9, bullet* ❷). *Note:* The park encompasses 15 museums, so try to start with the 2 or 3 that most appeal to you. START: **Bus 1, 3, 7, 7A/B, or 120 to Balboa Park.**

❶ ★ **Cabrillo Bridge.** Offering excellent views of downtown, the bridge straddles scenic, sycamore-lined Highway 163 and provides a dramatic entrance to the park. Built in 1915 for the Panama-California Exposition, it's patterned after a bridge in Ronda, Spain. Directly ahead are the distinctive California Tower of the Museum of Man and the park's main thoroughfare, El Prado. *This is the west-side entrance to the park; Laurel St. leads directly to the bridge.*

❷ ★ kids **San Diego Museum of Man.** This anthropological museum has an emphasis on the peoples of North and South America; there are also Egyptian mummies and relics, and a museum store with great folk art. The exterior doubled as part of Kane's mansion in the 1941 Orson Welles classic *Citizen Kane;* historical figures carved on the facade include conquistador Juan Rodríguez Cabrillo, Spanish Kings Charles I and Phillip III, and, at

Inside the Museum of Man.

The Alcazar Garden.

The Old Globe Theatre.

the very top, Father Junipero Serra. ⏱ *1 hr.* ☎ *619/239-2001. www. museumofman.org. Admission $8 adults, $6 seniors, $4 children 6–17, free for children under 6. Free 3rd Tues of the month. Daily 10am–4:30pm.*

③ ★★★ Old Globe Theatre.

This is actually a three-theater complex that includes the Old Globe, an outdoor stage, and a small theater-in-the-round. The Old Globe was built for the 1935 exposition as a replica of Shakespeare's Globe Theatre. It was meant to be demolished after the fair but was saved by a group of dedicated citizens. In 1978, an arsonist destroyed the theater, which was rebuilt into what you see today. *Backstage tours are offered select weekends at 10:30am and cost $5 for adults, $2 for students, seniors, and military. Performances are Tues–Sun, with weekend matinees. The box office is open Mon (and other nonperformance days) noon–6pm, Tues–Sun noon–8pm.* ☎ *619/234-5623. www.theoldglobe. org. Tickets $19–$65.*

④ ★ Alcazar Garden. This for-

mal garden is patterned after the ones surrounding the Alcazar Castle in Sevilla, Spain. The large tree at the rear is an Indian laurel fig, planted by Kate Sessions when the park was first landscaped.

⑤ ★★ Mingei International

Museum. The Mingei offers

changing exhibitions that celebrate human creativity expressed in textiles, costumes, jewelry, toys, pottery, paintings, and sculpture. The gift shop alone is worth a visit. ⏱ *30 min.–1 hr.* ☎ *619/239-0003. www. mingei.org. Admission $6 adults, $3 children 6–17 and students with ID, free for children under 6. Free 3rd Tues of each month. Tues–Sun 10am–4pm.*

⑥ ★ San Diego Museum of

Art. The exquisite facade was inspired by the famous university building in Salamanca, Spain. The three life-size figures over the scalloped entryway are the Spanish

The Mingei Museum.

painters Bartolomé Murillo, Francisco de Zurbarán, and Diego Velázquez. The museum holds San Diego's most extensive collection of fine art; major touring exhibitions are presented, as well. There's also an ongoing schedule of concerts, films, and lectures, usually themed with a current show. ⏱ *At least 1 hr.* ☎ *619/232-7931. www.sdmart.org. Admission $10 adults, $8 seniors and military, $7 college students, $4 children 6–17, free for children under 6. Admission to traveling exhibits varies. Free 3rd Tues of each month. The lovely Sculpture Garden is always free. Tues–Sun 10am–6pm (Thurs until 9pm).*

The San Diego Museum of Art.

❼ ★ Timken Museum of Art. This small, always-free museum houses a collection of 19th-century American paintings and works by European old masters, as well as a worthy display of Russian icons and San Diego's only Rembrandt painting. ⏱ *30 min.* ☎ *619/239-5548. www.timkenmuseum.org. Free admission. Tues–Sat 10am–4:30pm; Sun 1:30–4:30pm. Closed Sept.*

❽ Visitors Center. Pick up maps, souvenirs, and discount tickets to the museums; guided and self-guided tours begin here, too. In the courtyard behind the Visitors Center, you'll find the beautiful *Woman of Tehuantepec* fountain sculpture by Donal Hord, as well as the Prado restaurant, *see p 10, bullet* ❸.

❾ ★★ Palm Canyon. Fifty species of palm, plus magnolia trees and a Moreton Bay fig tree, provide a tropical canopy along this short, dead-end walkway. It's secluded, so exercise caution if walking here alone.

🔟 ★ Japanese Friendship Garden Tea Pavilion. This tranquil spot serves fresh sushi, noodle soups, and Asian salads—it also carries quirky

imported Japanese candies and beverages in addition to some familiar American snacks. The teahouse overlooks an 11½-acre (5-hectare) canyon that has been carefully developed to include traditional Japanese elements, including a small meditation garden. ☎ *619/ 231-0048. www.cohnrestaurants. com. Tea Pavilion admission is free; admission to the garden is $3 adults, $2.50 seniors, $2 students and military, free for children 6 and under. Free 3rd Tues of each month. Tues–Sun 10am–4pm (also on Mon 10am–4pm in summer).* ☎ *619/232-2721. www.niwa.org.*

A work from the Timken Museum of Art.

Palm Canyon.

⑪ ★ **Spreckels Organ Pavilion.** Donated to San Diego by brothers John D. and Adolph B. Spreckels, famed contralto Ernestine Schumann-Heink sang at the December 31, 1914, dedication. Free recitals featuring the largest outdoor organ in the world (its vast structure contains 4,518 pipes) are given Sundays at 2pm, with additional concerts and events scheduled during summertime.

⑫ **House of Pacific Relations International Cottages.** This cluster of 17 cottages disseminates information about the culture, traditions, and history of more than 30 countries. Special events are presented by one of the nations every Sunday, 2 to 3pm, March through October. ☎ *619/234-0739. Free admission. Sun noon–4pm; 4th Tues of each month 11am–3pm. The adjacent United Nations Building houses an international gift shop where you can buy jewelry, toys, books, and UNICEF greeting cards.* ☎ *619/233-5044. Daily 10am–4:30pm.*

⑬ ★ **San Diego Automotive Museum.** Whether you're a gearhead into muscle cars or someone who appreciates the sculptural beauty of fine design, this museum has something for everyone. It features a changing roster of exhibits, as well as a permanent collection of fabulous wheels. ⏱ *30–45 minutes.* ☎ *619/231-2886. www.sdautomuseum.org. Admission $8 adults, $6 seniors and active military, $5 students, $4 children 6–15, free for children under 6. Free 4th Tues of each month. Daily 10am–5pm (last admission 4:30pm).*

⑭ ★★ **kids** **San Diego Air & Space Museum.** This kid-pleaser has more than 60 aircraft on display, providing an overview of aeronautical history, from the days of hot-air

The Spreckels Organ Museum.

The Air & Space Museum.

balloons to the space age. Highlights include the *Apollo 9* Command Module and the new Planetary Theater, which allows visitors to take an interactive journey through the galaxy. ⏱ *1 hr.* ☎ *619/234-8291. www.sandiegoairandspace.org. Admission $10 adults, $8 seniors, $5 juniors 6–17, free for active military with ID and children under 6. Free 4th Tues of each month. Sept–May daily 10am–4pm; June–Aug daily 10am–5pm.*

⑮ San Diego Hall of Champions Sports Museum.
From baseball great Ted Williams to skateboard icon Tony Hawk, this slick museum celebrates San Diego's best-ever athletes and the sports they played. There are more than 25 exhibits, rotating art shows, and interactive stations where you can try out your play-by-play skills. ⏱ *1 hr.* ☎ *619/234-2544. www.sdhoc.com. Admission $8 adults, $6 seniors 65 and older, students and military, $4 children 7–17, free for children under 7. Free 4th Tues of each month. Daily 10am–4:30pm.*

⑯ ★ Botanical Building and Lily Pond.
This serene park within the park is a great retreat on a hot day. Ferns, orchids, impatiens, begonias, and other plants—about 2,100 tropical and flowering varieties, plus rotating exhibits—are sheltered beneath a domed lath house. The graceful 250-foot- (76m-) long building, part of the 1915 Panama-California Exposition, is one of the world's largest wood lath structures. The lily pond out front attracts sun worshippers, painters, and buskers. ⏱ *15 min.* ☎ *619/235-1100. Free admission. Fri–Wed 10am–4pm; closed Thurs and major holidays.*

⑰ ★★ Museum of Photographic Arts.
This is one of the few museums in the United States devoted exclusively to the photographic arts, encompassing not only traditional photography, but also cinema, video, and digital photography. There's also a plush cinema that screens classic films on an ongoing basis and a great bookstore. ⏱ *30 min–1 hr.* ☎ *619/238-7559. www.mopa.org. Admission $6 adults, $4 seniors, students and military, free for children under 12 with*

The lily pond at the Botanical Museum.

adult. Free 2nd Tues of each month. Tues–Sun 10am–5pm (Thurs until 9pm).

18 ★ kids **San Diego Model Railroad Museum.** Kids and train buffs will love the six scale-model railroads depicting Southern California's transportation history and terrain with an astounding attention to miniature details. 🕐 *30 min. Located in the Casa de Balboa, below the Museum of Photographic Arts.* ☎ *619/696-0199. www.sdmrm. com. Admission $6 adults, $5 seniors, $3 student, $2.50 military; free for children under 15. Free 1st Tues of each month. Tues–Fri 11am–4pm; Sat–Sun 11am–5pm.*

19 ★★ kids **Reuben H. Fleet Science Center.** A must-see for kids of any age, this tantalizing collection of interactive exhibits and rides is designed to stimulate the imagination and teach scientific principles. There is also an IMAX theater, which is used for planetarium shows the first Wednesday of each month at 7pm. 🕐 *At least 1 hr.* ☎ *619/238-1233. www.rhfleet.org. Fleet Experience admission includes an IMAX film and exhibit galleries: $12 adults, $10 seniors and children*

The Museum of Natural History.

The Spanish Village Art Center.

3–12 (exhibit gallery can be purchased individually); planetarium show: $8.50 adults, $7 seniors and kids 3–12. Free 1st Tues of each month (exhibit galleries only). Hours vary but always daily 9:30am–5pm; later closing times possible.

20 kids **San Diego Natural History Museum.** Founded in 1874, SDNHM is the oldest scientific institution in Southern California and focuses on the flora, fauna, and mineralogy of the region, including Mexico. The museum also presents special exhibitions, leads free nature hikes, and has a full schedule of classes, lectures, and overnight expeditions for both families and adults. 🕐 *At least 1 hr.* ☎ *619/232-3821. www.sdnhm.org. Admission $11 adults, $9 seniors, $7 students, youth age 13–17 and active-duty military, $6 children 3–12, free for children under 3. Two films in the museum's giant-screen theater are included with admission. Free 1st Tues of each month. Daily 10am–5pm.*

21 ★ **Spanish Village Art Center.** Nearly 40 artists are at work here, creating jewelry, paintings, and sculptures in tile-roofed studios

Passport to Balboa Park

If you plan to visit more than three of the park's museums, buy the Passport to Balboa Park—it allows entrance to 13 major museums (the rest are always free) and is valid for 1 week. It's $35 for adults, $19 for children 3 to 12. If you plan to spend a day at the zoo and return for the museums another day, buy the Deluxe Passport, which provides one ticket to the zoo (including guided bus tour and Skyfari aerial tram ride) and 7 days' admission to the 13 museums for $59 adults, $33 children. The passports can be purchased at any participating museum, at the visitor center, or online at www.balboapark.org.

around a charming courtyard. There are restrooms here, too. 🕐 *30 min.* ☎ *619/233-9050. www.spanish villageart.com. Daily 11am–4pm.*

㉒ kids San Diego Miniature Railroad and Carousel. The open-air railroad takes a 3-minute journey through a grove of eucalyptus trees, while the carousel, built in 1910, is one of the last to still offer a ring grab. *Zoo Dr., next to San Diego Zoo entrance. Railroad* ☎ *619/231-1515, ext. 4219; daily in summer 11am–6:30pm; 11am–4:30pm weekends and holidays only Sept–May. Carousel* ☎ *619/460-9000; in summer Mon–Sat 11am–5:30pm, Sun 11am–6pm; 11am–4:30pm weekends*

and holidays only Sept–May. www. balboapark.org. Admission $2 Railroad, $1.75 Carousel, free for children under 1.

㉓ ★★ Gardens. Cross Park Blvd. via a pedestrian overpass and you'll find, to your left, a **Desert Garden** for cacti and other plants at home in an arid landscape; and to your right, the **Inez Grant Parker Memorial Rose Gardens,** home to 2,400 roses. The World Rose Society voted the latter as one of the top 16 rose gardens in the world—blooms peak March through May (but there are almost always some flowers visible, except in January and February when they are pruned). 🕐 *20 min.*

Balboa Park's Desert Garden.

San Diego **with Kids**

1 San Diego Zoo
2 Corvette Diner
3 SeaWorld San Diego
4 San Diego Wild Animal Park
5 LEGOLAND California
6 Reuben H. Fleet Science Center
7 Birch Aquarium at Scripps
8 Whale watching
9 San Diego Model Railroad Museum
10 Chula Vista Nature Center
11 Children's Museum / Museo de los Niños
12 Belmont Park

Activities abound for kids from toddlers to teens in San Diego. From its renowned theme parks and zoo, to its kid-friendly museums (where unsuspecting young minds just might learn a thing or two), San Diego more than lives up to its reputation as an optimal family vacation destination. Best of all, these places won't bore the adults in tow either. START: **Bus 7 or 7A/B to the San Diego Zoo in Balboa Park.**

Meerkats at the San Diego Zoo.

❶ ★★★ **San Diego Zoo.** San Diego's world-famous zoo appeals to children of all ages, and the double-decker bus tours bring all the animals into easy view of even the smallest visitors. There's a Children's Zoo where kids can feed and pet the animals, as well as a popular show featuring trained sea lions. *See p 17, bullet* ❶.

❷ **Corvette Diner.** Travel back in time to the rockin' 1950s at this theme diner, where the jukebox is loud, the gum-snapping waitresses slide into your booth to take your order, and the decor is neon and vintage Corvette to the highest power. *3946 Fifth Ave. (between Washington St. and University Ave.).* ☎ *619/542-1001. www.cohn restaurants.com. $–$$.*

❸ ★★ **SeaWorld San Diego.** Crowd-pleasing shows and rides highlight this marine-life theme park, made politically correct with a nominally informative atmosphere. The 20-minute shows—starring orcas, otters, dolphins, household pets, and (in summer) human acrobats—run several times throughout the day. Several successive 4-ton (3,629kg) killer whales have functioned as the park's mascot, Shamu, who performs in a 7-million gallon pool with see-through walls. SeaWorld's real strength, though, are the simulated marine environments, including Wild Arctic (with beluga whales, walruses, and polar bears), Manatee Rescue, the Shark Encounter, and—everyone's favorite—the Penguin Encounter. ⏱ *At least 4 hr. 500 SeaWorld Dr.* ☎ *800/257-4268 or 619/226-3901. www.seaworld.com. Admission $56 adults, $46 children 3–9, free for children under 3. Hours vary seasonally, but always at least daily 10am–5pm; most weekends and during summer 9am–11pm. Parking $10. Bus: 8 or 9.*

Koala bears at the San Diego Zoo.

④ ★★★ San Diego Wild Animal Park. Originally a breeding facility for the San Diego Zoo, the 1,800-acre (728-hectare) Wild Animal Park now holds 3,500 animals representing some 430 different species. Many of the animals roam freely in vast enclosures, allowing giraffes to interact with antelopes, much as they would in Africa. Although the San Diego Zoo may be more famous, it's the Wild Animal Park that many visitors celebrate as their favorite. The Roar & Snore and Beastly Bedtime programs, which are held year-round (except Dec. and Jan.) on most Fridays and Saturdays—with extended dates in

Dolphins at Sea World.

summer—let you camp out next to the animal compound (reservations required). ⏱ *At least 4 hr. 15500 San Pasqual Valley Rd.* ☎ *760/747-8702. www.wildanimalpark.org. Admission $29 adults, $26 seniors 60 and over, $18 children 3–11, free for children under 3 and military in uniform. Daily 9am–4pm (grounds close at 5pm); extended hours during summer and Festival of Lights (2 weekends in Dec). Parking $8. Bus: 386 (Mon–Sat). The park is 34 miles (55km) north of downtown San Diego in a rural setting, making a car almost a necessity.*

⑤ ★ LEGOLAND California. This theme park in Carlsbad, 40 minutes north of downtown San Diego, offers a full day of entertainment for families. There are more than 50 rides, shows, and attractions, including hands-on interactive displays; a life-size menagerie of tigers, giraffes, and other animals; and scale models of international landmarks (the Eiffel Tower, Sydney Opera House, and so on), all constructed of LEGO bricks. The park is geared toward children ages 2 to 12, and there's just enough of a thrill-ride component that preteens will be amused. Most teenagers, however, will find LEGOLAND a bit of a snooze. ⏱ *4 hr. 1 Legoland Dr.* ☎ *877/534-6526 or 760/918-5346.*

Admission Discounts

San Diego's three main animal attractions offer combo tickets that can save you some cash. If you plan to visit both the zoo and Wild Animal Park, a two-park ticket (the "Best Value" zoo package, plus Wild Animal Park admission) is $59 for adults, $39 for children 3 to 11 (for a $62/$40 value). You get one visit to each attraction, to be used within 5 days of purchase. Or throw in SeaWorld within the same 5 days, and the combo works out to $107 for adults, $77 children ages 3 to 9 (a $118/$86 value).

Other value options include the **San Diego Passport** ($79 for adults, $45 for children 3–11), which includes zoo admission, an Old Town Trolley city tour, Hornblower bay cruises, and more; passports are sold at the attractions themselves. **City Pass** (☎ 707/256-0490, www.citypass.com) covers the zoo or Wild Animal Park, plus Sea-World, Disneyland Resorts, and Universal Studios in Los Angeles; passes are $235 for adults, and $189 for kids age 3 to 9 (a savings of more than 30%), valid for 14 days. The **Go San Diego Card** (☎ 800/887-9103; www.gosandiegocard.com) offers unlimited general admission to more than 25 attractions, including the zoo and LEGOLAND, as well as deals on shopping, dining, and day trips to Mexico and other locales. One-day packages start at $55 for adults and $45 for children (ages 3–12).

www.legoland.com. $57 adults, $44 seniors and children 3–12, free to children under 3. July–Aug daily 10am–8pm; June daily 10am–5 or 6pm; off-season Thurs–Mon 10am–5 or 6pm. Closed Tues–Wed Sept–May, but open daily during Christmas and Easter vacation periods. Parking $10. From San Diego, you'll need a car for this one.

6 ★ **Reuben H. Fleet Science Center.** With its hands-on exhibits, motion simulator rides, and an

A giraffe at the Wild Animal Park.

The Birch Aquarium at Scripps.

IMAX theater, this science funhouse draws kids like magnets. *See p 26, bullet* ⑲.

⑦ ★★ Birch Aquarium at Scripps. This beautiful facility is both an aquarium and a museum, operated as the interpretive arm of the world-famous Scripps Institution of Oceanography. The aquarium affords close-up views of the Pacific Northwest, the California coast, Mexico's Sea of Cortés, and the tropical seas, all presented in more than 60 marine-life tanks; the giant kelp forest is particularly impressive. The outdoor demonstration tide pool shows visitors marine coastal life and amazing coastal views. ⏱ *90 min. 2300 Expedition Way.* ☎ *858/534-3474. www.aquarium. ucsd.edu. Admission $11 adults, $9 seniors, $8 college students with ID, $7.50 children 3–17, free for children under 3. Daily 9am–5pm. Free parking. Bus: 30.*

⑧ ★★ Whale watching. The easiest (and cheapest) way to observe the migration of the Pacific gray whales every mid-December to mid-March is to head to Cabrillo National Monument (*see p 13, bullet* ①), where you'll find a glassed-in observatory and educational whale exhibits. Better yet, head to sea—there are a variety of options, including sailboats, large

ships with lots of amenities, and barebones kayaking. *Classic Sailing Adventures, based at Shelter Island (* ☎ *800/659-0141 or 619/224-0800; www.classicsailingadventures.com,) offers two trips per day (8:30am and 1pm); each lasts 4 hours and carries a maximum of six passengers. Cruises are $75 per person (minimum 2 passengers), including beverages and snacks. OEX Dive & Kayak Centers (* ☎ *858/454-6195; www. oexcalifornia.com) leads guided kayak tours in search of passing whales. It's about a 1-mile (1.6km) paddle that departs daily at noon from La Jolla Shores. $60 for single kayak, $110 for double. Embarcadero-based companies that offer engine-driven expeditions include Hornblower Cruises (* ☎ *888/467-6256 or 619/686-8715; www.horn blower.com) and San Diego Harbor Excursions (* ☎ *800/442-7847 or 619/ 234-4111; www.sdhe.com). Trips are 3 or 3½ hours, and fares run $27–$35 for adults, with discounts for kids.*

⑨ ★ San Diego Model Railroad Museum. This 27,000-square-foot (2,508 sq. m) space has six scale-model railroad dioramas, along with interactive multimedia displays, to fire the imaginations of train lovers, young and old alike. *See p 26, bullet* ⑱.

⑩ ★★ Chula Vista Nature Center. Overshadowed by Sea-World and the zoo, this wonderful, interactive nature center highlights the plants and animals native to San Diego Bay and the surrounding wetlands, featuring exhibits of stingrays and small sharks in kid-level open tanks. The center, about 15 minutes south of downtown, recently unveiled Turtle Lagoon, San Diego's only habitat for endangered green sea turtles. ⏱ *90 min. 1000 Gunpowder Point Dr.* ☎ *619/409-5900. www.chulavistanaturecenter.org. $6 adults, $5 seniors and students, $4 youth 12–17, $3 children 4–11, free for children 3 and under. Tues–Sun 10am–5pm. The (free) parking lot is located away from the center; a shuttle bus ferries guests between the two points every 10 to 15 minutes (last shuttle at 4pm). Bus: 932. Trolley: Blue Line to Bayfront/E St. (request shuttle at trolley info center).*

⑪ Children's Museum/Museo de los Niños. This $25 million, state-of-the-art facility—designed by the city's most acclaimed architect—is scheduled to open in May 2008. The downtown space will feature cultural and educational programs, including hands-on art projects, storytelling, music, and visual and performing arts. The museum will engage visitors of all ages, from toddlers to parents. *200 W. Island Ave. (at Front St.).* ☎ *619/233-8792. www.sdchildrensmuseum.org. Bus: 11 or 992. Trolley: Orange Line to Convention Center.*

⑫ Belmont Park. This seaside amusement park in Mission Beach first opened in 1925 as a means to lure people to the then-scarcely populated coastal areas. There are plenty of carnival-style rides, but the star attractions are the Giant Dipper roller coaster and the Plunge, a huge indoor pool. Both are Roaring '20s originals. Recent years have seen the addition of the Wavehouse, which features unique wave machines that produce rides for both novice and advanced surfers and bodyboarders. It's a blast to watch the pros in action. ⏱ *2 hr. 3146 Mission Blvd. (at W. Mission Bay Dr.).* ☎ *858/488-1549. www. belmontpark.com. Rides are $2–$6 each; unlimited-ride wristbands are $23 (for those over 50 inches/127cm) and $16 (under 50 inches/127cm); wave rides start at $15 per hour, with a one-time registration fee of $10. Daily 11am–7 or 8pm (weekend and summer hours later; closed weekdays Jan and Feb). Bus: 8 or 9.*

The Giant Dipper at Belmont Park.

Historic San Diego

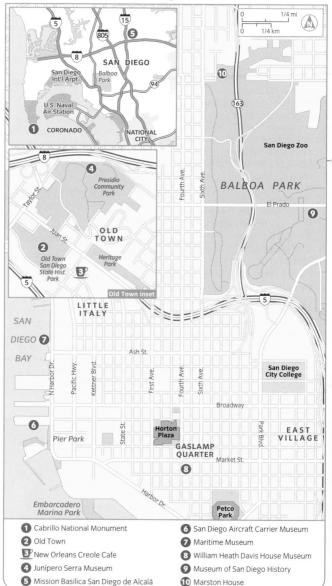

1 Cabrillo National Monument
2 Old Town
3 New Orleans Creole Cafe
4 Junípero Serra Museum
5 Mission Basilica San Diego de Alcalá
6 San Diego Aircraft Carrier Museum
7 Maritime Museum
8 William Heath Davis House Museum
9 Museum of San Diego History
10 Marston House

San Diego is where California began. Conquistador Juan Rodriguez Cabrillo first claimed the region in the name of Spain in 1542, but it would be more than 220 years before they sent an occupying force to colonize Alta California. In 1769, soldiers and missionaries, including Father Junípero Serra, set up camp on Presidio Hill overlooking what is now Old Town, making it the first European settlement in California. San Diego would eventually grow into a Wild West boomtown, complete with characters such as famed lawman Wyatt Earp. And even from the earliest days of the 20th century, the United States military coveted San Diego's strategic geographic location, making it the bastion of military heritage it remains today. If you like to bolster your trips with a little history, San Diego is an excellent choice with lots to offer. START: **Bus 28C from Old Town Transit Center.**

① ★★★ kids **Cabrillo National Monument.** From the park's location high atop Point Loma, you can overlook San Diego Bay and see the spot where Juan Cabrillo came ashore and met with some very concerned Kumeyaay Indians in 1542. There are also museum installations describing the point's long military history; the cemetery you pass on the way into the park is Fort Rosecrans National Cemetery, a military graveyard since the 1860s. *See p 13, bullet* ①.

The Cabrillo National Monument.

② ★ **Old Town.** The flags of Spain, Mexico, and the United States flew in succession over the dusty pueblo of San Diego, a rough and tumble outpost of frontier settlers. History comes alive daily in Old Town State Historic Park (*see p 9, bullet* ①), where you can wander the original town square, lined with reconstructed and original buildings re-creating the era from 1821–1872. The structures now serve as museums, shops, and restaurants. Directly south of the park, along San Diego Ave., you'll find more curio stores and dining options, as well as The Whaley House museum, which attracts attention far and wide for its reputation of being certifiably haunted. A little farther down the street is El Campo Santo, the town's original cemetery. A block east of the Whaley House is Heritage Park, a collection of seven gorgeously restored Victorian buildings, including Southern California's first synagogue. ***Whaley House:*** 🕐 *30 min. 2476 San Diego Ave.* ☎ *619/297-7511. www.whaleyhouse.org. Admission before 5pm $6 adults, $5 seniors over 54, $4 children 3–12; admission after 5pm $10 adults, $5 children 3–12. Mon–Tues 10am–5pm; Thurs–Sun 10am–10pm; daily in*

Temple Beth Israel in Old Town.

summer 10am–10pm. **Heritage Park:** ⏱ *20 min. 2450 Heritage Park Row (corner of Juan and Harney sts.).* ☎ *877/565-3600 or 858/694-3049. www.sdparks.org. Free admission. Trolley: Blue or Green Line to Old Town.*

③ New Orleans Creole Cafe.
When you're seated on the lovely patio of this small cafe, amid the shade trees of the Whaley House complex, you won't mind a little geographical incongruity one bit. You'll happily enjoy your po' boy, gumbo, or muffuletta while the throngs line up elsewhere for mediocre Mexican food. *2476 San Diego Ave. (behind the Whaley House gift shop).* ☎ *619/542-1698. neworleanscreolecafe.com. $–$$.*

④ ★ Junípero Serra Museum.
Perched on a hill above Old Town, this Spanish Mission–style structure is located where, in 1769, the first mission, first presidio, and first non-native settlement on the west coast of the United States were founded. This is the "Plymouth Rock of the Pacific Coast." The museum's exhibits introduce visitors to the Native American, Spanish, and

Mexican people who first called this place home; on display are their belongings, from cannons to cookware. Built in 1929, the stately building offers great views from its 70-foot (21m) tower. Presidio Park, which was established around the museum, is a nice place for a picnic, and has surprisingly extensive walking trails. ⏱ *1 hr. 2727 Presidio Dr.* ☎ *619/297-3258. www.sandiego history.org. Admission $5 adults; $4 seniors, students, and military; $2 children 6–17; free for children under 6. Mon–Fri 11am–3pm, Sat–Sun 10am–4:30pm. Park rangers lead a free outdoor tour the 2nd Sunday of every month from 1–2pm. Trolley: Blue or Green Line to Old Town.*

⑤ Mission Basilica San Diego de Alcalá.
This was the first link in a chain of 21 missions founded by Spanish missionary Junípero Serra. In 1774, the mission was moved from Old Town to its present site for agricultural reasons and to separate the indigenous converts from the fortress that included the original building. The mission was sacked by Native Americans a year after it was

Junípero Serra Museum.

Mission San Diego de Alcalá.

built—Father Serra rebuilt the structure using 5- to 7-foot- (1.5m- to 2.1m-) thick adobe walls and clay tile roofs, rendering it harder to burn. In the process, he inspired a bevy of 20th-century California architects. Mass is said daily in this active Catholic parish. 🕐 *30 min. 10818 San Diego Mission Rd.* ☎ *619/ 281-8449. www.missionsandiego. com. Admission $3 adults, $2 seniors and students, $1 children under 12. Free Sun and for daily Masses. Daily 9am–4:45pm; Mass daily 7am and 5:30pm. Trolley: Green Line to Mission San Diego.*

❻ San Diego Aircraft Carrier Museum. The USS *Midway* had a 47-year military history that began 1 week after the Japanese surrender of WWII in 1945. The carrier is now moored at the Embarcadero and has become the world's largest floating naval-aviation museum. A self-guided audio tour takes visitors to several levels of the ship, telling the story of life on board. The highlight is climbing up the superstructure to the bridge and gazing down on the 1,001-foot- (305m-) long flight deck, with various aircraft poised for duty. Check into docent tours, many given by Midway vets, to add insight to your visit. 🕐 *1 hr. 910 Harbor Dr. (at Navy Pier).* ☎ *619/ 544-9600. www.midway.org. Admission $15 adults; $10 seniors, students,*

and military; $8 children 6–17, free for children under 6 and military in uniform. Daily 10am–5pm. Trolley: Orange or Blue Line to America Plaza.*

❼ ★★ kids Maritime Museum. This flotilla of classic ships is led by the full-rigged merchant vessel *Star of India* (1863), a national historic landmark and the world's oldest ship that still goes to sea. Recent additions include the HMS *Surprise*, a painstakingly accurate reproduction of an 18th-century Royal Navy Frigate, which played a supporting role to Russell Crowe in the film *Master and Commander: Far Side of the World;* and a 300-foot- (91m-)

The sailor statue at the Air Carrier Memorial.

The USS Midway at the Aircraft Carrier Museum.

long Cold War–era B-39 Soviet attack submarine. You can board and tour each vessel. 🕐 *90 min. 1492 N. Harbor Dr.* ☎ *619/234-9153. www.sdmaritime.org. Admission $12 adults; $9 seniors over 62 and active military with ID; $8 children 6–17; free for children under 6. Daily 9am–8pm (till 9pm in summer). Bus: 2, 923, or 992. Trolley: Orange or Blue Line to America Plaza.*

❽ William Heath Davis House Museum. Shipped by boat to San Diego in 1850 from Portland, Maine, this is the oldest structure in the Gaslamp Quarter. It is a well-preserved example of a prefabricated "saltbox" family home and has remained structurally unchanged for more than 150 years, though it originally stood at another location. A museum on the first and second floors documents life in "New Town," and profiles some of the city's early movers and shakers. The Gaslamp Quarter Historical Foundation also makes its home here, and it has a nice gift store in the basement. 🕐 *30 min. 410 Island Ave. (at Fourth Ave.).* ☎ *619/233-4692. www. gaslampquarter.org. Admission $5; $4 seniors, military, and students. Tues–Sat 10am–6pm; Sun 9am–3pm. The Historical Foundation sponsors*

walking tours of the neighborhood for $10 ($8 for seniors, students, and military), Saturdays at 11am. Bus: 3, 120, or 992. Trolley: Gaslamp Quarter or Convention Center.

❾ Museum of San Diego History. Operated by the San Diego Historical Society, this Balboa Park museum offers permanent and changing exhibits on topics related to the history of the region. Many of the museum's photographs depict Balboa Park and the growth of the city. Books about San Diego's history are available in the gift shop, and the research library downstairs is open Thursday through Saturday. 🕐 *45 min. 1649 El Prado, in Casa del Balboa.* ☎ *619/232-6203. www. sandiegohistory.org. Admission $5 adults, $4 students, seniors and military with ID, $2 children 6–17, free for children 5 and under. Free 2nd Tues of each month. Daily 10am–5pm. Bus: 7 or 7A/B.*

❿ ★★ Marston House. Noted San Diego architects Irving Gill and William Hebbard designed this Craftsman house in 1905 for George Marston, a local businessman and philanthropist. Listed on the National Register of Historic Places and now managed by the San Diego

Spooks & Splashes

Those who want to take a walk on the supernatural side can stroll through Old Town with **"ghost hunter" Michael Brown** (☎ 619/972-3900; www.oldtownsmosthaunted.com). He leads tours in search of real paranormal activity on Thursday at 7 and 9pm, and Friday and Saturday at 7, 9, and 11pm. $19 adults, $10 children 6 to 12, kids under 5 are free. **Ghostly Tours in History** (☎ 877/220-4844; www.ghostlytoursinhistory.com) leads walking tours through both Old Town (Thurs–Sat, 7 and 8:30pm) and the Gaslamp Quarter (Fri–Sat, 7:15pm). The cost is $10, free for children under 5 (the Gaslamp tour may be inappropriate for small children).

The 90-minute amphibious SEAL tour departs from Seaport Village and motors along the Embarcadero until splashing into San Diego Bay. The narrated tour gives you the maritime and military history of San Diego from the right perspective. Trips are scheduled daily (except Mon in winter), from 10am to 4pm (till 5pm in summer). The cost is $30 for adults and $15 for kids 4 to 12. For information and tickets, call ☎ 619/298-8687, or visit www.historictours.com.

Historical Society, the home's interior is furnished with decor from the Arts and Crafts period, including Roycroft, Stickley, and Limbert pieces, as well as art pottery. ⏱ *45 minutes. 3525 Seventh Ave. (northwest corner of Balboa Park at* *Balboa Dr. and Upas St.).* ☎ *619/298-3142. www.sandiegohistory.org. Guided tour $5 adults, $4 seniors and students, $2 children 6–17, free for children 5 and under. Fri–Sun 11am–3pm. Bus: 1, 3, or 120.*

Inside the Davis House.

The Best Golf Courses

Balboa Park Municipal
  Golf Course 4
Coronado Municipal
  Golf Course 5
Four Seasons Resort Aviara
  Golf Club 1
Riverwalk Golf Club 3
Torrey Pines Golf Course 2

With its mild year-round climate and nearly 100 courses, half of them public, San Diego County is an ideal destination for golfers. This selection includes acclaimed courses for hardcore aficionados and easily accessed greens for casual duffers. All exploit the full range of San Diego's diverse ecosystems, from the desert to the sea. For a full list of San Diego courses, check out the **San Diego Golf Pages** (www.golfsd.com); **San Diego Golf Reservations** (☎ 866/701-4653 or 858/964-5980; www.sandiegogolf.com) can arrange tee times for you at the premier courses. START: **Bus 101.**

Balboa Park Municipal Golf Course. Surrounded by the beauty of Balboa Park, this 18-hole course features pure greens, fairways sprinkled with eucalyptus leaves, and distracting views of the San Diego skyline. It's convenient and affordable—the perfect choice for visitors who want to work some golf into their vacation, rather than the other way around. The course even rents clubs. *2600 Golf Course Dr. (off Pershing Dr. or 26th St. in the southeast corner of the park).* ☎ *619/239-1660. www.sandiego.gov/golf. Non-resident fees $34 weekdays, $43 weekends; twilight rate $20 weekdays, $26 weekends; cart rental $26, pull carts $5. Reservations are suggested at least a week in advance.*

Bus: 2, exit at C and 26th sts., head north into the park.

Coronado Municipal Golf Course. The postcard vistas will test your powers of concentration at this 18-hole, par-72 course overlooking Glorietta Bay, the Coronado Bridge, and the downtown San Diego skyline. There's also a coffee shop, pro shop, and driving range on site. Two-day prior reservations are strongly recommended; call after 7am up to 2 weeks in advance (the $38 advance registration charge is nonrefundable). *2000 Visalia Row.* ☎ *619/435-3121. www. golfcoronado.com. Greens fees $25 to walk, $40 to ride for 18 holes; after 4pm, $13 to walk, $28 to ride. Club rental $45 ($25 twilight rate);*

The Four Seasons Resort Aviara Golf Club.

pull-cart rental $5. Bus: 901, exit at Pomona Ave. and Glorietta Pl.

★★ Four Seasons Resort Aviara Golf Club.

In Carlsbad (40 min. north of downtown San Diego), Aviara is uniquely landscaped to incorporate natural elements compatible with the protected Batiquitos Lagoon nearby. The course is 7,007 yards (6,407m) from the championship tees, on rolling hillsides with plenty of bunker and water challenges (casual golfers may be frustrated). There are practice areas for putting, chipping, sand play, and driving, and the pro shop and clubhouse are fully equipped. Golf packages are available for guests of the Four Seasons. *7447 Batiquitos Dr.* ☎ *760/603-6900. www.fourseasons.com. Greens fees Mon–Thurs $205 (including mandatory cart); Fri–Sun $225; afternoon rates start at 1:30pm in winter, 3pm in summer ($130 weekday, $135 weekend). Coaster: Carlsbad Village Station; cab it from there.*

★ Riverwalk Golf Club.

Redesigned by Ted Robinson and Ted Robinson, Jr., these links wandering along the Mission Valley floor are the most convenient courses for anyone staying downtown or near the beaches. The course sports a slick, upscale clubhouse; four lakes with waterfalls (in play on 13 of the 27 holes); open, undulating fairways; and trolley tracks on which a bright red trolley speeds through now and then without proving too distracting. *1150 Fashion Valley Rd.* ☎ *619/296-4563. www.riverwalk gc.com. Nonresident greens fees, including cart, $95 Mon–Thurs, $120 Fri–Sun; senior, twilight, and bargain evening rates are available. Trolley: Green Line to Fashion Valley Transit Center.*

★★ Torrey Pines Golf Course.

These two gorgeous, municipal 18-hole championship courses, on the coast between La Jolla and Del Mar, are only 20 minutes from downtown San Diego. Home of the Buick Invitational Tournament, and the setting for the 2008 U.S. Open, Torrey Pines is second only to Pebble Beach as California's top golf destination. On a bluff overlooking the ocean, the north course is picturesque and has the signature hole (no. 6), but the south course is more challenging, has more sea-facing play, and benefits from a $3.5-million overhaul in 2002. *11480 Torrey Pines Rd.* ☎ *619/570-1234 or 800/ 985-4653 for the pro shop and lessons. www.torreypinesgolfcourse. com or www.sandiego.gov/torrey pines. Greens fees on the south course $130 weekdays, $163 weekends; on the north course $80 weekdays, $100 weekends; twilight rates available. Cart rentals $32. Tee times are taken by computer, starting at 7am up to 7 days in advance and by automated telephone only—it takes only 20 to 30 minutes for all tee times for a given day to sell out. Lessons assure you a spot on the course, and the pro shop rents clubs. Bus: 101.* ●

The Torrey Pines Golf Course.

3 The Best
Neighborhood Walks

44

Gaslamp Quarter

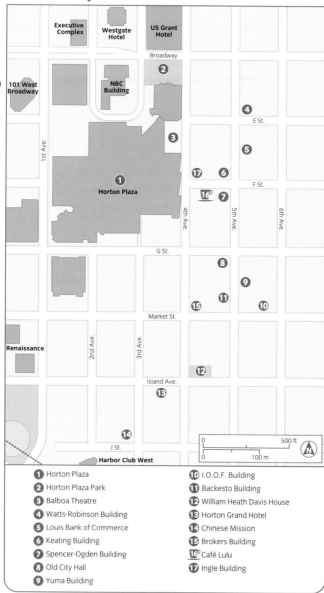

1 Horton Plaza
2 Horton Plaza Park
3 Balboa Theatre
4 Watts-Robinson Building
5 Louis Bank of Commerce
6 Keating Building
7 Spencer-Ogden Building
8 Old City Hall
9 Yuma Building
10 I.O.O.F. Building
11 Backesto Building
12 William Heath Davis House
13 Horton Grand Hotel
14 Chinese Mission
15 Brokers Building
16 Café Lulu
17 Ingle Building

A house in Hillcrest.

A National Historic District covering 16 city blocks, the Gaslamp Quarter features many Victorian-style commercial buildings built between the Civil War and World War I. The father of modern San Diego, Alonzo Horton, purchased 1,000 acres (405 hectares) of muddy, bay-front land for $260 in 1867 and ignited a real estate boom. Horton's "New Town" is today's Gaslamp Quarter, with its proliferation of restaurants, shops, clubs, and hotels making it a mirror image of its 1880s heyday. The Gaslamp Quarter is bound by Fourth Avenue to the west, Sixth Avenue to the east, Broadway to the north, and L Street and the waterfront to the south. It's all very walkable thanks to Horton's business savvy—he wanted to maximize his land sales, so he laid out small blocks (creating more desirable corner lots) with no alleys. START: **Any downtown bus to Horton Plaza, Blue or Orange Line trolley to Civic Center.**

1 ★ **Horton Plaza.** A colorful conglomeration of shops, eateries, and architecture, Horton Plaza spearheaded the revitalization of downtown when it opened in 1985. The ground floor is home to the Jessop Street Clock, designed by Joseph Jessop, Sr., and built primarily by Claude D. Ledger. It stood outside Jessop's Jewelry Store on Fifth Avenue from 1907 until being moved to Horton Plaza in 1985, and has reportedly only stopped three times in its history: once after being hit by a team of horses, once after an earthquake, and again on the day in 1935 when Ledger died. *Bound by Broadway, First, and Fourth aves., and G St.* ☎ *619/238-1596. www.westfield.com/hortonplaza.*

2 **Horton Plaza Park.** Its centerpiece is a fountain designed by well-known local architect Irving Gill. It was dedicated Oct. 15, 1910, and it was the first successful attempt to combine colored lights with flowing water. On the fountain's base are bronze medallions of San Diego's "founding fathers": Juan Rodríguez Cabrillo, Father Junípero Serra, and Alonzo Horton. *Corner of Fourth Ave. and Broadway.*

3 ★ **Balboa Theatre.** Constructed in 1924, the Spanish

Louis Bank.

Renaissance–style building has a distinctive tile dome, striking tile work in the entry, and two 20-foot- (6m-) high ornamental waterfalls inside. In the theater's early days, plays and vaudeville took top billing. After years of sitting dormant and decrepit, the Balboa is slated for an eagerly anticipated 2008 re-opening. *Southwest corner of Fourth Ave. and E St. www.ccdc.com.*

The Keating Building at night.

4 ★ Watts-Robinson Building. Built in 1913 in a Chicago School of Architecture style, this was one of San Diego's first skyscrapers. It once housed 70 jewelers and is now a boutique hotel (*see Gaslamp Plaza Suites, p 138*). Take a minute to look inside at the marble wainscoting, tile floors, ornate ceiling, and brass ornamentation. *903 Fifth Ave. (northeast corner of Fifth Ave. and E St.).*

5 ★★ Louis Bank of Commerce. Built in 1888, this proud building was the first in San Diego made of granite. It once housed the city's first ice cream parlor; an oyster bar frequented by Wyatt Earp (of OK Corral shootout fame); and, upstairs, the Golden Poppy Hotel, a brothel run by a fortuneteller, Madame Coara. After a fire in 1904, the original towers of the building were removed, and the iron eagles perched atop them disappeared. A 2002 renovation installed a new pair of eagles, cast at the same English foundry as the originals. *835 Fifth Ave.*

6 ★ Keating Building. A San Diego landmark dating from 1890,

this structure was nicknamed the "marriage building." It was developed by businessman George Keating, who died halfway through construction. His wife, Fannie, finished the project, changing some of the design along the way. She had her husband's name engraved in the top cornice as a tribute to him. Originally heralded as one of the city's most prestigious office buildings, it featured conveniences such as steam heat and a wire-cage elevator.

The Yuma Building.

A sleek boutique hotel, the Keating, is now ensconced here (*see p 140*). *432 F St. (northwest corner of Fifth Ave. and F St.).*

7 ★ **Spencer-Ogden Building.** Built in 1874, this is one of the oldest buildings in the Gaslamp Quarter—and it's lucky to still be standing. It escaped major damage after an explosion in 1887 caused by a druggist who was making firecrackers. Other tenants over the years included realtors, an import business, a home-furnishing business, and a "Painless Parker" dental office. Edgar Parker owned a chain of dental offices and legally changed his name to "Painless" in order to avoid claims of false advertising. *770 Fifth Ave.*

8 ★ **Old City Hall.** Also dating from 1874, when it was a bank, this Florentine Italianate building features 16-foot (5m) ceilings, 12-foot (4m) windows framed with brick arches, antique columns, and a wrought-iron cage elevator. Notice the windows on each floor are different. (The top two stories were added in 1887, when it became the city's public library.) The entire city government filled this building in 1900, with the police department on the first floor and the council chambers on the fourth. Incredibly, this beauty was completely stuccoed over in the 1950s in an attempt at modernization. It was restored in the 1980s. *664 Fifth Ave. (southwest corner of Fifth Ave. and G St.).*

9 ★★ **Yuma Building.** The striking edifice was built in 1888 and was one of the first brick buildings downtown. The brothel at the Yuma was the first to be closed during the infamous 1912 cleanup of the area. In the end, 138 women (and no men) were arrested. They were given a choice: join the Door of Hope charity and reform or take a one-way train ride to Los Angeles.

One hundred thirty-six went to LA (many were back within days); one woman was pronounced insane; and the last became San Diego's first telephone operator. *631 Fifth Ave.*

10 ★ **I.O.O.F. Building.** Finally finished in 1882 after 9 years of construction, this handsome building served as a joint lodge for the Masons and Odd Fellows. When the cornerstone was finally laid, a parade was held with King Kalakaua of Hawaii as the grand marshal. Gaslamp lore has it that, sitting on the balcony, he caught a cold and died soon after of pneumonia. *526 Market St.*

11 **Backesto Building.** Built in 1873, this classical revival and Victorian corner building was expanded to its present size and height over its first 15 years. At the turn of the last century, this part of the Gaslamp was known as the Stingaree, the city's notorious red-light district. Gambling, opium dens, and wild saloons were all part of the mix. *617 Fifth Ave. (northwest corner of Fifth Ave. and Market St.).*

The Ghirardelli marquee.

Touring the Town

Old Town Trolley Tours (☎ 619/298-8687; www.historictours.com) offer an easy way to get an overview of the city. These vehicles, gussied up like old-time trolleys, do a 30-mile (48km) circular route, and you can hop off at any one of eight stops, explore at leisure, and reboard when you please (the trolleys run every half-hour). Stops include Old Town, the Gaslamp Quarter and downtown area, Coronado, the San Diego Zoo, and Balboa Park. You can begin wherever you want, but you must purchase tickets before boarding (most stops have a ticket kiosk). The tour costs $30 for adults ($15 for kids 4–12, free for children 3 and under) for one complete circuit; the route by itself takes about 2 hours. The trolleys operate daily from 9am to 4pm in winter, and from 9am to 5pm in summer.

City Sightseeing (☎ 619/246-2400; www.citysightseeing-sd. com) conducts narrated tours aboard double-decker buses that continuously loop through the city, offering on-and-off privileges at Old Town, Balboa Park, the Gaslamp Quarter, and five other spots. The full tour is about 2 hours and your ticket is good for 48 hours; tours commence in Old Town, from City Sightseeing's office at 2415 Old Town Ave. Day tours are $25 to $30 for adults, $15 to $20 for children age 4 to 12; night tours are also available ($20 adults, $12 children). Coronado is not included in these tours, but passes for the Coronado ferry are included in some ticket prices.

⓬ ★ **William Heath Davis House.** Downtown's oldest surviving structure, this prefabricated lumber home was shipped to San Diego around Cape Horn from New England in 1850. Alonzo Horton lived in the house in 1867, at its original location at the corner of Market and State streets. Around 1873 it was moved to 11th Avenue and K Street, where it served as the county hospital. It was relocated to this site in 1984 and

Davis House.

completely refurbished. The entire house is now a museum and educational gift shop, and the small park next to it are open to the public (*see p 38, bullet* **8**). The Gaslamp Quarter Historical Foundation is also headquartered here. *410 Island Ave. (at Fourth Ave.).* ☎ *619/233-4692. www.gaslampquarter.org.*

13 ★ **Horton Grand Hotel.** Two 1886 hotels were moved here—very gently—from other sites, and then renovated and connected by an atrium; the original Grand Horton is to your left, the Brooklyn Hotel to your right. Now it's all one: the Horton Grand Hotel (*see p 139*). The life-size papier-mâché horse (Sunshine), in the sitting area near reception, stood in front of the Brooklyn Hotel when the ground floor was a saddlery. Wyatt Earp lived upstairs at the Brooklyn for most of his 7 years in San Diego. In the Palace Bar, look for the portrait of Ida Bailey, a local madam whose establishment, the Canary Cottage, once stood nearby. *311 Island Ave. (southwest corner of Island and Fourth aves.).*

14 **Chinese Mission.** Originally located on First Avenue, this brick building built in 1927 was a place where Chinese immigrants (primarily men) could learn English and find employment. Religious instruction and living quarters were also provided. The building was rescued from demolition and moved to its present location, where it now contains the San Diego Chinese Historical Museum. ⏱ *20 min. 404 Third Ave. (at J St.).* ☎ *619/338-9888. www.sdchm.org. Admission $2 adults, free for children under 12. Tues–Sat 10:30am–4pm; Sun noon–4pm.*

15 **Brokers Building.** Constructed in 1889, this building has 16-foot (5m) wood-beam ceilings and cast-iron columns. In recent years it was converted to artists' lofts, with the ground floor dedicated to the

The Horton Grand.

downtown branch of the Hooters chain. Due to the failure of many previous ventures here, as well as a fire and a structural collapse, this was thought of as a "cursed corner." *402 Market St.*

16 **Café Lulu.** Ostensibly a coffee bar, bohemian Café Lulu also makes a good choice for casual dining (the sidewalk tables are great for people-watching). It also serves later than just about any other place downtown. *419 F St. (near Fourth Ave.).* ☎ *619/238-0114. Cash only. Sun–Thurs 11am–1am; Fri–Sat 11am–3am. $.*

17 ★ **Ingle Building.** It dates from 1906 and now houses the Hard Rock Cafe. The mural on the F Street side of the building depicts a group of deceased rock stars (including Hendrix, Lennon, Joplin, and Elvis, of course) lounging at sidewalk tables. Stained-glass windows from the original Golden Lion Tavern (1907–32) front Fourth Avenue. Inside, the restaurant's stained-glass ceiling was taken from the Elks Club in Stockton, California, and much of the floor is original. *801 Fourth Ave. (northeast corner of Fourth Ave. and F St.).*

Old Town

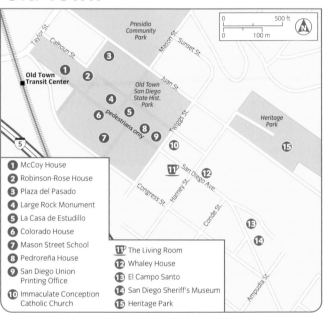

1 McCoy House
2 Robinson-Rose House
3 Plaza del Pasado
4 Large Rock Monument
5 La Casa de Estudillo
6 Colorado House
7 Mason Street School
8 Pedrorreña House
9 San Diego Union
   Printing Office
10 Immaculate Conception
   Catholic Church

11 The Living Room
12 Whaley House
13 El Campo Santo
14 San Diego Sheriff's Museum
15 Heritage Park

San Diego's Mexican and Spanish colonial history is vividly
evident in Old Town. A visit here will transport you to an era of
village greens and one-room schoolhouses, a time when *vaqueros*
and whalers, outlaws and officers, *Californios* and Yankees all min-
gled—sometimes uneasily—in this then-tiny pueblo. When you stroll
through Old Town State Historic Park, California's most popular state
park, you don't have to look hard to see traces of the past. The park
is just part of the Old Town experience, though. This compact neighborhood is home to other historic sites, as well as lots of shopping
and dining, much of it themed to California's frontier past. Admission
is free. START: **Blue or Green Line trolley to Old Town Transit Center.**

1 **McCoy House.** The interpretive center for Old Town State Historic Park (*see p 35, bullet* 2) is a
historically accurate replication of
the home of James McCoy, San
Diego's larger-than-life lawman/
legislator who lived on this site
until the devastating fire of 1872.
With exhibits, artifacts, and visitor

information, the house gives a great
overview of life in San Diego from
1821 to 1872. ⏱ *30 min. Wallace
and Calhoun sts. (northwest corner
of the park).*

2 **Robinson-Rose House.** Built
in 1853 as a family home, the park
visitor center was also once a newspaper and railroad office. Here you'll

A Spanish tile staircase in Old Town.

see a large model of Old Town the way it looked prior to 1872—the year a large fire broke out and destroyed much of the town, initiating the exodus to what is now downtown San Diego. Old Town State Historic Park contains seven original buildings, including the Robinson-Rose House, and replicas of other buildings that once stood here. ⏱ *15 min.*

❸ Plaza del Pasado. Colorful shops and restaurants spill into a flower-filled courtyard where costumed employees and weekend entertainment create an early California atmosphere. A motel in the 1930s, it was designed by acclaimed architect Richard Requa. *2754 Calhoun St. (at Juan St.).* ☎ *619/297-3100. www.plazadelpasado.com.*

❹ Large Rock Monument. This site commemorates the first U.S. flag flown in Southern California, on July 29, 1846.

❺ ★ La Casa de Estudillo. An original adobe building from 1827, this U-shaped house has covered walkways and an open central patio. The patio covering is made of corraza cane, from seeds brought by Father Serra in 1769. The walls are 3- to 5-feet (1- to 1.5m-) thick, holding up the heavy beams and tiles, and insulating against summer heat (in those days, the thicker the walls, the wealthier the family). The furnishings in the "upper-class" house are representative of the 19th century (note the beautiful four-poster beds); the original furniture came from the East Coast and from as far away as Asia. The Estudillo family, which then numbered 12, lived in the house until 1887; today family members still live in San Diego.

❻ Colorado House. Built in 1851, it was destroyed by fire in 1872, as were most buildings on this side of the park. Now the home of the Wells Fargo Historical Museum, it originally was San Diego's first two-story hotel. The museum features an original Wells Fargo stagecoach,

The road into Old Town.

Inside the Mason St. School.

numerous displays of the overland-express business, and a video show. Next-door to the Wells Fargo museum, and kitty-corner to La Casa de Estudillo, is the small, redbrick San Diego Court House & City Hall. ⏱ *15 min.*

7 ★ Mason Street School. An original building dating from 1865, this school was commissioned by Joshua Bean, uncle of the notorious "hanging judge" Roy Bean; Joshua Bean was also San Diego's first mayor. Inside, you'll notice the boards that make up the walls don't match; they were leftovers from the construction of San Diego homes.

Docents in period costume at the Casa de Estudillo.

Mary Chase Walker, the first teacher, ventured here from the East when she was 38 years old. She enjoyed the larger salary but hated the fleas, mosquitoes, and truancy; after a year, she resigned to marry the president of the school board.

8 Pedroreña House. No. 2616 is an original Old Town house built in 1869, with stained glass over the doorway. The shop inside now sells fossils, minerals, and gems. The original owner, Miguel Pedroreña, also owned the house next door.

9 San Diego Union Printing Office. The newspaper was first published in 1868. This house arrived in Old Town after being pre-fabricated in Maine in 1851 and shipped around the Horn (it has a distinctly New England–style appearance). Inside you'll see the original hand press used to print the paper, which merged with the *San Diego Tribune* in 1992.

10 Immaculate Conception Catholic Church. The corner-stone was laid in 1868, making it the first church built in California that was not part of the Mission system. With the movement of the community to New Town in 1872, it lost its parishioners and wasn't dedicated until 1919. Today the church serves about 300 families in the Old Town area. *2540 San Diego Ave. (at Twiggs St., which divides the park from the rest of Old Town).* ☎ *619/295-4148.*

11 The Living Room. Grab a patio table in the courtyard of this lovely old house and enjoy the people-watching, as well as light meals for breakfast, lunch, or dinner. *2541 San Diego Ave.* ☎ *619/325-4445. Sun–Thurs 7am–10pm; Fri–Sat 7am–midnight. $.*

12 Whaley House. The first two-story brick structure in Southern California, it was built from 1856 to 1857. The house is said to be haunted by several ghosts, including that of Yankee Jim Robinson, who was hanged on the site in 1852 for stealing a rowboat. The house is beautifully furnished with period pieces and also features the life mask of Abraham Lincoln. The house's north room served as the county courthouse for a few years, and the courtroom looks now as it did then. ⏱ *30 min. See p 35, bullet 2.*

13 El Campo Santo. Behind an adobe wall along San Diego Avenue is San Diego's first cemetery, established in 1850. This small plot is the final resting place for, among others, the unfortunate Yankee Jim Robinson (see above). Note the small, round brass markers along the sidewalk and in the street. They mark the still-buried remains of some of San Diego's earliest citizens, unknown souls paved over by the tide of progress. *One block south of the Whaley House on the east side of San Diego Ave.*

14 San Diego Sheriff's Museum. Exhibits trace the evolution of the department and its equipment since San Diego sheriffs first pinned a badge on in 1850. The building itself is a stone's throw from where the city's original cobblestone jail once stood. ⏱ *20 min. 2384 San Diego Ave.* ☎ *619/260-1850. www.sheriffmuseum.org. Free admission. Tues–Sat 10am–4pm.*

15 Heritage Park. The seven buildings in this grassy finger canyon, moved here from other parts of the city, are now used in a variety of ways: as a winsome bed-and-breakfast inn (in the Queen Anne shingle-style Christian House, built in 1889), a doll shop, a teahouse, a lingerie store, and offices. Toward the bottom of the hill is the classic revival Temple Beth Israel, dating from 1889. *2450 Heritage Park Row (corner of Juan and Harney sts.) See p 35, bullet 2.*

Old Town's Heritage Park.

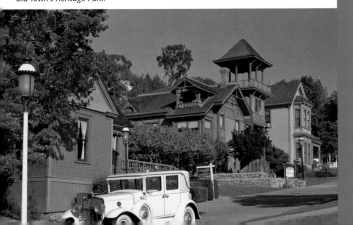

Embarcadero

SAN DIEGO BAY

B STREET PIER

BROADWAY PIER

NAVY PIER

Pier Park

Santa Fe Station

America Plaza

Embarcadero Marina Park

Manchester Grand Hyatt

1 Maritime Museum
2 County Administration Center
3 San Diego Cruise Ship Terminal
4 Harbor Cruises
5 Coronado Ferry
6 Santa Fe Depot
7 Museum of Contemporary Art San Diego
8 San Diego Aircraft Carrier Museum
9 U.S. Air Carrier Memorial
10 Seaport Village
11 Top of the Hyatt

Upon seeing San Diego Bay in 1602, the second European visitor to the area, Sebastián Vizcaíno, declared it to be "a port which must be the best to be found in all the South Sea." A walk along the waterfront, known as the Embarcadero, may convince you of Vizcaíno's opinion. Whalers, merchants with goods from Asia, and tanners (San Diego is the location of "Hide Park" in Richard Henry Dana's *Two Years Before the Mast*) made San Diego Bay a mid-19th century commercial hub. Up until the 1950s, the world's biggest tuna fleet was here, too. While things may be a little more genteel along the Embarcadero now than they were in 1850—tourism is the main commerce these days—it's still a world-class harbor. START: **Blue or Orange Line trolley to America Plaza.**

1 ★★ kids **Maritime Museum.** Making up part of the floating museum is the magnificent *Star of India*, built in 1863. It's the world's oldest merchant ship still afloat. The ship, whose billowing sails are a familiar sight along Harbor Drive, once carried cargo to India and immigrants to New Zealand, and braved the Arctic ice in Alaska to work in the salmon industry. Another component of the museum is the 1898 ferry *Berkeley,* which operated between San Francisco and Oakland. In service through 1958, it carried survivors to safety 24 hours a day for 4 days after the 1906 San Francisco earthquake. You can also check out the HMS *Surprise,* which had a star turn in the film *Master and Commander: The Far Side of the World;* a Soviet-era B-39 attack submarine; the *Californian,* a replica of a 19th-century revenue cutter; *Medea,* a

1904 steam yacht; and *Pilot,* which served as San Diego Bay's official pilot boat for 82 years. *See p 37, bullet* **7**.

2 ★ **County Administration Center.** Built in 1936 with funds from the Works Progress Administration, it was dedicated in 1938 by President Franklin D. Roosevelt. This Art Deco beauty is one of San Diego's most graceful buildings and is listed on the National Register of Historic Places; the waterfront side is presided over by the dignified 23-foot- (7m-) high granite statue, *Guardian of Water,* created by San Diego's most notable sculptor, Donal Hord. The building is even more impressive from the other side because of the carefully tended gardens; it's worth the effort and extra few minutes to walk around to Pacific Highway for a look. There are restrooms and a cafeteria with great

The Embarcadero marina.

The Maritime Museum.

harbor views inside. *1600 Pacific Hwy.* ☎ *619/531-5197. Mon–Fri 8am–5pm.*

③ San Diego Cruise Ship Terminal. Located on the B Street Pier, it has a large nautical clock at the entrance. The flag-decorated terminal's interior is light and airy; you'll also find a snack bar and gift shop.

④ ★ Harbor Cruises. Hornblower Cruises and San Diego Harbor Excursions run daily 1- and 2-hour sightseeing cruises around the bay, departing from near the Broadway Pier. There are a variety of vessels from which to choose, everything from antique yachts to three-deck behemoths, and both companies also offer evening dinner/dance cruises, as well as weekend champagne brunch

Richard Serra sculptures at the Museum of Contemporary Art San Diego.

packages. Ticket booths are right along the waterfront. *Hornblower Cruises* ☎ *888/467-6256 or 619/686-8715. www.hornblower.com. Harbor tours $17–$22 adults, $2 off for seniors and military, half price children 4–12. Dinner cruises start at $62; brunch cruise $45. San Diego Harbor Excursions* ☎ *800/442-7847 or 619/234-4111. www.sdhe.com. Harbor tours $17–$22 ($2 off for seniors and military, half price for children 4–12). Dinner cruises start at $58 adults, $36 children; brunch cruise $50 adults, $30 children.*

⑤ Coronado Ferry. It makes hourly trips between San Diego and Coronado. Buy tickets from the Harbor Excursion booth—you can make the round trip in about 50 minutes. *Sun–Thurs on the hour from 9am–9pm, Fri–Sat till 10pm. Return trips from the Ferry Landing in Coronado to the Broadway Pier are Sun–Thurs every hour on the half-hour from 9:30am–9:30pm, Fri–Sat till 10:30pm. The ride takes 15 minutes. $3 each way.*

⑥ ★ Santa Fe Depot. This mosaic-draped railroad station was built in 1915, and provides one of the city's best examples of Spanish Colonial Revival style. Check out the vaulted ceiling, wooden benches, and walls covered in striking green-and-gold tiles. A scale model of the aircraft carrier USS *Midway* is also on display.

7 ★★★ **Museum of Contemporary Art San Diego.** What was once the train station's baggage building has been transformed into a dynamic new space for this cutting-edge art museum. Designed by the same architect responsible for the Warhol museum in Pittsburgh and the Picasso museum in Spain, this is one of the city's new cultural flagships, featuring permanent, site-specific work by artists Richard Serra, Jenny Holzer, and others. Changing exhibitions are scheduled at both this space and MCASD's original downtown annex across the street. ⏱ *90 min. 1100 and 1001 Kettner Blvd. (between B St. and Broadway).* ☎ *858/454-3541 or 619/234-1001. www.mcasd.org. Admission $10 adults, $5 seniors and military, free for anyone 25 and under, free admission 3rd Tues of the month, paid ticket good for admission to MCASD La Jolla within 7 days. Sat–Tues 11am–6pm., Thurs–Fri 11am–9pm.*

8 **San Diego Aircraft Carrier Museum.** Decommissioned in 1991, the USS *Midway* saw 47 years of service, stretching from the end of WWII through to Desert Storm, where it acted as the flagship for that operation. Over the years, more than 225,000 men served aboard the Midway, and it's their stories

that are told on this floating naval museum. *See p 37, bullet* **6**.

9 **U.S. Air Carrier Memorial.** Erected in 1993, this compact black granite obelisk honors the nation's carriers and crews. It stands on the site of the old Navy fleet landing, where thousands of servicemen boarded ships over the years.

10 **kids** **Seaport Village.** This 14-acre (5.6-hectare) outdoor shopping center has more than 50 stores and restaurants, coupled with an unbeatable bay-front location (the New England–style architecture is completely out of place, but no one seems to mind). Kids love the classic carousel—Charles Looff of Coney Island carved the animals out of poplar in 1895; live entertainment is also often scheduled on weekends. *849 W. Harbor Dr. (at Kettner Blvd.).* ☎ *619/235-4014. www.seaport village.com. Daily 10am–9pm; restaurants have extended hours.*

11 ★★ **Top of the Hyatt.** There's no better place in San Diego for a sunset than the Top of the Hyatt, a 40th-floor lounge with sweeping views of the city and harbor. It's located in the eastern tower of the Manchester Grand Hyatt and opens at 3pm daily. *1 Market Pl.* ☎ *619/ 232-1234. $.*

The Pier Café at Seaport Village.

La Jolla

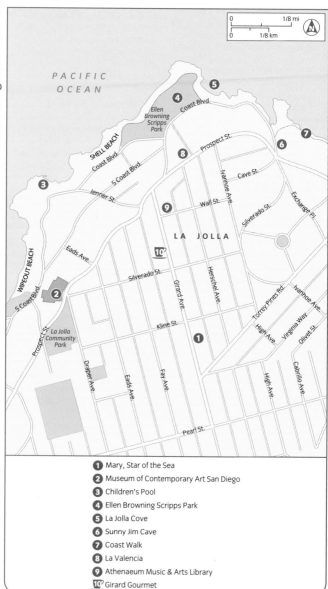

1 Mary, Star of the Sea

2 Museum of Contemporary Art San Diego

3 Children's Pool

4 Ellen Browning Scripps Park

5 La Jolla Cove

6 Sunny Jim Cave

7 Coast Walk

8 La Valencia

9 Athenaeum Music & Arts Library

10 Girard Gourmet

La Jolla is Southern California's Riviera. This seaside community of about 25,000 is home to an inordinate number of wealthy folk who could probably live anywhere. They choose La Jolla for good reason—it's surrounded by the beach, the University of California, San Diego, outstanding restaurants, boutiques, galleries, and some of the world's best medical facilities. The heart of La Jolla is referred to as the Village, roughly delineated by Pearl Street to the south, Prospect Street to the north, Torrey Pines Road to the east, and the rugged coast to the west; this picturesque neighborhood is an ideal place to simply stroll about. It's undetermined whether "La Jolla" (pronounced la-HOY-ya) is misspelled Spanish for "the jewel" or an indigenous word for "cave," but once you see it, you'll likely go with the first definition.
START: **Bus route 30 to Silverado St. and Girard Ave.**

1 ★ Mary, Star of the Sea. Dedicated in 1937, this beautiful little Mission-style Catholic church was designed by noted San Diego architect Carleton Winslow, Sr. Above the entrance, a striking mosaic re-creates the original fresco painted there by Mexican artist Alfredo Ramos Martínez. An influential art instructor in Mexico, Martínez once taught Rufino Tamayo and David Alfaro Siqueiros. Inside the church, the unique mural above the altar was painted by accomplished Polish artist John De Rosen. It depicts the Virgin Mary on a crescent moon, presiding over a storm-tossed sea. *7669 Girard Ave.* ☎ *858/454-2631. www.marystarlajolla.org.*

2 ★★★ Museum of Contemporary Art San Diego. Works produced since 1950 include noteworthy examples of minimalism, light and space work, conceptualism, installation, and site-specific art (the outside sculptures were designed specifically for this location). MCASD also offers lectures, cutting-edge films, and special events on an ongoing basis; the bookstore is a great place for contemporary gifts, and the cafe is a pleasant stop before or after your visit. The museum is on a cliff overlooking the Pacific Ocean, and the views from the galleries are gorgeous. The original building on the site, designed by Irving Gill in 1916, was the residence of Ellen Browning Scripps. ⏲ *90 min. 700 Prospect St.* ☎ *858/454-3541. www.mcasd.org. Admission $10 adults, $5 seniors and military, free 25 and under; free*

An Andy Goldsworthy sculpture at the Museum of Contemporary Art San Diego.

3rd Tues of the month; paid ticket good for admission to MCASD downtown within 7 days. Fri–Tues 11am–5pm; Thurs 11am–7pm.

③ ★★ kids Children's Pool. A seawall protects this pocket of sand—originally intended as a calm swimming bay for children, but serving since 1994 as a sanctuary for a colony of harbor seals; on an average day you'll spot dozens lolling in the sun. After much heated debate (and even acts of civil disobedience), people were allowed to swim here again—to the displeasure of many. While it is possible to now go in the water at the Children's Pool, keep in mind those are federally protected *wild* animals, and it is illegal to approach them or harass them in any way. Volunteers, with speed dials set to "lifeguard," keep watch to make sure bathers don't bother the colony.

④ ★★ Ellen Browning Scripps Park. This park and the bluffside walkway that courses through it afford some of California's finest coastal scenery. There's plenty of soft grass where you can toss a

Frisbee, have a picnic, or just laze. A series of rustic wooden shelters—popular with seagulls, pigeons, and pedestrians—overlooks La Jolla's shapely curves. The La Jolla Cove Bridge Club—a Works Project Administration structure dating to 1939, where card games still take place—must be one of the world's most view-enhanced card rooms. *La Jolla Cove Bridge Club.* ☎ *858/459-7000. www.lajollacovebridgeclub.com. Games Sun, Wed, Thurs, 11am–3pm.*

⑤ ★★★ kids La Jolla Cove. These protected calm waters, celebrated as the clearest along the coast, attract snorkelers, scuba divers, and families. The small sandy beach gets a bit cramped during the summer, but the cove's "look but don't touch" policy safeguards the colorful garibaldi, California's state fish, plus other marine life, including abalone, octopus, and lobster. The unique Underwater Park stretches from here to the northern end of Torrey Pines State Reserve and incorporates kelp forests, artificial reefs, two deep canyons, and tidal pools.

The coastwalk at Boomer Beach.

The Athenaeum.

6 kids **Sunny Jim Cave.** The only one of La Jolla's seven sea caves accessible by land, the Sunny Jim Cave is reached by a narrow, often slippery, staircase in the Cave Store. (Sunny Jim was a cartoon character created in 1902 for a cereal advertising campaign, and the cave opening resembles his profile.) Part art gallery, part antiques store, this cliff-top shop also rents snorkel equipment. The passageway with 145 steps was dug through the rock in 1902. *1325 Cave St. (just off Prospect St.).* ☎ *858/459-0746. www.cavestore.com. $4 adults, $3 kids 3–16, free for 2 and under.*

7 ★★ **Coast Walk.** As you face the ocean, continue past the Cave Store. You'll find two paths; one leads to a fabulous wood-platform overlook, the other continues along the bluffs. It's a cool little trail, affording expansive views of the coast. You can exit at a stairway that leads back to Prospect Street (before you come to the white wooden bridge) and circle back into town. If you continue along the trail, it will put you on Torrey Pines Road, an extra 10- to 15-minute walk back to the village.

8 ★★★ **La Valencia.** Within its bougainvillea-draped walls and wrought-iron garden gates, this bastion of gentility resurrects the golden age, when celebrities like Greta Garbo and Charlie Chaplin vacationed here. The blufftop hotel, which looks much like a Mediterranean villa, has been the centerpiece of La Jolla since opening in 1926. There are several lounges and restaurants, some with incredible vistas, which can be enjoyed by non-guests; the Whaling Bar is a classic, old-school haunt (see p 15, bullet **5**). *1132 Prospect St. (at Herschel Ave.).* ☎ *800/451-0772 or 858/454-0771. www.lavalencia.com.*

9 ★★ **Athenaeum Music and Arts Library.** One of only 17 nonprofit, membership libraries in the U.S., the Athenaeum hosts art exhibits, jazz and classical concerts, lectures, and special events open to the general public. Visitors can browse through the vast collection of books, music, and more, but only members can take something out. Founded in 1899, the library has expanded into adjacent buildings, including one built by Balboa Park architect William Templeton Johnson. *1008 Wall St. (at Girard Ave.).* ☎ *858/ 454-5872. www.ljathenaeum.org. Gallery exhibits are free. Tues, Thurs–Sat 10am–5:30pm, Wed 10am–8:30pm.*

10 ★ **Girard Gourmet.** This small bakery and restaurant always draws a crowd with its cookies, quiches, soups, salads, and deli sandwiches (the eight-grain bread is a must). The Belgian proprietor also whips up heartier fare such as lamb stew and duck *à l'orange*. It's the perfect place to gather goods for a picnic. *7838 Girard Ave.* ☎ *858/454-3325. www.girardgourmet.com. Mon–Sat 7am–8pm, Sun 7am–7pm.*

Hillcrest

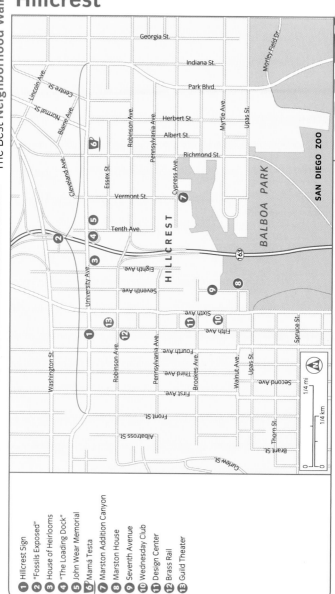

1 Hillcrest Sign
2 "Fossils Exposed"
3 House of Heirlooms
4 "The Loading Dock"
5 John Wear Memorial
6 Mamá Testa
7 Marston Addition Canyon
8 Marston House
9 Seventh Avenue
10 Wednesday Club
11 Design Center
12 Brass Rail
13 Guild Theater

Centrally located, brimming with popular restaurants and boutiques, Hillcrest is one of San Diego's most vibrant neighborhoods, thanks in no small part to its role as the heart of the local gay and lesbian community. In the 1920s, Hillcrest was the city's first self-contained suburb, making it a desirable address for bankers and businessmen, who built their mansions here. Despite the cachet of proximity to Balboa Park (home of the San Diego Zoo and numerous museums), the area fell into neglect in the 1960s. By the late 1970s, however, legions of preservation-minded residents began restoring Hillcrest, and the community is once again among San Diego's best places to live, work, and play. START: **Bus route 1 or 3 to Fifth and University aves.**

❶ **Hillcrest Sign.** Donated to the community in 1940 by a group of local businesswomen, this Art Deco Hillcrest landmark stretches 21 feet (6.5m) across University Ave., utilizing 240 feet (73m) of pink neon lighting. It went dark for some time, but was taken down and refurbished in 1983. Its relighting in August 1984 was the genesis for Hillcrest's annual street fair. Also of note, on the north side of University, is the neon sign for Jimmy Wong's Golden Dragon, a holdover from 1955 (the restaurant itself is defunct). *Corner of University and Fifth aves.*

❷ **"Fossils Exposed."** You can go on a bit of a scavenger hunt as you walk the neighborhood, searching for artist Doron Rosenthal's "Fossils Exposed." This 1998 public art project features 150 granite markers randomly embedded into the sidewalk along University Avenue, from First Avenue to Park Boulevard The 4½-inch (11cm) pieces are stylized representations of actual plant and animal fossils that would be found in this region.

❸ **House of Heirlooms.** Built in 1919, this building is now an antiques store but originally served as a surgery annex for St. Joseph's Sanitarium, a hospital opened by the Sisters of Mercy in 1891. Initially located across the street, it was moved to its present site in 1927, several years after the sisters relocated the hospital a few blocks away, where it continues to serve the community under the name Scripps Mercy Hospital. Preservationists have thus far been successful in saving the building from the concerted efforts of developers. *801 University Ave.* ☎ *619/298-0502.*

❹ **"The Loading Dock."** This detailed, trompe l'oeil mural was painted by artist Linda Churchill in 1999. *Corner of University and 10th aves.*

Hillcrest's Art Deco landmark sign.

Marston House.

⑤ John Wear Memorial. On December 13, 1991, 17-year-old John Wear was accosted and stabbed to death as he walked down the street with two friends because his assailants believed he was gay. This small plaque in the sidewalk in front of The Obelisk bookstore is dedicated to his memory and to the end of all hate crimes. *1029 University Ave.*

⑥ ★ Mamá Testa. A nearly overwhelming selection of tacos—soft, rolled, or hard-shell—featuring recipes from all over Mexico. You won't find better tacos anywhere, on either side of the border. *1417A University Ave.* ☎ *619/298-8226.*

Marston Addition Canyon.

www.mamatestataqueria.com. Mon–Thurs 11:30am–9pm, Fri–Sat 11:30am–10pm, Sun noon–9pm. $–$$.

⑦ ★ Marston Addition Canyon. Turn south down Vermont Street from University Avenue and head through part of residential Hillcrest. At the corner of Cypress Street, you'll come to the trailhead for this open-space oasis in the heart of the city. Follow the (usually) dry creek bed toward the sound of the ocean—actually it's the traffic on Highway 163. Take the footbridge over the freeway and head up the paved path into Balboa Park proper. ⏱ *20 min. Note: This is a very isolated part of the park. It's not recommended you attempt this after dark. If you are doing this walk in the evening, retrace your steps back to University and Sixth aves., and resume the tour there.*

⑧ ★★ Marston House. Built in 1905, this gorgeous Craftsman mansion designed by William Hebbard and Irving Gill was the home of one of San Diego's most prominent families. It's now a museum operated by the San Diego Historical Society. It sits on 5 beautifully landscaped acres (2 hectares) and the interior is filled with art and furniture from the Arts and Crafts period. *See p 38, bullet ⑩.*

9 ★ **Seventh Avenue.** Architecture buffs should continue on down Seventh Avenue for a concentrated dose of classic design. The 10 other houses on this short, shady street represent more brilliant work from architects Irving Gill and William Hebbard, who created the Marston House, as well as prominent San Diego architects Richard Requa and Frank Mead. All the homes were constructed between 1905 and 1913 in what was known as Crittenden's Addition, which dates back to 1887. *Note:* These are all private residences, so keep to the sidewalk. *3500 block of Seventh Ave.*

10 **Wednesday Club.** With the encouragement of architect Irving Gill, Hazel Waterman pursued a career in architecture following the death of her husband, who was the son of California governor Robert Waterman. With her only formal architectural education coming via a correspondence course, Gill hired her on and she helped with three of the houses on Seventh Avenue (see above). She moved on to design this structure in 1911, clearly influenced by Gill. *Sixth Ave. and Ivy Lane.*

11 **Design Center.** Fans of contemporary design will appreciate

this building by architect Lloyd Ruocco, San Diego's leading post-war modernist. Built in 1949, the structure served as Ruocco's office and as the location of his wife Ilse's interior decorating business and showroom. Fittingly, the space has been used by a succession of architectural and design firms ever since. *3611 Fifth Ave.*

12 **Brass Rail.** This is San Diego's oldest gay bar—it's been in the neighborhood since 1963 (although it was originally on the other side of the street, and prior to that, had been downtown). It has been in this spot since 1973. *3796 Fifth Ave. (at Robinson St.).* ☎ *619/298-2233. www.thebrassrailsd.com.*

13 **Guild Theater.** A series of failed enterprises has occupied what was once a beautiful, Spanish Revival–style movie house that first opened in 1913. Re-named the Guild in the late 1950s, the plug was finally pulled on it in 1997. A tragic event for many locals, the Guild was completely destroyed—what you see is a re-creation of the façade based on the original design. *3835 Fifth Ave.*

Hillcrest Village.

Coronado

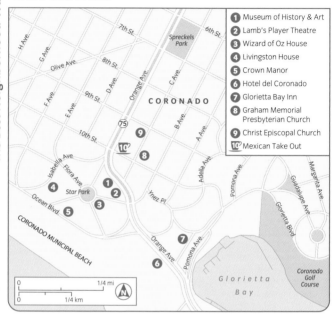

1. Museum of History & Art
2. Lamb's Player Theatre
3. Wizard of Oz House
4. Livingston House
5. Crown Manor
6. Hotel del Coronado
7. Glorietta Bay Inn
8. Graham Memorial Presbyterian Church
9. Christ Episcopal Church
10. Mexican Take Out

You may be tempted to think of Coronado as an island, but it's actually on a peninsula connected to the mainland by a narrow sand spit, the Silver Strand, traversed by the San Diego-Coronado Bay Bridge. It's a wealthy, self-contained community inhabited by lots of retired Navy brass who live on quiet, tree-lined streets. The northern portion of Coronado is home to the U.S. Naval Air Station, in use since World War I. The rest of the area has a history as an elite playground for snowbirds with plenty of big, beautiful homes. Shops and restaurants line the main street, Orange Avenue, which is reminiscent of a Midwestern town. You'll also find several ritzy resorts, including the landmark Hotel del Coronado, which fronts one of the area's finest beaches. START: **Bus route 901.**

1 Museum of History and Art. This museum offers archival materials about the development of Coronado, as well as tourist information. Exhibits include photographs of the Hotel Del in its infancy, the old ferries, Tent City (a seaside campground for middle-income vacationers from 1900 to 1939), and notable residents and visitors. You'll also learn about the island's military aviation history during World War I and II. ⏱ *30 min. 1100 Orange Ave.* ☎ *619/435-7242. www.coronadohistory.org. Suggested donation $4 adults, $3 seniors and military, $2 youths 9–18, free to* *children 8 and under. Mon–Fri 9am–5pm, Sat–Sun 10am–5pm.*

② ★ Lamb's Player Theatre.
This acclaimed troupe is one of the few professional theaters in the country with a year-round resident company. They perform a wide range of work, from classics to new musicals. The intimate theater space is in the heart of a Neo-classical structure known as the Spreckels Building. Constructed of reinforced concrete in 1917, it was designed by Harrison Albright, who also created the Organ Pavilion in Balboa Park and the downtown Spreckels Theater at the behest of sugar magnates John and A. B. Spreckels. *1142 Orange Ave.* ☎ *619/437-0600. www. lambsplayers.org.*

③ Wizard of Oz House. Author L. Frank Baum was a frequent visitor to Coronado, where he wrote several of his beloved *Wizard of Oz* books. It's believed he even patterned elements of the Emerald City after the architecture of the Hotel del Coronado. Baum occupied this colonial revival home, known as the Lemeche-Meade House, in the early 1900s. *1101 Star Park Circle.*

④ ★★ Livingston House. Also known as the Baby Del, this spectacular Queen Anne Revival home was originally located across the bay in San Diego. After 6 months of planning, it was moved to Coronado in 1983 for a cost of $120,000. Built in 1887, 6 months before the Hotel Del, it's believed the house was a training ground for carpenters who would work on the Del, and indeed, might have been designed by the Del's architects, working under a pseudonym. The house is privately owned, but it has its own website. *1144 Isabella Ave. www.babydel.com.*

⑤ ★★ Crown Manor. San Diego's all-star architectural team of William Hebbard and Irving Gill

The Coronado Bridge.

created the original designs for this amazing 27-bedroom, oceanfront estate in 1902. Also known as the Richards-Dupee Mansion, it covers 20,000 square feet (1,858 sq. m) and was commissioned by Bartlett Richards, a Nebraska cattle baron. Richards ran afoul of the law for questionable land schemes in his home state and died while in federal custody in 1911. He was elected to the National Cowboy Hall of Fame in 1970. *1015 Ocean Blvd.*

⑥ ★★★ Hotel del Coronado.
San Diego's romantic Hotel del Coronado is an unmistakable landmark with a colorful past. When it opened in 1888, it was among the first buildings rigged with Thomas Edison's new invention, electric light (its electrical power plant supplied the entire city of Coronado until 1922). Author L. Frank Baum, a frequent guest, designed the dining room's original crown-shaped chandeliers. The hotel has also played host to royalty and celebrities—Edward, Prince of Wales (later King Edward VIII, and then Duke of Windsor), caused a sensation with his visit in 1920, and of course, Marilyn

The Coronado Ferry gate.

Monroe, Tony Curtis, and Jack Lemmon famously frolicked here in the film *Some Like It Hot. See p 18, bullet ❹.*

❼ ★★ Glorietta Bay Inn. The Spreckels Mansion is now known as the Glorietta Bay Inn. It was designed by John Spreckels' go-to architect, Harrison Albright, and built in 1908. Spreckels, along with his family and money, abandoned San Francisco after the 1906 earthquake and set up shop in San Diego. He was particularly involved with Coronado, where he became sole owner of the Hotel Del. The Glorietta Bay Inn's 1950s motel-style annexes are lamentable, but the home's glory is still very much in evidence. *1630 Glorietta Blvd.* ☎ *800/283-9383 or 619/435-3101.* *www.gloriettabayinn.com.*

❽ ★ Graham Memorial Presbyterian Church. The founding fathers of Coronado were land speculators who purchased the peninsula—mostly inhabited by jackrabbits—for $110,000 in 1885. Their intent from the beginning was to create a resort community. This lovely little church was built by Hotel Del architect James Reid for one of those original investors, Elisha S. Babcock, Jr., in 1890. The church was then dedicated to the memory of Babcock's in-laws, John and Susan Graham. *975 C Ave.*

❾ ★ Christ Episcopal Church. James and Watson Reid, the brother architects who created the Hotel Del Coronado, designed this Gothic stone church. Completed in 1894, it features stained glass made by noted California artist, writer, and landscape designer Bruce Porter. The church was commissioned by Capt. Charles Hinde (the magnificent Kirk-Hinde residence, also designed by the Reid brothers, is across the street at 959 C Ave.). *900 C Ave.*

❿ Mexican Take Out. This no-frills, walk-in closet–sized space lacks any pretense of charm, which of course is its charm. Mexican Take Out (yes, that's actually the name) offers, well, Mexican take-out— there's no eating on the premises. *1107 10th St.(at Orange Ave., behind Clayton's Coffee Shop).* ☎ *619/437-8811. Mon–Sat 10:30am–9pm, Sun 11:30am–7:30pm. Cash only. $.* ●

The iconic Coronado Hotel.

Shopping Best Bets

Best **Jewelry That Doubles as Art**
★★★ Taboo Studio *1615½ W. Lewis St. (p 79)*

Best **Clothing That Doubles as Artwork**
★★★ La Jolla Fiber Arts *7644 Girard Ave. (p 77)*

Best **Urban-Fabulous Sneakers**
★★ Mint *525 University Ave. (p 77)*

Best **Vintage Clothing**
★★★ Wear It Again Sam *3823 Fifth Ave. (p 77)*

Best **Gallery for Local Artists**
★★★ David Zapf Gallery *2400 Kettner Blvd., Suite 104 (p 74)*

Best **Place to Find Dr. Seuss on the Loose**
★★ Fingerhut Gallery *1205 Prospect St. (p 75)*

Best **Place to Find Your Bearings**
★★★ Ruderman Antique Maps *1298 Prospect St., Suite 2C (p 74)*

Best **Place for Mid-Century Modernists**
★★★ Boomerang for Modern *2475 Kettner Blvd. (p 78);* and ★★★ Mid-Century *3795 Park Blvd. (p 79)*

Best **Place for Moms-to-Be**
★★ Baby Mabel's *111 S. Cedros Ave. (p 76)*

Best **Denim**
★★ G-Star Raw *470 Fifth Ave. (p 77)*

Best **Pop Culture Gifts**
★ Babette Schwartz *421 University Ave. (p 78)*

Best **Stuff From Out of Africa**
★★ Africa and Beyond *1250 Prospect St. (p 74)*

Best **Place to Buy a Trilobite**
★★ Dinosaur Gallery *1327 Camino del Mar (p 78)*

Best **Candle Store**
★★ Knorr Candle Shop *14906 Villa de la Valle (p 78)*

Best **Vintage Glass**
★★ Vetro *7605 Girard Ave. (p 74)*

Best **Toy Store**
★★ The Lily Pad *3746 Sixth Ave. (p 76)*

Best **Place for Surfer Girls and Boys**
★★ Quiksilver/Roxy *1111 Prospect St. (p 76)*

Best **Greek Gods**
★★ Column One *401 University Ave. (p 79)*

Best **New Retro Furnishings**
★★★ Design Within Reach *393 Seventh Ave. (p 79)*

Best **Shopping Center for Fashionistas**
★★ Fashion Valley Center *7007 Friars Rd. (p 80)*

Horton Plaza in the Gaslamp Quarter.

Downtown Shopping

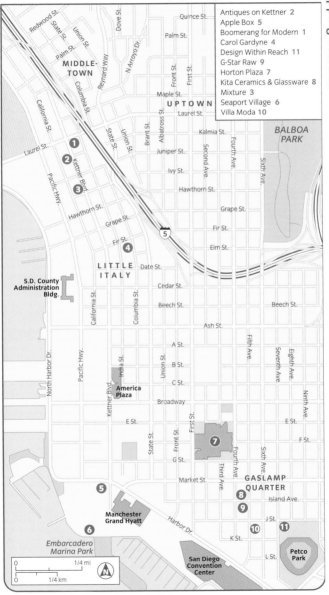

Antiques on Kettner 2
Apple Box 5
Boomerang for Modern 1
Carol Gardyne 4
Design Within Reach 11
G-Star Raw 9
Horton Plaza 7
Kita Ceramics & Glassware 8
Mixture 3
Seaport Village 6
Villa Moda 10

Hillcrest Shopping

La Jolla Shopping

Africa & Beyond **3**
Blondstone **7**
Emilia Castillo **2**
Fingerhut Gallery **5**
Joseph Bellows Gallery **11**
La Jolla Fiber Arts **10**
Laura Gambucci **12**
Morrison Hotel Gallery **4**
My Own Space **8**
Quiksilver/Roxy **6**
Quint Contemporary Art **9**
Ruderman Antique Maps **1**
Vetro **13**

North County Shopping

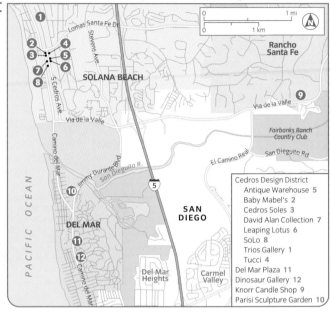

Cedros Design District
Antique Warehouse 5
Baby Mabel's 2
Cedros Soles 3
David Alan Collection 7
Leaping Lotus 6
SoLo 8
Trios Gallery 1
Tucci 4
Del Mar Plaza 11
Dinosaur Gallery 12
Knorr Candle Shop 9
Parisi Sculpture Garden 10

Shopping A to Z

Antiques & Collectibles
★ Antiques on Kettner LITTLE
ITALY   Nearly 30 individual dealers share this space with a wide selection of antiques and collectibles. *2400 Kettner Blvd., Suite 106 (at W. Kalmia St.).* ☎ *619/234-3332. www. antiquesonkettner.com. MC, V. Bus: 83. Map p 71.*

★★★ Ruderman Antique
Maps LA JOLLA   History buffs won't want to miss this place—it sells maps, atlases, and books that date from the 15th through 19th centuries. *1298 Prospect St., Suite 2C (at Ivanhoe Ave.).* ☎ *858/551-8500. www.raremaps.com. AE, DISC, MC, V. Bus: 30. Map p 73.*

★★ Vetro LA JOLLA   A rainbow
collection of vintage, hand-blown glass from America, Italy, and Scandinavia. *7605 Girard Ave. (at Torrey Pines Rd.).* ☎ *858/729-0045. www. vetrocollections.com. AE, MC, V. Bus: 30. Map p 73.*

Art
★★ Africa and Beyond LA JOLLA
A collection of contemporary and traditional African sculpture, textiles, jewelry, and furnishings. *1250 Prospect St. (east of Ivanhoe Ave.).* ☎ *858/454-9983. www.africaand beyond.com. AE, DISC, MC, V. Bus: 30. Map p 73.*

★★★ David Zapf Gallery LITTLE
ITALY   One of the city's leading

Vetro in La Jolla.

contemporary galleries, it focuses on local artists. *2400 Kettner Blvd., Suite 104 (at Kalmia St.).* ☎ *619/232-5004. Cash and checks only. Bus: 83. Map p 71, bullet ②.*

★★ **Fingerhut Gallery** LA JOLLA Theodor Geisel, aka Dr. Seuss, was a longtime resident of La Jolla. This gallery features his work, including plenty of pieces you won't find in a children's book. *1205 Prospect St. (at Ivanhoe Ave.).* ☎ *858/456-9900. www.fingerhutart.com. AE, DISC, MC, V. Bus: 30. Map p 73.*

★★★ **Joseph Bellows Gallery** LA JOLLA Devotees of photography will want to check out this gallery, which showcases both contemporary and vintage work. *7661 Girard Ave. (between Kline St. and Torrey Pines Rd.).* ☎ *858/456-5620. www.josephbellows.com. AE, DISC, MC, V. Bus: 30. Map p 73.*

★★ **Morrison Hotel Gallery** LA JOLLA I know, it's only rock 'n' roll photography, but I like it. *1230 Prospect St. (east of Ivanhoe Ave.).* ☎ *858/551-0835. www.morrison hotelgallery.com. AE, DISC, MC, V. Bus: 30. Map p 73.*

★★★ **Parisi Sculpture Garden and Gallery** DEL MAR A tranquil hideaway near the Del Mar Fairgrounds where you'll find contemporary, museum-quality pieces. *2002 Jimmy Durante Blvd., Suite 308 (north of the Camino del Mar junction).* ☎ *858/259-0031. www.parisi portfolio.com. Bus: 101. Map p 74.*

★★★ **Quint Contemporary Art** LA JOLLA A bit off the beaten tourist path, this gallery is worth seeking out for its roster of engaging artists. *7739 Fay Ave. (entrance on Drury Lane, between Silverado and Kline sts.).* ☎ *858/454-3409.*

Scott White Art Gallery.

Surfer and skater gear at Quiksilver/Roxy in La Jolla.

www.quintgallery.com. AE, MC, V. Bus: 30. Map p 73.

★★★ **Scott White Contemporary Art** LITTLE ITALY   Another leading light on the local gallery scene, Scott White deals in contemporary painting, sculpture, and photography by artists from around the world. *2400 Kettner Blvd., Suite 238 (at Kalmia St.).* ☎ *619/501-5689. www.scottwhiteart.com. AE, MC, V. Bus: 83. Map 71, bullet ❷.*

Children: Fashion & Toys
★★ **kids Apple Box** EMBAR-CADERO   This shop specializes in wooden toys. You'll find everything from puzzles and pull toys to rocking horses and toy chests. *Seaport Village, 837 W. Harbor Dr., Suite C (at Kettner Blvd.).* ☎ *800/676-7529. www.appleboxtoys.com. AE, DISC, MC, V. Trolley: Orange Line to Seaport Village. Map p 71.*

★★ **Baby Mabel's** SOLANA BEACH   Hip fashions and gifts for infants and style-conscious moms-to-be. *111 S. Cedros Ave. (south of Lomas Santa Fe Dr.).* ☎ *858/794-0076.*

www.babymabels.com. AE, DISC, MC, V. Bus: 101. Map p 74.

★★ **kids The Lily Pad** HILLCREST This small shop features old-fashioned toys that let creativity soar; performances, lectures, and workshops are also on tap. *3746 Sixth Ave. (south of Robinson Ave.).* ☎ *619/220-8555. www.thelilypad sd.com. AE, DISC, MC, V. Bus: 3 or 120. Map p 72.*

★★ **kids Quiksilver/Roxy** LA JOLLA   Teens and 'tweens will love the surf and skate gear at this conjoined boys/girls shop in the heart of La Jolla village. *1111 Prospect St. (at Herschel Ave.).* ☎ *858/459-1267. www.quiksilver.com. AE, DISC, MC, V. Bus: 30. Map p 73.*

Fashion
★★★ **Carol Gardyne** LITTLE ITALY One-of-a-kind and limited edition silk scarves and wall hangings, hand-painted at this studio/boutique. *1840 Columbia St. (at Fir St.).* ☎ *619/233-8066. www.carolgardyne.com. AE, DISC, MC, V. Bus: 83. Map p 71.*

★★ **Cedros Soles** SOLANA BEACH   Just try to resist the fabulous shoes for women here; there's

Baby Mabel's maternity clothes.

Tucci in Solana Beach.

also a great selection of handbags and other accessories. *143 S. Cedros Ave., Suite L (south of Lomas Santa Fe Dr.).* ☎ *858/794-9911. www. cedrossoles.com. AE, DISC, MC, V. Bus: 101. Map p 74.*

★★ **G-Star Raw** GASLAMP QUARTER   This international chain has a cool San Diego boutique, selling Euro-style denim. *470 Fifth Ave. (between Island Ave. and J St.).* ☎ *619/238-7088. www.g-star.com. AE, DISC, MC, V. Bus: 3, 11, 120, or 992. Map p 71.*

★★★ **La Jolla Fiber Arts** LA JOLLA   The hand-woven creations here make this store something of an art gallery, as well as a fashion outlet. *7644 Girard Ave. (between Kline St. and Torrey Pines Rd.).* ☎ *858/454-6732. www.lajollafiber arts.com. AE, DISC, MC, V. Bus: 30. Map p 73.*

★★★ **Laura Gambucci** LA JOLLA Bucking the conservative La Jolla trend, this women's boutique features unique, contemporary styles and sexy shoes and handbags. *7629 Girard Ave., Suite C3 (between Kline St. and Torrey Pines Rd.).* ☎ *858/551-0214. AE, DISC, MC, V. Bus: 30. Map p 73.*

★★ **Mint** HILLCREST   An excellent selection of urban sneakers and casual footwear for him and her. *525 University Ave. (between 5th and 6th aves.).* ☎ *619/291-6468. AE, MC, V. Bus: 1, 3, 10, 11, or 120. Map p 72.*

★★ **Tucci** SOLANA BEACH   This boutique is chic and sophisticated, offering contemporary, international designs in a comfortably mod space. *130 S. Cedros Ave., Suite 140 (south of Lomas Santa Fe Dr.).* ☎ *858/259-8589. www.tucciboutique.com. AE, MC, V. Bus: 101. Map p 74.*

★★ **Villa Moda** GASLAMP QUARTER   The Gaslamp's best spot for women's fashions and a sparkling array of jewelry, as well. *363 Fifth Ave. (between J and K sts.).* ☎ *619/236-9068. www.villamoda.com. AE, DISC, MC, V. Bus: 992. Trolley: Orange Line to Gaslamp Quarter. Map p 71.*

★★★ **Wear It Again Sam** HILLCREST   This classy vintage clothing store sells high-quality goods from the 1920s through the '50s. *3823 Fifth Ave. (between University and Robinson aves.).* ☎ *619/299-0185. www.wearitagainsamvintage.com. AE, MC, V. Bus: 1, 3, 10, 11, or 120. Map p 72.*

Villa Moda in the Gaslamp Quarter.

Gifts

★ Babette Schwartz HILLCREST Camp meets kitsch at this fun-loving gift store stocked with novelties, cards, and T-shirts. *421 University Ave. (between 4th and 5th aves.). ☎ 619/220-7048. www.babette. com. MC, V. Bus: 1, 3, 10, 11, or 120. Map p 72.*

★★ kids Dinosaur Gallery DEL MAR Own a piece of (pre)history—fossils, gems and minerals, and amber jewelry. Models, puzzles, and more for the kids, too. *1327 Camino Del Mar (between 13th and 14th sts.). ☎ 858/794-4855. AE, MC, V. Bus: 101. Map p 74.*

★★ Kita Ceramics & Glassware GASLAMP QUARTER *Objets d'art* from Italy, Japan, and San Diego, including Murano glass jewelry and lighting, pottery, and home accessories. *517 Fourth Ave., Suite 101 (at Island Ave.). ☎ 619/239-2600. www.kitaceramicsglass.com. AE, MC, V. Bus: 992. Map p 71.*

★★ Knorr Candle Shop DEL MAR This family-run business has been making beeswax candles here since 1928; it's one of the largest candle stores in the country. *14906*

Boomerang for Modern in Little Italy.

Via de la Valle (east of El Camino Real). ☎ 858/755-2051. www.knorr candleshop.com. AE, DISC, MC, V. Bus: 308. Map p 74.

Home Decor

★★★ Boomerang for Modern LITTLE ITALY Sleek vintage modern furniture and accessories by Herman Miller, Vitra, Eames, and Noguchi. *2475 Kettner Blvd. (at Laurel St.). ☎ 619/239-2040. www. boomerangformodern.com. AE, DISC, MC, V. Bus: 83. Map p 71.*

★★★ Cedros Design District SOLANA BEACH More than two-dozen chic and eclectic shops. Highlights include **Antique Warehouse** (212 S. Cedros Ave.; ☎ 858/755-5156; DISC, MC, V); **David Alan Collection** (241 S. Cedros Ave.; ☎ 858/481-8044; www.thedavid alancollection.com; MC, V); **Leaping Lotus** (240 S. Cedros Ave.; ☎ 858/720-8283; www.leapinglotus.com; AE, MC, V); **SoLo,** (309 S. Cedros Ave.; ☎ 858/794-9016; www.solo cedros.com; AE, DISC, MC, V); and **Trios Gallery** (404 N. Cedros Ave.; ☎ 858/793-6040; www.triosgallery. com; AE, DISC, MC, V). *Primarily the*

Design Within Reach.

100 and 200 blocks of S. Cedros Ave. (south of Lomas Santa Fe Dr.). www. cedrosdesigndistrict.com. Bus: 101. Map p 74.

★★ **Column One** HILLCREST Classical and contemporary statuary and fountains for the home and garden. *401 University Ave., Suite C. (at 4th Ave.).* ☎ *619/299-9074. MC, V. Bus: 1, 3, 10, 11, or 120. Map p 72.*

★★★ **Design Within Reach** EAST VILLAGE The source for official reproductions of classic furnishings and accessories by companies such as Herman Miller, Knoll, and Vitra. *393 Seventh Ave. (at J St.).* ☎ *619/744-9900. www.dwr.com. AE, DISC, MC, V. Bus: 992. Trolley: Orange Line to Gaslamp Quarter. Map p 71.*

★★★ **Mid-Century** HILLCREST Cool pottery, light fixtures, cocktail accessories, furniture, and more from the 1940s, '50s, and '60s. *3795 Park Blvd.* ☎ *619/295-4832. AE, DISC, MC, V. Bus: 7. Map p 72.*

★★ **Mixture** LITTLE ITALY This old brick warehouse has been beautifully transformed into a repository of modern design and decor. *2210 Kettner Blvd. (at Ivy St.).* ☎ *619/239-4788. www.mixturedesigns.com. AE, MC, V. Bus: 83. Map p 71.*

★★ **kids My Own Space** LA JOLLA Hello Kitty meets mid-century modernism at this whimsical furniture and accessories boutique. *7840 Girard Ave. (between Silverado and Wall sts.).* ☎ *858/459-0099. www.mosmyownspace.com. MC, V. Bus: 30. Map p 73.*

Jewelry
★★ **Blondstone** LA JOLLA Creative jewelry designs, including one-of-a-kind rings, pendants, earrings, and bracelets incorporating seashells and tumbled sea-glass "mermaid tears." *925 Prospect St. (at Drury Lane).* ☎ *858/456.1994.*

www.blondstone.com. AE, MC, V. Bus: 30. Map p 73.

★★ **Emilia Castillo** LA JOLLA From her home studio in Taxco, Mexico, Emilia Castillo produces fantastic silver creations, including necklaces, cuffs, belt buckles, and tableware. *1273 Prospect St. (east of Ivanhoe Ave.).* ☎ *858/557-9600. www.emiliacastillojewelry.com. AE, DISC, MC, V. Bus: 30. Map p 73.*

★★★ **Taboo Studio** MISSION HILLS The jewelry here is more than just simple ornamentation, these pieces are works of art created by nationally and internationally known jewelry artists. *1615½ W. Lewis St. (between Stephens St. and Palmetto Way).* ☎ *619/692-0099. www.taboostudio.com. AE, DISC, MC, V. Bus: 83. Map p 72.*

Shopping Centers
★★★ **Del Mar Plaza** DEL MAR With its ocean-view terraces, fountains, destination restaurants, and open-air wine bar, this might be the nicest mall you've ever seen. There are more than 30 stores. *1555*

My Own Space in La Jolla.

Camino Del Mar (at 15th St.).
☎ 858/792-1555. www.delmar
plaza.com. Bus: 101. Map p 74.

★★ **Fashion Valley Center** MIS-
SION VALLEY   This upscale shopping
center features Nordstrom, Neiman
Marcus, and Saks Fifth Avenue
department stores, as well as more
than 200 specialty shops and an 18-
screen movie theater. 7007 Friars Rd.
(between Hwy. 163 and Fashion Valley
Rd.). ☎ 619/688-9113. www.simon.
com. Bus: 6, 14, 20, 25, 41, 120, or
928. Trolley: Blue or Green Line to
Fashion Valley. Map p 72.

★★ **Horton Plaza** GASLAMP
QUARTER   This colorful shopping
center has more than 180 specialty
shops, a performing arts venue,
a 14-screen cinema, two major
department stores, and a variety of
restaurants and short-order eateries. 324 Horton Plaza (bounded by
Broadway, 1st and 4th aves., and
G St.). ☎ 619/238-1596. www.
westfield.com/hortonplaza. Bus: 2,
3, 5, 7, 11, 15, 20, 30, 50, 120, 150,
210, 901, 923, 929, or 992. Trolley:
Blue or Orange Line to Civic Center.
Map p 71.

Mission Valley Center MISSION
VALLEY   This old-fashioned outdoor
mall has budget-minded offerings
such as Nordstrom Rack outlet store
and Target; there's also a 20-screen
movie theater and 150 other stores
and places to eat. 1640 Camino del
Rio N. (alongside I-8 at Mission Center Rd.). ☎ 619/296-6375. www.
westfield.com/missionvalley. Bus: 6
or 14. Trolley: Blue or Green Line to
Mission Valley Center. Map p 72.

★ kids **Seaport Village** EMBAR-
CADERO   This 14-acre (5.5-hectare)
bayfront outdoor mall provides an
idyllic setting that visitors love.
Many of the more than 50 shops are
of the Southern California cutesy
variety, but the atmosphere is pleasant, and there are a few gems. 849
W. Harbor Dr. (at Kettner Blvd.).
☎ 619/235-4014. www.seaport
village.com. Trolley: Orange Line
to Seaport Village. Map p 71.

★ **Westfield UTC** LA JOLLA   This
outdoor shopping complex has a
shady, landscaped plaza and more
than 180 stores, including Nordstrom and Macy's. It's also home to
a year-round ice-skating rink. 4545
La Jolla Village Dr. (at Genesee Ave.).
☎ 858/546-8858. www.westfield.
com/utc. Bus: 30, 31, 41, 48, 49, 50,
89, 105, 101, 310, 921, or 960. ●

Seaport Village outdoor mall.

The Best **Beaches**

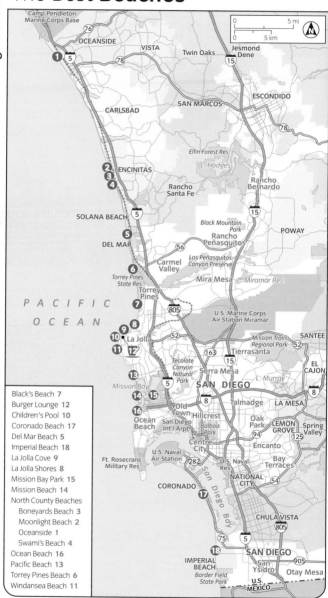

Black's Beach **7**
Burger Lounge **12**
Children's Pool **10**
Coronado Beach **17**
Del Mar Beach **5**
Imperial Beach **18**
La Jolla Cove **9**
La Jolla Shores **8**
Mission Bay Park **15**
Mission Beach **14**
North County Beaches
  Boneyards Beach **3**
  Moonlight Beach **2**
  Oceanside **1**
  Swami's Beach **4**
Ocean Beach **16**
Pacific Beach **13**
Torrey Pines Beach **6**
Windansea Beach **11**

A game of volleyball at DelMar Beach.

San Diego County is blessed with 70 miles (113km) of sandy coastline and more than 30 individual beaches. Even in winter and spring, when water temperatures drop into the 50s, the beaches are great places to walk, jog, and surf. In summer, when the beaches teem with locals and visitors alike, bikinis bust out, pecs are bared, and a spring-break atmosphere threatens to break loose.

★★★ **Black's Beach.** Located at the base of steep, 300-foot- (91m-) high cliffs, this 2-mile- (3km-) long beach is out of the way and not easy to reach, but it draws scores with its secluded beauty and good swimming and surfing conditions—the graceful spectacle of paragliders launching from the cliffs above adds to the show. This is the area's unofficial nude beach, though technically nude sunbathing is illegal. Citations are rarely issued—lifeguards will either ignore it or just ask you to cover up (they will write tickets if you disregard their request). There are no facilities here. *Bus: 101 to the Torrey Pines Gliderport; hike down the trail. You can also walk to Black's from beaches south (La Jolla Shores) or north (Torrey Pines).*

Take a Break

☕ **Burger Lounge.** A fast-food joint—La Jolla-style. This sleek and modern burger spot has plenty of panache—it's casual but fashionable, serving grass-fed, organic beef burgers, as well as hand-cut fries and salads. Milkshakes, wine, and beer are also on the short menu. *1101 Wall St. (at Herschel Ave.).* ☎ *858/456-0196. Daily 11am–9pm, with later closing on Fri–Sat. www. burgerlounge.com. $.*

★★ **kids Children's Pool.** Think clothing-optional Black's Beach is the city's most controversial sun-sea-sand situation? Think again—the Children's Pool is currently home to the biggest man-vs.-beast struggle since *Moby*

Sea lions loll on the beach at the Children's Pool.

Del Mar Beach.

Dick. A seawall shields this pocket of sand, originally intended as a calm swimming bay for children, but since 1994, when a rock outcrop off the shore was designated as a protected mammal reserve, the beach has been cordoned off for the resident harbor seal population. Swimming has been reinstated here—under the watchful eye of seal-loving volunteers—but most people just come to observe the colony. *See p 60, bullet* ❸ . *Bus: 30 to Girard Ave. and Silverado St.*

Del Mar Beach.

Walk 2 blocks down Girard Ave., cross Prospect St. to Ocean Lane.

★★ kids Coronado Beach.

Lovely, wide, and sparkling, this beach is conducive to strolling and lingering, especially in the late afternoon. At the north end, you can watch fighter jets flying in formation from the Naval Air Station, while just south is the pretty section fronting Ocean Boulevard and the Hotel del Coronado. Waves are gentle here, so the beach draws many Coronado families—and their dogs, which are allowed off-leash at the most north-westerly end. South of the Hotel Del, the beach becomes the beautiful, often deserted Silver Strand. The islands visible from here, Los Coronados, are 18 miles away and belong to Mexico. *Bus: 901 or 904 to the Hotel Del Coronado.*

★★ kids Del Mar Beach. The Del

Mar Thoroughbred Club's slogan, as famously sung by DMTC founder Bing Crosby, is "where turf meets the surf." This town beach represents the "surf" portion of that phrase. It's a long stretch of sand backed by grassy cliffs and a playground area. This area is not

La Jolla Shores.

heavily trafficked, and there are several restaurants where you can dine right alongside the beach. Del Mar is about 15 miles (24km) from downtown San Diego. *Bus: 101.*

★ **Imperial Beach.** A half-hour south of downtown San Diego by car or trolley, and only a few minutes from the Mexican border, Imperial Beach is popular with surfers and local youth, who can be somewhat territorial about "their" sands in summer. The beach has 3 miles (5km) of surf breaks plus a guarded "swimmers only" stretch; check with lifeguards before getting wet, though, since sewage runoff from nearby Mexico can sometimes foul the water. I.B. also plays host to the annual U.S. Open Sandcastle Competition in late July—the best reason to come here—with world-class sand creations ranging from nautical scenes to dinosaurs. *Trolley: Blue Line to Palm Ave., transfer to Bus 933.*

★★★ kids **La Jolla Cove.** The star of postcards for more than a century, the tropical-hued waters of La Jolla Cove represent San Diego at its most picture-perfect. Part of the

San Diego–La Jolla Underwater ecological reserve, the Cove is a perfect place to do a little snorkeling. If this small beach gets a little too crowded, classy, grassy Ellen Browning Scripps Park on the bluff above it provides a great alternative. *See p 60, bullets ④ and ⑤. Bus: 30. Walking directions same as previous.*

★★ kids **La Jolla Shores.** The wide, flat mile of sand at La Jolla Shores is popular with joggers, swimmers, kayakers, novice scuba divers, and beginning body- and board-surfers, as well as families. Weekend crowds can be enormous, quickly claiming fire rings and occupying both the sand and the metered parking spaces in the lot. There are restrooms, showers, and picnic areas here, as well as palm-lined Kellogg Park across the street. *Bus: 30 to La Jolla Shores Dr. and Avenida de la Playa. Walk 5 blocks down Avenida de la Playa.*

★ kids **Mission Bay Park.** This 4,600-acre (1,862-hectare) aquatic playground contains 27 miles (43km) of bayfront, picnic areas, children's playgrounds, and paths for biking, in-line skating, and jogging. The bay lends itself to windsurfing, sailing,

La Jolla Cove.

The pier at Imperial Beach.

water-skiing, and fishing. There are dozens of access points; one of the most popular is off I-5 at Clairemont Drive. Also accessed from this spot is Fiesta Island, where the annual softball-cum-beach party spectacle known as the Over the Line Tournament is held to raucous enthusiasm in July; a 4-mile (6.5km) road loops around the island. Vacation Island, in the center of the bay, is home to Paradise Point Resort (*see p 143*) and Ski Beach. Parts of the bay have been subject to closure over the years due to high levels of bacteria, so check for posted warnings. Personally, I'd rather sail on Mission Bay than swim in it. *Bus: 8 (west Mission Bay), 9 (Vacation Island), or 105 (east Mission Bay). See p 92.*

★ **Mission Beach.** While Mission Bay Park is a body of saltwater surrounded by land and bridges, Mission Beach is actually a beach on the Pacific Ocean, anchored by the Giant Dipper roller coaster and the Belmont Park amusement center. Always popular, the sands and wide cement boardwalk sizzle with activity and great people-watching in summer; at the southern end there's always a volleyball game in play. The long beach and path

extend from the jetty north to Belmont Park and Pacific Beach Drive. Parking is often tough, with your best bets being the public lots at Belmont Park or at the south end of West Mission Bay Drive. Busy Mission Boulevard is the centerline of a 2-block-wide isthmus that separates the ocean and Mission Bay; it stretches a mile north to Pacific Beach. *Bus: 8 to Mission Beach.*

North County Beaches. Those inclined to venture farther north in San Diego County won't be disappointed. Pacific Coast Highway leads to inviting beaches, such as these in Encinitas: peaceful ★★ **Boneyards Beach,** ★★★ **Swami's Beach** for surfing, and ★★ **Moonlight Beach,** popular with families and volleyball buffs. Farthest north is ★★ **Oceanside,** which has one of the West Coast's longest wooden piers, wide sandy beaches, and several popular surfing areas. *Bus: 101.*

★ **Ocean Beach.** Officially known as Dog Beach, the northern end of Ocean Beach Park is one of only a few in the county where your pooch can roam freely on the sand and frolic with several dozen other people's pets. Surfers generally congregate around the O.B. Pier, mostly in the water but often at the snack shack on the end. Rip currents can be strong here and sometimes discourage swimmers from venturing beyond waist depth (check with the lifeguard stations). Facilities at the beach include restrooms, showers, picnic tables, volleyball courts, and plenty of metered parking lots. *Bus: 35 or 923 to Newport Ave.*

★ **Pacific Beach.** There's always action here, particularly along Ocean Front Walk, a paved promenade featuring a human parade akin to that at L.A.'s Venice Beach boardwalk. It runs along Ocean Boulevard (just west of Mission Blvd.) to the pier. Surfing is popular year-round here, in marked sections, and the beach is well staffed with lifeguards. You're on your own to find street parking. Pacific Beach is also the home of Tourmaline Surfing Park, a half-mile (.8km) north of the pier, where the sport's old guard gathers to surf waters where swimmers are prohibited; reach it via Tourmaline Street, off Mission Boulevard. *Bus 8/9.*

★★★ **Torrey Pines Beach.** At the foot of Torrey Pines State Reserve is this fabulous, underused strand, accessed by a pay parking lot at the entrance to the park. In fact, combining a visit to the park with a day at the beach makes for the quintessential San Diego outdoor experience. It's rarely crowded, though you need to be aware of high tide (when most of the sand gets a bath). In almost any weather, it's a great beach for walking. *Note:* At this and any other bluff-side beach, never sit at the bottom of the cliffs. The hillsides are unstable and could collapse. *Bus: 101.*

★★ **Windansea Beach.** The fabled locale of Tom Wolfe's *Pump*

Hang gliding at Torrey Pines.

House Gang, Windansea is legendary to this day among California's surf elite and remains one of San Diego's prettiest strands. This is not a good beach for swimming or diving, so come to surf (no novices, please), watch surfers, or soak in the camaraderie and party atmosphere. Windansea has no facilities, and street parking is first-come, first-served. *Bus: 30 to Nautilus St.*

A crab shack on Pacific Beach.

Cabrillo National Monument

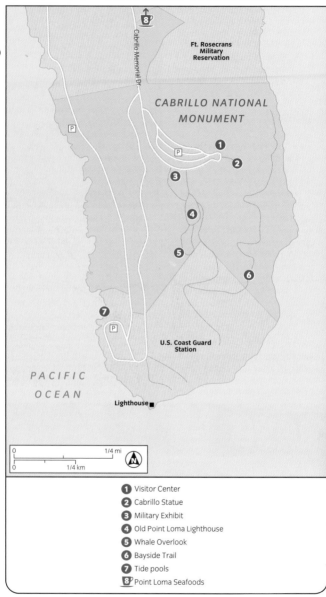

Cabrillo Memorial Dr.

Ft. Rosecrans
Military
Reservation

*CABRILLO NATIONAL
MONUMENT*

P

PACIFIC
OCEAN

U.S. Coast Guard
Station

Lighthouse ■

0 ___ 1/4 mi
0 ___ 1/4 km

1. Visitor Center
2. Cabrillo Statue
3. Military Exhibit
4. Old Point Loma Lighthouse
5. Whale Overlook
6. Bayside Trail
7. Tide pools
8. Point Loma Seafoods

"**On this day, Thursday, September 28, 1542,** we discovered a port, closed and very good." When Juan Rodríguez Cabrillo led his three galleons into that sheltered harbor nearly 470 years ago, he became the first European to set eyes on what would become the West Coast of the United States. Point Loma, the spit of land that protected Cabrillo and his flotilla from an oncoming storm, is now the site of Cabrillo National Monument, a 160-acre (65-hectare) national park that is rich not only in history, but in natural wonders as well. START: **Bus route 28C.**

❶ ★★ Visitor Center. Start your tour here. The visitor center has a bookstore with hundreds of publications on San Diego history, marine life, and the age of exploration in the 16th century. There's also a glassed-in observation area offering stellar panoramas, including views of the actual spot where Cabrillo's party came ashore. The park's auditorium has ongoing screenings of films about Cabrillo's journey, whale migration, and more; a small museum features interactive exhibits about the conquistador and Spain's far-flung empire. Declared a National Monument in 1913 by President Woodrow Wilson, the park is also the site of special events, including a reenactment of Cabrillo's landing every late September and early October, and whale-related festivities every winter. *See p 13, bullet* **❶**.

Cabrillo statue.

❷ ★★ Cabrillo Statue. This 15-foot (4.5m) statue portrays Cabrillo looking steadfast and resolute; he doesn't seem to be much enjoying the 360-degree view from his privileged position. The flesh-and-blood Cabrillo was Portuguese (actual name, João Rodrigues Cabrilho), and as a soldier serving Spain he made a name for himself as a crossbowman during Hernán Cortés' siege of Tenochtitlán (now Mexico City), and also participated in the conquest of Guatemala. His adventuring would come to an end several months after his visit to San Diego, though, when he died from an injury suffered in a skirmish with Chumash Indians on one of Southern California's Channel Islands.

❸ Military Exhibit. Point Loma's strategic importance has long been recognized, and the area was established as a military reserve in 1852. Long-range gun batteries bristled from this plateau during both World Wars, and their remnants are still

The new Point Loma Lighthouse.

The Old Point Loma Lighthouse.

here. In a small building once used as an army radio station, there is an exhibit documenting San Diego's 19th Coast Artillery and the war hysteria that gripped the city after the attack on Pearl Harbor.

④ ★★ **Old Point Loma Lighthouse.** This lighthouse had a relatively short lifespan, from 1855 to 1891, its seemingly perfect location compromised by low clouds and fog that often rendered the sweeping beam of light useless. The New Point Loma Lighthouse, situated nearby at sea level, has been in continuous operation since 1891. An interactive exhibit details what life was like for the keepers who lived here in the 19th century, far from the relative comforts of Old Town; the lighthouse itself is filled with period furnishings.

⑤ ★ **Whale Overlook.** From this sheltered space, you can spot Pacific gray whales as they make their amazing, 10,000-mile (16,093km) journey from the Bering Sea to the warm lagoons of Mexico's Sea of Cortés, and back again, every mid-December through mid-March. These 40-ton (36T), 50-foot (15m) behemoths (with calves in tow on the return trip) are making the longest migration of any mammal. The overlook is outfitted with recorded information and high-powered telescopes; if you don't manage to see a whale, you can still have your picture taken with the scaled-down whale sculpture nearby.

Bayside Trail at sunset.

Federally protected tide pools.

6 ★★★ **Bayside Trail.** This trail meanders through a coastal sage ecosystem that has all but disappeared from Southern California. The hiking is easy—the trail is only 2.5 miles (4km) roundtrip—but the bay views are spectacular, and there are informative signs posted along the way, identifying and explaining the local flora and fauna. Audio stations providing historical details in six different languages are located at various sites throughout the park. Rangers and docents often present a variety of talks and guided walks.

7 ★★★ **kids** **Tide pools.** Cabrillo National Monument has the only federally protected tide pools on the Southern California mainland. This rocky, intertidal ecosystem hosts a variety of sea life, including crabs, starfish, octopi, and anemones. For the best tide pooling, call ahead to find out when low tide is happening, otherwise there may not be much to see—other than the awe-inspiring cliffs and ocean vistas. ☎ 619/557-5450. *Exercise caution when exploring tide pools, the rocks are slippery; do not handle the animals; expect to get a little bit wet.*

8 ★★ **Point Loma Seafoods.** There are no food facilities at Cabrillo National Monument so consider stopping by this San Diego institution before or after visiting the park. It's usually chaos at this deli-style seafood market, especially around lunchtime, but this is the place for fresh-off-the-boat fish. *2805 Emerson St. (at Scott St.).* ☎ *619/223-1109. www.pointloma seafoods.com. Mon–Sat 9am–6:30pm, Sun 11am–6:30pm. $–$$.*

Rough surf at Cabrillo National Monument.

Mission Bay Park

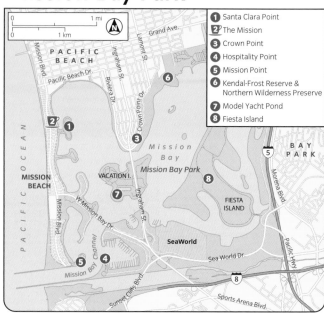

1 Santa Clara Point
2 The Mission
3 Crown Point
4 Hospitality Point
5 Mission Point
6 Kendal-Frost Reserve & Northern Wilderness Preserve
7 Model Yacht Pond
8 Fiesta Island

Originally known as False Bay, this swampy marshland was transformed in the 1940s into Mission Bay Park. This vast outdoor playground encompasses more than 4,200 acres (1,700 hectares)—about half of it water, half of it land—with 27 miles (43km) of shoreline, 19 sandy beaches, grassy parks, wildlife preserves, boat docks and launches (with rental facilities), basketball courts, and an extensive system of pathways. Locals and visitors alike flock to Mission Bay for everything from kite flying to power-boating. START: **Bus 8/9 to Santa Clara Pl.**

1 ★★ kids **Santa Clara Point.** Recreation centers don't get any cooler than the city-run facility here. Surrounded by the bay waters, it features tennis courts, a softball field, lighted basketball courts, a playground, and weight room. Also located on the point is Mission Bay Sports Center, where you can rent sailboats, catamarans, pedal boats, sailboards, kayaks, wave runners,

motorboats, or surfboards. The Sportcenter also offers lessons on how to use the gear. *Recreation Center, 1008 Santa Clara Pl.* ☎ *858/ 581-9928. Mon/Wed/Fri noon–7pm, Tues/Thurs noon–7:30pm, Sat 10am– 2pm, closed Sun. Mission Bay Sportcenter, 1010 Santa Clara Pl.* ☎ *858/ 488-1004; www.missionbaysport center.com. Daily 9am–7pm. Bus: 8/9.*

Santa Clara Point.

2 ★ **The Mission.** The menu features all-day breakfasts, from traditional pancakes to nouvelle egg dishes to burritos and quesadillas. At lunch, the menu expands for sandwiches, salads, and a few Chino-Latino items like ginger-sesame chicken tacos. *3795 Mission Blvd. (at San Jose Pl.).* ☎ *858/488-9060. www.themission1.signonsandiego. com. Daily 7am–3pm. $.*

3 ★ **kids Crown Point.** You'll find everything you need here for a

day of outdoor recreation: large grassy expanses, a white-sand beach, picnic tables, fire rings, barbecue grills, basketball courts, and a boat launch. This swimming area has a lifeguard on duty during the summer months; there are also restrooms and showers here. *Crown Point Dr. (there are several large parking lots off this street). 4am–2am, but parking lots close at 10pm. As with all city beaches, no glass containers are allowed and alcohol is permitted from noon–8pm only. Bus: 8/9.*

4 ★ **Hospitality Point.** Located at the confluence of the Mission Bay Channel and the San Diego River, this popular spot lacks a beach, but draws visitors with its ocean, bay, and channel views. The walking and bike path will take you alongside the Flood Control Channel, which doubles as the Southern Wildlife Preserve. The preserve provides a landing for more than 100 different species of birds migrating along the Pacific Flyway. Look for herons, egrets, osprey, and the endangered California least tern. *South end of Quivira Rd. Bus: 8/9 to Dana Landing at W. Mission Bay Dr., then it's a little less than a mile on Quivira Rd. to the point.*

Mission Bay cyclists.

Hospitality Point.

5 ★ kids **Mission Point.** For those who want to combine an ocean and bay experience, Mission Point will do the trick. Situated at the Southern end of Mission Boulevard, this grass-and-sand recreation area is just a short walk from the Mission Beach jetty and the Pacific. Mission Point offers fire rings, picnic tables, a children's playground, and restrooms with showers. This is a swimming area, but there is no lifeguard on duty. *Bayside Lane. 4am–10pm. Bus 8/9 to Mission Blvd. at W. Mission Bay Dr., then about a mile south.*

6 ★★★ **Kendal-Frost Reserve and Northern Wilderness Preserve.** Due to its fragile nature, most of this 30-acre (12-hectare) area is off-limits to the public. You can get close to it, though, via the pathway that extends north from Crown Point (*see bullet* **3**) or by kayak. This saltwater marsh provides sanctuary to a wide variety of birds: avocets to vireos, coots to loons. Two endangered, non-migratory species, the light-footed clapper rail and Belding's savannah sparrow, even live out their entire lives within this small ecosystem. Like many of the estimated 15 million people who flock to Mission Bay Park every year, the clapper rail takes advantage of the bay's calm waters, too—it builds a floating nest among the stands of cordgrass.

Skaters on the waterfront.

Palms in Mission Bay.

7 ★ kids Model Yacht Pond.
Sailboats and powerboats are ubiquitous features on Mission Bay, but many people are unaware of the flotilla that plies the waters of the Model Yacht Pond in the middle of Vacation Island. Just about any weekend you can find hobbyists with their sophisticated, radio-controlled craft competing or just having fun. Some of these models are amazingly detailed replicas of historic ships such as Spanish galleons or World War II battleships; others are ferocious little hydroplanes capable of speeds in excess of 60 mph (97kmph). *Alcohol is prohibited here. Bus: 8/9 to W. Vacation Rd.*

8 Fiesta Island. If you've got Fido in tow, this is a great place to let him run leash-free to his heart's content. This is the largest individual piece of Mission Bay Park, a rather barren island at the eastern edge of the bay, often used for events such as the Over-the-Line softball tournament in July and cycling time trials and races. There is a 4-mile (6.5km)

road that loops around the island, and fire rings are situated throughout. *Picnics are not permitted; there are no restrooms. 6am–10pm. Bus: 105 to Sea World Dr.*

Catamarans in De Anza Cove.

The Best **Hiking**

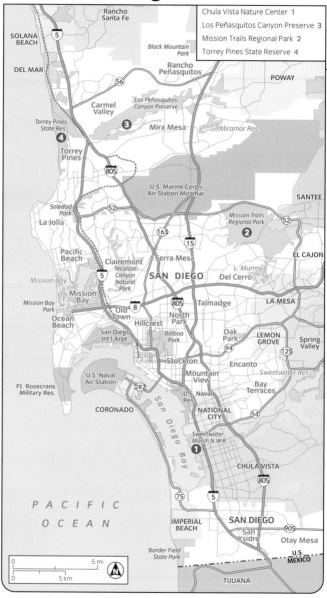

Chula Vista Nature Center 1
Los Peñasquitos Canyon Preserve 3
Mission Trails Regional Park 2
Torrey Pines State Reserve 4

Even from downtown, you don't have to venture far to discover San Diego's wild side. Whether you're looking for solitude along an oak-shaded trail or want to spot an endangered species in its natural habitat, you'll find nearby open-space preserves and parks that will satisfy a range of outdoor enthusiasts. START: **Bus 101 to Torrey Pines State Reserve.**

★★ kids **Chula Vista Nature Center.** This interpretive center set in the Sweetwater Marsh National Wildlife Refuge is just a 15-minute drive from downtown San Diego. There is a 1.5-mile (2.5km) loop trail through coastal wetlands where more than 220 different species of birds have been identified. The trail also features a photo blind and posted information on the flora and fauna. See p 33, bullet ⑩.

★★ **Los Peñasquitos Canyon Preserve.** Stretching for nearly 7 miles (11km), this 4,000-acre (1,619-hectare) preserve is an oasis amid the suburbia that it surrounds. The area was part of the first Mexican land grant in San Diego, and the historic Santa Maria de los Peñasquitos adobe ranch home (1823) still stands at the east end of the park (tours are Sat at 11am and Sun at 1pm). Along the trail are beautiful stands of oak and sycamore; there's also a waterfall that flows year-round. *12020 Black Mountain Rd.*

☎ *858/484-7504. www.sandiego. gov/park-and-recreation. Free admission. Daily 8am–sunset. Bus: 210 to Mira Mesa Blvd. and Black Mountain Rd., 1.3 miles (2k) farther north on Black Mountain Rd.*

★★ **Mission Trails Regional Park.** This is one of the nation's largest urban parks, a 5,800-acre (2,347-hectare) spread that includes abundant bird life, two lakes, a picturesque stretch of the San Diego River, the remains of the Old Mission Dam (probably the first irrigation project in the West), and 1,592-foot (485m) Cowles Mountain, the summit of which reveals outstanding views over much of the county. There are trails up to 4 miles (6.5km) in length—including a 1.5-mile (2.5km) interpretive trail—some of which are designated for mountain bike use. *1 Father Junipero Serra Trail.* ☎ *619/668-3275 or 619/668-3281. www.mtrp.org. Free admission. Daily sunrise to sundown (visitor center 9am–5pm). Bus: 115 to*

Hikers in Los Peñasquitos Canyon Reserve.

Into the Wild

Those in search of a wilderness experience will find ample room to roam in 600,00-acre (242,820-hectare) ★★★ **Anza-Borrego Desert State Park,** California's largest state park, less than a 2-hour drive away from downtown San Diego.

The terrain at Anza-Borrego incorporates dry lakebeds, sandstone canyons, granite mountains, palm groves fed by year-round springs, and more than 600 kinds of desert plants. The best time to come is in spring, when thousands of wildflowers burst into bloom, transforming the desert into a brilliant palette of pink, lavender, red, orange, and yellow. Your first stop here should be the architecturally striking **Visitor Center** (☎ 760/767-4205 or 760/767-5311; www.parks.ca.gov). This small museum offers information, maps, and audiovisual presentations; an interpreted loop trail is also on site. The visitor center is open October through May daily from 9am to 5pm, June through September weekends from 9am to 5pm.

Jackson Dr. and Navajo Rd., then 1.4 miles (2.25km) to the West Gate.

★★★ Torrey Pines State Reserve.
One of San Diego's most treasured spots, this reserve is home to the country's rarest tree, the Torrey pine, which grows only here and on an island off the coast of

The Anza-Borrego Desert.

Santa Barbara. The 1,750-acre (708-hectare) reserve was established in 1921, from a gift by Ellen Browning Scripps, and encompasses dramatic 300-foot- (91m-) high, water-carved limestone bluffs, the beach below them, and a lagoon immediately north. There are six different trails, none longer than 1.3 miles (2km), and the aptly named Beach Trail provides access to the ocean; pick up a trail map at the small visitor center, built in the traditional adobe style of the Hopi Indians. Interpretive nature walks are held weekends and holidays at 10am and 2pm. *Hwy. 101 (between La Jolla and Del Mar).* ☎ *858/755-2063. www.torreypine. org. There are no facilities for food or drinks inside the park; you can bring a picnic lunch, but you have to eat it on the beach—food and drink (other than water) are not allowed in the upper portion of the reserve. Admission $6 per car weekday, $8 per car weekend; seniors $5 weekday, $7 weekend. Daily 8am–sunset. Bus: 101.* ●

Dining Best Bets

Best **Business Lunch**
★ Dobson's Bar & Restaurant $$ *956 Broadway Circle (p 107)*

Best **Mexican Food**
★★★ El Agave Tequileria $$–$$$ *2304 San Diego Ave. (p 107);* and ★★★ Candelas $$$ *416 Third Ave. (p 106)*

Best **Breakfast With a View**
★ Brockton Villa $–$$ *1235 Coast Blvd. (p 106)*

Best **Lunch With a View**
★★★ Bertrand at Mister A's $$$$ *2550 Fifth Ave. (p 105)*

Best **Dinner With a View**
★★★ Georges California Modern $$$$ *1250 Prospect St. (p 109)*

Best **Use of Local Product (Sea)**
★★ Zenbu $$–$$$ *7660 Fay Ave. (p 112)*

Best **Use of Local Product (Land)**
★★★ Market Restaurant + Bar $$$ *3702 Via de la Valle (p 110)*

Best **California Cuisine**
★★★ Blanca $$$$ *437 S. Highway 101 (p 105)*

Best **Modern American Cuisine**
★★★ Jack's La Jolla $$$$ *7863 Girard Ave. (p 109)*

Best **Eclectic Menu**
★★ Parallel 33 $$–$$$ *741 W. Washington St. (p 111)*

Best **Pan-Asian Cuisine**
★★ Red Pearl Kitchen $$–$$$ *440 J St. (p 111)*

Best **Pizza**
★★ Bronx Pizza $–$$ *111 Washington St. (p 106)*

Best **Desserts**
★★★ Extraordinary Desserts $ *2929 Fifth Ave. and 1430 Union St. (p 107)*

Best **Bistro**
★★ Café Chloe $$–$$$ *721 Ninth Ave. (p 106)*

Best **Picnic Fare**
★★ Bread & Cie $ *350 University Ave. (p 105)*

Most **Romantic Dining Room**
★★★ The Marine Room $$$$ *2000 Spindrift Dr. (p 110)*

Best **Sushi**
★★★ Sushi Ota $$ *4529 Mission Bay Dr. (p 112)*

Best **Place for Hipster Foodies**
★★ Modus $$–$$$ *2202 Fourth Ave. (p 110)*

Café Pacifica.

Downtown Dining

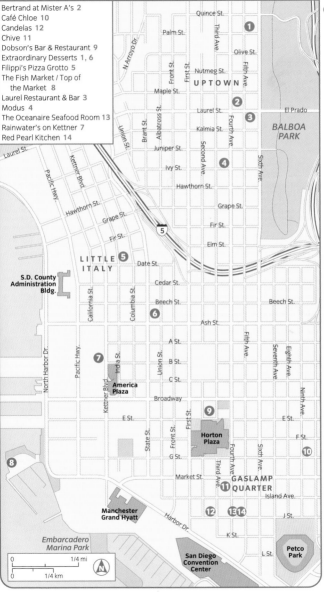

Hillcrest & Old Town Dining

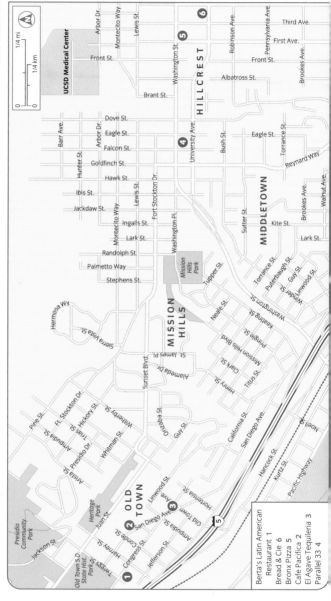

Berta's Latin American
Restaurant 1
Bread & Cie 6
Bronx Pizza 5
Cafe Pacifica 2
El Agave Tequileria 3
Parallel 33 4

Dining **at the Beaches**

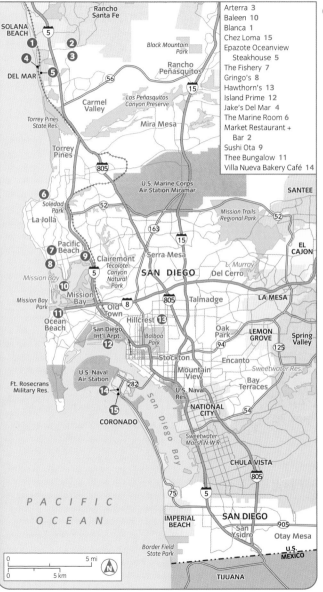

Arterra 3
Baleen 10
Blanca 1
Chez Loma 15
Epazote Oceanview
  Steakhouse 5
The Fishery 7
Gringo's 8
Hawthorn's 13
Island Prime 12
Jake's Del Mar 4
The Marine Room 6
Market Restaurant +
  Bar 2
Sushi Ota 9
Thee Bungalow 11
Villa Nueva Bakery Café 14

La Jolla Dining

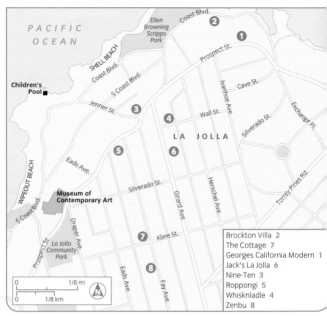

PACIFIC OCEAN

Ellen Browning Scripps Park

Coast Blvd.

Prospect St.

SHELL BEACH

Coast Blvd.

S Coast Blvd.

Children's Pool

Jenner St.

Ivanhoe Ave.

Cave St.

Exchange Pl.

Wall St.

LA JOLLA

Silverado St.

WIPEOUT BEACH

Eads Ave.

Herschel Ave.

Torrey Pines Rd.

Silverado St.

S Coast Blvd.

Museum of Contemporary Art

Girard Ave.

Prospect St.

Draper Ave.

La Jolla Community Park

Kline St.

Eads Ave.

Fay Ave.

0   1/8 mi
0   1/8 km

Brockton Villa 2
The Cottage 7
Georges California Modern 1
Jack's La Jolla 6
Nine-Ten 3
Roppongi 5
Whisknladle 4
Zenbu 8

Dining A to Z

★★ **Arterra** DEL MAR *CALIFORNIAN* The menu is regularly adapted to meet the schedule of Mother Earth, featuring top products from local farms. *11966 El Camino Real (next to I-5 in the Marriott Del Mar).* ☎ *858/369-6032. Entrees $8–$18*

Arterra in Del Mar.

breakfast, $14–$24 lunch, $27–$38 dinner. AE, DC, DISC, MC, V. Breakfast daily; lunch Mon–Fri; dinner Mon–Sat; bar menu daily. Bus: 89.

★★ **Baleen** MISSION BAY *SEAFOOD/ CALIFORNIAN* This attractive waterfront eatery is located right in the middle of Mission Bay—the perfect place to savor a selection of seafood simply grilled, wood-roasted, or sautéed. *1404 Vacation Rd. (Paradise Point Resort).* ☎ *858/490-6363. Entrees $19–$60. AE, DC, DISC, MC, V. Dinner daily. Bus: 8/9.*

★ **Berta's Latin American Restaurant** OLD TOWN *LATIN AMERICAN* Faithfully re-creating

Bread & Cie in Hillcrest.

the flavors of Central and South America, Berta's provides welcome relief from the nacho-and-fajita places that dominate Old Town. *3928 Twiggs St. (at Congress St.). ☎ 619/295-2343. Entrees $7–$10 lunch, $11–$16 dinner. AE, MC, V. Tues–Sun lunch & dinner. Bus: 10, 14, 30, or 150. Trolley: Old Town.*

★★★ Bertrand at Mister A's
BALBOA PARK *AMERICAN/MEDITER-RANEAN* The seasonal menu is modern American with a French/Mediterranean twist. A bar/patio menu gives diners on a budget access to the million-dollar vistas. *2550 Fifth Ave. (at Laurel St.), Hillcrest. ☎ 619/239-1377. Entrees $15–$27 lunch, $20–$45 dinner. AE, DC, MC, V. Lunch Mon–Fri; dinner daily. Bus: 3 or 120.*

★★★ Blanca SOLANA BEACH
CALIFORNIAN/FRENCH Sleek and sophisticated, this cosmopolitan space may be the best restaurant in San Diego County. Blanca uses only top, seasonal products, preparing creative California cuisine with a modern French touch. *437 S. Highway 101 (north of Via de la Valle). ☎ 858/792-0072. Entrees $30–$95. AE, DC, DISC, MC, V. Dinner daily. Bus: 101.*

★★ Bread & Cie HILLCREST *LIGHT FARE/MEDITERRANEAN*
The traditions of European artisan bread-making are proudly carried on here. You can get a light breakfast or a great sandwich, as well as loaves of specialty breads. *350 University Ave. (at Fourth St.). ☎ 619/683-9322. Sandwiches and light meals $4–$9. DISC,*

Brockton Villa in La Jolla.

MC, V. Breakfast, lunch & early supper daily. Bus: 1 or 3.

★ **Brockton Villa** LA JOLLA *BREAKFAST/CALIFORNIAN* A restored 1894 beach bungalow, this charming cafe occupies a breathtaking perch overlooking La Jolla Cove. *1235 Coast Blvd. (across from La Jolla Cove).* ☎ *858/454-7393. Entrees $7–$12 breakfast, $9–$15 lunch, $15–$30 dinner. AE, DISC, MC, V. Breakfast & lunch daily; dinner Tues–Sun. Bus: 30.*

★★ **Bronx Pizza** HILLCREST *ITALIAN* This tiny pizzeria serves up San Diego's best pies—other than calzones, that's all they make. There's usually a line out the door. *111 Washington St. (at First Ave.).* ☎ *619/291-3341. Phone orders accepted for full pies. Pies $12–$18; $2.50 by the slice. Cash only. Lunch & dinner daily. Bus: 3, 10, or 11.*

★★ **Thee Bungalow** OCEAN BEACH *FRENCH* The fanciest restaurant in laid-back Ocean Beach, Thee Bungalow features an excellent wine list and house specialties such as crispy roast duck and dessert soufflés for two. *4996 W. Point Loma Blvd. (at Bacon St.).*

Café Chloe in the East Village.

Candelas in the Gaslamp Quarter.

☎ *619/224-2884. Entrees $20–$37, early bird specials $15–$19. AE, DC, DISC, MC, V. Dinner daily. Bus: 35 or 923.*

★★ **Café Chloe** EAST VILLAGE *FRENCH* The conviviality of this bistro—combined with a short-but-sweet French-inspired menu covering breakfast, lunch, and dinner—makes for a winning dining experience. *721 Ninth Ave. (at G St.).* ☎ *619/232-3242. Entrees $8–$13 breakfast, $9–$13 lunch, $15–$28 dinner. AE, MC, V. Lunch & dinner daily; breakfast Tues–Sun. Bus: 3, 5, 11, 210, 901, or 929.*

★★ **Cafe Pacifica** OLD TOWN *CALIFORNIAN/SEAFOOD* This cozy eatery serves upscale, imaginative seafood at decent prices; arrive before 6:30pm and you can take advantage of the early bird special for $26. *2414 San Diego Ave. (at Congress St.).* ☎ *619/291-6666. Entrees $14–$34. AE, DC, DISC, MC, V. Dinner daily. Bus: 10, 30, or 150. Trolley: Old Town.*

★★★ **Candelas** GASLAMP QUARTER *MEXICAN* If you're looking for tacos and burritos, go somewhere else. If you're in the mood for a sophisticated, romantic fine dining experience, look no further. *416 Third Ave. (at J St.).* ☎ *619/702-4455. Entrees $11–$15 lunch, $22–$35 dinner. AE, DC, DISC, MC, V. Lunch Mon–Fri; dinner daily. Bus: 3, 11, or 992. Trolley: Convention Center.*

★ **Chez Loma** CORONADO *FRENCH* Tables are scattered throughout this classic Victorian house and on the enclosed garden terrace. Early birds enjoy specially priced meals—$25 for a three-course meal before 6pm. *1132 Loma (off Orange Ave.), Coronado.* ☎ *619/435-0661. Entrees $22–$34. AE, DC, DISC, MC, V. Dinner Tues–Sun. Bus: 901 or 904.*

★★★ **Chive** GASLAMP QUARTER *CALIFORNIAN* The cuisine is as modern as the decor, taking a global approach with small-plate dishes such as a Moroccan-spiced chicken kebab and Kung Pao–style sweetbreads. *558 Fourth Ave. (at Market St.).* ☎ *619/232-4483. Entrees $10–$36. AE, DISC, MC, V. Dinner daily. Bus: 3, 11, 120, or 992. Trolley: Convention Center.*

★ **The Cottage** LA JOLLA *BREAKFAST/LIGHT FARE* Maybe La Jolla's best breakfast, served at a turn-of-the-20th-century bungalow on a shady corner. The housemade granola is a favorite. *7702 Fay Ave. (at Kline St.).* ☎ *858/454-8409. Entrees $7–$10 breakfast, $8–$12 lunch, $12–$22 dinner. AE, DISC, MC, V. Breakfast & lunch daily; dinner June–Aug Tues–Sat. Bus: 30.*

★ **Dobson's Bar & Restaurant** GASLAMP QUARTER *CALIFORNIAN* By day it buzzes with the energy of movers and shakers; in the evening it segues from happy-hour watering hole to sophisticated pre- and post-theater American bistro. *956 Broadway Circle (at Broadway).* ☎ *619/231-6771. Entrees $10–$18 lunch; $18–$39 dinner. AE, DC, MC, V.*

Lunch Thurs–Fri; dinner Thurs–Sat; happy hour Mon–Fri. Bus: 7, 929, 992.

★★★ **El Agave Tequileria** OLD TOWN *MEXICAN* The regional Mexican cuisine and rustic elegance here leave the touristy joints of Old Town far behind. It also boasts more than 850 tequilas and mezcals, and some of the best margaritas in town. *2304 San Diego Ave. (at Old Town Ave.).* ☎ *619/220-0692. Entrees $8–$11 lunch, $16–$32 dinner. AE, MC, V. Lunch & dinner daily. Bus: 10, 30, or 150. Trolley: Old Town.*

★ **Epazote Oceanview Steakhouse** DEL MAR *AMERICAN* The unimpeded sea views here are regal. And the bar whips up a wicked house margarita. *1555 Camino del Mar (at 15th St.), Del Mar Plaza.* ☎ *858/259-9966. Entrees $9–$15 brunch, $11–$24 lunch, $20–$45 dinner. AE, DC, DISC, MC, V. Lunch & dinner daily; brunch Sun. Bus: 101.*

★★★ **Extraordinary Desserts** HILLCREST *DESSERTS* Dozens of divine creations are available daily; there's also an exclusive line of jams,

Dobson's Bar & Restaurant in the Gaslamp Quarter.

El Agave Tequileria in Old Town.

syrups, spices, and confections for sale. This location also serves panini, salads, and artisan cheeses, as well as wine and beer. *2929 Fifth Ave. (between Palm and Quince sts.)* ☎ *619/294-2132. Desserts $2–$9. MC, V. Breakfast, lunch & dinner daily. Bus: 3. Other location: Little Italy, 1430 Union St. (between Beech and Ash sts.),* ☎ *619/ 294-7001. Bus: 11 or 30.*

★ **Filippi's Pizza Grotto** LITTLE ITALY *ITALIAN* Walk through an Italian grocery and deli to get to the dining room, where the menu offers more than 15 pizzas, plus huge portions of spaghetti, lasagna, and other pasta. *1747 India St. (between Date and Fir sts.).* ☎ *619/232-5094. Entrees $6–$13. AE, DC, DISC, MC, V. Lunch & dinner daily; deli opens daily at 8am. Bus: 83. Trolley: Little Italy. Other location: Pacific Beach, 962 Garnet Ave. (between Cass and Bayard sts.),* ☎ *858/483-6222, Bus: 8/9.*

★ **The Fishery** PACIFIC BEACH *SEAFOOD* You're pretty well guaranteed fresh-off-the-boat seafood at this off-the-beaten-track establishment. It's really a wholesale warehouse and retail fish market with a casual restaurant attached. *5040 Cass St. (at Opal St.).* ☎ *858/272-9985. Entrees $8–$21 lunch, $9–$28 dinner. AE, DC, DISC, MC, V. Lunch & dinner daily. Bus: 8/9.*

★ **The Fish Market/Top of the Market** EMBARCADERO *SEAFOOD/ SUSHI* This San Diego institution with enhanced views is always packed. Upstairs, fancy Top of the Market offers sea fare with souped-up presentations. *750 N. Harbor Dr.* ☎ *619/232-3474. Entrees $10–$25 lunch, $13–$32 dinner (Top of the Market main courses $13–$35 lunch, $18–$45 dinner). AE, DC, DISC, MC,*

Extraordinary Desserts in Little Italy.

V. Lunch & dinner daily. Bus: 992. Trolley: Seaport Village. Other location: Del Mar, 640 Via de la Valle (between S. Cedros Ave. and Solana Circle E), ☎ 858/755-2277, Bus: 308.

★★ **Fresh** LA JOLLA *CALIFORNIAN/SEAFOOD* You'll find a menu of small and large plate fare created from top quality products (like Chino Farm veggies and Kobe beef) at modest sums, and retail pricing on wine. *1044 Wall St. (at Hershel Ave.). ☎ 858/551-7575. Entrees $9–$17 lunch, $18–$31 dinner. AE, DISC, MC, V. Lunch & dinner daily. Bus: 30.*

★★★ **Georges California Modern** LA JOLLA *CALIFORNIAN* This place has it all: stunning ocean views, style, impeccable service, and above all, a world-class chef. Those seeking fine food and incomparable views at more modest prices can head upstairs to Georges Ocean Terrace Bistro and Pacific View Bar. *1250 Prospect St. (east of Ivanhoe Ave.). ☎ 858/454-4244. Entrees $26–$42. AE, DC, DISC, MC, V. Dinner daily.* **Ocean Terrace Bistro** *entrees $10–$15 lunch, $14–$22 dinner. Lunch & dinner daily. Bus: 30.*

★ **Gringo's** PACIFIC BEACH *MEXICAN* The menu at this upscale space runs the gamut from the typical fare to regional specialties from Oaxaca, the Yucatan, and Mexico's Pacific Coast. There are also more than 100 tequilas available. *4474 Mission Blvd. (at Garnet Ave.). ☎ 858/490-2877. Entrees $6–$20 lunch, $10–$23 dinner, $7–$11 Sun brunch. AE, DC, DISC, MC, V. Lunch & dinner daily. Bus: 8/9, 27, or 30.*

★ **Hawthorn's** NORTH PARK *CALIFORNIAN* Set within a magnificently rehabilitated 1928 vaudeville theater just east of Hillcrest, this longtime favorite offers great deals on prix fixe and early-bird meals.

2895 University Ave. (at 29th St.). ☎ 619/544-0940. Entrees $19–$32 dinner. AE, MC, V. Dinner daily; Sun brunch 10am–2pm. Bus: 7 or 7A/B.

★★ **Island Prime** EMBARCADERO *SEAFOOD* Given the spectacular bay and skyline vistas here, it would be easy to understand if Island Prime didn't even bother to make its food interesting—but the views actually have some competition. *880 Harbor Island Dr. ☎ 619/298-6802. Entrees $11–$25 lunch; $22–$39 dinner. AE, DC, DISC, MC, V. Lunch & dinner daily. Bus: 923, 992.*

★★★ **Jack's La Jolla** LA JOLLA *AMERICAN* This multistory Epicurean funhouse rises from sidewalk coffee stop to third-floor sushi bar, with a fine dining component and a couple of bars and lounges thrown in for good measure. *7863 Girard Ave. (at Wall St.). ☎ 858/456-8111. Entrees $28–$42. AE, DC, DISC, MC, V. Dinner Tues–Sun.* **Jack's Grille** *entrees $10–$34. Dinner daily.* **Ocean Room** *entrees $8–$14 lunch, $12–$44 dinner. Lunch & dinner daily.* **Sidewalk Cafe** *Breakfast, lunch & dinner daily.* **Bars and lounges** *daily 5:30pm–2am (Wall St. Bar and sushi bar closed Mon). Bus: 30.*

Island Prime in the Embarcadero.

Laurel Restaurant & Bar in Balboa Park.

★ **Jake's Del Mar** DEL MAR
SEAFOOD/CALIFORNIAN This
seafood-and-view restaurant has a
perfect seat next to the sand—the
predictable menu can't live up to
the panorama, but it's prepared
competently. *1660 Coast Blvd. (at
15th St.).* ☎ *858/755-2002. Entrees
$9–$18 lunch, $10–$46 dinner. AE,
DC, DISC, MC, V. Lunch Tues–Sat; dinner daily; brunch Sun. Bus: 101.*

★★★ **Laurel Restaurant & Bar**
BALBOA PARK *FRENCH/MEDITER-
RANEAN* Look for game entrees
such as elk, boar, and rabbit, as well
as a wonderful cassoulet, a main-
course vegetable sampler, and a
seven-course chef's tasting meal.
505 Laurel St. (at Fifth Ave.). ☎ *619/
239-2222. Entrees $22–$39. AE, DC,
DISC, MC, V. Dinner daily. Bus: 3
or 120.*

★★★ **The Marine Room** LA
JOLLA *FRENCH/CALIFORNIAN* This
shorefront institution has been San
Diego's most celebrated dining
room. Executive chef Bernard Guillas
sees to it that the food lives up to
this room with a view. *2000 Spindrift
Dr. (at Torrey Pines Rd.).* ☎ *858/459-
7222. Entrees $28–$44. AE, DC,
DISC, MC, V. Dinner daily. Bus: 30.*

★★★ **Market Restaurant + Bar**
DEL MAR *CALIFORNIAN* This comfortably elegant restaurant specializes in regional San Diego cuisine,
showcasing the best ingredients
from the area's top farms, ranches,
and seafood providers. The wine list
focuses on small and non-traditional
wineries. *3702 Via de la Valle (at El
Camino Real).* ☎ *858/523-0007.
Entrees $22–$40. AE, MC, V. Dinner
daily. Bus: 308.*

★★ **Modus** BANKERS HILL *CALI-
FORNIAN* There's mood lighting, a
zigzagging bar, mod fireplace, DJs,
and a patio with water-wall feature;
there's also modern European bistro
cuisine with a California flair, incorporating fresh, local, organic products. *2202 Fourth Ave. (at Ivy St.).*
☎ *619/236-8516. Entrees $24–$32.
AE, DISC, MC, V. Dinner daily. Bus: 3,
11, or 120.*

★★★ **Nine-Ten** LA JOLLA *CALI-
FORNIAN* The seasonal menu at
this stylish spot is best enjoyed via
small-plate grazing; better yet, turn
yourself over to the "Mercy of the
Chef," a five-course tasting menu.
*910 Prospect St. (between Fay and
Girard).* ☎ *858/964-5400. Entrees
$6–$16 breakfast, $9–$14 lunch,*

$19–$40 dinner. AE, DC, DISC, MC, V. Breakfast, lunch & dinner daily. Bus: 30.

★★ The Oceanaire Seafood Room GASLAMP QUARTER
SEAFOOD   Featuring top local products as well as fish brought in daily from around the globe, the menu incorporates elements of Pacific Rim, Italian, classic French, and Asian cuisine. *400 J St. (at Fourth Ave.).* ☎ 619/858-2277. *Entrees $15–$50. AE, DISC, MC, V. Dinner daily. Bus: 3, 11, or 992. Trolley: Convention Center.*

★★ Parallel 33 MISSION HILLS
INTERNATIONAL   This very cool restaurant brings together the unique flavors of far-flung locales along the 33rd parallel (which includes San Diego). *741 W. Washington St. (at Falcon).* ☎ 619/260-0033. *Entrees $19–$34. AE, DISC, MC, V. Dinner daily. Bus: 3 or 10.*

★★ Rainwater's on Kettner
DOWNTOWN *AMERICAN*   A long-time favorite for power lunches, this East Coast–style chophouse has a spectacular wine list. *1202 Kettner Blvd. (at B St., next to the Santa Fe depot).* ☎ 619/233-5757. *Entrees $10–$18 lunch, $25–$50 dinner. AE, DISC, MC, V. Lunch Mon–Fri; dinner*

Parallel 33 in Mission Hill.

Modus in Banker's Hill.

daily. Bus: 83, 901, or 929. Trolley: Santa Fe Depot or American Plaza.

★★ Red Pearl Kitchen
GASLAMP QUARTER *CHINESE/ASIAN FUSION*   This sexy restaurant and bar specializes in dim sum dishes with a contemporary, pan-Asian flair. *440 J St. (between Fourth and Fifth aves.).* ☎ 619/231-1100. *Entrees $10–$18. AE, MC, V. Dinner daily. Trolley: Convention Center. Bus: 3, 120, 929, or 992.*

★ Roppongi LA JOLLA *ASIAN FUSION/PACIFIC RIM*   The cuisines of Japan, Thailand, China, Vietnam,

Red Pearl Kitchen in the Gaslamp Quarter.

Korea, and India collide, via a menu of tapas-style portions designed for sharing. *875 Prospect St. (at Fay Ave.).* ☎ *858/551-5252. Entrees $11–$19 lunch, $9–$19 tapas, $22–$37 dinner. AE, DC, DISC, MC, V. Lunch & dinner daily. Bus: 30.*

★★★ **Sushi Ota** PACIFIC BEACH *SUSHI* Masterful chef-owner Yukito Ota creates San Diego's finest sushi in a nondescript location in a mini-mall. Discerning regulars look for the daily specials posted behind the counter. *4529 Mission Bay Dr. (at Bunker Hill).* ☎ *858/270-5670. Entrees $6–$12 lunch, $9–$20 dinner, sushi $4–$12. AE, MC, V. Lunch Tues–Fri; dinner daily. Bus: 8/9.*

★ **Villa Nueva Bakery Café** CORONADO *BREAKFAST/LIGHT FARE*

Locals rave about the "Yacht Club" sandwich, a croissant filled with yellowfin tuna, and the breakfast croissant, topped with scrambled ham and eggs and cheddar cheese. *956 Orange Ave. (between 9th and 10th sts.).* ☎ *619/435-4191. Entrees $5–$8. AE, DISC, MC, V. Breakfast, lunch & dinner daily. Bus: 901 or 904.*

★★ **Zenbu** LA JOLLA *SUSHI/ SEAFOOD* You can order something from the sushi bar or maybe an entree such as steak of locally harpooned swordfish. *7660 Fay Ave. (at Kline St.).* ☎ *858/454-4540. Entrees $22–$30. AE, DC, DISC, MC, V. Dinner daily. Happy hour all night Sun–Tues; Wed–Thurs until 6:30pm. Lounge Thurs–Sat 7pm– 1am. Bus: 30.* ●

Nightlife Best Bets

Best Bar With a View
★★★ Top of the Hyatt *1 Market Pl.*
(p 119)

Best Concert Venue (Indoor)
★★★ Belly Up Tavern *143 S.
Cedros Ave. (p 120)*

Best Concert Venue (Outdoor)
★★ Humphrey's *2241 Shelter Island
Dr. (p 121)*

Best Rock 'n' Roll Club
★★ The Casbah *2501 Kettner Blvd.
(p 120)*

Best After-Hours Dance Club
★★★ Club Montage *2028 Hancock
St. (p 120)*

Best Dive Bar
★★ Nunu's *3537 Fifth Ave. (p 118)*

Best Wine Bar
★★★ 3rd Corner *2265 Bacon St.
(p 122)*

Best Megaclub
★★★ Stingaree *454 Sixth Ave. (p 122)*

Best Shoes-Optional Bar
★★★ Beach *421 B St. (p 117)*

Best Open-air Bar (High-Rise)
★★★ Altitude Skybar *660 K St.
(p 117)*

Best Open-air Bar (Low-Rise)
★★★ J6Bar *616 J St. (p 117)*

Most Thrilling Patio
★★★ Airport *2400 India St. (p 117)*

Best Supper Club
★★★ Anthology *1337 India St.
(p 121)*

Best 2-for-1 Experience
★★★ The Onyx Room/Thin *852
Fifth Ave. (p 118)*

Best Art Collection
★★★ House of Blues *1055 Fifth
Ave. (p 121)*

Coolest Pool Room
★★★ On Broadway *615 Broadway
(p 119)*

Best Spot for Latin Music
★★ Sevilla *555 Fourth Ave. (p 122)*

**Best Place to Launch Your
Weekend (Gay)**
★★★ Top of the Park *525 Spruce
St. (p 120)*

**Best Place to Launch Your
Weekend (Straight)**
★★★ Side Bar *536 Market St.
(p 118)*

Anthology Supper Club. *Previous page: Airport in Little Italy.*

Downtown Nightlife

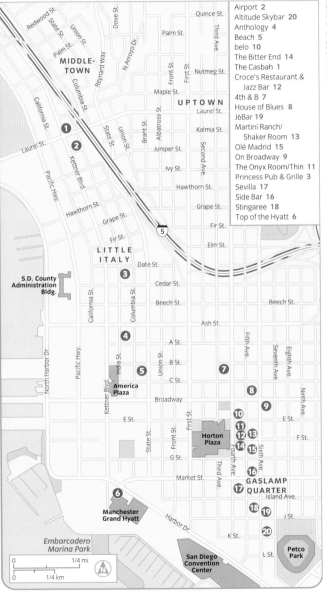

Airport 2
Altitude Skybar 20
Anthology 4
Beach 5
belo 10
The Bitter End 14
The Casbah 1
Croce's Restaurant &
    Jazz Bar 12
4th & B 7
House of Blues 8
J6Bar 19
Martini Ranch/
    Shaker Room 13
Olé Madrid 15
On Broadway 9
The Onyx Room/Thin 11
Princess Pub & Grille 3
Sevilla 17
Side Bar 16
Stingaree 18
Top of the Hyatt 6

Hillcrest Nightlife

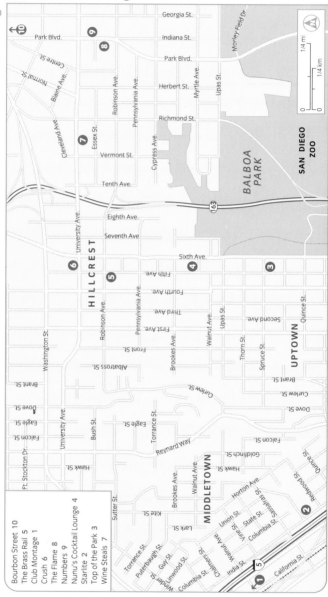

Nightlife **on the Beaches**

Nightlife A to Z

Bars

★★★ **Airport** LITTLE ITALY   This sexy, minimalist gem has one of the best shows in town—from its very cool interior patio, you can almost touch the planes as they come roaring in for a landing at nearby Lindbergh Field. *2400 India St. (south of Laurel St.).* ☎ *619/685-3881. www. airportsd.com. Bus: 83. Map p 115.*

★★★ **Altitude Skybar** GASLAMP QUARTER   Twenty-two stories up in a Marriott hotel, this long, narrow open-air space looks down on PETCO Park and the Convention Center. *660 K St. (between 6th and 7th aves.).* ☎ *619/696-0234. www. atltitudeskybar.com. Bus: 3, 11, 120,* or 992. Trolley: Orange Line to Gaslamp Quarter. Map p 115.

★★★ **Beach** DOWNTOWN   This is the rooftop bar of the W hotel. Go ahead and kick off your shoes—the sand is heated. The hotel's two other bars, Living Room and Magnet, are also stylish venues. *421 B St. (at State St.).* ☎ *619/398-3100. www.wbeachbar.com. Bus: 7, 901, or 929. Trolley: Blue or Orange Line to American Plaza or Civic Center. Map p 115.*

★★★ **J6Bar** GASLAMP QUARTER   On the 4th-floor pool deck of the Hotel Solamar, there are fire pits, cabanas, comfy lounges, and views of the Gaslamp Quarter action. *616 J St. (at 6th Ave.).* ☎ *619/531-8744.*

Altitude Skybar in the Gaslamp Quarter.

www.jsixsandiego.com. Bus: 3, 11, or 992. Trolley: Orange Line to Gaslamp Quarter. Map p 115.

★ **Martini Ranch/Shaker Room** GASLAMP QUARTER   The split-level bar at Martini Ranch boasts more than 50 kinds of martinis (or martini-inspired concoctions). The Shaker Room is a dance club next door. *528 F St. (at 6th Ave.).* ☎ *619/235-6100. www.martini ranchsd.com. Bus: 3, 11, or 992. Map p 115.*

★★ **Nunu's Cocktail Lounge** HILLCREST   Lots of 1960s Naugahyde style, plus a kitchen that

whips up burgers, liver-and-onions, and other grilled standards for an eclectic crowd. *3537 Fifth Ave. (at Ivy Lane).* ☎ *619/295-2878. Bus: 3 or 120. Map p 116.*

★★★ **The Onyx Room/Thin** GASLAMP QUARTER   At subterranean Onyx the atmosphere is lounge, the music is cool. Live jazz is featured on Tuesdays. At street level is hyper-modern Thin, run by the same crew. *852 Fifth Ave. (between E and F sts.). Onyx* ☎ *619/235-6699, www.onyxroom.com; Thin* ☎ *619/ 231-7529, www.thinroom.com. Bus: 3, 120, or 992. Map p 115.*

★ **Princess Pub & Grille** LITTLE ITALY   A local haunt for Anglophiles and others hankering for a pint o' Watney's and some bangers 'n' mash. *1665 India St. (at Date St.).* ☎ *619/ 702-3021. www.princesspub.com. Bus: 83. Trolley: Blue Line to County Center/Little Italy. Map p 115.*

★★★ **Side Bar** GASLAMP QUARTER   Too cool for signage, Side Bar has roomy lounges and a sidewalk patio; plus you can get slices of New York–style pizza. *536 Market St. (northwest corner of 6th Ave. and Market St.).* ☎ *619/696-0946. www. sidebarsd.com. Bus: 3, 11, or 992. Map p 115.*

The Bitter End in the Gaslamp Quarter.

Belo dance club in the Gaslamp Quarter.

★★★ Top of the Hyatt EMBARCADERO
Perched on the 40th floor of the West Coast's tallest waterfront building, this is San Diego's ultimate bar with a view. *1 Market Pl. (at Harbor Dr.).* ☎ *619/232-1234. Trolley: Orange Line to Seaport Village. Map p 115.*

Dance Clubs

★ Bar West PACIFIC BEACH
With its bottle service, VIP booths, and dinner service, Bar West looks to bring some downtown chic to the beach. *959 Hornblend St. (between Cass and Bayard sts.).* ☎ *858/273-4800. www.barwestsd.com. Bus: 8/9. Map p 117.*

★★ belo GASLAMP QUARTER
Located below street level, this three-room circus features a retro design in pop-art hues and a restaurant (if you can manage to sit still). *Entrance on E St., between Fourth and Fifth aves.* ☎ *619/231-9200. www.belosandiego.com. Bus: 3, 120, or 992. Map p 115.*

★★ The Bitter End GASLAMP
QUARTER With three floors, this hot spot manages to be a sophisticated martini bar, dance club, and relaxing cocktail lounge all in one. *770 Fifth Ave. (at F St.).* ☎ *619/338-9300. www.thebitterend.com. Bus: 3, 120, or 992. Map p 115.*

★★★ On Broadway GASLAMP
QUARTER This dress-to-impress hangout in an old bank has five rooms covering the musical gamut, plus a sushi bar, and a billiards room in the former vault. *615 Broadway (at 6th Ave.).* ☎ *619/231-0011. www.obec.tv. Bus: 2, 7, 15, 20, 30, 50, 150, 210, 901, 929, or 923. Trolley: Blue or Orange Line to 5th Ave. Map p 115.*

Gay & Lesbian Bars & Clubs

★★ Bourbon Street UNIVERSITY
HEIGHTS There's an outdoor patio, a game room for darts or pool, a performance area (karaoke, drag shows, bingo, live music), and a lounge where DJs spin house music.

Bourbon Street in University Heights.

4612 Park Blvd. (near Adams Ave.). ☎ *619/291-4043. www.bourbon streetsd.com. Bus: 11. Map p 116.*

★★ **The Brass Rail** HILLCREST San Diego's oldest gay bar, it's been remodeled and refreshed, and now features VIP rooms, bottle service, and live music. *3796 Fifth Ave. (at Robinson St.).* ☎ *619/298-2233. www.thebrassrailsd.com. Bus: 1, 3, 11 and 120. Map p 116.*

★★★ **Club Montage** MIDDLE-TOWN One of San Diego's first urban-glam venues, this three-level dance club thumps away till the wee after-hours. *2028 Hancock St. (north of Washington St. between Pacific Hwy. and I-5).* ☎ *619/294-9590. www.clubmontage.com. Bus: 30 or 150. Trolley: Blue Line to Washington St. Map p 116.*

★★ **The Flame** HILLCREST It's usually boy's night on Friday, girls on Saturday, with a Goth gathering every second Saturday. There's classic neon out front. *3780 Park Blvd. (at Robinson Ave.).* ☎ *619/295-4163. www.flamesd.com. Bus: 1, 7, or 10. Map p 116.*

★★ **Numbers** HILLCREST It's a predominantly male crowd at this

Olé Madrid in the Gaslamp Quarter.

busy dance emporium, located just up the street from The Flame; Friday is Bad Kitties (ladies') night. *3811 Park Blvd. (at University Ave.).* ☎ *619/294-9005. www.numbers-sd. com. Bus: 1, 7, or 10. Map p 116.*

★★★ **Top of the Park** HILLCREST The weekend party scene officially begins here at the penthouse bar of the Park Manor Hotel, Friday evenings from 5 to 10pm. *525 Spruce St. (at Fifth Ave.).* ☎ *619/ 291-0999. www.parkmanorsuites. com. Bus: 3 or 120. Map p 116.*

Live Music Venues

★ **4th & B** DOWNTOWN In a former bank building, this venue has great sound and eclectic booking—everything from comedy to a wide range of musical artists. *345 B St. (at 4th Ave.).* ☎ *619/299-2583. www. 4thandB.com. Ticket prices vary. Trolley: Blue Line to 5th Ave. Map p 115.*

★★★ **Belly Up Tavern** SOLANA BEACH A 30-minute drive from downtown, this funky beach bar hosts international artists of all genres and is arguably San Diego's best spot for live music. *143 S. Cedros Ave. (south of Lomas Santa Fe Dr.).* ☎ *858/481-9022 (recorded info) or 858/481-8140 (box office). www. bellyup.com. $15–$25. Bus: 101. Map p 117.*

Canes MISSION BEACH A killer beachfront location, right alongside the Mission Beach amusement park—the rooftop restaurant may be more compelling than the bands on stage. *3105 Ocean Front Walk (at Mission Blvd. and W. Mission Bay Dr.).* ☎ *858/488-1780. www.canes barandgrill.com. Ticket prices vary. Bus: 8/9. Map p 117.*

★★ **The Casbah** LITTLE ITALY This rockin' club has a well-earned rep for showcasing alternative and punk bands that either are, were, or will be famous. Expect to hear live music at least 6 nights a week. *2501 Kettner Blvd. (at Laurel St.).* ☎ *619/ 232-4355. www.casbahmusic.com. Cover charge usually under $15. Bus: 83. Map p 115.*

★★ **Humphrey's** SHELTER ISLAND This locally beloved 1,300-seat outdoor venue is set on the water next to bobbing yachts. An indoor lounge, Humphrey's Backstage, also has music nightly. *2241 Shelter Island Dr.* ☎ *619/523-1010 (general info) or 619-224-3577 (reservations). www. humphreysconcerts.com. Ticket prices vary. Bus: 28. Map p 117.*

Supper Clubs
★★★ **Anthology** LITTLE ITALY Celebrity chef Bradley Ogden has put his imprimatur on the kitchen, while a host of marquee-name jazz, blues, and world-music artists take care of the entertainment. *1337 India St. (between Ash and A sts.).* ☎ *619/595-0300. www.anthology sd.com. Dinner packages $65 plus ticket (prices vary); $20 minimum food/beverage for first floor and mezzanine. Bus: 2, 11, or 923. Trolley: Blue or Orange Line to America Plaza. Map p 115.*

★★ **Croce's Restaurant & Jazz Bar** GASLAMP QUARTER A

Stingaree in the Gaslamp Quarter.

crowded, mainstream place where you'll find a variety of jazz and rhythm 'n' blues 7 nights a week. *802 Fifth Ave. (at F St.).* ☎ *619/ 233-4355. www.croces.com. Cover $5–$10 (cover is waived if you eat at the restaurant). Bus: 3, 20A, 120, or 992. Map p 115.*

★★★ **House of Blues** DOWNTOWN Filled with cool art, there's an 1,100-person capacity concert space and a restaurant serving Southern-inspired cuisine (also open for lunch and Sunday Gospel brunch). *1055 Fifth Ave.(between Broadway and C St.).* ☎ *619/299-2583. www.hob.com/sandiego. Ticket prices vary. Trolley: Blue Line to 5th Ave. Map p 115.*

★★ **Olé Madrid** GASLAMP QUARTER This dressy restaurant and dance club features salsa on

Wine Steals in Hillcrest.

3rd Corner in Ocean Beach.

Wednesday night and a flamenco show on Friday and Saturday. *751 Fifth Ave. (between F and G sts.).* ☎ *619/557-0146. www.olemadrid. com. Cover $10–$15 after 10pm. Bus: 3, 11, or 992. Map p 115.*

★★ **Starlite** MIDDLETOWN This hip restaurant and bar eschews the large-scale dine and dance scene that's popular in the Gaslamp Quarter for an intimate, mondo-exotica lounge feel. *3175 India St.* ☎ *619/ 358-9766. www.starlitesandiego. com. No cover. Bus: 83. Trolley: Blue Line to Middletown. Map p 116.*

★★ **Sevilla** GASLAMP QUARTER This Latin-themed club is the spot for salsa and samba lessons; there's also a tapas bar and dining room. Live flamenco dinner shows take place Friday to Sunday. *555 Fourth Ave (at Market St.).* ☎ *619/233-5979. www.cafesevilla.com. Cover $5–$15. Bus: 3, 11, or 992. Map p 115.*

★★★ **Stingaree** GASLAMP QUARTER This 3-level club has more than 22,000 square feet (2,044 sq. m) of space, a fine dining component, a handful of bars and private nooks, and a rooftop deck with cabanas and fire pit. *454 Sixth Ave. (between Island Ave. and J St.).* ☎ *619/544-9500. www.stingsan diego.com. Cover $20. Bus: 992.*

Trolley: Orange Line to Gaslamp Quarter. Map p 115.

Wine Bars

★★ **Crush** HILLCREST Hip and stylish, Crush also has specialty cocktails and tasty food. *530 University Ave. (at 6th Ave.).* ☎ *619/291-1717. www.crushsd.com. Bus: 1, 3, 11, 83, or 120. Map p 116.*

★★★ **3rd Corner** OCEAN BEACH This convivial wine bar multitasks as a restaurant and as a wine shop where you can meander through racks of wines looking for the right one to uncork. *2265 Bacon St. (between Voltaire St. and W. Point Loma Blvd.).* ☎ *619/223-2700. www.the3rdcorner. com. Bus: 923. Map p 117.*

★★ **The Vine** OCEAN BEACH Wine and beer drinkers can find common ground here—there's a great selection of suds, as well as an eclectic menu of small-plate offerings. *1851 Bacon St. (at Niagara Ave.).* ☎ *619/222-8463. www.theobvine. com. Bus: 35 or 923. Map p 117.*

★★ **Wine Steals** HILLCREST This casual neighborhood spot also has a wine-shop component and is conveniently attached to a cheese store. *1243 University Ave.(between Richmond and Vermont sts.).* ☎ *619/ 295-1188. www.winestealssd.com. Bus: 1, 10, or 11. Map p 116.* ●

A&E Best Bets

Best **Classical Music Festival**
★★★ La Jolla Music Society
SummerFest *various locations*
(p 126)

Best **Sports Venue**
★★★ San Diego Padres' PETCO
Park *100 Park Blvd. (p 129)*

Best Place for **Culture in a Mall**
★★ San Diego Repertory Theatre
Horton Plaza (p 130)

Best **Place for Foreign and
Indie Film**
★★ Hillcrest Cinema *3965 Fifth
Ave. (p 127)*

Best **Restored Venue**
★★★ North Park Theatre *2891 University Ave. (p 127)*

Most **Anticipated Restored
Venue**
★★ Balboa Theatre *850 Fourth
Ave. (p 126)*

Best **Use of Strings and
Pyrotechnics**
★★ San Diego Symphony Summer
Pops *Embarcadero Marina Park
South (p 126)*

Best **Broadway-Bound Fare**
★★★ La Jolla Playhouse *2910 La
Jolla Village Dr. (p 129)*; and ★★★
Old Globe Theatre *Balboa Park
(p 130)*

Best **Place to Get Your
Dance On**
★★ Dance Place at NTC Promenade *2650 Truxton Rd. (p 127)*

Most **Extreme Screen**
★★★ Fleet Science Center IMAX
Dome Theater *Balboa Park (p 127)*

Best **Place for Tragic Heroines**
★★★ San Diego Opera *1200 Third
Ave. (p 128)*

Best **Place for Horsing Around**
★★★ Del Mar Races *2260 Jimmy
Durante Blvd. (p 128)*

Del Mar Race Track.   *Previous Page: PETCO PARK, home of the San Diego Padres.*

Downtown/Balboa Park A&E

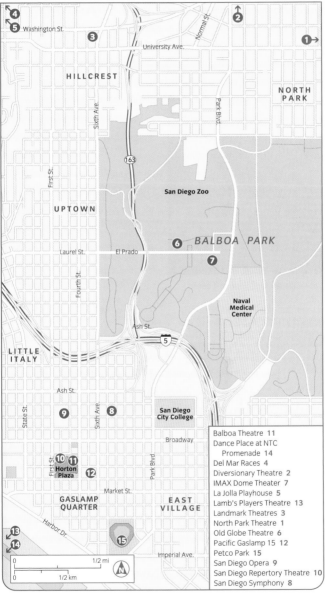

Balboa Theatre 11
Dance Place at NTC
  Promenade 14
Del Mar Races 4
Diversionary Theatre 2
IMAX Dome Theater 7
La Jolla Playhouse 5
Lamb's Players Theatre 13
Landmark Theatres 3
North Park Theatre 1
Old Globe Theatre 6
Pacific Gaslamp 15 12
Petco Park 15
San Diego Opera 9
San Diego Repertory Theatre 10
San Diego Symphony 8

A&E A to Z

The San Diego Symphony, downtown.

SummerFest in August is always highly anticipated, featuring concerts, lectures, and workshops. *Performances at Sherwood Auditorium at the Museum of Contemporary Art in La Jolla, Neurosciences Institute, Copley Symphony Hall, and North Park Theatre.* ☎ *858/459-3728. www.ljms.org. Tickets $20–$95.*

★★ San Diego Symphony

DOWNTOWN/EMBARCADERO Top talent performs at Copley Symphony Hall, then transfers to the waterfront for an open-air summer pops season. *Symphony Hall, 750 B St. (at 7th Ave.).* ☎ *619/235-0804. www.san diegosymphony.com. Bus: 3 or 120; Trolley: Blue or Orange Line to 5th Ave.; Embarcadero Marina Park South (behind the Convention Center), Trolley: Orange Line to Gaslamp Quarter. Tickets $20–$85. Map p 125.*

Classical Music
★★★ La Jolla Music Society
VARIOUS LOCATIONS This well-respected organization has been bringing marquee names to San Diego since 1968; the annual

Concert & Performance Venues
★★ Balboa Theatre
GASLAMP QUARTER Scheduled to reopen in January 2008, the restoration of this beautiful 1920s-era theater has been

What a Deal

Half-price tickets to theater, music, and dance events are available at the ARTS TIX booth in Horton Plaza Park, at Broadway and Third avenues. The kiosk is open Tuesday through Thursday at 11am, Friday to Sunday at 10am. The booth stays open until 6pm daily except Sunday, when it closes at 5pm. Half-price tickets are available only for same-day shows, except for Monday performances, which are sold on Sunday. For a daily listing of offerings, call ☎ 619/497-5000 or check www.sandiegoperforms.com; the website also sells half-price tickets for some shows. Full-price advance tickets are also available—the booth doubles as a Ticketmaster outlet.

The San Diego Opera, downtown.

a hard-fought battle for preservationists. *850 Fourth Ave. (between E and F sts.). Check www.ccdc.com for contact info. Bus: 3, 120, 992, or all Broadway routes. Map p 125.*

★★★ North Park Theatre

NORTH PARK   This gloriously restored vaudeville house is home to Lyric Opera San Diego and also hosts a variety of performances and film presentations by other groups. *2891 University Ave. (at Kansas St.) ☎ 619/239-8836. www.lyricopera sandiego.org. Ticket prices vary. Bus: 2 or 7. Map p 125.*

Dance

★★ Dance Place at NTC Promenade POINT LOMA   This former military base is now the heart of the city's dance scene, providing studio, performance, and educational space for **San Diego Ballet** (☎ 619/294-7378; www.sandiegoballet.org), **Malashock Dance** (☎ 619/260-1622; www.malashockdance.org), and **Jean Isaacs San Diego Dance Theater** (☎ 858/484-7791; www.san diegodancetheater.org). *2650 Truxton Rd. (at Dewey Rd.). ☎ 619/226-1491. www.ntcpromenade.org. Bus: 28. Map p 125.*

Film

★★★ IMAX Dome Theater BALBOA PARK   The Reuben H. Fleet Science Center features movies in the early evening projected onto the 76-foot (23m) tilted-dome screen (later shows on weekends). *Balboa Park (adjacent to Park Blvd.). ☎ 619/ 238-1233. www.rhfleet.org. Tickets $7.50–$17. Bus: 7. Map p 125.*

★★ Landmark Theatres HILLCREST/LA JOLLA   Indie and foreign films play at these multiscreen (five at Hillcrest, four at La Jolla) cinemas. *Hillcrest Cinema, 3965 Fifth Ave.*

San Diego Chargers.

PETCO Park in the East Village.

(between University Ave. and Washington St.). Bus: 1, 3, 10, 11, 83, or 120. La Jolla Village, 8879 Villa La Jolla Dr. (at Nobel Dr.). Bus: 30 or 150. ☎ 619/819-0236. www. landmarktheatres.com. Tickets $7.25–$9.50. Map p 125.

★★ Pacific Gaslamp 15

GASLAMP QUARTER   Located in the heart of the Gaslamp, these 15 theaters all offer stadium seating with large screens and great sound systems. 701 Fifth Ave. (at G St.). ☎ 619/232-0400. www.pacific theatres.com. Tickets $7–$10.50. Bus: 3, 11, 120, or 992. Map p 125.

Diversionary Theatre.

Opera

★★ San Diego Opera DOWN-

TOWN   A season of both well-trod warhorses and edgier works runs from late January to mid-May, per-formed at the Civic Theatre by local singers and name talent from around the world. 1200 Third Ave. (at B St.). ☎ 619/533-7000 (box office) or ☎ 619/232-7636 (admin). www.sdopera.com. Tickets $27–$182. Bus: 30, 50, 150, 923, or 992. Trolley: Blue or Orange Line to Civic Center. Map p 125.

Spectator Sports

★★★ Del Mar Races DEL MAR

Thoroughbred racing takes place at the Del Mar Race Track from mid-July to early September. Party crowds come for post-race concerts and other special events; there's year-round satellite wagering at the fairgrounds' Surfside Race Place (☎ 858/755-1167; www. surfsideraceplace.com). 2260 Jimmy Durante Blvd. (at Via de la Valle). ☎ 858/755-1141. www.delmar racing.com. Tickets $5–$15. Bus: 101. Map p 125.

★★ **San Diego Chargers** MISSION VALLEY   The city's NFL team plays at Qualcomm Stadium; the season runs from August to December. *9449 Friars Rd. (between the 805 and 15 freeways).* ☎ *877/242-7437. www.chargers.com. Tickets $54–$290. Trolley: Green Line or special event Blue Line to Qualcomm Stadium.*

★★★ **San Diego Padres** EAST VILLAGE   Major League Baseball action at PETCO Park, an architecturally striking downtown facility; season runs April to September. *100 Park Blvd. (bordered by 7th and 10th aves. at J St.).* ☎ *877/374-2784 or 619/795-5000. www.padres.com. Tickets $5–$67. Trolley: Orange or special event line to Gaslamp Quarter; Blue or Orange Line to 12th & Imperial Transit Center or Park & Market. Map p 125.*

Theater

★★ **Diversionary Theatre** UNIVERSITY HEIGHTS   This 104-seat theater focuses on plays with gay and lesbian themes. *4545 Park Blvd. (between Madison and Monroe aves.).* ☎ *619/220-0097. www.diversionary.org. Tickets $27–$29, $9 student rush 1 hour prior to curtain. Bus: 11. Map p 125.*

★★★ **La Jolla Playhouse** LA JOLLA   The Tony Award–winning Playhouse is known for its contemporary takes on classics and commitment to *commedia dell'arte* style, as well as producing Broadway-bound blockbusters. *2910 La Jolla Village Dr. (at Torrey Pines Rd.).* ☎ *858/550-1010. www.lajollaplayhouse.org. Tickets $28–$72. Bus: 30, 41, 48, 49, 101, 150, or 921. Map p 125.*

★★ **Lamb's Players Theatre** CORONADO   Featuring a true resident ensemble, Lamb's presents both premieres and classics, keeping things on the safe, noncontroversial side. *1142 Orange Ave. (at C Ave.).* ☎ *619/437-0600. www.lambsplayers.org. Tickets $26–$48. Bus: 901 or 904. Map p 125.*

Lowell Davies Festival Theater, part of the Old Globe Theatre complex.

Sure Bets

San Diego has 18 Native American tribes, half of which operate casinos. The most accessible from downtown is **Viejas Casino** (5000 Willows Rd., Alpine; ☎ 800/847-6537; www.viejas.com)—it's a straight shot out I-8 (exit Willows Rd.), less than a half-hour's drive away. Viejas also has an outlet center with more than 50 brand-name retailers. **Barona Valley Ranch Resort and Casino** (1932 Wildcat Canyon Rd., Lakeside; ☎ 888/722-7662 or 619/443-2300; www.barona.com), has 2,000 Vegas-style slots, nearly 70 table games, and an off-track betting area. The resort includes 400 guest rooms, a spa, and an 18-hole championship golf course. Take I-8 east to Highway 67 north; at Willows Road, turn right and continue to Wildcat Canyon Road; turn left, and continue 6 miles (10km) to the reservation (allow 40 min. from downtown). **Sycuan Resort & Casino** is outside El Cajon, at 5469 Casino Way (☎ 800/279-2826 or 619/445-6002; www.sycuan.com). Follow I-8 east for 10 miles (16km) to the El Cajon Boulevard exit. Take El Cajon 3 blocks to Washington Avenue, turning right and continuing on Washington as it turns into Dehesa Road. Stay on Dehesa for 5 miles (8km), and follow the signs (allow 30 min. from downtown). Sycuan features 2,000 slots, 65 game tables, a 1,200-seat bingo palace, an off-track betting area, and a 450-seat theater that features name touring acts; Sycuan's 54 holes of golf are also some of San Diego's best.

★★★ The Old Globe Theatre

BALBOA PARK   This Tony Award–winning, three-theater complex attracts big-name playwrights and performers, and has spawned a number of Broadway hits. The summer Shakespeare Festival features three works by the Bard. *Balboa Park (behind the Museum of Man).* ☎ *619/234-5623. www. theoldglobe.org. Tickets $19–$65. Bus: 3, 7, or 120. Map p 125.*

Lamb's Players.

★★ San Diego Repertory Theatre

GASLAMP QUARTER   The Rep mounts plays and musicals with a strong multicultural bent, performing in the two-stage Lyceum Theatre at Horton Plaza. *79 Broadway Circle, in Horton Plaza.* ☎ *619/544-1000. www.sandiegorep.com. Tickets $28–$43. Bus: All Broadway routes. Map p 125.* ●

Lodging Best Bets

Best **Historic Hotel**
★★★ Hotel Del Coronado $$$$
1500 Orange Ave. (p 139)

Best **for a Romantic Getaway**
★★★ The Lodge at Torrey Pines
$$$$ *11480 N. Torrey Pines Rd.
(p 142)*

Best **for Families**
★★ Paradise Point Resort & Spa
$$$ *1404 Vacation Rd. (p 143)*

Best **Moderately Priced Hotel**
★ Horton Grand Hotel $$ *311
Island Ave. (p 139)*

Best **Budget Hotel**
★ La Pensione Hotel $ *606 W. Date
St. (p 141)*

Best **Bed & Breakfast**
★★★ Britt Scripps Inn $$$$ *406
Maple St. (p 137)*

Best **Boutique Inn**
★★★ Hotel Parisi $$$$ *1111
Prospect St. (p 140)*

Best **Place to Stay on the
Beach**
★★ Tower 23 $$$$ *723 Felspar St.
(p 143)*

Best **Place to Stay Over the
Beach**
★★ Crystal Pier Hotel $$$ *4500
Ocean Blvd. (p 137)*

Best for **Travelers With
Disabilities**
★ Manchester Grand Hyatt $$$$
1 Market Pl. (p 142)

Best **Place to Watch a Concert
From Your Room**
★★★ The Hard Rock Hotel $$$
207 Fifth Ave. (p 139)

Best **Pool**
★★ Hotel Solamar $$$$ *435 Sixth
Ave. (p 140)*

Best **Golf Resort**
★★★ Four Seasons Resort
Aviara $$$$ *7100 Four Seasons
Point (p 138)*

Best **Place to Adjust Your
Chakras**
★★ La Costa Resort and Spa $$$$
2100 Costa del Mar Rd. (p 141)

Best for **Baseball Fans**
★★ Omni San Diego Hotel $$$$
675 L St. (p 143)

Best for **Modernists**
★★ Keating Hotel $$$$ *432 F St.
(p 140)*

Best for **Traditionalists**
★★ The Westgate Hotel $$$$
1055 Second Ave. (p 144)

Best **Retreat from the World**
★★ Loews Coronado Bay Resort
$$$$ *4000 Coronado Bay Rd. (p 142)*

Aviara Four Seasons.   *Previous page: The pool at Paradise Point.*

Downtown Lodging

Best Western Bayside Inn 5
Britt Scripps Inn 1
Embassy Suites Hotel San Diego
  Bay–Downtown 20
Gaslamp Plaza Suites 9
Hard Rock Hotel San Diego 15
Hilton San Diego Gaslamp
  Quarter 16
Holiday Inn on the Bay 4
Horton Grand 17
Hotel Occidental 2
Hotel Solamar 12
Ivy Hotel 11
Keating Hotel 10
La Pensione Hotel 3
Manchester Grand Hyatt 19
Marriott San Diego
  Gaslamp Quarter 13
Marriott San Diego Hotel &
  Marina 18
Omni San Diego Hotel 14
The US Grant 8
W San Diego 6
The Westgate Hotel 7

Mission Bay Lodging

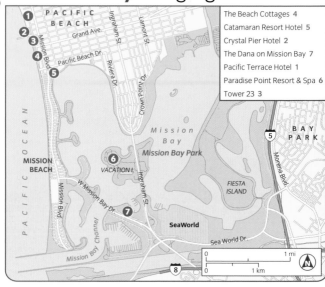

The Beach Cottages 4
Catamaran Resort Hotel 5
Crystal Pier Hotel 2
The Dana on Mission Bay 7
Pacific Terrace Hotel 1
Paradise Point Resort & Spa 6
Tower 23 3

La Jolla Lodging

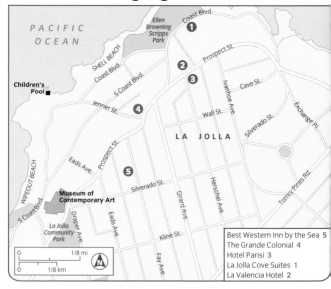

Best Western Inn by the Sea 5
The Grande Colonial 4
Hotel Parisi 3
La Jolla Cove Suites 1
La Valencia Hotel 2

Hotels **on the Beaches**

Balboa Park Inn 11
Coronado Inn 13
Del Mar Motel on the Beach 3
El Cordova Hotel 14
Estancia La Jolla Hotel & Spa 9
Four Seasons Resort Aviara 1
Glorietta Bay Inn 15
The Grand Del Mar 7
Hotel del Coronado 16
La Costa Resort & Spa 2
La Jolla Shores Hotel 10
L'Auberge Del Mar Resort & Spa 4
Les Artistes 6
The Lodge at Torrey Pines 8
Loews Coronado Bay Resort 17
Park Manor Suites 12
Wave Crest 5

Lodging A to Z

Britt Scripps Inn.

★ **Balboa Park Inn** HILLCREST Popular with gay travelers. The hotel's specialty accommodations, such as the "Greystoke" suite, are over-the-top. *3402 Park Blvd. (at Upas St.).* ☎ *800/938-8181. www. balboaparkinn.com. 26 units. Doubles $99 w/breakfast. AE, DC, DISC, MC, V. Bus: 7. Map p 135.*

The Beach Cottages PACIFIC BEACH This family-owned operation has been around since 1948

Coronado Bay Inn.

and offers a variety of guest quarters, including cottages just steps from the sand. *4255 Ocean Blvd. (1 block south of Grand Ave.).* ☎ *858/ 483-7440. www.beachcottages.com. 61 units. Doubles $135–$155. AE, DC, DISC, MC, V. Bus: 8, 9, or 30. Map p 134.*

Best Western Bayside Inn DOWNTOWN Accommodations here are basic chain-hotel issue, but they are well maintained and have balconies overlooking the bay or downtown. *555 W. Ash St. (at Columbia St.).* ☎ *800/341-1818. www.baysideinn.com. 122 units. Doubles $189 w/breakfast. AE, DC, DISC, MC, V. Bus: 7, 11, 30, 50, 810, or 820. Trolley: Blue or Orange Line to America Plaza. Map p 133.*

★ **Best Western Inn by the Sea** LA JOLLA Occupying an enviable location in the heart of La Jolla's charming village, this property is just a short walk from the cliffs and beach. *7830 Fay Ave. (between Prospect and Silverado sts.).* ☎ *800/526-4545. www.best western.com/innbythesea. 132 units.*

Doubles $159–$239 w/breakfast. AE, DC, DISC, MC, V. Bus: 30. Map p 134.

★★★ **Britt Scripps Inn** BANKERS HILL   A glorious Victorian house lovingly converted into an intimate "estate hotel"—part B&B, part luxury hotel. *406 Maple St. (at 4th Ave.).* ☎ *888/881-1991. www.britt scripps.com. 9 units. Doubles $435–$525 w/breakfast and afternoon wine and hors d'oeuvres. AE, DC, MC, V. Bus: 3 or 120. Map p 133.*

★★ kids **Catamaran Resort Hotel** PACIFIC BEACH   Right on Mission Bay, this Polynesian-themed resort has its own beach, complete with watersports facilities. *3999 Mission Blvd. (4 blocks south of Grand Ave.).* ☎ *800/422-8386. www. catamaranresort.com. 315 units. Doubles $254–$409. AE, DC, DISC, MC, V. Bus: 8, 9, 27. Map p 134.*

★ **Coronado Inn** CORONADO This tropically flavored 1940s motel is centrally located and terrifically priced, and maintains a friendly ambience. *266 Orange Ave. (corner of 3rd St.).* ☎ *800/598-6624. www. coronadoinn.com. 30 units. Doubles $165 w/breakfast. AE, DISC, MC, V. Bus: 901 or 904. Map p 135.*

★★ kids **Crystal Pier Hotel** PACIFIC BEACH   This utterly unique cluster of cottages literally sits over the surf on the vintage Crystal Pier. *4500 Ocean Blvd. (at Garnet Ave.).* ☎ *800/748-5894. www.crystalpier. com. 29 units. Doubles $300–$375. DISC, MC, V. Bus: 8, 9, 27, or 30. Map p 134.*

★ **The Dana on Mission Bay** MISSION BAY   Some rooms here overlook bobbing sailboats in the recreational marina; beaches and SeaWorld are a 15-minute walk away. *1710 W. Mission Bay Dr. (off Ingraham St.).* ☎ *800/345-9995. www.thedana.net. 270 units. Doubles $229–$319. AE, DC, DISC, MC, V. Bus: 8 or 9. Map p 134.*

Del Mar Motel on the Beach DEL MAR   The only property in Del Mar right on the beach, this simply furnished little white-stucco motel has been here since 1946. *1702 Coast Blvd. (at 17th St.).* ☎ *800/223-8449. www.delmarmotelonthebeach. com. 44 units. Doubles $259–$299. AE, DC, DISC, MC, V. Bus: 101. Map p 135.*

★ **El Cordova Hotel** CORONADO With its courtyard, meandering pathways, and prime location across from the Hotel del Coronado, this Spanish hacienda is a popular option. *1351 Orange Ave. (at Adella Ave.).* ☎ *800/229-2032. www.el cordovahotel.com. 40 units. Doubles*

Grand Del Mar.

Grand Colonial.

$169–$215. AE, DC, DISC, MC, V. Bus: 901 or 904. Map p 135.

★★ Embassy Suites Hotel San Diego Bay–Downtown EMBAR-CADERO

At this modern, neoclassical high-rise every room is a suite with kitchenette and bay or city views. *601 Pacific Hwy. (at N. Harbor Dr.).* ☎ 800/362-2779. www.embassy suites.com. 337 units. Suites $279–$389 w/breakfast and afternoon cocktail. AE, DC, DISC, MC, V. Bus: 7, 923, 929, or 992. Trolley: Orange Line to Seaport Village. Map p 133.

★★★ Estancia La Jolla Hotel and Spa LA JOLLA

This California rancho-style property is built on the remains of a horse farm, and was named one of the world's hottest new hotels in 2005 by *Condé Nast Traveler.* *9700 N. Torrey Pines Rd. (north of Almahurst Row).* ☎ 877/437-8262. www.estancialajolla.com. 210 units. Doubles $249–$399. AE, DC, DISC, MC, V. Bus: 101. Map p 135.

★★★ kids Four Seasons Resort Aviara CARLSBAD

This ocean-view resort, a AAA 5 Diamond property, hits the trifecta—its spa, restaurant, and golf course are all outstanding. A surf concierge is available for lessons. *7100 Four Seasons Point (at Aviara Pkwy.).* ☎ 800/332-3442. www.fourseasons.com/aviara. 329 units. Doubles $405–$585. AE, DC, DISC, MC, V. No public transportation. Map p 135.

★★ Gaslamp Plaza Suites GASLAMP QUARTER

At 11 stories, this was San Diego's first skyscraper, built in 1913. Most rooms are spacious and offer luxuries rare in this price range. *520 E St. (corner of 5th Ave.).* ☎ 800/874-8770. www.gaslampplaza.com. 64 units. Doubles $109–$159 w/breakfast. AE, DC, DISC, MC, V. Bus: 3, 120, 992, or any Broadway route. Trolley: Blue or Orange Line to Fifth Ave. Map p 133.

★★ Glorietta Bay Inn CORON-ADO

Across the street from the Hotel del Coronado, this pretty hotel consists of the charmingly historic John D. Spreckels mansion (1908) and several younger, motel-style buildings. *1630 Glorietta Blvd. (near Orange Ave.).* ☎ 800/283-9383. www.gloriettabayinn.com. 100 units. Doubles $170–$650 w/breakfast. AE, DC, DISC, MC, V. Bus: 901 or 904. Map p 135.

★★★ The Grand Del Mar DEL MAR

In the foothills of Del Mar, this new luxury resort is a fanciful Spanish Revival creation with lushly landscaped courtyards and gardens; it also incorporates a Tom Fazio–designed golf course. *5200 Grand Del Mar Way (off Carmel Country Rd.).* ☎ 858/314-2000. www.thegranddelmar.com. 249 units. Doubles from $575. AE, DC, DISC, MC, V. No public transportation. Map p 135.

★★ The Grande Colonial LA
JOLLA This refined hotel possesses an old-world European flair that's more London or Georgetown than seaside La Jolla. *910 Prospect St. (between Fay and Girard aves.).* ☎ *800/826-1278. www.thegrande colonial.com. 75 units. Doubles $285–$460. AE, DC, DISC, MC, V. Bus: 30. Map p 134.*

★★★ Hard Rock Hotel San Diego GASLAMP QUARTER This
12-story condo-hotel has a sweet location, a celebrity-chef restaurant, and an outdoor concert space. The Black Eyed Peas designed one of the "Rock Star" suites. *207 Fifth Ave. (between K and L sts.).* ☎ *888/593-6177. www.hardrockhotelsd.com. 420 units. Doubles $250–$500. AE, DC, DISC, MC, V. Bus: 992. Trolley: Orange Line to Gaslamp Quarter. Map p 133.*

★★★ Hilton San Diego Gaslamp Quarter GASLAMP
QUARTER This handsome hotel incorporates elements of a historic building. It's also a great place for guests who want to be in the heart of the Gaslamp action. *401 K St. (at 4th Ave.).* ☎ *800/445-8667. www. hilton.com. 282 units. Doubles $329. AE, DC, DISC, MC, V. Bus: 992. Trolley: Orange Line to Gaslamp Quarter or Convention Center. Map p 133.*

★★ kids Holiday Inn on the Bay EMBARCADERO This three-
building high-rise complex has a scenic location across from the harbor and the Maritime Museum, only 1½ miles (2.4km) from the airport. *1355 N. Harbor Dr. (at Ash St.).* ☎ *800/465-4329. www.holiday-inn. com/san-onthebay. 600 units. Doubles $224. AE, DC, MC, V. Bus: 2, 210, 810, 820, 850, 860, 923, or 992. Trolley: Blue or Orange Line to America Plaza. Map p 133.*

★ Horton Grand GASLAMP
QUARTER The charming Horton Grand combines two hotels built in 1886. Both were saved from demolition and moved to this spot. *311 Island Ave. (at 4th Ave.).* ☎ *800/ 542-1886. www.hortongrand.com. 132 units. Doubles $169–$199. AE, DC, MC, V. Bus: 3, 11, 120, or 992. Trolley: Orange Line to Convention Center. Map p 133.*

★★★ Hotel del Coronado
CORONADO Opened in 1888 and designated a National Historic Landmark in 1977, the Hotel Del is the last of California's stately old seaside hotels and a monument to Victorian grandeur. *1500 Orange Ave. (at Dana Pl.).* ☎ *800/468-3533. www.hoteldel.com. 688 rooms. Doubles $245–$545. AE, DC, DISC, MC, V. Bus: 901 or 904. Map p 135.*

Hard Rock San Diego.

La Costa.

★ **Hotel Occidental** BANKERS HILL   Just a block from Balboa Park, this attractive Mission-style building has been restored to its 1923 glory. *410 Elm St. (between 4th and 5th aves.).* ☎ *800/205-9897. www.hoteloccidental-sandiego.com. 54 units. Doubles $99 w/breakfast. AE, MC, V. Bus: 3 or 120. Map p 133.*

★★★ **Hotel Parisi** LA JOLLA   Feng shui principles hold sway at this boutique hotel; the Italy-meets-Zen composition is carried into the 20 rooms, where custom furnishings are modern yet comfy. *1111 Prospect St. (at Herschel Ave.).* ☎ *877/472-7474. www.hotelparisi. com. 28 units. Doubles $265–$425*

w/breakfast. AE, DC, DISC, MC, V. Bus: 30. Map p 134.

★★ **Hotel Solamar** GASLAMP QUARTER   This stylishly urban and sophisticated property provides excellent Gaslamp digs. The 4th-floor pool bar is a hot spot. *435 Sixth Ave. (between J St. and Island Ave.).* ☎ *877/230-0300. www.hotel solamar.com. 235 units. Doubles $379. AE, DC, DISC, MC, V. Bus: 3, 11, or 992. Trolley: Orange Line to Gaslamp Quarter. Map p 133.*

★★ **Ivy Hotel** GASLAMP QUARTER   A dowdy old hotel has been magically transformed into a world-class, high-style luxury destination. It features a four-level nightclub and rooftop pool/entertainment area. *650 F St. (between 6th and 7th aves.).* ☎ *619/814-1000. www.ivyhotel.com. 159 units. Doubles $450–$550. AE, DC, DISC, MC, V. Bus: 3, 120, or 992. Map p 133.*

★★ **Keating Hotel** GASLAMP QUARTER   The Italian design group behind Ferrari and Maserati has made its first foray into hotel design with this ultra-contemporary project, set in a gorgeous structure built in 1890. *432 F St. (between 4th and 5th aves.).* ☎ *877/753-2846. www. keatinghotel.com. 35 units. Doubles $429–$459. AE, DC, DISC, MC, V. Bus: 3, 120, or 992. Map p 133.*

The Keating Hotel.

Hotel Solamar.

★★★ L'Auberge Del Mar Resort & Spa DEL MAR

An excellent spa and one of the area's finest restaurants are highlights of this elegant hotel, situated across from Del Mar's shopping and dining scene, and a short jog from the sand. *1540 Camino del Mar (at 15th St.).* ☎ *800/245-9757. www.lauberge delmar.com. 120 units. Doubles $325–$470. AE, DC, MC, V. Bus: 101. Map p 135.*

★★ kids La Costa Resort and Spa CARLSBAD

This campuslike golf and tennis resort has a California ranch style. There's also a 42-room spa, the new-age Chopra Center for adults, waterslides, and entertainment for the kids. *2100 Costa del Mar Rd. (at El Camino Real).* ☎ *800/854-5000. www.la costa.com. 511 units. Doubles $300–$500. AE, DC, DISC, MC, V. Bus: 309. Map p 135.*

La Jolla Cove Suites LA JOLLA

Sitting across from Ellen Browning Scripps Park, this family-run 1950s-era hotel has to-die-for ocean views and is steps away from the Cove. *1155 Coast Blvd. (across from the Cove).* ☎ *888/525-6552. www.la jollacove.com. 90 units. Doubles $219–$429 w/breakfast. AE, DC, DISC, MC, V. Bus: 30. Map p 134.*

★ kids La Jolla Shores Hotel LA JOLLA

Spend time on the beach or the tennis court at this three-story 1960s hotel in a mainly residential enclave. *8110 Camino del Oro (at Avenida de la Playa).* ☎ *866/392-8762. www.ljshoreshotel.com. 128 units. Doubles $309–$579. AE, DC, DISC, MC, V. Bus: 30. Map p 135.*

★ La Pensione Hotel LITTLE ITALY

This place has a lot going for it: modern amenities, remarkable value, a convenient location, a friendly staff, and free parking. *606 W. Date St. (at India St.).* ☎ *800/232-4683. www.lapensionehotel. com. 80 units. Doubles $90. AE, DC, DISC, MC, V. Bus: 83. Trolley: Blue Line to County Center/Little Italy. Map p 133.*

★★★ La Valencia Hotel LA JOLLA

This bluff-top hotel, which looks like a Mediterranean villa, has been the centerpiece of La Jolla since opening in 1926; La V's clubby

L'auberge del Mar.

Torrey Pines Lodge.

Whaling Bar is a classic. *1132 Prospect St. (at Herschel Ave.).* ☎ *800/451-0772. www.lavalencia. com. 117 units. Doubles $275–$575. AE, DC, DISC, MC, V. Bus: 30. Map p 134.*

Les Artistes DEL MAR   A funky, informal hotel, just a few blocks from downtown Del Mar, where the rooms have been redone as tributes to favored artists like Diego Rivera. *944 Camino del Mar (between 9th and 10th sts.).* ☎ *858/755-4646. www.lesartistesinn.com. 12 units. Doubles $85–$195 w/breakfast. DISC, MC, V. Bus: 101. Map p 135.*

★★★ The Lodge at Torrey Pines LA JOLLA   This AAA 5 Diamond resort is a Craftsman-style fantasy brimming with clinker-brick masonry, Stickley furniture, and exquisite pottery. Some rooms overlook the golf course and the ocean.

Manchester Grand Hyatt.

11480 N. Torrey Pines Rd. (at Callan Rd.). ☎ *800/656-0087. www.lodge torreypines.com. 175 units. Doubles from $575. AE, DC, DISC, MC, V. Bus: 101. Map p 135.*

★★ kids Loews Coronado Bay Resort CORONADO   Located on its own private peninsula 4 miles (6.5km) south of downtown Coronado, this isolated resort destination has a plethora of water-related activities. *4000 Coronado Bay Rd. (off Silver Strand Blvd.).* ☎ *800/235-6397. www.loewshotels/sandiego. com. 438 units. Doubles $319–$369. AE, DC, DISC, MC, V, JCB. Bus: 901. Map p 135.*

★ Manchester Grand Hyatt EMBARCADERO   This twin-towered behemoth is adjacent to the Convention Center and Seaport Village shopping center, creating a neatly insular, if touristy, little world. *1 Market Place (Market St. at Harbor Dr.).* ☎ *800/233-1234. www.manchester grand.hyatt.com. 1,625 units. Doubles $299–$374. AE, DC, DISC, MC, V. Trolley: Orange Line to Seaport Village. Map p 133.*

★ Marriott San Diego Gaslamp Quarter GASLAMP QUARTER   A massive renovation transformed this property into a stylish destination with a boutique feel. Check out the open-air bar on the 22nd floor. *660 K St. (between 6th and 7th aves.).* ☎ *888/800-8118.*

www.sandiegogaslamphotel.com.
306 units. Doubles $259–$359 double. AE, DC, DISC, MC, V. Bus: 992.
Trolley: Orange Line to Gaslamp
Quarter. Map p 133.

★★ Marriott San Diego Hotel & Marina EMBARCADERO Convention goers are drawn to the scenic 446-slip marina, lush grounds, waterfall pool, and breathtaking bay-and-beyond views. *333 W. Harbor Dr. (at Front St.).* ☎ *800/228-9290. www.marriott.com. 1,408 units. Doubles $215–$515. AE, DC, DISC, MC, V. Trolley: Orange Line to Convention Center. Map p 133.*

★★ Omni San Diego Hotel GASLAMP QUARTER This swank 32-story high-rise has lots of baseball memorabilia and a 4th-floor "skybridge" that connects it with PETCO Park. It's baseball fan heaven. *675 L St. (at 6th Ave.).* ☎ *800/843-6664. www.omnihotels. com. 511 units. Doubles $299–$750. AE, DC, DISC, MC, V. Bus: 992. Trolley: Orange Line to Gaslamp Quarter. Map p 133.*

★ Pacific Terrace Hotel PACIFIC BEACH More upscale than most of the casual places nearby, this boardwalk hotel features a South Seas–meets–Spanish Colonial ambience. *610 Diamond St. (west of Mission*

Blvd.). ☎ *800/344-3370. www. pacificterrace.com. 73 units. Doubles $359–$444 w/breakfast. AE, DC, DISC, MC, V. Bus: 30. Map p 134.*

★★ kids Paradise Point Resort & Spa MISSION BAY Smack dab in the middle of Mission Bay, this hotel complex is almost as much a theme park as its closest neighbor, SeaWorld (a 3-min. drive). *1404 Vacation Rd. (off Ingraham St.).* ☎ *800/344-2626. www.paradise point.com. 457 units. Doubles $329–$495. AE, DC, DISC, MC, V. Bus: 8 or 9. Map p 134.*

★ Park Manor Suites HILLCREST This eight-story property, built in 1926, occupies a prime corner overlooking Balboa Park; a few rooms have glassed-in terraces. *525 Spruce St. (between 5th and 6th aves.).* ☎ *800/874-2649. www.parkmanor suites.com. 74 units. Doubles $149–$189 w/breakfast. AE, DC, DISC, MC, V. Bus: 3 or 120. Map p 135.*

★★ Tower 23 PACIFIC BEACH This modernist beach resort sits right alongside the boardwalk in Pacific Beach. *723 Felspar St. (west of Mission Blvd.).* ☎ *866/869-3723. www.t23hotel.com. 44 units. Doubles $389–$469. AE, DC, DISC, MC, V. Bus: 8, 9, 27, or 30. Map p 134.*

Tower 23.

The US Grant.

★★★ The US Grant DOWNTOWN

Built in 1910, this grandiose 11-story property is one of San Diego's most historic hotels. It reopened in 2006 following a 20-month, $52 million renovation. *326 Broadway (between 3rd and 4th aves., main entrance on 4th Ave.).* ☎ *800/237-5029. www.usgrant.net. 270 units. Doubles $249–$549. AE, DC, DISC, MC, V. Bus: 2, 3, 120, 992, and all Broadway routes. Trolley: Orange or Blue Line to Civic Center. Map p 133.*

★★ W San Diego DOWNTOWN

There's an adventurous restaurant,

W San Diego.

lively nightspots, and accommodations that are bright and cheery—like mod beach cabanas. *421 W. B St. (at State St.).* ☎ *888/625-5144. www.whotels.com/sandiego. 259 units. Doubles $349–$469. AE, DC, DISC, MC, V. Bus: 30, 50, 150, 810, or 820. Trolley: Blue or Orange Line to America Plaza. Map p 133.*

★★ Wave Crest DEL MAR

On a bluff overlooking the Pacific, these gray-shingled bungalow condominiums are beautifully maintained and wonderfully private. *1400 Ocean Ave. (at 15th St.).* ☎ *858/755-0100. www.wavecrestresort.com. 31 units. Studios $195–$260. MC, V. Bus: 101. Map p 135.*

★★ The Westgate Hotel

DOWNTOWN With its regal and lavish decor, this is about as "old world" as San Diego gets. It's a hub of cultural and culinary activities as well. *1055 Second Ave. (between Broadway and C St.).* ☎ *800/522-1564. www.westgatehotel.com. 223 units. Doubles $340–$435. AE, DC, DISC, MC, V. Bus: 2, 7, 923, 929, and all Broadway routes. Trolley: Blue or Orange Line to Civic Center. Map p 133.* ●

North County

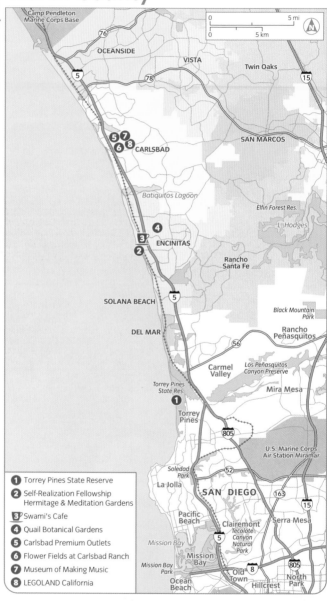

1. Torrey Pines State Reserve
2. Self-Realization Fellowship Hermitage & Meditation Gardens
3. Swami's Cafe
4. Quail Botanical Gardens
5. Carlsbad Premium Outlets
6. Flower Fields at Carlsbad Ranch
7. Museum of Making Music
8. LEGOLAND California

Carlsbad Ranch in bloom.

Don't be fooled by the laidback, surf-dude ethic that prevails amid the string of picturesque coastal communities north of La Jolla. For decades, the area's slower pace and stunning physical beauty have attracted serious and accomplished artists, writers, celebrities, spiritualists, and others who could afford a piece of coastal solitude. The result is a casual sophistication and territorial pride that distinguishes this region from the county's lower reaches.
START: **Del Mar is 18 miles (29km) north of downtown San Diego, Carlsbad about 33 miles (53km), and Oceanside approximately 36 miles (58km). If you're driving, follow I-5 north; Del Mar, Solana Beach, Encinitas, Carlsbad, and Oceanside all have freeway exits. The northernmost point, Oceanside, will take about 45 minutes. The other choice by car is to wander up the old coast road, known as Camino del Mar, "PCH" (Pacific Coast Highway), Old Highway 101, and County Highway S21. The Breeze 101 bus route traverses 101 from La Jolla to Oceanside. From San Diego, the Coaster commuter train provides service to Solana Beach, Encinitas, Carlsbad, and Oceanside, and Amtrak stops in Solana Beach and Oceanside. The Coaster makes the trip a number of times (6:30am–7pm) on weekdays, four times on Saturday; Amtrak passes through about 11 times daily each way. Call ☎ 619/685-4900 for transit information or check with Amtrak (☎ 800/872-7245 or www.amtrak.com). If you are driving, beware of rush-hour traffic.**

① ★★★ **Torrey Pines State Reserve.** Simply one of the most breathtaking locations in San Diego County, this forest is home to the gnarled little evergreen that's the rarest native pine in North America. See p 87.

② ★★ **Self-Realization Fellowship Hermitage and Meditation Gardens.** Paramahansa Yogananda, a guru born and educated in India, opened this retreat with the exotic

Torrey Pines State Reserve.

lotus domes in 1937. He lived for many years in the Hermitage and today the site serves as a spiritual sanctuary for his followers. The gift shop sells distinctive arts and crafts from India; the serene meditation gardens offer spectacular ocean views and are a terrific place to cool off on a hot day (and no disciples will give you a sales pitch). ⏱ *45 min. 215 W. K St. (off S. Coast Hwy. 101). ☎ 760/753-2888. www.yoganandasrf.org. Free admission. Tues–Sat 9am–5pm, Sun 11am–5pm (Hermitage open Sun 2–5pm).*

③ ★ **Swami's Cafe.** Locals crowd into this casual eatery for tasty, health-conscious breakfasts and lunch. It gets its name from the legendary surf spot across the highway, which in turn was named for the yogi's retreat on the clifftop. *1163 S. Coast Hwy. 101 (at W. K St.). ☎ 760/944-0612. Daily 7am–4pm. $.*

A hang glider over Torrey Pines.

4 ★★ **Quail Botanical Gardens.** Featuring 35 acres (14 hectares) of California natives, exotic tropicals, palms, bamboo, cacti, Mediterranean, Australian, and other unusual collections, this serene compound is crisscrossed

Legoland Tower

with scenic walkways and trails. There's also a gift shop and nursery, and a variety of special events and classes are scheduled throughout the year. ⏱ *90 min. 230 Quail Gardens Dr. (off Encinitas Blvd.).* ☎ *760/436-3036. www.qbgardens.com. Admission $10 adults, $7 seniors and military, $5 children 3–12, free for children under 3, free admission the first Tues of the month. Daily 9am–5pm. Guided tours Sat at 10am.*

5 ★★ **Carlsbad Premium Outlets.** From Adidas to Swarovski, some of the biggest names in fashion and retail are elbow to elbow here. This smart, upscale outlet mall features some 90 stores—everything from soup (Le Gourmet Chef) to nuts (Sweet Factory). It even has a fine-dining component, Bellefleur Winery & Restaurant, anchoring one end of the center. ⏱ *2 hr. 5620 Paseo del Norte (off Palomar Airport Rd.).* ☎ *888/790-7467. www.premiumoutlets.com. Daily 10am–8pm.*

6 ★ **Flower Fields at Carlsbad Ranch.** One of the most arresting sights in North

Grape Escape

Over the line in Riverside County, 60 miles (97km) north of San Diego via I-15, is the wine country of Temecula (pronounced "ta-*meck*-you-la"). Some believe Franciscan friars planted the first grapevines here in the early 1800s, and there are now 20-plus wineries in the region (most are along Rancho California Road). Harvest time is generally from mid-August to September, but visitors are invited year-round to tour, taste, and stock up. For more information contact the Temecula Valley Winegrowers Association (☎ 800/801-9463; www.temeculawines.org) or the Temecula Valley Chamber of Commerce (☎ 866/676-5090; www.temecula.org), which can provide information on accommodations, golf, fishing, and the Temecula Valley Balloon & Wine Festival, held in June.

County is the blossoming sea of giant ranunculuses that occurs every March to mid-May. It creates a striped blanket of color covering some 50 acres (20 hectares). Visitors are welcome to tour the grounds and enjoy special floral installations. This is a working nursery the rest of the year. ⏱ *1 hr. 5704 Paseo del Norte (off Palomar Airport Rd.).* ☎ *760/431-0352. www.theflower fields.com. Admission $9 adults, $8 seniors, $5 children 3–10. In season, daily 9am–6pm.*

⑦ ★ Museum of Making Music. Visitors go on a journey from Tin Pan Alley to MTV, stopping along the way to learn historic anecdotes about the American music industry and the instruments it created. There's an interactive portion where you can try your hand at playing drums, guitars, or a digital keyboard. ⏱ *1 hr. 5790 Armada Dr. (off Palomar Airport Rd.).* ☎ *877/551-9976. www.museumofmaking music.org. Admission $5 adults, $3 children ages 4–18, seniors, students, and military. Tues–Sun 10am–5pm.*

⑧ ★ kids LEGOLAND California. A child's most important work is play, and that credo is vigorously pursued at LEGOLAND. See p 30, bullet ⑤.

A Lego car in Legoland.

Julian

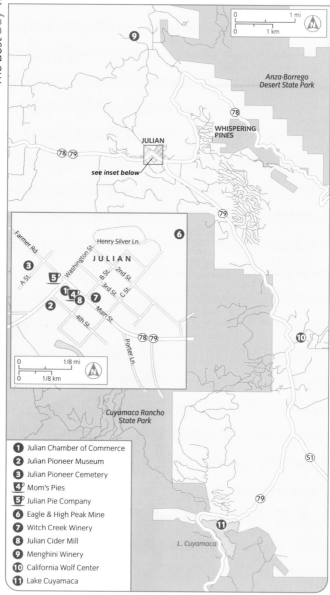

Anza-Borrego
Desert State Park

WHISPERING
PINES

JULIAN

see inset below

JULIAN

Henry Silver Ln.

Farmer Rd.

A St.

Washington St.

2nd St.

B St.

3rd St.

C St.

Main St.

4th St.

Porter Ln.

Cuyamaca Rancho
State Park

L. Cuyamaca

1 Julian Chamber of Commerce
2 Julian Pioneer Museum
3 Julian Pioneer Cemetery
4 Mom's Pies
5 Julian Pie Company
6 Eagle & High Peak Mine
7 Witch Creek Winery
8 Julian Cider Mill
9 Menghini Winery
10 California Wolf Center
11 Lake Cuyamaca

In October 2003, the devastating Cedar Fire virtually engulfed the historic mountain hamlet of Julian. Firefighters made a desperate stand to protect the town against what seemed insurmountable odds. For a few days it was touch-and-go, and 15 lives and some 800 homes in the surrounding hillsides were lost. But the central part of this Old West gold-mining town was saved, and today you can stand on Main Street without knowing a catastrophe visited just a few hundred yards away. Prospectors first ventured into these fertile hills (elevation 4,225 feet/1,288m) in search of gold in the late 1860s. Within 10 years, 18 mines were operating, producing up to an estimated $13 million worth of gold. After the rush played out, Julian (pop. 3,000) renewed its fame after striking another mother lode: apples. START: **Julian is not accessible via public transportation. You can make the 90-minute drive on Highway 78 or I-8 to Highway 79; try taking one route going and the other on the way back (Highway 79 winds through Rancho Cuyamaca State Park, while Highway 78 traverses open country and farmland). Weekend crowds can be heavy, especially during the fall apple harvest season.**

1 Julian Chamber of Commerce. The Chamber in the foyer of the creaky old Town Hall, built in 1913. Staffers here always have enthusiastic suggestions for local activities. Be sure to duck into the auditorium itself to check out the photos of Julian's bygone days. Main Street is only 6 blocks long, and shops, cafes, and some lodgings are on it or a block away. Town maps and accommodations fliers are available on the Town Hall porch. Public restrooms are behind the building. *2129 Main St. (at Washington St.).* ☎ *760/765-1857. www.julianca.com. Daily 10am–4pm.*

2 Julian Pioneer Museum. This small museum is dedicated to illuminating the life and times of Julian's townspeople from 1869 to 1913. It exhibts clothing, tools, gold-mining equipment, household and military items, and a fine

A horse-drawn carriage in the streets of Julian.

The Julian Pioneer Museum.

collection of lace doilies, quilts, and scarves. Look out back for the Julian Transportation Garage museum, with its vintage machinery and vehicles. ⏲ *30 min. 2811 Washington St. (south of 4th St.).* ☎ *760/765-0227. $3 donation requested. Apr–Nov, Wed–Sun, 10am–4pm; weekends 10am–4pm the rest of the year.*

③ ★ Julian Pioneer Cemetery. This small, hillside graveyard is straight out of *Our Town.* Julian's citizens have been laid to rest here since 1870, when the only way to deliver caskets to the gravesite was to carry them up the long, stone staircase in front. If you don't want to huff and puff up the stairs (just imagine carrying a casket), there's now a parking lot behind the cemetery that provides easy access. ⏲ *20 min. A St. (at Farmer Rd).*

④ You've waited long enough—it's time for some pie. You can observe the mom-on-duty rolling crust and crimping edges at **★★ Mom's Pies** (2119 Main St.; ☎ 760/765-2472; www.momspiesjulian.com; $). The shop routinely bakes several varieties of apple pie and will, with advance notice, whip up any one of a number of specialties. *Mon–Fri, 8am–5pm; weekends 8am–6pm.*

⑤ ★★ Julian Pie Company (2225 Main St.; ☎ 760/765-2449; www. julianpie.com; $) has outdoor seating where overhanging apples are literally up for grabs. Among its specialties is a no-sugar-added pie; light lunches of soup and sandwiches are also available. *Daily 9am–5pm. Lunch 11am–2pm.*

⑥ ★ kids Eagle and High Peak Mine. Although it's seemingly a tourist trap, this mine, which dates from around 1870, affords an interesting and educational look at the town's one-time economic mainstay. Tours take you underground to the 1,000-foot (305m) hard-rock tunnel to see the mining and milling process; antique engines and authentic tools are on display. ⏲ *1 hr. End of C St. (at Old Miner's Trail).* ☎ *760/765-0036. $10 adults, $5 children 6–16, $1 for children under 6. Hour-long tours are usually given beginning at 10am, but hours vary so it's best to call ahead.*

⑦ Witch Creek Winery. There are a handful of wineries in the Julian area, but this is the only wine-tasting operation right in town. What it lacks in ambience, it makes up for in convenience and friendliness. *2100 Main St. (between B and*

C sts.). ☎ 760/765-2023. www.
witchcreekwinery.com. Daily
11am–5pm.

⑧ ★★ Julian Cider Mill. You can
see cider presses at work here October through March. It offers free
tastes of the fresh nectar, and jugs
to take home. Throughout the year,
the mill also carries the area's
widest selection of food products,
from apple butters and jams to
berry preserves, several varieties of
local honey, candies, and other
goodies. ⏱ 30 min. 2103 Main St.
(at B St.). ☎ 760/765-1430.
Mon–Thurs 9:30am–5pm, Fri–Sun
9:30am–5:30pm.

⑨ ★★ Menghini Winery. The
rustic facilities and rolling picnic
grounds of this winery make it a
popular spot for wine tasting as well
as special events such as the annual
Grape Stomp Festa and Menghini
Arts and Music Festival in September, and the Apple Days Festival in
October. It's located about 3 miles
(5km) out of town. ⏱ 1 hr. 1150
Julian Orchards Dr. (at Wynola Rd.).
☎ 760/765-2072. Mon–Fri 10am–
4pm, Sat–Sun 10am–5pm.

**⑩ ★★ kids California Wolf
Center.** Animal lovers should look
into this education and conservation
center, located about 4 miles
(6.5km) from town, where you can
learn about wolves and visit with
the resident wolf pack. Reservations
required. ⏱ 1 hr. 18457 Hwy. 79 (at
KQ Ranch Campground, look for
Wolf Center sign). ☎ 760/765-0030.
www.californiawolfcenter.org. $10
adults, $7 seniors, $6 kids. Sat at
2pm; private tours can be arranged
during the week ($25 per person).

⑪ ★ kids Lake Cuyamaca.
Eight miles (13km) south of Julian
this 110-acre (45-hectare) lake
offers boating, fishing, and camping.
Anglers try for bass, catfish, crap-
pie, bluegill, and trout (stocked

*You're never far from first-rate apple pie
in Julian.*

year-round). There's also a general
store and restaurant at the lake's
edge. 15027 Hwy. 79 (between Milk
Ranch and Wolahi rds.). ☎ 877/581-
9904. www.lakecuyamaca.org. Fishing fee $6 per day, $3.50 per day for
ages 8–15, free for children under 8.
A California fishing license is required
and sold here: $12 per day, $37 per
year. Rowboats $15 per day, motor-
boat $40 per day ($30 after 1pm),
canoes and paddleboats (summer
only) $10 per hour. Daily 6am–sunset
(weather permitting); Dec–Jan,
closed Wed and Sun till noon.

*Julian's most famous product, fresh from
the oven.*

Tijuana

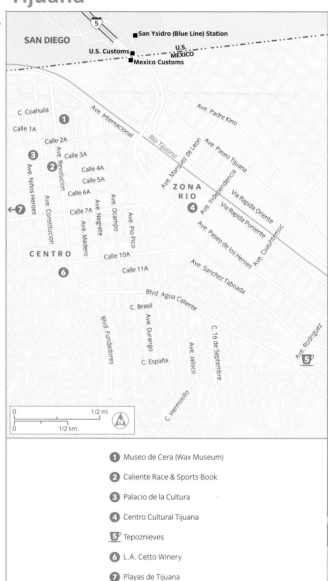

SAN DIEGO

San Ysidro (Blue Line) Station

U.S. Customs

U.S. MEXICO

Mexico Customs

Ave. Padre Kino

C. Coahuila

Calle 1A

Ave. Internacional

Rio Tijuana

Ave. Marquez de Leon

Ave. Paseo Tijuana

Calle 2A

Ave. Niños Heroes

Ave. Revolucion

Calle 3A

Calle 4A

Calle 5A

Calle 6A

Ave. Independencia

ZONA RIO

Via Rapida Oriente

Calle 7A

Ave. Ocampo

Ave. Constitucion

Ave. Negrete

Ave. Pio Pico

Via Rapida Poniente

Ave. Cuauhtemoc

Ave. Madero

Ave. Paseo de los Heroes

CENTRO

Calle 10A

Calle 11A

Ave. Sanchez Taboada

Blvd. Agua Caliente

C. Brasil

Ave. Durango

Blvd. Fundadores

C. España

Ave. Jalisco

C. 16 de Septiembre

Ave. Rodriguez

C. Hermosillo

0   1/2 mi

0   1/2 km

1. Museo de Cera (Wax Museum)
2. Caliente Race & Sports Book
3. Palacio de la Cultura
4. Centro Cultural Tijuana
5. Tepoznieves
6. L.A. Cetto Winery
7. Playas de Tijuana

Vibrant, chaotic, colorful, and confounding, Tijuana is Mexico's fourth largest city and just a 20-minute drive from downtown San Diego. With a population of more than two million, it's the West Coast's second largest city, trumped only by Los Angeles. "T.J.," as San Diegans call it, was little more than a village at the turn of the 20th century, but it grew explosively in response to the needs of San Diego and the rest of California, providing a workforce for factories and fields, especially during World War II. It also offered succor, becoming a decadent playground for Americans deprived of booze and gambling by Prohibition and moral reformers. The city's economic engine now hums along, driven by free-trade policies that gave rise to the foreign-owned factories known as *maquiladoras*. Tijuana's urban landscape isn't attractive, but its beauty lies within its fabulous restaurants, burgeoning art and music scene, plentiful shopping opportunities, and legendary nightlife. START: **Take the Blue Line trolley to San Ysidro (it's the last stop). From the trolley, cross the street and head up the ramp that accesses the border-crossing bridge.**

1 Museo de Cera (Wax Museum).

This creepy sideshow is filled with characters from Mexican history and lore, and includes a few incongruous figures such as Bill Clinton and Whoopi Goldberg. And despite her wax likeness here, there was no kindly rancho matriarch named Tía Juana (aunt Jane) for whom the city was named. Tijuana derives its name from *tycuan,* an indigenous word meaning "near the water," a reference to a broad, shallow river that is now little more than a trickle (except during storms) running down a concrete wash. *8281*

Calle 1 (between aves. Revolución and Maderas). ☎ *664/688-2478. Admission $1.60. Daily 10am–6pm.*

2 Caliente Race & Sports Book.

Opened in 2006, this attractive, flagstone-fronted space has all the bells and whistles of a Vegas sports book. You can bet on international sporting events including NFL, NBA, and soccer games; there's also electronic gaming. About a 10-minute cab ride away is Hipódromo Caliente (Caliente Racetrack), at Blv. Agua Caliente and Tapachula (☎ 664/633-7300), where there's daily greyhound

Caliente Race & Sports Book.

Crossing the World's Busiest International Border

As of January 1, 2008, a valid U.S. passport is required for all land arrivals, as well as air and sea arrivals; non–U.S. citizens need a passport, an I-94, a multiple-entry visa, or a Resident Alien Card to return to the U.S. Waits of up to 2 hours are not uncommon when crossing back to the U.S.

If you walk across to Mexico, the first structure you'll see on your left is a Visitor Information Center (☎ 664/607-3097), open daily 9am to 6pm. They have maps, safety tips, and brochures that cover the city's highlights. There's also an information booth on the east side of Avenue Revolución at Third. The Tijuana Convention & Visitors Bureau (☎ 664/684-0537; www.tijuanaonline.org) is across the street from the Centro Cultural, Paseo de los Héroes 9365, Suite 201. It's open Monday to Friday 9am to 6pm. For English-speaking tourist assistance, dial ☎ 078. When calling numbers from the U.S., dial 011-52 then the 10-digit number.

English is widely spoken and dollars are accepted just about everywhere; Visa and MasterCard are accepted in many places, but never assume they will be—ask before dining or purchasing. You're permitted to bring $800 worth of purchases back across the border duty-free, including 1 liter of alcohol per person (for adults 21 and older). You can also bring back about a month's supply (50 dosages) of any medicine that requires a prescription in the U.S. Possession of illegal drugs or firearms is a very serious offense in Mexico.

The following countries have consulate offices in Tijuana: the United States (☎ 664/622-7400), Canada (☎ 664/684-0461), and the United Kingdom (☎ 664/681-7323).

racing (Mon, Wed–Fri at 7:45pm; Sat–Sun at 1pm; Tues at 2pm and 7:45pm) and another sports book. *Ave. Revolución at Calle 4.* ☎ *664/688-3425. www.caliente.com.mx. Hours vary but usually daily 11am–midnight.*

③ ★ **Palacio de la Cultura.** This large gallery complex opened in late 2006. Showcasing the work of local artists, it's set in the Antigua Palacio Municipal, which served as a seat of government from 1921 to 1986, and is one of the area's few remaining historical buildings. This is a great side trip off touristy Revolución—adjacent are the

A Tijuana horse farm.

A street vendor.

Cathedral and Mercado el Popo, a quintessentially Mexican marketplace selling nuts, candy, and produce. ⏱ *1 hr. Calle 2 at Ave. Constitución.* ☎ *664/687-687-1391 www.imactijuana.com. Free admission. Hours vary but usually daily 10am–6pm.*

④ ★★ Centro Cultural Tijuana. A short cab ride away in the Zona Río is Tijuana's cultural icon, which opened in 1982. You'll easily spot the ultramodern complex with its gigantic, sand-colored sphere that houses an IMAX Dome Theater (some English-language films on weekends). CECUT also has a museum that covers the history of Tijuana and Baja, from pre-Hispanic times through the modern era (descriptions are in both Spanish and English); there is also a gallery for visiting exhibits. Music, theater, and dance performances are held in the center's acoustically excellent concert hall; and there's a cafe and a great museum bookshop. At press time, CECUT was working to complete a new wing that is expected to host major traveling art shows. *Paseo de los Héroes, at Ave. Independencia.* ☎ *664/687-9600. www.cecut.gob.mx. Museum admission $2.20; IMAX tickets $4.50 adults, $2.50 children. Tues–Sun 10am–6pm; extended hours for films and special events.*

⑤ ★ Tepoznieves. In the heart of town you'll find this unique ice-cream parlor. It serves up flavors that are sure to intrigue and delight, like *nardos,* concocted from the tangy tuberose flower; *nopal,* made from cactus; or *petalo de rosas* (rose petals). *Blvd. Sánchez Taboada 4002 (at Ave. Rodriguez).* ☎ *664/634-6532. $.*

Travel Tip

Tijuana's shopping and nightlife district, Avenida Revolución, is a $5 taxi ride from the border, or you can walk the mile (.6km) into the tourist area. The trolley takes about 40 minutes from downtown San Diego; the one-way fare is $2.50. The last trolley to San Ysidro departs downtown around midnight (1am on Sat); the last returning trolley from San Ysidro is at 1am (2am on Sat). Unless you plan to drive farther into Mexico, it's best to park your car on the U.S. side and walk across. Taxis are cheap, plentiful, and safe in Tijuana (you will need to negotiate a price with cab drivers; the white taxis with red stripes are metered and a better deal). If you do drive, take I-5 south. We highly recommend that you purchase Mexican auto insurance north of the border.

Street musicians.

6 ★★ L.A. Cetto Winery (Cava de Vinos). This barrel-shaped winery and visitor center provides an introduction to the Mexican wine industry. The Valle de Guadalupe, a fertile region southeast of Tijuana, produces most of Mexico's wine, and many high-quality vintages are exported to Europe; most are unavailable in the United States. L.A. Cetto also sells fine tequila, brandy, olive oil, and more. ⏱ *1 hr. Ave. Cañón Johnson 2108 (at Ave. Constitución Sur).* ☎ *664/685-3031. www.cettowines. com. Admission $2 for tour and tasting (18 and over; under 18 are admitted free with an adult but cannot taste the wines), $5 with souvenir wine glass. Mon–Fri 10am–6:30pm, Sat 10am–5pm.*

7 ★★ Playas de Tijuana. This large, sandy beach is popular with families. It features a line of ramshackle restaurants and cafes sitting on a bluff overlooking the surf, offering great spots for lunch and a cold beer. A stone's throw away is the bullring-by-the-sea known as Plaza Monumental. Perhaps the most notable thing here, though, is the imposing, rusting fence of unevenly spaced girders of different heights that disappears into the ocean, dividing the U.S. and Mexico. It provides a stark contrast to the laughing children splashing in the water next to it. *About 6 miles (9.5km) west of the Zona Centro, off the scenic toll road that heads toward Rosarito and Ensenada (but before you reach the first toll booth).* ●

Tijuana Safety Alert

Violence has risen dramatically in Tijuana, mostly due to the presence of organized crime—but tourists are not the targets. There is petty crime, too, so observe the same precautions as in any large city: Don't flash a lot of cash or expensive jewelry, and stick to populated areas. *Mordida,* "the bite," is also still known to occur. That's when uniformed police officers extort money in exchange for letting you off some infraction, like a traffic ticket. If you do find yourself dealing with an official, never offer a bribe—you may find yourself in much more trouble than you bargained for. And if you do meet up with corruption, you have little recourse but to comply, and then report the incident to your consulate.

The
Savvy Traveler

Before You Go

Tourist Offices

Contact the **San Diego Convention & Visitor's Bureau** (2215 India St., San Diego, CA 92101, mailing address only; ☎ 619/232-3101; www.sandiego.org). The *Visitors Planning Guide* features excellent maps and information on accommodations, activities, and attractions. The *San Diego Travel Values* insert is full of discount coupons for hotels at all price levels, restaurants, attractions, cultural and recreational activities, and tours. It's available online, too. Convis' **International Visitor Information Center** (☎ 619/236-1212; www.sandiego.org) is on the Embarcadero at 1040⅓ W. Broadway, at Harbor Drive. Daily summer hours are from 9am to 5pm; for the remainder of the year it's open daily 9am to 4pm. Convis also operates a walk-up–only facility at the **La Jolla Visitor Center**, 7966 Herschel Ave., near the corner of Prospect Street. This office is open daily in summer, from 10am until 7pm (until 6pm Sun); from September to May the center is open daily but with more limited hours. The **Mission Bay Visitor Information Center,** on 2688 E. Mission Bay Dr. (☎ 866/746-8440; www.infosandiego.com), is between Mission Bay and I-5, at the Clairemont Drive exit. This private facility books hotels and sells discounted admission tickets to a variety of attractions; hours are 9am to dusk. The **Coronado Visitors Center** (1100 Orange Ave.; ☎ 619/437-8788; www.coronadovisitors.com) dispenses maps, newsletters, and information-packed brochures. Inside the Coronado Museum, they're open Monday through Friday 9am to 5pm, Saturday 10am to 5pm, and Sunday from 11am to 4pm. The

San Diego North Convention and Visitors Bureau (☎ 800/848-3336; www.sandiegonorth.com) can answer your questions about **North County** as well as the **Anza-Borrego Desert.** For more information about Del Mar, contact or visit the **Del Mar Regional Chamber of Commerce Visitor Information Center,** 1104 Camino del Mar (☎ 858/755-4844; www.delmar chamber.org), which distributes a detailed folding map of the area. The hours of operation vary, but usually approximate weekday business hours. There's also a city-run website at www.delmar.ca.us. The **Solana Beach Visitor Center** is near the train station at 103 N. Cedros Ave. (☎ 858/350-6006; www.solanabeachchamber.com). The **Encinitas Visitors Center** is in a nondescript shopping mall immediately west of the I-5, at 138 Encinitas Blvd. (☎ 800/953-6041; www. encinitaschamber.com). The **Carlsbad Visitor Information Center** in the old Santa Fe Depot, 400 Carlsbad Village Dr. (☎ 800/227-5722; www.carlsbadca.org), has information on flower fields and nursery touring. **Oceanside's California Welcome Center,** 928 N. Coast Hwy. (☎ 800/350-7873; www. oceansidechamber.com), provides information on local attractions, dining, and accommodations.

The Best Times to Go

With its coastal setting, the city of San Diego maintains a moderate climate year-round. Although the temperature can change 20°F to 30°F between day and evening, it rarely reaches a point of extreme heat or cold; daytime highs above 100°F (38°C) are unusual, and times when

Balboa Park by scooter.

AVERAGE MONTHLY TEMPERATURES (°F & °C) & RAINFALL (IN.)

	JAN	FEB	MAR	APR	MAY	JUNE	JULY	AUG	SEPT	OCT	NOV	DEC
High (°F)	65	66	66	68	70	71	75	77	76	74	70	66
(°C)	18	19	19	20	21	21	24	25	25	23	21	19
Low (°F)	46	47	50	54	57	60	64	66	63	58	52	47
(°C)	8	9	10	12	14	15	17	19	17	15	10	8
Rainfall	2.1	1.4	1.6	0.8	0.2	1	0	0.1	0.2	0.3	1.1	1.4

the mercury drops below freezing can be counted in mere hours once or twice each year. San Diego receives very little precipitation (just 10 in./103cm of rainfall in an average year); what rain does fall comes primarily between November and April. Fall and spring are great times to be here; but beach bunnies should note that late spring and early summer tanning sessions are often compromised by a local phenomenon called **May Gray** and **June Gloom**—a layer of low-lying clouds or fog along the coast that doesn't burn off until noon (if at all) and returns before sunset. San Diego is busiest between Memorial Day and Labor Day; if you visit in summer, expect fully booked beachfront hotels and crowded parking lots. The only slow season is from Thanksgiving to early February.

Festivals & Special Events

SPRING. Wildflowers bloom in the desert between late February and the end of March, at **Anza-Borrego Desert State Park** (☎ 760/767-4205; www.parks.ca.gov). The peak of blooming lasts for a few weeks and timing varies from year to year, depending on the winter rainfall. The **San Diego Latino Film Festival** (☎ 619/230-1938; www.sdlatino film.com), held in mid-March, has grown to become one of the largest and most successful Latino film events in the country. More than 100 movies from throughout Latin America and the United States

are shown, complemented by gala parties, seminars, a music series, and art exhibits. The **St. Patrick's Day Parade** (☎ 858/268-9111; www.stpatsparade.org) takes place the Saturday prior to March 17; it's followed by a festival in Balboa Park. The **Flower Fields at Carlsbad Ranch** (☎ 760/431-0352; www.the flowerfields.com) provide one of the most spectacular sights in North County: the yearly blossoming of a gigantic sea of bright ranunculuses during March and April. Visitors are welcome to view and tour the fields. **ArtWalk** (☎ 619/615-1090; www. artwalkinfo.com) is the largest art event in the San Diego/Tijuana region, showcasing hundreds of visual and performing artists. It takes place along the streets of Little Italy in late April. Held the weekend closest to May 5, **Fiesta Cinco de Mayo** (☎ 619/260-1700; www. fiestacincodemayo.com) commemorates the 1862 triumph of Mexican soldiers over the French. The festivities include a battle re-enactment, mariachi music, and margaritas galore.

SUMMER. The **Rock 'n' Roll Marathon** (☎ 800/311-1255; www. rnrmarathon.com) in early June offers runners a unique course through Balboa Park, downtown, and around Mission Bay, and pumps them (and spectators) up with live bands on 26 stages along the course. There is a pre-race fitness expo and post-race concert, featuring big-name talent. Annually, the biggest local event is the **San Diego County Fair** (☎ 858/793-5555; www.sdfair.com), mid-June to early July. Livestock competitions, thrill rides, flower-and-garden shows, gem and mineral exhibits, food and crafts booths, carnival games, and home arts exhibits dominate the event. There are also grandstand concerts by name performers. The **World Championship Over-the-Line Tournament** (☎ 619/688-0817; www.ombac.org) in mid-July is a San Diego original. It's a beach softball event renowned for boisterous, beer-soaked, anything-goes behavior. The **San Diego Lesbian and Gay Pride Parade, Rally, and Festival** (☎ 619/297-7683; www.sdpride.org), held the third or fourth weekend in July, is one of San Diego's biggest draws. It begins Friday night with a rally in Balboa Park, reconvenes at 11am on Saturday for the parade through Hillcrest, followed by a massive 2-day festival in the park. The "turf meets the surf" in Del Mar during the **thoroughbred racing season** at the Del Mar Race Track (☎ 858/792-4242; www.dmtc.com). The ponies run mid-July to early September. Upward of 60,000 people attend America's largest comic-book convention, **Comic-Con International** (☎ 619/491-2475; www.comic-con.org), each late July. It's a long weekend of auctions, dealers, autographs, and seminars focusing on graphic novels, fantasy, and sci-fi movies. In late July and early August, the **Acura Classic** (☎ 760/438-5683; www.acuraclassic.com) gathers the greatest female tennis players in the world at the La Costa Resort & Spa. **La Jolla SummerFest** (☎ 858/459-3728; www.ljms.org) is perhaps San Diego's most prestigious annual music event. It features a wide spectrum of classical and contemporary music, with guest composers and

musicians ranging from the likes of Chick Corea to Yo-Yo Ma. SummerFest also offers master classes, open rehearsals, and workshops.

FALL. The country's largest rough-water swimming competition, the **La Jolla Rough Water Swim** (☎ 858/456-2100; www.ljrws.com) began in 1916. It takes place the Sunday after Labor Day at La Jolla Cove. Up in the mountain town of Julian (☎ 760/765-1857; www.julianca.com), the **fall apple harvest** from mid-September to mid-November draws big crowds. Every weekend local artisans display their wares, and there's plenty of cider and apple pie, plus entertainment and brilliant fall foliage. **Fleet Week** (☎ 800/353-3893; www.fleetweeksandiego.org) is a bit of a misnomer. It's the nation's largest military appreciation event and it lasts the entire month of October. It includes Navy ship tours, a college football game, an auto race of classic speedsters, and the renowned Miramar Air Show. More than 20 bands from around North America and beyond perform at the **San Diego Thanksgiving Dixieland Jazz Festival** (☎ 619/297-5277; www.dixielandjazzfestival.org). This annual festival is held over the long Thanksgiving weekend and features vintage jazz sounds like ragtime, swing, and, of course, pure New Orleans Dixieland.

WINTER. During the first Friday and Saturday nights of December, San Diego's fine urban park is decked out in holiday splendor for **Balboa Park December Nights** (☎ 619/239-0512; www.balboapark.org). There's a candlelight procession, caroling, entertainment, and ethnic food; park museums are all free, too. **Whale-watching season** begins in mid-December and continues until about mid-March, as more than 25,000 Pacific gray whales make the trek from the chilly Alaskan seas to the warm-water breeding lagoons of Baja California, and then back again. There are a variety of ways to witness the procession, from both land and sea (www.sandiego.org). San Diego is home to two college football bowl games: the **Holiday Bowl** (☎ 619/283-5808; www.holidaybowl.com) and the **Poinsettia Bowl** (☎ 619/285-5061; www.poinsettiabowl.net), both held in late December. The Holiday Bowl pits top teams from the Pac 10 and Big 12 Conferences; the Poinsettia Bowl pits a team from the Mountain West Conference against an at-large opponent. The Holiday Bowl features several special events, including the nation's biggest balloon parade of giant inflatable characters. The PGA Tour's **Buick Invitational** (☎ 800/888-2842; www.buickinvitational.com) in late January features 150 of the finest professional golfers in the world. An annual event since 1952, it draws more than 100,000 spectators to Torrey Pines Golf Course. **Mardi Gras in the Gaslamp Quarter** (☎ 619/233-5227; www.gaslamp.org) is the largest Mardi Gras party on the West Coast. The celebration of "Fat Tuesday" features a Mardi Gras parade and an outdoor celebration in downtown's historic Gaslamp Quarter.

Useful Websites

- **www.sandiego.org** is maintained by the San Diego Convention & Visitors Bureau and includes up-to-date weather data, a calendar of events, and a hotel booking engine.

- **www.sandiegoartandsol.com** is the link for cultural tourism. You'll find a list of art shows and music events, plus intriguing touring itineraries that delve into the city's culture.

- **www.sandiego-online.com**, the *San Diego Magazine* website, offers abbreviated stories and dining and events listings.

- **www.sdreader.com**, the site of the free weekly *San Diego Reader*, is a great resource for club and show listings. It has printable dining and other coupons you can really use, plus arts, eats, and entertainment critiques.

- **www.signonsandiego.com** is where CitySearch teams up with the *San Diego Union-Tribune*, catering as much to locals as to visitors. It offers plenty of helpful links, plus reviews of restaurants, music, movies, performing arts, museums, outdoor recreation, beaches, and sports.

- **www.gosddowntown.com** is SignOnSanDiego's Gaslamp Quarter site, offering information on downtown events, restaurants, nightlife, and shopping.

- **www.digitalcity.com/sandiego** is a lifestyle guide targeted at locals, and therefore yields occasional off-the-beaten-tourist-path recommendations. You'll find everything from personal ads to constantly changing restaurant spotlights and daily top picks.

- **www.wheresd.com** provides information on arts, culture, special events, shopping, and dining for San Diego, Orange County, and Los Angeles. You can also make hotel reservations through the site.

- **www.voiceofsandiego.org** is an excellent online news source that offers sober information on what's happening in the city politically and culturally.

- **www.blogsandiego.com** is a hip spot for local music reviews and previews, and other musings from the cultural underground.

Getting **There**

By Plane

San Diego International Airport (☎ 619/231-2100; www.san.org), also known as Lindbergh Field (airport code: SAN), is just 2 miles (3km) northwest of downtown San Diego. It isn't a connecting hub for domestic airlines, and most international travel arrives via Los Angeles or points east. Planes land at Terminal 1 or 2, though most flights to and from Southern California airports use the Commuter Terminal, a half-mile (.8km) away; the Airport Flyer ("red bus") provides free service from the main airport to the Commuter Terminal, or there's a footpath. General **information desks** with visitor materials, maps, and other services are near the baggage claim areas of both Terminal 1 and 2. You can exchange foreign currency at **Travelex America** (☎ 619/295-1501; www.travelex usa.com) in Terminal 1 across from the United Airlines ticket counter, or in Terminal 2 on the second level (*inside* the security area, near the gates). **Hotel reservation** and **car-rental courtesy phones** are in the baggage-claim areas of Terminal 1 and 2. Major airlines flying into San Diego include **AeroMéxico** (☎ 800/ 237-6639; www.aeromexico.com), **Air Canada** (☎ 888/247-2262; www.aircanada.com), **Alaska Airlines** (☎ 800/252-7522; www.alaska air.com), **Aloha Airlines** (☎ 800/ 367-5250; www.alohaairlines.com), **America West** (☎ 800/235-9292; www.americawest.com), **American Airlines** (☎ 800/433-7300; www.aa. com), **Continental Airlines** (☎ 800/ 525-0280; www.continental.com), **Delta Airlines** (☎ 800/221-1212; www.delta.com), **Express Jet** (☎ 888/958-9538; www.xjet.com), **Frontier Airlines** (☎ 800/432-1359; www.frontierairlines.com), **Hawaiian Airlines** (☎ 800/367-5320; www. hawaiianair.com), **JetBlue** (☎ 800/ 538-2583; www.jetblue.com), **Midwest Airlines** (☎ 800/452-2022; www.midwestairlines.com), **Northwest Airlines** (☎ 800/225-2525; www.nwa.com), **Southwest Airlines** (☎ 800/435-9792; www.south west.com), **Sun Country Airlines** (☎ 800/359-6786; www.suncountry. com), **United Airlines** (☎ 800/864-8331; www.ual.com), and **US Airways** (☎ 800/428-4322; www.us airways.com). The Commuter Terminal, a half-mile (.8km) from the main terminals, is used by regional carriers **American Eagle** and **United Express** and for connecting flights to Los Angeles (for flight info, contact the parent carriers).

By Bus & Train

Greyhound buses (☎ 800/231-2222; www.greyhound.com) from Los Angeles, Phoenix, Las Vegas, and other points in the southwest United States arrive at the station in downtown San Diego at 120 W. Broadway. Local buses stop in front and the San Diego Trolley line is nearby. San Diego's Santa Fe Station is at the west end of Broadway, on Kettner Boulevard between Pacific Highway and India Street, within a half-mile (.8km) of most downtown hotels and the Embarcadero. Taxis line up outside the main door, the trolley station is across the street, and a dozen local bus routes stop on Broadway or Pacific Highway.

The **Metropolitan Transit System** (☎ 619/233-3004; www.sdmts. com) operates the San Diego Transit Flyer—bus route no. 992—providing service between the airport and downtown San Diego, running along Broadway then down into the

Gaslamp Quarter along 4th and 5th avenues. Bus stops are at each of Lindbergh Field's three terminals. The one-way fare is $2.25, and exact change is required. Request a transfer if you're connecting to another bus or the San Diego Trolley route downtown. The ride takes about 15 minutes and buses come at 10- to 15-minute intervals.

By Taxi
Taxis line up outside both terminals, and the trip to a downtown location, usually a 10-minute ride, is about $10 (plus tip); budget $20 to $25 for Coronado or Mission Beach, and about $30 to $35 for La Jolla.

By Shuttle
Several airport shuttles run regularly from the airport to points around the city; you'll see designated pick-up areas outside each terminal. The fare is about $8 per person to downtown hotels; Mission Valley and Mission Beach hotels are $10 to $12; La Jolla and Coronado hotels are around $15 to $19. Rates to a residence are about double the

above rates, for the first person. One company that serves all of San Diego County is **Cloud 9 Shuttle** (☎ 800/974-8885; www.cloud9 shuttle.com).

By Car
If you're driving to downtown from the airport, take Harbor Drive south to Broadway, the main east–west thoroughfare, and turn left. To reach Hillcrest or Balboa Park, exit the airport toward I-5, and follow the signs for Laurel Street. To reach Mission Bay, take I-5 north to I-8 west. To reach La Jolla, take I-5 north to the La Jolla Parkway exit, bearing left onto Torrey Pines Road. Three main interstates lead into San Diego. **I-5** is the primary route from San Francisco, central California, and Los Angeles; it runs straight through downtown to the Tijuana border crossing. **I-8** cuts across California from points east like Phoenix, terminating just west of I-5 at Mission Bay. **I-15** leads from the deserts to the north through inland San Diego; as you enter Miramar, take **Highway 163** south to reach the central parts of the city.

Getting **Around**

By Car
Most downtown streets run one-way, in a grid pattern. However, outside downtown, canyons and bays often make streets indirect. Finding a parking space can be tricky in the Gaslamp Quarter, Old Town, Mission Beach, and La Jolla, but parking lots are often centrally located. Rush hour on the freeways is generally concentrated from 7 to 9am and 4:30 to 6pm (for up-to-the-minute traffic info, dial ☎ 511). A few things to note: San Diego's gas prices are often among the highest in the country; California has a seat-belt

law for both drivers and passengers; and as of July 1, 2008, state law will require drivers to use hands-free cell phone technology. You may turn right at a red light after stopping unless a sign says otherwise; likewise, you can turn left on a red light from a one-way street onto another one-way street after coming to a full stop. Penalties in California for drunk driving are among the toughest in the country; the main beach arteries (Grand, Garnet, and Mission) sometimes have random checkpoints set up to catch impaired drivers. If you plan to drive to Mexico, be sure to check with your insurance company at home to verify exactly the limits of your policy. Mexican car insurance is available from various agencies (visible to drivers heading into Mexico) on the U.S. side of the border.

All the major car-rental firms have an office at the airport and several have them in larger hotels. Some of the national companies include **Alamo** (☎ 800/462-5266; www.alamo.com), **Avis** (☎ 800/230-4898; www.avis.com), **Budget** (☎ 800/527-0700; www.budget.com), **Dollar** (☎ 800/800-3665; www.dollar.com), **Enterprise** (☎ 800/736-8222; www.enterprise.com), **Hertz** (☎ 800/654-3131; www.hertz.com), **National** (☎ 800/227-7368; www.nationalcar.com), and **Thrifty** (☎ 800/847-4389; www.thrifty.com). Some companies, including Avis, will allow their cars into Mexico as far as Ensenada, but other rental outfits won't allow you to drive south of the border.

By Bus

The **MTS Transit Store,** 102 Broadway at First Avenue (☎ 619/234-1060), dispenses multiday passes, tokens, timetables, maps, brochures, and lost-and-found information. It issues ID cards for seniors 60 and older, and for travelers with disabilities, all of whom pay $1 per ride. Request a copy of the useful brochure *San Diego Fun Places,* which details the city's most popular tourist attractions and the buses that will take you to them. The office is open Monday through Friday 9am to 5pm. Most bus **fares** are $2.25. Buses accept dollar bills and change, but drivers can't give change. Transfers must be used within 90 minutes, and you can return to where you started (meaning a quick round-trip might cost just the one-way fare). If transferring from the trolley, your validated

ticket serves as a transfer onto the bus, good for up to 2 hours from validation. For assistance with route information from a living, breathing entity, call ☎ 619/233-3004. You can also view timetables, maps, and fares online at www.sdmts.com. There is also a downloadable version of *San Diego Fun Places*. If you know your route and just need schedule information—or automated answers to FAQs—call **Info Express** (☎ 619/685-4900) from any touch-tone phone, 24 hours a day.

By Trolley

The San Diego Trolley is great for visitors, particularly if you're staying downtown or plan to visit Tijuana. There are three routes. The **Blue Line** travels from the Mexican border (San Ysidro) north through downtown and Old Town, with some trolleys continuing into Mission Valley. The **Orange Line** runs from downtown east through Lemon Grove and El Cajon. The **Green Line** runs from Old Town through Mission Valley to Qualcomm Stadium, San Diego State University, and on to Santee. The trip to the border takes 40 minutes from downtown; from downtown to Old Town takes 10 to 15 minutes. Trolleys operate on a self-service fare-collection system; riders buy tickets from machines in stations before boarding. The machines list fares for each destination (ranging from $1.25 for anywhere within downtown, to $3 for the longest trips) and dispense change. Tickets are valid for 2 hours from the time of purchase, in any direction. Fare inspectors board trains at random to check tickets. A round-trip ticket is double the price, but is valid all day between the origination and destination points. The lines run every 15 minutes during the day and every 30 minutes at night; during peak weekday rush hours the Blue Line runs every

10 minutes. There is also expanded service to accommodate events at PETCO Park and Qualcomm Stadium. Trolleys stop at each station for only 30 seconds. To open the door for boarding, push the lighted green button; to open the door to exit the trolley, push the lighted white button. For recorded transit information, call ☎ 619/685-4900. To speak with a customer service representative, call ☎ 619/233-3004 (TTY/TDD 619/234-5005), daily from 5:30am to 8:30pm. For wheelchair lift info, call ☎ 619/595-4960. The trolley generally operates daily from 5am to about midnight; the Blue Line provides limited but additional service between Old Town and San Ysidro throughout the night from Saturday evening to Sunday morning; check the website at www.sdmts.com for details.

By Train
San Diego's express rail commuter service, the **Coaster,** travels between the downtown Santa Fe Depot station and the Oceanside Transit Center, with stops at Old Town, Sorrento Valley, Solana Beach, Encinitas, and Carlsbad. Fares range from $4 to $5.50 each way, depending on how far you go, and can be paid by credit card at vending machines at each station. Eligible seniors and riders with disabilities pay $2 to $2.75. The scenic trip between downtown San Diego and Oceanside takes 1 hour. Trains run Monday through Friday, from about 6:30am to 7pm, with four trains in each direction on Saturday; call ☎ 800/262-7837 or log on to www.sdmts.com for info. **Amtrak** (☎ 800/872-7245; www.amtrak.com) trains run between San Diego and downtown Los Angeles, about 11 times daily each way. Trains to Los Angeles depart from the Santa Fe Depot and stop in Solana Beach, Oceanside, San Juan Capistrano, Santa Ana, and Anaheim (Disneyland). Two trains per day also stop in San Clemente. The travel time from San Diego to Los Angeles is about 2 hours and 45 minutes (for comparison, driving time can be as little as 2 hr., or as much as 4 hr. during rush hour). A one-way ticket to Los Angeles is $32 to $45; a one-way ticket to Solana Beach is $10, to Oceanside $14, to San Juan Capistrano $17, and to Anaheim $23.

By Taxi
Rates are based on mileage and can add up quickly in sprawling San Diego—a trip from downtown to La Jolla will cost about $30 to $35. Other than in the Gaslamp Quarter after dark, taxis don't cruise the streets as they do in other cities, so you have to call ahead for quick pickup. Among the local companies are **Orange Cab** (☎ 619/291-3333), **San Diego Cab** (☎ 619/226-8294), and **Yellow Cab** (☎ 619/234-6161). The **Coronado Cab Company** (☎ 619/435-6211) serves Coronado.

By Ferry & Water Taxi
There's regularly scheduled ferry service between San Diego and Coronado (☎ 619/234-4111 for information). Ferries leave from the Broadway Pier (1050 N. Harbor Dr., at the intersection of Broadway) Sunday through Thursday on the hour from 9am to 9pm, and Friday and Saturday until 10pm. They return from the Ferry Landing in Coronado to the Broadway Pier Sunday through Thursday every hour on the half-hour from 9:30am to 9:30pm and Friday and Saturday until 10:30pm. The ride takes 15 minutes. The fare is $3 each way (50¢ extra if you bring a bike). Buy tickets at the Harbor Excursion kiosk on Broadway Pier or at the Ferry Landing in Coronado. Water taxis (☎ 619/235-8294) will pick you up from any dock around San Diego

Bay, and operate Monday through Friday from 2 to 10pm, on weekends, and in summer from 11am to 11pm. If you're staying in a downtown hotel, this is a great way to get to Coronado. Boats are sometimes available at the spur of the moment, but reservations are advised. Fares are $7 per person to most locations.

By Bicycle

San Diego is ideal for exploration by bicycle, and many roads have designated bike lanes. Bikes are available for rent in most areas. San Diego Ridelink publishes a comprehensive map of the county detailing bike *paths* (for exclusive use by bicyclists), bike *lanes* (alongside motor vehicle ways), and bike *routes* (shared ways designated only by bike-symbol signs). It's available at visitor centers; to receive a copy in advance, call ☎ 800/266-6883.

Fast **Facts**

AREA CODES   San Diego's main area code is **619,** used primarily by downtown, uptown, Mission Valley, Point Loma, Coronado, La Mesa, El Cajon, and Chula Vista. The area code **858** is used for northern and coastal areas, including Mission Beach, Pacific Beach, La Jolla, Del Mar, Rancho Santa Fe, and Rancho Bernardo. Use **760** to reach the remainder of San Diego County, including Encinitas, Carlsbad, Oceanside, Escondido, Ramona, Julian, and Anza-Borrego.

ATMS & BANKS   One of California's most popular banks is Wells Fargo, a member of the Star, PLUS, Cirrus, and Global Access systems. It has hundreds of ATMs at branches and stores (including most Vons supermarkets) throughout San Diego County. Other statewide banks include Bank of America (which accepts PLUS, Star, and Interlink cards), and First Interstate Bank (Cirrus). Banks are open weekdays, 9am to 4pm or later, and sometimes Saturday morning.

BABYSITTERS   **Marion's Childcare** (☎ 888/891-5029; www.hotelchild care.com) has bonded babysitters available to come to your hotel room; rates start at $16 per hour with a 3-hour minimum. **Panda Services** (☎ 858/292-5503; www. sandiegobabysitters.com) is also available.

B&BS   Check with the **San Diego Bed & Breakfast Guild** (☎ 619/ 523-1300; www.bandbguildsan diego.org).

BEACH & SURF REPORT   Call ☎ 619/ 221-8824.

CONSULATES & EMBASSIES   All embassies are in the nation's capital, Washington, D.C. Some consulates are in major U.S. cities, and most nations have a mission to the United Nations in New York City. For addresses and phone numbers of embassies in Washington, D.C., call ☎ 202/555-1212 or log on to www.embassy.org/embassies. The **British Consulate** in San Diego is at 7979 Ivanhoe Ave., La Jolla CA 92037 (☎ 858/353-3633). The **Mexican Consulate** is at 1549 India St., San Diego CA 92101 (☎ 619/231-8414).

DENTISTS   For dental referrals, contact the **San Diego County Dental Society** at ☎ 800/201-0244, or call ☎ 800/DENTIST.

DISABLED TRAVELERS   **Accessible San Diego** (☎ 858/279-0704;

www.accessandiego.org) has an info line that helps travelers find accessible hotels, tours, attractions, and transportation. If you call long distance and get the answering machine, leave a message, and the staff will call you back collect. Ask for the annual *Access in San Diego* pamphlet, a citywide guide with specifics on which establishments are accessible for those with visual, mobility, or hearing disabilities (cost is $5). Manual wheelchairs with balloon tires are available free of charge daily at the main lifeguard stations in Ocean Beach, Mission Beach, Pacific Beach, and La Jolla. The Mission Beach lifeguard station also has four electric wheelchairs available Fri to Sun, 11:30am to 3:30pm, beach conditions permitting (☎ 619/525-8247). Airport transportation for travelers with disabilities is available in vans holding one or two wheelchairs from **Cloud 9 Shuttle** (☎ 800/974-8885; www.cloud9shuttle.com).

DOCTORS   **Hotel Docs** (☎ 800/468-3537) is a 24-hour network of physicians, dentists, and chiropractors. They accept credit cards, and their services are covered by most insurance policies.

ELECTRICITY   Like Canada, the United States uses 110–120 volts AC (60 cycles), compared to 220–240 volts AC (50 cycles) in most of Europe, Australia, and New Zealand. Downward converters that change 220–240 volts to 110–120 volts are difficult to find in the United States, so bring one with you.

EMERGENCIES   Call ☎ **911** for fire, police, or ambulance. The main **police station** is at 1401 Broadway, at 14th Street (☎ 619/531-2000, or TTY/TDD 619/531-2065). If you encounter serious problems, contact the San Diego chapter of **Traveler's Aid International** at ☎ 619/295-8393, or log on to

www.travelersaid.org to help direct you to a local branch. This nationwide, nonprofit, social-service organization is geared to helping travelers in difficult straits, including reuniting families separated while traveling, providing food and/or shelter to people stranded without cash, or emotional counseling.

HOSPITALS   Near downtown San Diego, **UCSD Medical Center–Hillcrest** (200 W. Arbor Dr.; ☎ 619/543-6400) has the most convenient emergency room. In La Jolla, **UCSD Thornton Hospital** (9300 Campus Point Dr.; ☎ 858/657-7600) has a good emergency room, and you'll find another in Coronado, at **Sharp Coronado Hospital** (250 Prospect Pl., opposite the Marriott Resort; ☎ 619/435-6251).

HOT LINES   HIV Hot Line (☎ 619/236-2352); Alcoholics Anonymous (☎ 619/265-8762); Debtors Anonymous (☎ 619/525-3065); Mental Health referral and Suicide Crisis Line (☎ 800/479-3339); or Traveler's Aid Society (☎ 619/295-8393).

INSURANCE/LOST LUGGAGE   On flights within the U.S., checked baggage is covered up to $2,500 per ticketed passenger. On flights outside the U.S. (and on U.S. portions of international trips), baggage coverage is limited to approximately $9 per pound, up to approximately $635 per checked bag. If you plan to check items more valuable than what's covered by the standard liability, see if your homeowner's policy covers your valuables, get baggage insurance as part of your comprehensive travel-insurance package, or buy Travel Guard's "Bag-Trak" product. If your luggage is lost, immediately file a lost-luggage claim at the airport, detailing the luggage contents. Most airlines require that you report delayed, damaged, or lost baggage within 4 hours of arrival. The airlines are required to deliver luggage, once found, directly to your house or destination free of charge.

INSURANCE/MEDICAL   Unlike many European countries, the United States does not usually offer free or low-cost medical care to its citizens or visitors. Doctors and hospitals are expensive, and in most cases will require advance payment or proof of coverage before they render their services. Good policies will cover the cost of an accident, repatriation, or death. Packages, such as **Europ Assistance's Worldwide Healthcare Plan,** are sold by European automobile clubs and travel agencies at attractive rates. **Worldwide Assistance Services, Inc.** (☎ 800/777-8710; www.worldwide assistance.com) is the agent for Europ Assistance in the United States. Though lack of health insurance may prevent you from being admitted to a hospital in nonemergencies, don't worry about being left on a street corner to die: The American way is to fix you now and bill the living daylights out of you later.

INSURANCE FOR BRITISH TRAVELERS Most big travel agents offer their own insurance and will probably try to sell you their package when you book a holiday. Think before you sign. **Britain's Consumers' Association** recommends that you insist on seeing the policy and reading the fine print before buying travel insurance. **The Association of British Insurers** (☎ 020/7600-3333; www. abi.org.uk) gives advice by phone and publishes *Holiday Insurance,* a free guide to policy provisions and prices. You might also shop around for better deals: Try **Columbus Direct** (☎ 0870/033-9988; www. columbusdirect.net).

INSURANCE FOR CANADIAN TRAVELERS Canadians should check with their provincial health plan offices or call

Health Canada (☎ 866/225-0709; www.hc-sc.gc.ca) to find out the extent of their coverage and what documentation and receipts they must take home in case they are treated in the United States.

INSURANCE/TRIP CANCELLATION   This will help retrieve your money if you have to back out of a trip or depart early, or if your travel supplier goes bankrupt. Permissible reasons for trip cancellation can range from sickness to natural disasters to the State Department declaring a destination unsafe for travel. For more information, contact one of the following recommended insurers: **Access America** (☎ 866/807-3982; www.accessamerica.com), **Global Alert** (☎ 800/423-3632; www.tripinsurance.com), **Travel Guard International** (☎ 800/826-4919; www.travelguard.com), **Travel Insured International** (☎ 800/243-3174; www.travel insured.com), and **Travelex Insurance Services** (☎ 888/457-4602; www.travelex-insurance.com).

INTERNET   Cafes, coffeehouses, and hotels provide a multitude of wireless options to travelers with laptops. For those without a computer, cybercafes have dwindled here, but you can find terminals at all **public libraries,** including the downtown central library (820 E St., ☎ 619/236-5800; www.sandiegolibrary. org), the Pacific Beach branch (4275 Cass St., ☎ 858/581-9934); and La Jolla (7555 Draper Ave., ☎ 858/552-1657). **Internet Place** charges $1.50 for 6 minutes, $2.30 for 15, $3.50 for 30, and $5.50 per hour; they have two locations: downtown in Horton Plaza, on the ground floor near Broadway Circle (☎ 619/702-4643), and Hillcrest, 3834 Fifth Ave. (☎ 619/299-9360).

LIQUOR LAWS   The legal age for purchase and consumption of alcoholic beverages in California is 21.

Proof of age is a necessity—it's often requested at bars, nightclubs, and restaurants, even from those well into their 30s, so always bring ID when you go out. Beer, wine, and hard liquor are sold daily from 6am to 2am and are available in grocery stores. Do not carry open containers of alcohol in your car or any public area that isn't zoned for alcohol consumption—the police can fine you on the spot. Alcohol in a can, *not* a bottle, is allowed at most, but not all, San Diego beaches from noon to 8pm, on the sand only—check signs at beach entrances for exact rules.

MAIL   Domestic postage rates are 26¢ for a postcard and 41¢ for a letter. For international mail, a first-class letter of up to 1 ounce costs 90¢ (69¢ to Canada and Mexico); a first-class postcard costs 90¢ (69¢ to Canada and Mexico). For more information go to **www.usps.com** and click on "Calculate Postage."

San Diego's main post office is located in the boondocks, but the former main office, located just west of Old Town at 2535 Midway Dr., is a good alternative; it's open Monday through Friday, 8am to 5pm, and Saturdays, 8am to 4pm. Post offices are downtown, at 815 E St. and at 51 Horton Plaza at Broadway Circle. There is also a post office in the Mission Valley Shopping Center, next to Macy's. These branch offices are generally open Monday through Friday during regular business hours, plus Saturday morning; for specific branch information, call ☎ 800/275-8777 or log on to www.usps.com.

PASSPORTS   Always keep a photocopy of your passport with you when traveling. If it's lost or stolen, a copy will facilitate the reissuing process at a local consulate or embassy. Keep your passport and other valuables in the hotel or room safe.

RESTROOMS   Horton Plaza and Seaport Village downtown, Balboa Park, Old Town State Historic Park, and the Ferry Landing Marketplace in Coronado all have well-marked public restrooms. In general, you won't have a problem finding one (all restaurants, including fast-food outlets, are required to have one). Restrooms are usually clean and accessible, though a small purchase is usually expected.

SAFETY   San Diego is a relatively safe destination, by big-city standards. Of the 10 largest cities in the United States, it historically has had the lowest incidence of violent crime, per capita. Virtually all areas of the city are safe during the day. In Balboa Park, caution is advised in areas not frequented by regular foot traffic (particularly off the walkways on the Sixth Avenue side of the park). Transients are common in San Diego—especially downtown, in Hillcrest, and in the beach area. They are rarely a problem, but can sometimes be unpredictable. Downtown areas to the east of PETCO Park are sparsely populated after dusk, and poorly lit. Parts of the city that are usually safe on foot at night include the Gaslamp Quarter, Hillcrest, Old Town, Mission Valley, La Jolla, and Coronado.

SMOKING   Smoking is prohibited in nearly all indoor public places, including theaters, hotel lobbies, and enclosed shopping malls. In 1998, California enacted legislation prohibiting smoking in all restaurants and bars, except those with outdoor seating. San Diego has also banned smoking from all city beaches and parks, which includes Mission Bay Park and Balboa Park, as well as piers and boardwalks.

TAXES   Sales tax in restaurants and shops is 7.75%. Hotel tax is 10.5%.

TELEPHONES **Local calls** made from public pay phones cost either 35¢ or 50¢. Pay phones do not accept pennies, and few will take anything larger than a quarter. Most long-distance and international calls can be dialed directly from any phone. **For calls within the United States and to Canada,** dial 1 followed by the area code and the seven-digit number. **For other international calls,** dial 011 followed by the country code, city code, and the number you are calling. For **reversed-charge or collect calls,** and for person-to-person calls, dial the number 0 then the area code and number; an operator will come on the line, and you should specify whether you are calling collect, person-to-person, or both. If your operator-assisted call is international, ask for the overseas operator. For **local directory assistance** ("information"), dial 411; for long-distance information, dial 1 and then the appropriate area code and 555-1212.

TIME ZONE San Diego, like the rest of the West Coast, is in the Pacific Standard Time zone, which is 8 hours behind Greenwich Mean Time. Daylight-saving time is observed. To check the time, call ☎ 619/853-1212.

TIPPING In hotels, tip **bellhops** at least $1 per bag ($2–$3 if you have a lot of luggage) and tip the **chamber staff** $1 to $2 per day (more if you've left a disaster area to clean up). Tip the **doorman** or **concierge** only if he or she has provided you with some specific service (for example, calling a cab for you or obtaining difficult-to-get theater tickets). Tip the **valet-parking attendant** $1 every time you get your car. In restaurants, bars, and nightclubs, tip **service staff** 15% to 20% of the check, tip **bartenders** 10% to 15%, tip **checkroom attendants** $1 per garment, and tip **valet-parking attendants** $1 per vehicle. Tip **cab drivers** 15% of the fare; tip **skycaps** at airports at least $1 per bag ($2–$3 if you have a lot of luggage); and tip **hairdressers** and **barbers** 15% to 20%.

TRANSIT INFORMATION Call ☎ 619/233-3004 (TTY/TDD 619/234-5005). If you know your bus route and just need schedule information, call ☎ 619/685-4900.

WEATHER Call ☎ 619/289-1212.

A Brief **History**

It's believed that humans first arrived in San Diego's coastal areas some 20,000 years ago, while others settled in the desert about 8,000 years later. The first cultural group, which is now referred to as the San Dieguito people, date back to 7,500 BCE. They were followed by the La Jollan culture, which populated the coastal mesas until about 1,000 to 3,000 years ago. The Diegueños followed about 1,500 years ago, and existed in two groups: the Ipai, who lived along the San Diego River and northeast toward what is now Escondido, and the Tipai, or Kumeyaay, who lived south of the river into Baja California and east toward Imperial Valley.

In 1542, a Portuguese explorer in the employ of Spain, **Juan Rodriguez Cabrillo,** set out from the west coast of Mexico, principally in search of a northwest passage that might provide an easier crossing between the Pacific Ocean and Europe. En route he landed at a place he charted as San Miguel, spending 6 days to wait out a storm and venture ashore, doing a meet-and-greet with three fearful Kumeyaay (who had heard tales of white men killing natives to the east and south) before heading north along the coast. Although Cabrillo wrote favorably about what he saw, it would be 60 years before Europeans visited San Miguel again. When Spanish explorer Sebastián Vizcaíno sailed into the bay on the feast day of San Diego de Alcalá in 1602, he renamed it in honor of the saint. But despite Vizcaino calling it "a port which must be the best to be found in all the South Sea," San Diego Bay was all but ignored by invaders for the next century and a half.

In 1768, Spain, fearing that Russian enclaves in Northern California might soon threaten Spanish settlements to the south, decreed the founding of colonies in Southern California. The following year, following an arduous 110-day voyage from the tip of Baja California, the *San Carlos* arrived into San Diego Bay on April 29, 1769, leading "the sacred expedition" of **Father Junipero Serra,** a priest who had been charged with the task of spreading Christianity to the indigenous people. Serra would arrive about 2 months later via an overland route.

The site for a mission was selected just above the San Diego River, on a prominent hill that offered views onto plains, mesas, marshes, and the sea. The **Presidio de San Diego** was the first of what would be 21 missions in Alta California (the first mission in Baja California was established in 1697); a fort was built to surround and protect the settlement. After 4 years, Father Serra requested permission to relocate the mission to Nipaguay, a site 6 miles (10km) up the valley, next

to an existing Kumeyaay village. Although the mission provided the indigenous people with a more sustainable existence, it came at a price: Their culture was mostly lost; communities were shattered by foreign diseases from which they had no natural immunities; and those who defied the Spaniards or deserted the new settlements were punished by whipping or confinement.

In 1821, as what is now known as **Old Town** started to take shape, Mexico declared independence from Spain. California's missions were secularized; the Mexican government lost all interest in the native people and instead focused on creating sprawling rancheros. The Mexican flag flew over the Presidio, and in 1825, San Diego became the informal capital of the California territory.

The **Mexican-American War** took root in 1846, spreading from Texas west, creating brutal battles between the Californios and the Americans. By 1847 the Californios had surrendered, the treaty of Guadalupe-Hidalgo was signed a year later, and Mexico was paid $15 million for what became the southwestern United States. In 1848, gold was discovered near Sacramento and the **gold rush** began. In 1850, California was made the 31st state, and San Diego was established as both a city and county.

In 1850, William Heath Davis, a San Francisco financier, purchased 160 acres (65 hectares) of bayfront property with plans to develop a "new town." Residents of Old Town scoffed, and despite Davis' construction of several prefabricated houses and a wharf, the citizens stayed rooted at the base of the Presidio and labeled the project "Davis' Folly." But in 1867, another developer, Alonzo Horton, also saw the potential of the city and bought 960 acres (389 hectares) of bayfront land for

$265. This time, people started moving into the new town, and by 1869 San Diego had a population of 3,000; a devastating fire in Old Town in 1872 proved to be the final blow for the original settlement.

In 1915, despite a competing event in San Francisco, San Diego's **Panama-California Exposition** was a fabulous success, and it spurred the development of 1,400-acre (567-hectare) **Balboa Park** into fairgrounds of lasting beauty. The barrage of publicity from the 2-year fair touted San Diego's climate and location, and helped put the city on the map.

Toward the end of the 19th century, the **U.S. Navy** began using San Diego as a home port. In 1908 the Navy sailed into the harbor with its battleship fleet and 16,000 sailors—the War Department laid plans to dredge the bay to accommodate even larger ships. Aviator Glenn Curtiss convinced the Navy to designate $25,000 to the development of aviation, and soon after he opened a flying school at North Island, the northwestern lobe of the Coronado peninsula. World War I meant construction projects, and North Island was established as a Marine base. The Navy built a shipyard at 22nd Street in downtown, and constructed a naval training station and hospital in 1921. America's first aircraft carrier docked in San Diego in 1924.

Aviator T. Claude Ryan started Ryan Aviation to build military and civilian aircraft and equipment, and in 1927 he built The Spirit of St. Louis for Charles A. Lindbergh, a young airmail pilot. Only a few weeks after taking off from North Island, Lindbergh landed in Paris and was toasted as the first to fly solo across the Atlantic. In 1928, San Diego's airport was dedicated as **Lindbergh Field.**

A second world's fair, the 1935–36 **California-Pacific International Exposition,** allowed the Spanish colonial architecture in Balboa Park to be expanded, and many tourists became residents. In the decades to come, though, downtown stumbled the way many urban centers did in the 1960s and 1970s, filled after dark with the homeless and inebriated. In 1974, the **Gaslamp Quarter**—the new name for Alonzo Horton's New Town—was designated as a historic district. Little occurred to revitalize downtown at first, but a redevelopment plan was established and the first step was taken when **Seaport Village,** a waterside shopping complex at the south end of the Embarcadero, opened in the early '80s. In 1985, a $140-million shopping center next to Horton Plaza opened to raves, and San Diegans responded immediately, coming downtown to shop and dine as they hadn't in a generation. Another wave of downtown development saw the opening of the $474-million ballpark **PETCO Park** in 2004.

Today's San Diego owes a lot to **medical and high-tech industries**—biotechnology, pharmaceutical, and telecommunications in particular. One economic think tank declared the city to be the nation's number one "biotech cluster," supported by a steady flow of research from academic institutions like the University of California, San Diego, the Scripps Research Institute, and the Salk Institute. The biotech industry here also provides a home base for 13 science-based Nobel Prize winners and is directly responsible for nearly 39,000 jobs and some $8.5 billion in local economic impact.

San Diego's motto of "America's Finest City" was quietly retired several years back following a tragicomic series of political scandals, some of which are still playing out. There was a tainted mayoral election (and the ensuing ascension of three different mayors over an 8-month period); the conviction of two city council members on charges of doing the bidding of a strip-club operator, with a third accused councilman dropping dead before he went to trial; and one spectacularly thieving U.S. congressman—Rep. "Duke" Cunningham, currently serving out his 8-year sentence for his infamous "bribe menu."

That's all topped by an estimated $1.4 to $2 *billion* deficit in the city-employee pension fund. Creative bookkeeping is suspected, prompting city, U.S. attorney, FBI, IRS, and Securities and Exchange Commission investigations, and leading the *New York Times* to dub San Diego "Enron by the sea." Stay tuned.

Index

Photo **Credits**

p 23, top: © Brett Shoaf/Artistic Visuals; p 23, bottom: © Brett Shoaf/Artistic Visuals; p 24, top: © Brett Shoaf/Artistic Visuals; p 24, bottom: © Charlie Manz/Artistic Visuals; p 25, top: © Brett Shoaf/Artistic Visuals; p 25, bottom: © Brett Shoaf/Artistic Visuals; p 26, top: © Brett Shoaf/Artistic Visuals; p 26, bottom: © Brett Shoaf/Artistic Visuals; p 27: © Thomas Shjarback/Alamy; p 29: © Brett Shoaf/Artistic Visuals; p 30, top: © Brett Shoaf/Artistic Visuals; p 30, bottom: © Brett Shoaf/Artistic Visuals; p 31: © Brett Shoaf/Artistic Visuals; p 32: © Brett Shoaf/Artistic Visuals; p 33: © Thomas Shjarback/Alamy; p 35: © Brett Shoaf/Artistic Visuals; p 36, top: © Richard Cummins/Lonely Planet Images; p 36, bottom: © Richard Cummins/SuperStock; p 37, top: © Mark E. Gibson/Ambient Images; p 37, bottom: © Brett Shoaf/Artistic Visuals; p 38: © Charlie Manz/Artistic Visuals; p 39: © Brett Shoaf/Artistic Visuals; p 41: Courtesy Four Seasons Resort Aviara North San Diego; p 42: © Jan Butchofsky-Houser/Corbis; p 43: © Richard Cummins/Lonely Planet Images; p 45: © Brett Shoaf/Artistic Visuals; p 46, top: © Brett Shoaf/Artistic Visuals; p 46, bottom: © Brett Shoaf/Artistic Visuals; p 47: © Richard Cummins/Lonely Planet Images; p 48: © Brett Shoaf/Artistic Visuals; p 49: © Brett Shoaf/Artistic Visuals; p 51, top: © David Forbert/SuperStock ; p 51, bottom: © Joe Sohm/Visions of America, LLC/Alamy; p 52, top: © Richard Cummins/SuperStock; p 52, bottom: © Peter Bennett/Ambient Images; p 53: © Brett Shoaf/Artistic Visuals; p 55: © Brett Shoaf/Artistic Visuals; p 56, top: © Joanne Montenegro/eStock Photo; p 56, bottom: © Lorenz Kienzle/Courtesy Museum of Contemporary Art San Diego; p 57: © Brett Shoaf/Artistic Visuals; p 59: © Philipp Scholz Rittermann/Courtesy Museum of Contemporary Art San Diego; p 60: © Brett Shoaf/Artistic Visuals; p 61: © Brett Shoaf/Artistic Visuals; p 63: © Charlie Manz/Artistic Visuals; p 64, top: © Peter Bennett/Ambient Images Inc./Alamy; p 64, bottom: © Brett Shoaf/Artistic Visuals; p 65: © Charlie Manz/Artistic Visuals; p 67: © Gistimages/Alamy; p 68, top: © Brett Shoaf/Artistic Visuals; p 68, bottom: © Travel Pix Collection/AGE Fotostock; p 69: © Peter Bennett/Ambient Images Inc./Alamy; p 75, top: © Gary Conaughton; p 75, bottom: © Gary Conaughton; p 76, top: © Gary Conaughton; p 76, bottom: © Gary Conaughton; p 77, top: © Gary Conaughton; p 77, bottom: © Gary Conaughton; p 78, top: © Gary Conaughton; p 78, bottom: © Gary Conaughton; p 79: © Gary Conaughton; p 80: © Gary Conaughton; p 81: © Brett Shoaf/Artistic Visuals; p 83: © Brett Shoaf/Artistic Visuals; p 84, top: © Brett Shoaf/Artistic Visuals; p 84, bottom: © Brett Shoaf/Artistic Visuals; p 85, top: © Joerg Boetel/AGE Fotostock; p 85, bottom: © Gary Crabbe/Alamy; p 86: © Ron Niebrugge/Alamy; p 87, top: © Brett Shoaf/Artistic Visuals; p 87, bottom: © Richard Cummins/Lonely Planet Images; p 89, middle: © Lowell Georgia/Corbis; p 89, bottom: © Jupiterimages; p 90, top: © Brett Shoaf/Artistic Visuals; p 90, bottom: © Charlie Manz/Artistic Visuals; p 91, top: © Richard Cummins/Lonely Planet Images; p 91, bottom: © Richard Cummins/SuperStock; p 93, top: © Brett Shoaf/Artistic Visuals; p 93, bottom: © Brett Shoaf/Artistic Visuals; p 94, top: © Brett Shoaf/Artistic Visuals; p 94, bottom: © Gary Crabbe/Alamy; p 95, top: © Ron Niebrugge/Alamy; p 95, bottom: © Brett Shoaf/Artistic Visuals; p 97: © Brett Shoaf/Artistic Visuals; p 98: © Darrell Gulin/DanitaDelimont.com; p 99: © Gary Conaughton; p 104: © Gary Conaughton; p 105, top: © Gary Conaughton; p 105, bottom: © Gary Conaughton; p 106, top: © Gary Conaughton; p 106, bottom: © Gary Conaughton; p 107: © Gary Conaughton; p 108, top: © Gary Conaughton; p 108, bottom: © Gary Conaughton; p 109: © Gary Conaughton; p 110:

The new way to get AROUND town.

Make the most of your stay. Go Day by Day

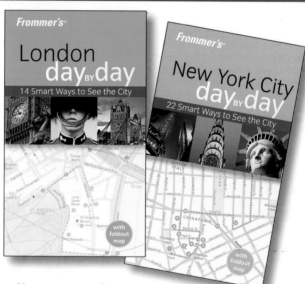

The all-new Day by Day series shows you the best places to visit and the best way to see them.

- Full-color throughout, with hundreds of photos and maps
- Packed with 1–to–3–day itineraries, neighborhood walks, and thematic tours
- Museums, literary haunts, offbeat places, and more
- Star-rated hotel and restaurant listings
- Sturdy foldout map in reclosable plastic wallet
- Foldout front covers with at-a-glance maps and info

The best trips start here. *Frommer's*

A Branded Imprint of ⑭WILEY
Now you know.

A UNIVERSAL/AMBLIN Entertainment Production

HARRY
AND THE HENDERSONS

A WILLIAM DEAR Film

JOHN LITHGOW "HARRY AND THE HENDERSONS"
MELINDA DILLON DON AMECHE DAVID SUCHET MARGARET LANGRICK JOSHUA RUDOY
with LAINIE KAZAN and KEVIN PETER HALL Music by WILLIAM DEAR Written by WILLIAM E. MARTIN & EZRA D. RAPPAPORT

AMBLIN
ENTERTAINMENT

Produced by RICHARD VANE Story by WILLIAM DEAR Directed by WILLIAM DEAR   A UNIVERSAL Picture

CALKINS

HARRY
AND THE HENDERSONS

A NOVEL BY JOYCE THOMPSON
BASED ON A SCREENPLAY BY WILLIAM DEAR
AND WILLIAM E. MARTIN & EZRA D. RAPPAPORT

Ⓑ
®
BERKLEY BOOKS, NEW YORK

HARRY AND THE HENDERSONS

A Berkley Book / published by arrangement with
MCA Publishing Rights, a Division of MCA, Inc.

PRINTING HISTORY
Berkley edition / June 1987

ISBN: 0-425-10155-X

A BERKLEY BOOK ® TM 757,375
Berkley Books are published by The Berkley Publishing Group,
200 Madison Avenue, New York, New York 10016.
The name "BERKLEY" and the stylized "B" with design
are trademarks belonging to Berkley Publishing Corporation.

PRINTED IN THE UNITED STATES OF AMERICA

1

Every year the Hendersons took their family vacation the last week of summer. The weather was too iffy in June, and July and August were the busiest months of the year at the sporting goods store where Mr. Henderson worked. George Henderson knew more about boots, backpacks, tent flaps, Coleman stoves and the fifteen brands of insect repellent the store sold than any other employee of Seattle Sport and Game. Which was only natural, of course. He was the boss's son.

George had been the boss's son for— count 'em—twenty years, longer if he added in the summers he'd worked for his father when he was still in high school. Old George wasn't about to let young George take to the woods in peak camping season, when he could be selling sleeping bags to somebody else. In fact, it was only after he'd worked for his dad ten years and sold maybe two thousand Swiss Army knives that George got to take his vacation in summer at all. He always recommended the model with the fish-hook remover and the portable toothpick.

George got the last week of August the same year his mom and dad traded their Jeep in on a Winnebago and started spending February in Palm Springs. February was always rainy in Seattle and slow in sporting goods. When the old man finally gave him August, George and his family burned their snowshoes and bought a four-man tent. Every summer since, just before Labor Day, they headed for the woods.

Old George had always taken young George camping when he was a boy. He'd taught him to fish and hunt, to clean his catch and skin his kill. On these trips, George had learned to be a sportsman, and something else besides. He'd come to see the beauty of the forest, to appreciate the uncomplicated quiet of life in the woods. As a kid, George hid a notebook and a pencil stub in the pocket of his chamois shirt and made quick little sketches of squirrels and rabbits and birds when his father wasn't looking. Now, when he took his family camping, George packed a Strathmore sketchbook and charcoal right alongside his shotgun and didn't care who knew it.

It was important to George that his children learn to love the woods as much as he did. For ten years now, even the summer Nancy was pregnant with Ernie and nervous the whole time that the baby might come early, the Hendersons had spent the last week of August in their tent somewhere in the Mt. Rainier National Forest. George saw no reason to part with tradition. When Nancy suggested, gently, that they might, just once, do something different on their vacation, like go to Disneyland, he was genuinely shocked.

"Why would anybody want to spend their vacation with thousands of other people? Besides, the air stinks down there in southern California."

Sarah, who was in ninth grade looked up from her homework. "If you ask me, Dad, camping stinks."

George looked at his daughter in alarm. "Sarah!"

Sarah held her ground. "It does, Daddy. Nobody takes a bath for a whole week. Everybody smells like smoke and fish. Except Ernie. He smells like the dump."

Above Sarah's head, George looked to Nancy for

support. Nancy looked away. Sarah said, "Tell him, Mom."

Nancy said, "You tell him."

"You promised, Mom."

"I chickened out. Maybe next year."

George looked from his wife to his daughter. "Tell me what?" he said.

Sarah stared at her math book.

"Nancy, what's going on here?"

Slowly, Nancy turned from the sink to face George. "Nothing really. It's just that apparently Sarah would rather not go camping this year."

"Not apparently," Sarah said. "Definitely."

The idea was so new and so shocking to George that all he could manage to say was "But . . ."

"Sasha's mom already said I could stay with them," Sarah informed her father.

"But . . ." George said.

"Besides, that way I could get a job and work all summer. I wouldn't have to stop before school started."

"But . . ." said George.

"That way everybody could have a good time. Not just you and Ernie." Sarah was on a roll.

"We all have a good time," George said. "You like camping. Remember when you caught your first trout? You were so excited you made us keep it in the freezer for a whole year. You used to take it out and show your friends."

"I was just a little kid then," Sarah said.

"What do you think you are now, a senior citizen?" George said.

Sarah sat up straighter at the table. "In three weeks, I'm going to be fifteen years old. I start high school next year. High school, Daddy. Nobody in high school goes camping with their family."

This was news to George. "Why not?" he asked.

Sarah sighed. She would have to explain the obvious. "First of all, there's no hot water in the woods. There's no telephone. There's no cable television. No bus service. No electricity."

"Of course not. That's what I love about camping. No distractions."

"Exactly," Sarah said.

George looked at his daughter. "What do you need electricity for, anyway?"

"To plug in my curling iron."

"Oh my God," George said.

"And then," Sarah went on, "there's Ernie."

Ernie picked just that moment to arrive home from baseball practice. His sneakers and jeans were caked with dirt. Nancy held up her palm like a school crossing guard. "Not in here, young man. I just mopped the kitchen floor. Take those filthy things off before you come inside."

Ernie retreated to the back stoop and kicked off his tennis shoes. His sweat socks were moderately clean—light gray with darker toes. He padded back into the kitchen, bound for the refrigerator. "What's to eat?"

"Have an apple and some milk," Nancy advised. "Don't spoil your appetite."

"He's spoiled my appetite," Sarah said. "Ernie, don't you ever wash your feet?"

Ernie bit loudly into a crisp Granny Smith. "What's the matter with her?"

George felt a little more confident with another male in the house. "Your sister," he said, "just informed me that she'd rather not go camping with the family this summer. She'd rather stay with her friend Sasha in the hot dirty city than spend a week in the woods with her family."

"Yo," Ernie said. "All right! You're going to let her, aren't you, Dad?"

In that instant, George made up his mind. It was

important to be firm with teenagers. They appreciated it. He'd read that somewhere. "Absolutely not," he said.

Sarah threw down her pencil so hard it bounced across the table and rolled down to the floor. "Mom . . ." she wailed.

"Coordinated," Ernie said.

Nancy surveyed her family with a sad smile. "It's months till vacation," she said. "There's plenty of time to talk about this later."

The Hendersons talked about it a lot. They talked about it the rest of the spring and most of the summer. Sarah still didn't want to go camping, and George still insisted that she had to. Nancy hated it. Usually, family fights blew over fast. Usually, someone gave in, or both parties compromised and peace was restored. But this was more than a skirmish. It was a war. Sarah was growing up and her father didn't want her to. That's how Nancy saw it. She didn't especially want her daughter to grow up, either, but she was willing to accept it as inevitable. And George. His stubbornness worried her. In spite of his six feet four inches, in spite of his weird enthusiasm for football and hunting, he was really the gentlest of men. This wasn't like him.

Ernie loved it. His big sister, who could do no wrong, was wrong. Dead wrong. Wrong enough to make Ernie right sometimes. Whenever he and Sarah got into a fight bad enough that their parents stepped in, Ernie brought up camping. Whenever Sarah wanted to do something that Ernie was too little to do himself, he brought up camping. Whenever Sarah was getting on his nerves, he mentioned camping. It was wonderful to have a new weapon in the brother-sister war. Of course, Ernie secretly hoped that Sarah would wear their father down. At nine, Ernie was still young enough to like the idea of having his parents all to himself. And he absolutely loved the idea of a whole week

in the woods without his sister. For once, he wanted her to
get her own way.

Most of the spring and summer, Sarah didn't think much
about camping at all. It annoyed her the way Ernie brought
it up all the time, to get her in trouble and himself out of it.
She certainly wasn't looking forward to spending a whole
boring week in the wilderness while her hair turned to
string, but mostly, she had other things to think about. Her
fifteenth birthday, for one thing. Since her birthday was in
May and junior high school graduation in June, the
Hendersons let her have one big party to celebrate both.

Then, as soon as school was out, Sarah got a job at
Burger King. In June, she was a trainee. By July, the
assistant manager decided she was smart and honest enough
to work the cash register, so she didn't even have to wear a
hairnet. The second week of August, she was picked
Cashier of the Week and got her name up on the wall.
Summer turned out hot after a rainy June, and Burger King
was so busy that Sarah had to work every day and every
weekend. By the time vacation rolled around, Sarah was
ready for it, even if she did have to spend it in the woods.
She planned to sleep the whole time anyway.

George was, well, a little sad that summer. He didn't
know why, exactly, except that here he was looking at his
fortieth birthday, the big four-oh, come February, and still
working for his dad, still taking orders, still selling
expensive toys to tenderfoots and greenhorns, guys who
wouldn't know the difference between an elk and a moose if
you drew them a picture.

That's what George wanted to do — draw pictures. At
twenty-four, right around the time Sarah was born, George
was sure he'd be a famous artist by the time he was forty. In
his daydreams, he was a kind of Frederic Remington of the
Pacific Northwest. The job was open. Mark Tobey had
made some post-expressionist squiggles and said they were

the Pike Place Market, and Morris Graves did a nice job with birds, but no one had ever really captured the grandeur of God's country as George believed it should be done. With each year that went by, it seemed less likely he'd be the one to do it.

He didn't like to blame his father, but Old George had a lot to do with it. George was accepted at the University of Washington right out of high school, but the old man said he wasn't paying for his son to learn to color—he should have gotten that out of his system in kindergarten. It was Business Administration, Engineering school or nothing. George didn't want to be an engineer or an accountant. He went to work at the store, planning to quit as soon as he'd saved his own tuition. Then he met Nancy. They got married. Then Sarah came.

Sarah. That was another thing. At her fifteenth birthday party, with her first orchid pinned to her shoulder, she looked like one of those dolls she used to play with when she was little. What were they called? She looked just like a Barbie. And she didn't want to go camping with the family this summer. His little girl wasn't just growing up, she was growing away.

When the Henderson station wagon, packed to the gills, backed out of the driveway that August, everyone in it had mixed feelings about the coming week. Except Ernie. Ernie couldn't wait to get to the woods and set up camp. His grandfather had given him a brand new rifle of his very own, and his dad was going to teach him how to shoot it.

2

Blam! Blam! Pow!

Bullets slammed into the trunk of the fir tree. Once in a while, they even hit the homemade target George had nailed up, right at Ernie's eye level. Ernie knelt in the dirt about five yards from the tree, the rifle butt planted in his shoulder. Since Ernie couldn't keep his left eye shut, George had taped a patch of Kleenex over the left lens of his glasses. He looked for all the world like a myopic pirate, kneeling there. Every time he hit the target, never mind the bull's eye, Ernie let out a blood-curdling yelp. Every time the gun went off, his mother winced.

The tent flap opened and Sarah stuck her head out. Her eyes were puffy and her hair mussed. Nancy smiled hopefully at her daughter. "Good morning, dear."

"Mom, do they have to start so early? It's practically the middle of the night."

Nancy looked at her digital wristwatch. "Actually, dear, it's almost 7:30."

Sarah groaned.

Ernie ran up to the tree trunk and ripped the target down, then took it to the tent. He waved the paper in his sister's face. "Look at that. It's practically confetti."

"Great," Sarah said. "What do you move on to next—books?"

9

"Animals," Ernie said. "I'm going to get me a bear."

"Sure," Sarah said.

"Aw, you can't even shoot a rubber band."

"Why would I want to?" Sarah asked. It wasn't really a question. She crawled out of the tent and squinted into the morning sun. "Another exciting day at Camp Deerfly," she said. "What's for breakfast, Mom?"

"The rest of us have already eaten," Nancy told her. "I saved you some oatmeal."

"Grody. Can I just have some toast?"

"Of course."

"At least I won't gain weight this vacation," Sarah said.

Nancy handed her daughter a loaf of Langendorf and the toasting fork. "The boys are going off in search of big game this afternoon. I thought maybe you and I could head off in the opposite direction and collect some wildflowers."

"Maybe so, Mom," Sarah said. "But I was planning to wash my hair in the creek. And if they're gone, maybe I can actually get some sleep around here."

"We'll leave just after lunch," Nancy said.

Sarah squatted on the ground next to the camp fire and held the toasting fork over the coals. "Okay, as long as we're back in time for *General Hospital*."

Nancy looked at the little portable battery-operated Sony TV set up on a milk crate next to the tent. George had given it to her for her birthday, but Nancy suspected it was really intended to keep Sarah happy in the woods. "I wish your father had never bought that thing," she said. "But don't tell him."

Ernie raced ahead. Somehow, he managed to snap every twig on the forest floor. An Indian scout he wasn't. Any animal within a mile would hear him coming. Still, George smiled at his son's enthusiasm. It helped bring back his own. He remembered the summer his father taught him how to shoot for the first time. George felt like Davy Crockett and Lewis and Clark rolled into one. He bagged a squirrel. That next Christmas, he'd asked for and got a coonskin cap. George loved that hat. So much that he insisted on wearing it in class. His fourth grade teacher, Mrs. Bundlesmith, had taken it away from him and kept if locked up in the bottom drawer of her desk until June. By then, it was all squished and smelled musty. He never wore it again.

George called ahead to Ernie. "Shhh. You have to move quietly in the woods. The idea is to surprise the animals."

Ernie slowed down and waited for his father to catch up. "I was being quiet."

George ruffled Ernie's hair. Ernie squirmed. He was pretty sure big game hunters didn't do that sort of thing. "Hey, Dad," he said. "You think there's any wild boars around here?"

George smiled. "I know there's possum," he said.

Ernie looked disappointed. "Aw, Dad, there's possums in the city. I want to kill something wild my first time. You know, something big."

Ernie's blood lust made George a little bit uneasy. He decided it was time to give Ernie the talk his father had given him. "You know, son, hunting is more than a sport. It's . . . well, it's only all right to kill animals if you eat what you kill."

Ernie hopped impatiently in the underbrush. "I know all that stuff, Dad."

"What I'm saying is, I don't think your mother has any recipes for wild boar."

Ernie cocked his head back so he could look his father in the eye. "When was the last time we had possum stew for supper?"

All in all, it was a long week. Sarah didn't hide her boredom, and she didn't get her sleep. The mosquitos were

big and swarmed around the Hendersons. Because Sarah
refused to put on the Old Woodsman's Fly Dope her father
brought, she was soon covered head to toe with nasty bites.
It wasn't so bad during the day, when she had the television
to distract her, but she scratched all night. This kept the rest
of the family, in their small tent, awake.

Ernie didn't bag his boar. On Tuesday, crouched to fire,
he lost his balance when the gun went off and toppled
backwards into a patch of poison ivy. George decided that,
under the circumstances, it might be smarter to fish than
hunt, but the trout, full of mosquitos, were slow to take
their bait. The ones that did bite were the runts, not keepers.
It was the kind of fishing that required patience. George
enjoyed it. He could laze on the stream bank, his back
against a tree, and sketch while he waited for a bite—but all
the waiting drove Ernie crazy. Like his grandfather, he
wanted results, *now*. Thursday afternoon, after almost half
an hour of unexpected peace, George looked downstream to
see his son, waist deep, aiming his rifle into the water.

"Ernie!" George called. "What the hell are you doing?"

Ernie looked upstream at him. "If you can't hook 'em,
shoot 'em," he said. Dead serious. George laughed. Ernie
was offended.

When they finally did manage to catch a respectable
supper, two legal trout, Sarah refused to eat them. The only
kind of fish she liked came frozen and breaded, from
Safeway. Sarah didn't like to be reminded her dinner had
once had heads and tails. She lived the week on toast,
raisins and Noodle-Roni.

Nancy was the only one of the family who enjoyed any
real success. Always careful to head away from her
menfolk, she roamed and climbed in search of flora. On one
of her expeditions, while George and Ernie were stalking
snipes and Sarah was watching the afternoon soap operas,
Nancy stumbled upon a meadow bright with wildflowers.

Guide book in hand, she identified cow parsnip, foxglove, bleeding heart, wild iris. Carefully, she pressed her specimens between sheets of wax paper and filled her pockets with them. No one else in the family thought they were the least bit wonderful. Sunday was a long time coming.

Sarah lifted the boiling kettle off the firepit and poured some in the dishpan. The steam was going to make her bangs frizz. "I don't see why Ernie never has to do the dishes," she complained.

Nancy sighed. "Because he does a lousy job, that's why."

"That's no excuse."

"Look, Sarah," Nancy said, "just be glad we're going home." Nancy was profoundly glad the family vacation was drawing to a close. One more day in close quarters might cost her her sanity. She loved her children dearly, but after six nights in a four-person tent, she wasn't sure she liked them very well.

"I can't wait to get back to civilization," Sarah said. "By the way, do you suppose you could drive me out to Southcenter tomorrow afternoon? I've still got some school shopping to do."

"Ask me tomorrow afternoon," Nancy said. She crawled inside the tent, lay down and rolled across the sleeping bags, to squish the air out, then stuffed them one by one, like big down sausages, into their duffel bags. She was always amazed that they fit. Underneath the sleeping bags there was a stratum of stray socks and dirty underwear—a week's worth. These she crammed into a big plastic garbage bag and sealed it tight against the smell. She tried to picture the laundry room cabinet. Was there enough bleach in the whole world to get Ernie's socks white again?

Suddenly, outside the tent, there sounded a terrific scream, Sarah. Nancy crawled out of the tent, half expecting to find her daughter being bear-hugged by a grizzly, only to see George and Ernie topping the rise beyond the campsite. The corpse of a rabbit dangled from Ernie's hand. When he saw Nancy, he lifted the dead rabbit aloft.

"Lunch," George announced.

"And I killed it!" Ernie beamed with pride.

Beside Nancy, Sarah made a gagging sound. "There's no way I'm eating a dead rabbit. You said we were leaving. Will this never end?"

The limp rabbit wiggled sadly as Ernie drew closer with his prize. Nancy put her hand on Sarah's arm. "We are leaving. Before lunch." She turned to George. "What happened to 'home before dark . . . grab a bite on the road?' "

George gave her his best "be reasonable" smile. "Come on, Nan, it's Ern's first kill."

"Yeah, Mom. It's my first blood." Ernie bounced up and down in his excitement. As he did, a trickle of blood spat from the rabbit's mouth.

Nancy was pretty sure her appetite would never return. Into the look she threw George, she packed all the disapproval that would fit. "Well, I hope you're real proud of yourself," she said.

"You're a butcher, Ernie," Sarah said. She *sounded* disgusted, but she looked a little green around the gills.

Ernie advanced, grinning. He waved the rabbit in his sister's face. "Back off, Sarah. It was him or me."

Dramatically, Sarah turned her back on Ernie and his prey. "In that case," she said, "I wish the rabbit had won."

3

Nancy hit upon a compromise. She usually did. To make up to Sarah for one more meal au naturel, she promised to take her shopping the following afternoon. To George, she said, "Okay, you're right. A boy should get to eat his first kill. In fact, he should *have* to. Where's your skinning knife?"

George pulled the curved knife from the scabbard on his belt. "Right here."

Ernie jumped up and down. "Oh boy. Am I hungry."

Nancy took the knife from George and handed it to Ernie. Ernie blinked at her behind his glasses. "Go on," his mother said. "You kill it, you clean it."

"That's women's work," Ernie said. He looked to his father. "Isn't it, Dad?"

George knew he was treading on quicksand. He could feel his wife's and daughter's eyes upon him. There were just waiting for him to say something sexist. He put his hand on Ernie's shoulder. "Come on, son. We'll show them how it's done."

"I'd rather not watch, thank you," Nancy said. "Come on, Sarah. There's some cheese left in the cooler. Let's make ourselves some sandwiches."

Ernie liked cleaning the rabbit a whole lot less than he'd liked shooting it. He wondered if Rambo ever felt a little sick when he had to touch guts. They never showed you that

15

in the movies. But then, Rambo killed mostly people, not rabbits. Ernie tried to think about other things while he skinned the rabbit. He thought about school starting. He thought about baseball. He thought about telling the guys about his hunting trip. In his imagination, the rabbit turned into a wolf. When he looked down, it was still small, bloody and slimy in his hands. Finally, it was ready to cook.

Nancy had already doused the campfire, so George had to build a new one. There was no time to wait for coals. He skewered the rabbit and charbroiled it over open flames. For lunch, George and Ernie ate charred rabbit carcass. For pride's sake, they pretended to enjoy it. When Nancy and Sarah were out of earshot, George promised Ernie they'd find a place to stop for burgers on the way home. They saved the rabbit skin so they could get it stuffed.

On the way home, everyone was cranky, except for Ernie, who was hyper. The station wagon was less like a passenger car than a badly packed moving van. Whenever George rounded a sharp curve, the camping gear shifted precariously. Restless, Ernie kept crawling back and forth from the back seat to the way back.

"Sit still, Ernie, and fasten your seat belt," Nancy said. "If a cop sees you without your seat belt, your father could get a ticket."

"Aw, Mom. That's bunk. Cops have better things to do than give kids tickets."

In the front seat, Nancy nudged George's knee. "Your mother's right, Ernie," George responded. "It's the law."

In the back seat, Sarah said weakly, "I think I'm going to throw up."

Nancy half turned, to find her daughter looking pale. "Open the window, honey. A little air will do you good."

"It's the fish," Sarah said. "Ernie, close the cooler."

Nancy assumed her detective voice. "Ernie, what are you doing in the fish?"

"Looking for my baseball glove. Hey, Dad?"

George looked for his son in the rearview mirror but couldn't see him around the sleeping bags. "Yeah?"

"You think I can get a pair of real major league–type cleats when we get back?"

George grinned. One thing you had to say for Ernie—he was enthusiastic. "You bet."

"Great! I'm gonna spike Frankie McDowell."

Nancy was unmoved by Ernie's enthusiasm. "Don't you dare," she said. Once again, her hand nudged George's thigh. Once again, George performed on cue. "Listen to your mom, Ernie," he said.

Ernie's voice rang with protest. "But he spiked me twice."

"Well, that's different. Go ahead, then."

"George!" Nancy's voice was indignant. Her gaze burned like a laser beam on George's cheek. She was a good woman, a good mother, George thought, but there were some things she just didn't understand. In the city, the difference between the sexes didn't seem to matter so much. It took a week in the woods to really bring it out. "That's just smart baseball, Nan," he explained, even though he knew she'd never agree.

"All right!" Ernie chirped. "Did anybody see my baseball?"

"Just be careful of my drawings," George called back. "And don't step on the trout."

"Or my flowers," Nancy added.

"Or the flowers," George said. He wasn't much for dried flowers, but he was glad Nan had found them. He smiled sideways at her. "Roughing it wasn't so bad, was it?"

Beside him, Nancy shrugged. "You know me. Nature is growing a potato in a glass. I'm just not cut out for camping."

George's smile deepened. Nancy always said that. Either

she hated camping less than she let on or loved him more than she admitted. Either way, she was a brick. Much as he regretted not going to art school, George never regretted marrying Nan. At thirty-five, she was still trim, blonde as ever, still fun. Even the old man had to admit she was a keeper.

The sun was low through the trees, their shadows long across the road. It was the time of day photographers call the magic hour. George mellowed out with the light. He was glad they'd gotten a late start, not just because it gave Ernie a last chance at hunting. This way they'd have the pleasure of late afternoon in the forest and hit the city after dark, when it looked its best. Seattle was beautiful on a clear night. Life was beautiful, at least until tomorrow morning. George pushed thoughts of tomorrow from his mind and studied the light. He'd have to try capturing that—the way the low sun raked through the branches of the firs.

Suddenly, a doe broke from cover and dashed across the road. George hit the brakes. The rear end fishtailed a little, but the deer made it safely to the other side of the road. Her tail bobbed white among the underbrush before she disappeared into the trees. George congratulated himself on his quick reactions.

Nancy was tense beside him. "George, please. Slow down."

"Come on, Nan. I know these roads like the back of my hand."

Nancy clutched the dashboard and peered out through the windshield, alert as the copilot in a fighter plane. "And I know Seattle will still be there if we get home fifteen minutes later," she said.

George sighed. His peaceful mood was gone. He goosed the accelerator, just a little, and watched his wife's knuckles turn white.

"George, please."

He glanced at the speedometer. "I'm only doing fifty."

"The curve caution sign said twenty-five."

The sign was right. Going round, the tires squealed a little. In the back of the wagon, the camping gear shifted and scattered. Coming out of the curve, they were headed due west. The sun was big and blindingly bright in front of them. Nancy slammed her visor down and rummaged through the glove box.

"George, do you need your sunglasses?"

"I'm fine, dear."

Nancy whacked the glove compartment shut and turned her attention to the back of the wagon, via the rearview mirror. The rifle had landed squarely in Ernie's lap. Nan put on her boot-camp voice. "Ernie, don't even touch that gun."

"Rifle, dear," George said.

"If you can shoot with it, then it's a *gun*."

In the mirror, George saw Ernie grin. "Hey, Dad. Maybe there's still a chance you could blast something."

"Ernie, don't give your dad any ideas. I couldn't face another stuffed bunny."

"Did I bring my rifle?" George protested. "Did I? No." Darn sun *was* bright. He put his visor down. He put his arm around Nancy and felt her relax inside it. Her voice was softer when she said, "You're right, George. We'll always remember this as the first camping trip that Ernie killed something and you didn't."

George saw her head jerk up. His own eyes followed, slamming into the sun, so bright it hurt.

"Oh my God," Nancy said.

Something huge and dark flickered in the glare. Instinctively, George braked. Again, the shape appeared, huge, black, gone. A man? It looked something like a man but it was big. Too big. George's insides lurched. He swerved away from where he imagined the thing had gone. Then, whap. Even as he felt impact and heard the fender crumple, George saw it, big and dark and manlike, rising up, hurtling away.

It, whatever it was, landed in a big black heap beside the road.

4

Ernie waited for somebody to say something. For a long time, no one did. His dad just sat there, still as a statue, holding on to the wheel. Finally, he let go and gave his head a little shake. Ernie saw him peek into the side mirror. Then his dad rolled down his window and looked out. Ernie looked too. A big furry mountain of a thing lay beside the road. It didn't move.

His dad blew out a long breath. "My god, I thought I hit a man." Ernie could tell he was glad the thing in the road wasn't human. "Everybody all right?" his dad asked. "Nancy?"

His mom said, "I'm okay. Kids?" She looked around at them. Sarah was huddled against the car door, wrapped up tight in her own arms. Girls had no sense of adventure. Once Ernie realized he was in one piece, he let out a yelp of excitement. "My first car crash. All right! Too bad you weren't going faster, Dad. We could have rolled it!"

His mom was still looking at Sarah, and Sarah was still looking scared. It was obvious to Ernie that she was faking, but his mom asked her again if she was okay. Finally, Sarah nodded.

"What was it, George?" his mom asked, and his dad answered in that same funny flat voice. "I don't now. It all happened so fast. Must be a bear."

Ernie knew it was no bear. It was too big to be a bear. Besides, he was sure the thing had been running on two legs, not four. Bears only did that in circuses, not in the woods. His mom didn't buy the bear stuff, either. "Could it have been a gorilla?" she asked.

His dad shook his head. "I don't think they get that big around here," he said.

Sarah finally came back to life. She leaned forward and said, "I think we should get out of here, Daddy." Typical Sarah, chicken through and through.

Then Ernie had an inspiration. Hitting something with a car wasn't quite the same as blasting it, but what the heck. A trophy was a trophy, right? The thing in the road was even bigger than the humongous stuffed grizzly his grandfather kept in the store, the one everybody called Claws. "Hey," he said, "if Grandpa doesn't want the head, can I have it? I can keep my cassettes in it." His grandfather had an end table that was really an elephant's foot and a hat rack made out of moose antlers. For a minute, Ernie pictured the thing's head in his bedroom, with tapes between its teeth.

His mom turned around and tried to see out the back window over the camping stuff, which was impossible. "What if it's still alive? What if it's in pain, George?"

"If it's still alive, it's probably not in a very good mood," his dad said.

Ernie couldn't believe it. They'd just had a car crash and bagged a monster, and his folks were sitting there talking like they were trying to decide what kind of pizza to order. Grown-ups. He couldn't take it anymore. "No way it's alive," he told them. "You trashed him, Dad. There's probably guts and eye balls hanging off the bumper."

Beside Ernie, Sarah shuddered. She rolled her window down fast and stuck her head outside. What a wimp. Worse yet, his dad got mad at *him*. It wasn't fair.

• • •

George's heartbeat was almost back to normal. After the rush came the shakes. His hands were slippery with sweat. Nan kept telling him they couldn't just leave it there in the road, like "it" was the neighbor's dachshund or something. Just pop it in the back seat and take it to the vet. No way. George saw it with his own eyes. He felt the front end crumple like a piece of Kleenex when they hit the thing. Whatever "it" was, and George's best guess was a lost steer, about three thousand pounds of raw hamburger on the hoof, they weren't talking small.

"George, it could be suffering," Nan said.

"Yeah," George said. He sat tight. No use in doing anything hasty. There was still a possibility he might wake up. This felt too much like a dream to be real. He breathed deep, like he did when he was trying to outfox a nightmare, and tried to imagine himself back in bed. Nothing changed. Ernie was still breathing down his neck, Sarah was still gagging out the window, and Nancy was still urging him to try CPR on a three-ton fur ball. Slowly, George started the car and turned it around in the narrow road.

The thing lay smack in the middle of the road. It sort of reminded George of the guest bedroom, where all the wives pile up their fur coats at Christmas parties. He kept his eyes glued to it, looking for signs of life, but it didn't move. He stopped the car and opened his door an inch or two. "I want everybody else to stay inside."

Wide-eyed, Nan looked at him. "Be careful, dear." George promised he would. He climbed out of the car and slammed the door shut behind him. First things first. He checked out the front end and felt his heart drop into his Nikes. He'd had this car for fifteen years—just five more and they were talking genuine antique. Fifteen years and hardly a scratch on her. Fifteen years of regular wash jobs, fifteen years of Turtle Wax, and now the hood was corrugated like one of those old-fashioned washboards. All because some darn dumb animal decided to jaywalk. For a moment, George was indignant. Then he wised up. The darn dumb animal was out there with him, and it was bigger than a horse. He glanced through the windows at his family. They stared at him expectantly. You figure it out, Dad. George edged toward the creature.

Were his insurance premiums paid up? Would Nancy remember where to find their will? Poor thing, she hadn't worked in fifteen years, not since Sarah was born. Actually, George didn't think dying would be so bad, but he was allergic to pain. What if the creature didn't finish him off? The heap of fur in the road didn't move, but the closer George got, the more it smelled. Sort of like the monkey house at the zoo.

Nan stuck her head out the window. "Shouldn't we call a ranger?"

"Not yet." Closer, closer. George kept his eyes glued to the heap. Maybe it wasn't dead, just playing possum. No sense in taking unnecessary risks. George kept his eye on the thing as he moved around to the back of the wagon and felt around inside. His own rifle, the big one, the one Nan thought he didn't bring, was carefully concealed under the family's foul-weather gear. He pulled it out and checked the chamber.

"You did bring it!" Ernie was exultant. And loud. "Doncha need some back up, Dad?"

"No! I want you all to stay in the car." George glanced at Nan. Her look could have fried an egg. He motioned to the creature. "This is exactly why I brought it. Protection."

"You didn't need to lie," Nan said.

This was no time to argue. George didn't answer. Instead, he moved toward the creature. Again, the smell hit him. If George had had another hand, he would have held his nose. At last, he stood beside the thing.

No telling which end was up. With the rifle, he poked the

fur ball. Nothing. Then he spotted something like an arm, and at its end, what appeared to be a paw. Paw, wrist. Wrist, pulse.

"Shoot it, Dad." Ernie's shrill boy voice broke so deep a silence it startled George. At first, he thought it might have been the creature. "It's already dead," he yelled back to his son.

"Shoot it anyway!"

He was going to have to have a little talk with Ernie, if he made it back alive. The boy had to understand you don't just go around blasting things, Rambo and Dirty Harry notwithstanding. George crouched low enough to reach the creature's paw. The back of it was hairy, but when George turned it over, five huge fingers uncurled to show a palm that might have been his own. Well, bigger, but human. A real hand. Gently, George lay the hand back in the dirt and called his wife.

Nancy leaned out the car window. "What is it?"

"I think you better come take a look."

Ernie took that for permission, too. The whole family piled out of the car. The creature's smell hit Sarah's queasy stomach, but Ernie marched right up. "Holy Toledo," he said. Then he apologized.

Under the circumstances, George overlooked the slip. "It's okay, Ern. I was looking for the right words myself."

They stared at the creature. Again, Ernie spoke George's thoughts. "Dad, do bears have fingers?"

"Maybe," George said. "But not thumbs." Thumbs were important. George remembered that from biology, way back at Franklin High. Thumbs were an evolutionary signpost. Only primates and people had them.

"Dad, what if it's . . ." Ernie's voice was tight with excitement. "You know. What if it's *him*?"

"Him?" George said. "Him who?"

"Bigfoot," Ernie said. "What if it's Bigfoot?"

What if it's Bigfoot? Ernie's words repeated loudly and slowly inside his father's head. George looked at the creature, at its strangely human hand. Four fingers and one opposable thumb. Well, it wasn't Mickey Mouse. "Bigfoot," George said aloud, considering.

That was enough for Ernie. "Bigfoot!" he confirmed. "Nice goin', Dad. You didn't even wreck the hide or anything!"

Nancy and Sarah joined them near the corpse. "It smells gross," Sarah said.

As Nancy studied the creature, George could tell that she too saw its human elements. "What is it, George?"

Good question, Nan. George had hoped she wouldn't ask, because the only answer he could think of sounded just plain looney. "A Bigfoot, I guess," he said. He waited for her to laugh. He sort of hoped she would. When she didn't, he said it again, inside his own head. Bigfoot. Nobody had ever seen one. God knows, they'd looked hard enough. Why, every few years, some crackpot claimed to have spotted one, and whole troops took to the woods. They beat the bushes, they followed the footprints, they . . . It always turned out to be a hoax. That, or the person who saw Bigfoot turned out to be recently released from a mental hospital.

On the other hand, the legend lived on. Where had it come from? Indians, most likely. The thing in the road was certainly real—the whole family saw it—and it certainly wasn't like any other animal George had ever seen or heard of. Bigfoot? "I don't know what else it could be," George said. "This is a big deal. It's a major discovery. I bet we could sell it to a museum for a lot of money, or do something like that."

George looked at Nan. She looked as stunned as he felt, and somewhat disapproving. Were those tears in her eyes? For a moment, George felt guilty. But he hadn't meant to hurt the thing. It was all an accident, anybody could see that. The creature had no business running out in the road like that. Didn't Bigfoots—Bigfeet?—teach their children not to play in traffic? It wasn't his fault the thing didn't stop, look and listen before it crossed the road. And if there was profit to be had from its misfortune, well, so be it. George hoped it would be enough to pay for fixing the car.

George turned to his son. "Ernie, you and Sarah take the stuff off the top of the car and put it in the back." Ernie raced off. "And tell your sister she'll have to help us lift this thing."

Ernie was on it. "Right, Dad. I can't wait to see her face when she hears that!" Jogging back to the car, Ernie called out in his sweetest voice, "Ohhh, Saaaahhraaah . . ."

George had to smile.

Ernie figured his dad was probably the smartest guy in the whole world. Most people's dads would have just left the Bigfoot lying there in the road, or called a tow truck or something, but not his father. His father walked around the thing a few times and stroked his chin and figured it all out. Now, George and Ernie, strong as they were, couldn't have lifted that Bigfoot up on the roof of the car no matter how hard they tried, and they couldn't expect much help from Mom or Sarah. Sarah couldn't even lift a bowling ball, much less a Bigfoot. But what they lacked in brawn, his dad made up in brains. He built a pulley out of a rope and a branch and let the car engine do the work. All they had to do was guide the body up onto the roof.

Ernie stood on one side and Sarah on the other while his dad drove slowly forward. The invention worked like a charm. Up the creature came. Ernie sank his hands into the creature's fur and helped. Sarah looked like she was going to puke. The creature's head moved up, its big arms and giant chest, thighs like Conan the Barbarian. Then its feet.

They were the biggest feet Ernie had ever seen. "What do you say, Dad? They must be at least size twenty!"

The thing must have weighed at least a ton. The hood buckled under it and the rope stretched out and almost broke, but at last the thing was balanced on the roof. His dad tied it down tight, head on the hood and feet in the back, and covered the whole thing up with the tarp.

"Good job, Dad!" Ernie said.

His father studied their handiwork, then put his hand on Ernie's shoulder. "Thanks, son. You know what they always say. There's more than one way to skin a cat."

"Right, Dad," Ernie said. "Can I help you skin him when we get home?"

His dad squeezed Ernie's shoulder, then let go. "We'll see, son," he said. Then he turned to Mom and Sarah. "Well, I guess we better hit the road. All the extra weight up there is going to slow us down."

The family settled back in the car and his dad drove off. Sarah was totally grossed out. Mom didn't seem exactly thrilled with the whole idea of taking a dead Bigfoot home, but Ernie was delighted. He always liked it when his dad gave him reason to be proud.

5

LaFleur chuckled deep in his throat. The sound that came out was something like the caw of a crow, or the croak of a frog. His name may have meant flower, but there was nothing pretty or soft about old Jacques. Most people thought he was mad. This proved he wasn't.

"This" was a footprint, a big clear deep authentic print. Six feet away, there was another. And another. The beast was running.

Ha! Let him run. He wasn't getting away from Jacques LaFleur. Not this time. This was it. Jacques patted his rifle, clean and well oiled, as always. Loaded. He had no interest in taking the animal alive. A corpse would just as easily prove him right.

The tracks went on and on. Not even the cleverest joker could have faked such prints. For one thing, they were too far apart. Too deep—there was real weight behind them. LaFleur's heart hammered in his chest. He was running now, running toward his moment of glory. He had been waiting for it most of his life.

The tracks headed down toward the road. LaFleur had never known his quarry to head for civilization, but he wasn't about to argue with the evidence of the prints. He followed, a surefooted tracker, after so many years spent in the woods. The prints led him out of the woods and onto the

road. And there they stopped. Stopped dead. LaFleur
looked up and down the road. He scanned the ground, but
there was no trace of his prey.

Weary, LaFleur sank to his knees. Outsmarted again.
Under his breath, he muttered curses in his native French.
And then. Then his eye settled on something interesting.
Something promising. On hands and knees, Jacques
crawled to the spot and rubbed his hand across the surface
of the road. Blood. And hair. And something else, too. A
skid mark on the road.

LaFleur smiled grimly to himself. Bigfoot would be his
yet.

6

Dusk was dim and grainy. For once, the kids were quiet. Nancy tried hard to think about safe, ordinary things like school lunches and bridge parties and the Japanese flower-arranging class she planned to take, but it was impossible. Her thoughts kept coming back to the thing strapped to the top of the car.

The problem was, of course, that Nancy guessed it was not a thing at all. It looked so human it might have been a distant relative. It even had toenails. Maybe it had Bigfoot parents out there somewhere, or even Bigfoot babies. Maybe it loved them, the way she loved her kids, no matter how exasperating they could be sometimes. Nancy leaned forward and stretched up a little, so she could glimpse her children in the rearview mirror. Half asleep, both of them. They both looked pale and dazed. She felt a little dazed herself.

Then an even worse thought struck her.

"Oh, George, what if it was the last one? I feel so guilty."

"It's not like I tried to hit it, Nan. It was just luck."

When George turned to look at her, he was smiling. His smile exasperated her. She wished she could make him understand her concern. "What if we've just rendered an entire species extinct?" she asked him.

Neatly, George sidestepped guilt. His smile became a grin. "One of a kind. Hmmmm. This thing might be worth something." Nancy shot him a look she usually reserved for the kids, to let them know their behavior was out of line. George shrugged his innocence. "Come on, Nan. It's all in how you look at it."

Well, he had that right. She just wished George wouldn't insist on looking at it inside out and backwards.

"Well, the way I see it," Nancy began, but she never finished telling him, because all of a sudden a big face pressed itself against the windshield, a hairy face with two big upside-down eyes, an upside-down nose and, when it opened its mouth to growl at them, an enormous set of upside-down teeth.

In chorus, the whole family screamed. George braked. The car rocked sharply and the creature rolled off the top. When the car skidded to a stop on the shoulder, they watched the creature roll down the road away from them. Once it stopped rolling, it didn't move again.

Nancy spoke first. "Oh, my God. It's alive."

"Did you see those big honkin' teeth, Dad?" Ernie chirped.

Sarah said nothing. George asked Ernie to give him his rifle.

"George, you're not going out there," Nancy said.

George flashed her a tiny, reluctant smile. "We can't just leave it in the road. What if it's suffering?"

Somehow, this time, Nancy was a little suspicious of George's concern.

George wasn't sure if he hoped the creature was alive or dead. A living Bigfoot was probably more valuable than a dead one—he really hadn't had time to think it through— and even though George had done his share of hunting, the idea of exterminating a rare animal didn't really appeal to him. On the other hand, if the thing *was* alive, he'd probably have to kill it, before it got him. "Ernie, pass my rifle," he said. The stock slid over the seat back. Armed, George felt better. He got out of the car.

The thing lay motionless. George poked his rifle into its ribs, not hard enough to hurt it, but enough to tickle it out of imitation sleep. When the creature didn't respond, George knelt beside it. Its big furry hand was cooling fast when he lifted it into his lap to feel for a pulse. His fingers combed through the creature's fur in search of a vein. Nothing. Just to be doubly sure, George felt along the tendons of its neck. Even for a layman, the carotid artery should be easy to find. Big animal, big pulse. No pulse. George guessed he was relieved. He called back to the family, waiting in the car. "Dead!"

"Are you sure?" Nancy asked him through her half-closed window.

"Yes!"

"But are you really sure? Remember, you were sure before."

George wished she'd just take his word for it. "Nancy, I'm not a doctor. But it doesn't have a pulse, it isn't breathing, and it's as cold as a Popsicle. Believe me, honey, it's dead."

That seemed to satisfy her. Ernie rolled down his window. "Dad, if it's dead, can I get out of the car now?"

"Sure, son," George said. "Everybody out. We've got to get this baby loaded."

"Oh, George, do you think that's wise?" Nan asked him.

"Don't we have enough stuffed animals at home?" Sarah wanted to know.

Only Ernie shared George's enthusiasm for the task. Mostly without help from the ladies, they rebuilt their makeshift hoist and hefted the beast back on top of the station wagon. George tied it down with every inch of rope and chain he could find among their gear. This time he wanted to be sure Bigfoot stayed where it belonged. When he was done, he stood back to survey the job.

Ernie stood beside him and slapped George on the back, as high up as he could reach. "Good job, Dad. If it tries to go anywhere now, it's gonna have to take the car with it."

George looked at his crippled fender, his crumpled hood. Just three hours before, the car had been impeccable. George looked down at Ernie. "Oh joy," he said.

Ernie dreamed of baseball. His team was the same as usual, but they took the field against nine large, hairy monsters. The monsters looked more or less like people, except bigger. They played without shoes and their yellow jerseys all said FEET. The FEET were up to bat in the bottom of the fifth. Ernie was on the mound. He sent a fastball whizzing over the plate. The monster swung. Ernie heard bat and ball connect. The ball went sailing out of the park, probably out of the state. The bat was split in two. The monster looked at it curiously for a while before he lumbered off for first.

Ernie woke up confused. At first he thought he really might be dead, but then he recognized the towers of old newspapers and stacks of dusty tools and camping gear that lined his own garage back home. Home. Ernie leaned back against the seat and took a deep breath, trying to sort out what was real and what was dream from the strange images inside his head. Pretty soon, his dad came out of the house and started rummaging around in the back for another load of stuff.

He stuck his head in the back seat, where Ernie still rested his head against the window. "Are you awake, son?"

"Yeah, Dad. I think so. I was having one weird dream."

His dad reached over the seat for another load of gear,

then laid it down again. "It's been a long day. You look beat. You want a ride to bed?"

Ernie thought about it for a minute and decided it would be all right. It wasn't like anybody was going to see them in the middle of the night. "Sure," he said.

His dad bent down and scooped up Ernie in his arms. Ernie wrapped his own arms around his father's neck. When his dad lifted him out of the car and stood up, Ernie saw a huge shape under the tarpaulin, lashed to the roof of the car. He whistled. "It really happened, huh, Dad?"

His dad looked at the giant lump and nodded. "Yes, Ern. It really did," he said.

"Wow," Ernie said. His father carried him upstairs to bed.

7

Jacques LaFleur was not used to stalking his prey by car. That was fine for those slick TV detectives, but he preferred to do his hunting on foot. Still, all the evidence suggested that his quarry was not on foot. There was nothing to do but take his rig.

It was not long before the light was gone. By his best estimation, the vehicle LaFleur was following was heading west, toward the interstate. He too headed west, his headlights on high beam. When faster-moving traffic jammed up behind him, he swerved onto the shoulder and traveled in the emergency lane. His eyes scanned constantly, alert to any clue.

Thirty slow miles later, a long set of skid marks caught his eye. He stopped the powerwagon and climbed out to investigate. Something big and rather violent had happened here, and LaFleur's instinct told him it had something to do with him. Some thirty feet west of the skid marks, there was a large depression in the hard-packed roadside dirt, as if something very large and very heavy had landed there. His imagination failed him when he tried to deduce just what had occurred, and how.

Darn. So close, and yet . . . The site told him nothing. Nothing. Who were these people? Who? How? Why? LaFleur drew a flask from an inside pocket of his hunting vest and took a long swig, hoping the whiskey would clear his thoughts. Then he chuckled. "Perhaps, Jacques, you expect they would leave a business card, to make your searching easy?"

Once more, he aimed his flashlight down the skid mark and into the roadside brush beyond. This time, he was rewarded by the glint of metal. He retrieved the object. Yes, there was blood, just as before, and hairs, a few coarse black hairs. LaFleur threw back his head and laughed a hearty laugh, deep and genuine.

The thing in his hands was almost as good as a business card, after all. It was a license plate.

8

George was exhausted. Almost as soon as his head hit the pillow, he was out. But it isn't easy to sleep soundly with blood on your bumper and a Bigfoot in your garage. All night, he tossed and turned, holding nightmares at bay. When his eyes popped open at 5:49 a.m., George knew he was awake for the day.

Beside him, deeply asleep, Nancy snored softly. George wished she would wake up so they could talk. He was even tempted to rouse her but then thought better of it. He didn't imagine she'd be thrilled. She hadn't wanted to bring the Bigfoot home in the first place. He was pretty sure she wasn't going to want to sell it.

On the other hand, if fate, or kismet or whatever you wanted to call it, was going to drop a golden goose in their laps, it would be foolish not to make a profit off the eggs. How else was George Henderson going to get rich? Not working for his father, that was sure. The old man was tighter than a ukelele string. Probably thought he could take it with him to the big game preserve in the sky. And George was sick, just plain sick of selling sporting goods. The more he thought about it, the more he began to believe there was a reason the Bigfoot had chosen to kamikaze against his car and not someone else's.

There had to be folks out there who'd pay a bundle for a

Bigfoot hide. Look at all the people who came into the store wanting to buy Claws. And they had more to sell than just a carcass. There was their story, too. Movie rights. George wondered who would play him. Paul Newman, maybe. He imagined a fat stock portfolio. He imagined Sarah's coming out party, Ernie's graduation from Harvard.

Of course, George had no idea if his son was smart enough for Harvard—it was really too soon to tell—but it was nice to think that if he got in, they'd be able to pay his way. Nancy shifted from her back to her side and muttered something in her sleep. George wondered, suddenly, if he were being sexist. What the heck. Let Sarah go to Harvard, too. But only if she wanted to. George promised himself he would never tell *his* kids what to do with their lives. They could join the circus, as far as he was concerned.

A terrible thought struck him. What if they *wanted* to be engineers or accountants when they grew up? George sighed. Much as he would be disappointed, he wouldn't interfere, even with that.

Best of all, George imagined himself in his own studio, painting all day long. If he could paint all the time, he'd get better and better until he was really good. Then he would get famous. Maybe he'd open a gallery of his own, too. No sense in paying some greedy agent a fifty- or sixty-percent commission to sell his pictures. Nancy could manage the gallery while he painted. If she wanted, it could be a flower shop, too.

No, scratch that. He couldn't very well paint nature if he was stuck in the city all the time. Let somebody else take care of business. They'd build themselves a little A-frame in the woods.

All that daydreaming made George impatient. He wanted it to be nine o'clock so he could start making the phone calls that would make them rich. Who should he call first? Well, time enough for that later. It was only 6:15. George decided to have a look at his golden goose. Not that anything was wrong—what could be wrong? Just to make sure.

He crawled out of bed and crept down the stairs, then pawed through the junk drawer in the kitchen. The flashlight had to be in there. Candles, keys, a hammer, a cheese grater, a roll of duct tape . . . gotcha. His hand closed on the flashlight. Just beyond it, he felt the cool casing of his metal measuring tape. Might as well get the big guy's stats straight while he was at it. He took the tape.

It was still dark outside, and just a little spooky. Those new haloid streetlights made everything look green or purple. Every dog in the neighborhood seemed to be awake and howling. Already there was a nip of fall in the air, and George shivered in his bathrobe. When he got to the garage, he turned on the flashlight and shined it through the window.

The ropes were broken. The tarp was thrown aside. Except for the car, which looked like it might not ever go anywhere again, the garage was empty.

Then came the crash. It was hard to imagine just what could crash so loud. The sound came from the house. George turned toward it. A small, pale, ghostly light blinked on and off inside the kitchen. By the time George got there, the light had stopped. He dropped his flashlight. The dark was deep and ominous. After his eyes adjusted, he saw the shadow, huge and moving, more ominous still. More from curiosity than courage, he followed it, past the sink, past the dishwasher, past the cupboards and the ironing-board closet.

George found himself staring into a very large pair of very widely spaced eyes, kind of greenish turquoise eyes, with light brown centers. They were embedded in a very large and hairy face. It was the Bigfoot and it wasn't dead. Apparently, it *was* hungry, because the refrigerator lay on its side, wide open, and the Bigfoot was wearing the biggest milk moustache George had ever seen. When the creature opened its mouth to growl at George, he would have been impressed by its big white teeth, if only he hadn't been so scared.

When the creature stood, George found himself looking up. Way up. The Bigfoot dropped the milk carton and reached for George. George backed away. He tried his voice, but it wasn't working very well. The creature came and he went, back, back, until he backed into the kitchen table. This time his voice worked just fine. He yelled for help. Somebody! Anybody! Helllllllllllp!

Ernie flew down the stairs. What he saw inside the kitchen stopped him short. There was his father, backed against the wall. There was the Bigfoot, amazingly, wonderfully, *enormously* alive! "All right!" he hollered. "I knew you weren't dead."

"Not yet, Ernie," his dad called back. "Quick, get my rifle."

"Not you, dad," Ernie said. "Him. He's still alive."

"Ernie!"

"He looks so much bigger standing up." It was true. The Bigfoot was even taller than the stuffed gorilla at the Museum of History and Industry. "He's got you beat by a couple of feet. How tall are you, Dad?"

His father yelled for help again. His mother came downstairs. "Oh, my God! George, are you all right?"

"Nancy, get my rifle. Quick."

The Bigfoot turned and took a good look at Ernie's mother. Ernie thought he almost looked glad to see her.

"What do you want your rifle for?" his mom asked his dad.

"Because I'm about to be eaten by a . . . by a . . ."

Ernie decided to help his father out. "Bigfoot, Dad. I think it's a Bigfoot for sure. What do you think, Mom?"

His mom agreed with him. Then Sarah came in and got all worked up about the way the Bigfoot smelled. Actually, Ernie kind of liked how he smelled. His dad got mad at Sarah. "Your father is about to be devoured by a wild, vicious, savage beast; your poor mother is obviously in a state of shock; and you complain about a smell. This is unbearable. Nancy! Do something!"

Ernie hadn't heard his dad yell so much at one time since last year's Super Bowl. He was really upset. Meanwhile, his mom started to sort of inch her way toward the sink, real slow, and they all watched her do it. She called out to his dad, "I think I know what to do, dear." His dad seemed real glad because he obviously didn't know what to do. What his mom did was corner the room deodorizer and start spraying it all around the room. It was called Glade and smelled just like the woods, only stronger. Ernie thought the Bigfoot kind of liked it.

Then Sarah let out one of her first-class Sarah shrieks. It was so loud even the Bigfoot stared at her. She moved toward the refrigerator, the creature, and the mess on the kitchen floor. Maybe the Bigfoot thought she was playing some kind of game. He watched her closely as she squatted down and reached for something right in the middle of the mess. Sarah picked up her grody old flowers that had been rotting in the refrigerator for months. The Bigfoot grabbed the box away from her. Ernie felt like cheering.

"Oh, Mom," Sarah wailed. "My corsage."

Then the Bigfoot did something really neat. He ate Sarah's stupid old corsage. Ernie wished he'd thought of it himself. It would have been worth the bellyache, just to see that look on Sarah's face. The Bigfoot apparently thought the flowers tasted just fine, even without hot fudge.

"My orchid. My beautiful orchid. It's eating my fifteenth birthday corsage. The one I've saved for months!" Ernie had to admire his sister's lung power, even if she did use it to complain all the time. Even the Bigfoot was impressed. He spat out the rest of her dumb orchid right then and there. It was too late, though. Sarah really let him have it.

"I was going to keep that flower for the rest of my life, but you ate it! I don't care how big and ugly and smelly you are, you can't go around eating other people's corsages. It was a *bad* thing you did. A bad, bad thing! Do you hear me?"

No way the Bigfoot couldn't hear. They could probably hear her downtown, the way she was carrying on. She certainly had his attention, Ernie had to hand her that. Then she started wagging her finger in its face, just like she always did to Ernie when she was really mad and trying to act like mom.

"Even if you *are* an animal, you can't go around acting like one in this house." Ernie thought the Bigfoot looked kind of sheepish, the way *he* always felt when his mother let him have it. The creature backed away from Sarah. But that wasn't enough for his sister. Oh, no. She threw back her head and let out a bloodcurdling scream. The Bigfoot looked her right in the eye and screamed back. He won. Sarah went running to her mother. His dad ordered them to evacuate the house.

Ernie thought the Bigfoot looked pretty confused. On his way out the door, Ernie stopped to explain. "She didn't mean it. All girls are weird, you know?" As his mother pushed him out into the yard, Ernie secretly hoped the creature would stay around long enough to give him some lessons in handling his big sister. With an ally like that, he'd never lose a fight again.

9

The Hendersons filed into the backyard. The predawn chill cooled Sarah down a little. Once she stopped being quite so angry, she realized her knees felt watery and weak. She'd just lambasted a Bigfoot. Well, he deserved it. That animal had worse manners than Ernie, and that was saying a lot.

"Boy, Sarah," Ernie said. "You really made him mad."

Sarah told her brother to shut up. Maybe if they were really lucky, the beast would eat the little creep or something. Their mother told them both to shut up. The whole family gathered at the picture window to watch the Bigfoot remodel their house.

First it was the living room door. Too low. The creature bumped its head when it tried to go through, so it just reached up, pushed, and raised the door frame a foot or two. No problem.

"Bummer," Ernie said.

His mom said, "Shouldn't we run?" Nobody ran.

Bigfoot moved on to the living room. The family scuttled around the side of the house to get a better view. They arrived in time to see the creature sampling leaves from a variety of their mother's fancy foreign plants. Even Ernie knew better than to mess with Mom's plants. The Bigfoot was munching them down like they were potato chips— betcha can't eat just one.

"George," their mom hollered, "those are my *passiflora corriacea*!"

The Bigfoot especially liked *passiflora corriacea*. He ate half the plant before he discovered the aquarium. So much for salad, on to the main course. He crouched down and eyed the goldfish. Through the glass sides of the tank, they could see him lick his lips. At that point, their mom broke the food chain. She knocked on the window. The creature stood up and gave them a dirty look. For a minute there, Sarah thought maybe he was going to smash through the glass and eat *them*, but then the beast dropped what was left of the *passiflora corriacea*, pot and all, into the aquarium and wandered off.

What'd caught its eye was their dad's pride and joy—the dead deer head with the fake eyes and big antlers that hung on the wall between the living room and the dining room. It was a ten-point buck, or something. Her dad thought it was a big deal, but Sarah thought it was gross. Whenever they ate dinner in the dining room, she made sure to sit with her back to it. Otherwise, it watched you eat with those sad plastic eyes. The Bigfoot tiptoed up and tried to pet it. When the deer didn't respond, he looked upset.

"Oh-oh," their father said.

Oh-oh was right. The Bigfoot wanted to find out what had happened to the rest of the deer. He smashed his fist through the wall and felt around the other side. No good. The Bigfoot had obviously never seen a deer without a rump before. He stood under the archway between the two rooms and looked on one side and then the other, like he thought maybe the deer was tricking him, moving back and forth, and he was going to catch it in the act. After a while, he either figured it out or decided he never would and gave up. Then it was time to see what he could do to improve the second floor. Even from outside, they could hear the stairs splintering when the Bigfoot stepped on them.

Dad wasn't too pleased. He said, "That's it," in the same voice he used when Sarah and Ernie were arguing and he wanted them to stop. It was a voice that meant business—you had five seconds to obey or lose your allowance for the week. He strode off toward the back of the house. By the time the rest of them got there, Dad was leaning their tallest ladder against the house. When it was steady, he cocked his rifle and started up.

"What's that for, George?" Mom said. "Why don't we just call someone?"

Dad kept right on climbing. "I know what I'm doing. I'm not going to stand around while some animal destroys our home."

Sometimes Ernie didn't know when to keep his mouth shut. This was one of them. "Dad, it's not an animal."

Dad was in no mood to be corrected for his choice of words. Mom hustled Sarah and Ernie back around the side of the house, where they couldn't get on his nerves. Sarah was glad. She didn't want to watch the showdown. "It if goes in my room," she said, "I'll definitely have to burn my clothes."

"I've got matches," Ernie volunteered. Sarah started to punch him in the stomach, but Mom pulled them close and told them to be quiet, please.

By the time George got to the top of the ladder, the creature was already in the master bedroom, fondling the mink stole Nancy's mother gave her. When the stole didn't wake up and start purring, the Bigfoot got upset. He gave the stole a good shake. This was as good a time as any. George raised the rifle, planted the butt on his shoulder. The high-powered scope brought the creature close enough that George could see the texture of his fur. Too bad about the window, but then, what was a little glass compared to an entire house? George leaned against the porch to brace himself. It was going to be an easy shot.

It was, until the ladder slipped a little and the barrel of his rifle tapped against the window glass. That was when the creature looked at him. Looked curious. Interested. Maybe a little afraid. Looked, in fact, all the ways George could imagine himself looking, if their situations were reversed. The scope's hairs crossed right in the middle of the creature's forehead. One shot and he'd be dead meat. George knew how to aim a rifle, all right. The trouble was, he couldn't shoot it. Not at something that looked so inquisitive, so intelligent, so . . . human.

He lowered the rifle. George Henderson, humanitarian. Okay. So he couldn't shoot it. Now what? He looked down to check his footing and found his family staring up at him. George looked away from their questioning faces. He started to climb down.

"George!" Nancy said.

"I'm okay," George said. His voice came out gruffer than he meant it to.

Nobody said anything as they watched him climb down. Sarah was glad he hadn't killed the Bigfoot. It wasn't that she had tender feelings about the stinky thing, but she hated the sight of blood and she didn't like to see her father playing Rambo. It was so uncouth. For once, even Ernie had the good sense to keep his comments to himself.

Almost as soon as Dad stepped off the bottom rung, they heard a tremendous crash. It came from inside the house. Before they could go investigate, the Bigfoot came marching out into the yard, cradling something dark and furry in its arms.

"Oh, God," Mom said. "It's mother's stole."

The creature crunched into the garden, trampling the tomato plants, and then knelt down and started to dig a hole. This was one strange animal. Sarah couldn't figure him out. "What's it doing, Mom?"

"It's burying Grandma's mink."

"This is too intense," Sarah said. It truly was. Something in her voice must have caught the creature's attention, because right then it stopped burying the mink and looked at their mom. Sarah and Ernie did, too.

Their mom looked guilty. "Well, I didn't kill the poor little things." She turned to the creature in the garden. "Stop looking at me that way!" The creature didn't stop looking. Their mom kept trying to explain. "Grandma didn't kill them. Some ranchers raised them, and then they killed them. They only did it because they knew someone would *buy* it." Mom stopped talking and looked embarrassed.

Sarah decided right then and there she was never ever going to have a fur coat, as long as she lived. Not even a fur collar. Not even earmuffs. The creature patted a mound of garden dirt smooth over the stole, so it could rest in peace.

While Bigfoot was busy administering last rites to half a dozen ranch minks, George addressed the family. "Quick! Everybody back in the house."

They all ran for the kitchen door. It was a good plan. Except the creature decided to come in with them. He didn't feel like hanging out in the kitchen, though. He marched on into the other room and ripped George's ten-point buck right off the wall, no by-your-leave or anything. He carried it out the back door to the pet cemetery where the kitchen garden used to be and started digging.

George realized that if he didn't move fast, every stuffed animal in the house was going to end up six feet deep. He asked Nancy to keep an eye on the gravedigger and hustled to the den. Down came the elk. Down came the moose. Down came the young buck and the cougar.

"George, he's coming back," Nancy called from the kitchen.

"Stall him! Show him the pasta maker!" George opened the closet door and unceremoniously stuffed his treasures inside. He hoped the Bigfoot was too unsophisticated to notice that the wall paint was darker where the heads used to be. He stashed the wolf. The closet was so full of dead animals he could barely shut the door.

"Company, George!" Nancy called out.

George caught up with the creature just as he was about to enter the den. He rubbed his hands together. "Well, that wraps up the old funeral, huh?" The creature's nose wrinkled as he sniffed the air, but George held firm in the doorway, and pretty soon the thing moved on to the next room. He peered into the workroom George and Nancy shared. George did his drawing there, while she planted and transplanted her pet plants. Nancy was not about to let Bigfoot sample any more horticultural delicacies. "Not in here," she said firmly. "George, he's not coming in here. This is my space."

George turned to the creature. "Sorry. That's her space."

The Bigfoot was evidently not familiar with the concept of personal space. He sauntered past Nancy and helped himself to a handful of tasty leaves. George whispered to Nancy, "Keep him in here."

"Are you kidding? He'll eat all my plants."

"So let him," George said. He raised a mime telephone to his ear and pretended to dial. Nancy got the message. She joined the Bigfoot at her potting table, picked up a scrawny coleanthus, and offered the pot to her guest. "Here. Try these. They are from the dime store."

The Bigfoot was no snob. He consumed the coleanthus and emitted a polite burp. In the doorway, Sarah clapped her hand to her brow. "I'm dying. This is death."

Behind his sister, Ernie said, "I know just the place for you. It's out back."

While Sarah was slugging her brother, George made for the living room phone, as stealthily as he could. 911 answered promptly. "Downtown, Sergeant Mancini."

Before George could respond, the Bigfoot ambled into the living room. For a moment, he looked curiously at George and the telephone, then began to browse around among the magazines and knickknacks. George cleared his throat and spoke quietly into the receiver.

"My name is George Henderson. I live at 437 Manning and I want to report . . ." George paused, looking for an accurate description. He settled on "something."

"What kind of something, Mr. Henderson?"

"A *big* something. My family is in danger."

"Mr. Henderson, do you have someone in your house? A burglar? A prowler?"

The creature dangled his long fingers in the fishtank. George lowered his voice. "Look, don't think I'm crazy, but it's Bigfoot, sergeant."

Even from downtown, he could hear Mancini's long exhalation. His voice changed from serious to seriously sarcastic. "Well, of course, pal. They sure can be a nuisance. Tell you what, Mr. Henderson. Run a hose on him, he'll melt right down."

The creature's hairy fingers closed around a goldfish. He plucked it deftly from the tank and popped it in his mouth. George bellowed, "Hey!"

"Ouch," Mancini said.

"Sorry, sergeant. Look, I hit a Bigfoot with my car. I thought it was dead. I was going to call you guys in the morning. But it must have been hungry, because I found it in the kitchen."

"Whoa. Back up a minute. You hit a Bigfoot with your car? In your kitchen?"

"No. I mean yes." George was getting seriously confused. And if he was confused, Mancini must be in far

worse shape. He tried again. "I'm under a lot of stress here.
I mean, it wasn't dead anymore. It just walked into our
kitchen. It was eating out of our refrigerator, then I thought
it was going to eat me, but it ate my daughter's corsage
instead, and then a *passiflora corr*—well, one of my wife's
exotic plants, and it just ate our goldfish." George was glad
he wasn't under oath. Nancy's look told him he was being
something less than coherent. Well, let her try to tell it
straight.

"And where is it now, Mr. Henderson?"

George wanted to give accurate testimony. The Bigfoot
was headed for the bathroom. "In the bathroom," George
reported.

"Of course, how stupid of me," Mancini said. Then his
voice got very no-nonsense. "Look, this has gone far
enough. Let me explain something to you. The charge for
creating a nuisance over the telephone isn't worth the
paperwork involved. So, let's say I believe you have a
Bigfoot in your house. First, we cordon off your neighborhood. Second, we evacuate your neighbors. Third, we'd
send a truckload of cops to deal with the thing."

George started to protest, but the crash from the bathroom stopped him. A few seconds later, the Bigfoot
emerged from the bathroom. He was carrying the medicine
cabinet and making faces at himself in the mirror. Meanwhile, the cop talked on.

"And I mean fully armed and ready, Mr. Henderson. So,
unless you want to be responsible for wrongfully turning
your neighborhood into a war zone, a charge that *is* well
worth the paperwork, I suggest you drop the whole thing
right now."

The Bigfoot held the medicine cabinet in his left hand.
With the fingers of his right, he lifted his upper lip to get a
better look at his teeth. He must have thought they looked
pretty good. He seemed to be smiling.

"A war zone," George said.

"Very well, then . . ."

"Huh? Oh, no sergeant. No Bigfoot here. Just a bad joke." George felt the eyes of his family on him. The Bigfoot looked, too. George had the feeling they thought he'd blown it. There was no telling what the policeman thought. George tried to undo the damage. "Look, I'm sorry. Actually, I'm not even George Henderson. Just a prank. I'm really sorry. Thanks for being so understanding. Thank you. You must have the wrong number. Goodbye." George talked as fast as he could and hung up even faster.

Nancy gave him one of those mocking looks he'd always hated. "If you aren't George Henderson, just who are you? Superman?"

Actually, George felt like the Lone Ranger. And he'd always believed policemen were his friends. Another childhood myth down the tubes. If the best they could do was send out a SWAT team to blow Bigfoot away, he was better off without their help. On to Plan B. There was only one problem—George had absolutely no idea what Plan B was.

He looked into the expectant faces of his family. Even the Bigfoot looked back with absolute attention. "We're on our own," George told them.

10

"I guess the cops aren't coming, huh, Dad," Ernie said. He was glad. The police would probably have taken the Bigfoot away, just when things were getting interesting. Now that Ernie wasn't afraid of the big guy anymore, he was looking forward to getting to know him better. Maybe they could keep him. Ernie imagined the Bigfoot walking him to school every day, waiting for him when the bell rang every afternoon. He could even come to all their baseball games. Like a mascot.

His father shook his head. "At least, I hope not."

From the expression on his dad's face, Ernie guessed this wasn't the right time to ask him if they could keep Bigfoot for a pet. When the phone rang, they all jumped. His dad answered.

"No Bigfoot here, sergeant. What? Oh, hello, Irene. Just fine. We had a wonderful time. You're what? No, wait . . ." His dad stared at the receiver. "She hung up. It was Irene. She's bringing Little Bob back."

Ernie's mother looked out the window. "It's the crack of dawn, George."

His father shrugged. "I couldn't stop her."

Ernie sympathized. Nobody could stop Mrs. Moffitt. He could never stop her from tousling his hair, or pinching his cheeks. She thought he was cute. Ernie thought she was too much. She was always on some weird new diet, and she always wanted to tell you all about it, whether you wanted to hear or not. Thanks to their next-door neighbor, Ernie was the only kid in fourth grade who knew exactly how many calories there were in eggplant pâté. Mrs. Moffitt never lost any weight, either. Ernie figured the only thing that would help would be sewing her mouth shut for a month or so.

His mom sprang into action. "I'll go meet her halfway."

It was too late. They could hear Mrs. Moffitt knocking and Little Bob barking outside the front door.

"Just take the dog and get rid of her," his dad said.

"Easy for you to say," his mom said. "This is Irene Moffitt, remember? Our live-in neighbor."

Little Bob was barking like crazy outside the door. The Bigfoot started for the door, like he was going to let him in, but then the doorbell rang. Bigfoot didn't know about doorbells. The ringing stopped him dead.

"Oh, my God," Ernie's dad said. "What are we going to do with this thing?" He looked to the Bigfoot. "No offense."

By this time, Ernie could see Mrs. Moffitt trying to peek in through the curtains on the window by the door. "It's no use hiding, Nancy. I know you're in there."

"I could take him up to my room," Ernie volunteered.

His mom looked at the smashed stairs and shook her head. "The basement," she said.

That suited Ernie. He didn't care where they were going, as long as he got the creature to himself for a while. He reached out and took the creature's hand. It was some big hand. Ernie tugged on it. "The basement. You'll love it down there. It's like a cave, only with a pool table." The Bigfoot started to follow him. Ernie turned back to his dad. "It's okay if I teach him to play pool isn't it, Dad?"

His father nodded. The doorbell rang again. Then Mrs. Moffitt popped up at the side window, snooping. The woman was a terrible snoop. His mother said so.

"Just a minute, Irene," Mom called out.

Sarah leaned against the wall like maybe she was going to faint or something. "This is it," she said. "The beginning of the end. Mrs. Moffitt will see it, the whole world will know, and I'll be a social outcast for the rest of my life. I'll go to the prom and the kids will throw pig's blood on me." She looked at their father. "Thank you, Dad."

"Cheer up," Ernie said. "You'd be a social outcast anyway. At least now you have an excuse."

"Mom," Sarah wailed, but Mom wasn't listening. Mrs. Moffitt knocked again, at the window this time.

"Come on, big guy," Ernie said. "We don't want her to see us." The Bigfoot stopped walking and looked curiously at the window. "No, no. You don't want to see her either," Ernie told him. "She's a creep." Ernie looked over his shoulder at his mother. She didn't like him bad-mouthing grown-ups, even if what he said was true, but this time she wasn't listening. She and George were too busy pulling the drapes shut.

Ernie led the Bigfoot into the kitchen. There was food and garbage all over the floor. As they passed the sink, the Bigfoot reached out and snared an African violet from the windowsill. He was about to munch it down when Ernie's mom caught him. "Oh, no, you don't." She looked around the mess and picked up a head of lettuce that had been in the refrigerator since before they went on vacation. It looked pretty sad, all brown and limp. "Here, eat this." Mom grabbed her plant and handed the lettuce to the Bigfoot. He stared at the wilted lettuce, sniffed it, then tossed it back on the floor. Ernie chuckled. This Bigfoot was nobody's fool.

"Hurry up, Ernie," his dad called. Ernie pulled the

creature toward the basement door. When he saw the steep steps with no railing, the Bigfoot stopped cold.

"It's okay," Ernie told him. "Come on, big guy. Follow me." Ernie raced down the stairs. He'd just reached the bottom when the Bigfoot arrived beside him, on his butt. The stairs rained down around them, and years of dust rose up. The Bigfoot sneezed. Ernie heard his mom calling from the top of the stairs. "We're okay, Mom," Ernie hollered. "It was just the stairs."

Dust settled like dandruff on the Bigfoot's dark fur. He sneezed again, at hurricane force. Ernie felt sneeze droplets spray his face. They fogged his glasses. "Sorry about the stairs," he said. "You know, if you're gonna stay around here, you might want to think about losing a little weight."

The Bigfoot didn't look too happy with this suggestion. Ernie punched his mammoth shoulder. "Joke," he said.

George slammed the basement door, while Nancy opened the kitchen door. Nancy winced at the sight of Irene's bathrobe. It was louder than a brass band. Her hair was still in curlers. She stood expectantly in the doorway, Little Bob in one hand and the week's mail in the other. Little Bob jumped down from Irene's arms and headed straight for the basement door.

"Lil Bob must be in heat," Irene said. "Every dog in the neighborhood's out there."

Nancy stuck her head out the door and saw it was true. There was a whole pack gathered in the backyard—little dogs, big dogs, you name it. Hard to believe that Irene had kept Little Bob for a week without noticing he was a boy. Nancy thanked God for small blessings. "Yeah," she said. "I guess we better take him . . . uh, her . . . to the vet." Nancy shut the kitchen door behind Irene and swooped down to pick up Little Bob. "Take it easy, little guy. Uh, little girl."

Sarah and George had fallen into a defensive line to block Irene. Nancy fell in beside them. Irene strained to see past them. Her nose wrinkled. "God! What is that smell?"

She stepped up to Nancy. Nancy moved aside, letting Irene see the kitchen in all its glory. "What the hell happened here?" Irene demanded.

"We were just defrosting the fridge," Nancy said. Discreetly, she elbowed George.

"Oh, yeah," he said. "Spoiled food. We had a little trouble moving it out."

George was such a champion of understatement. Still, Nancy couldn't come up with a better lie. She smiled nervously at their neighbor.

Irene surveyed the battle scene, then looked searchingly at the Hendersons. "Is everything okay with you kids?" They didn't have to answer, because Irene had already moved on to the next question. Now she was crouching down, searching through the wreckage on the floor. "Nan, I don't suppose you've got any peanut butter and brewer's yeast? I found a new diet . . ."

Nancy handed Little Bob to George and knelt beside Irene, searching. She thought they had some peanut butter. She hoped. "Sarah," she said, "how about taking Little Bob out of here?"

Sarah disappeared with the dog. After some serious digging, they managed to exhume a half-full jar of peanut butter. Nancy picked it up and read the label. "Crunchy. This is the best I can do. No yeast."

Irene seized the jar and clutched it to her flowered robe. "No matter. Got to go to the market for Tabasco and cod liver oil anyway." She patted George's stomach. "It's an energy diet. You might want to try it."

Accompanied by a loud cracking sound, the floor buckled upwards under George's feet, then collapsed. George responded to Irene's inquisitive look by dipping deep into a

kneebend. One, two, three. "Exercise, Irene. That's the
only diet. Plenty of energy here." Up and down he went
until the floor leveled out. Nancy went to stand beside him
and flashed their neighbor her biggest smile.

Irene sniffed the air. "Probably rotten meat or eggs."

"Just what we thought," George said. "Well, no use
standing here breathing it."

"Yeah," Nancy said. "Sure glad we could be of help,
Irene. And thanks so much for taking care of Little Bob. He
just hates camping."

"No problem," Irene said. She and the peanut butter
made for the door. George smile hopefully at Nancy. Just
then the crash came.

Bigfoot loved the basement. He studied the Maytags for a
while and then sat down on one. Luckily it was a heavy-
duty dryer. The top hardly caved in at all. "Not too soft,
huh?" Ernie said. He took the creature's hand again.
"Come on, there's something I wanna show you."

What Ernie had in mind was the pool table, but the
creature spotted the hot water heater first. Ernie's dad had
wrapped it with insulation to save electricity. Ernie had to
admit it looked like a fat lady with no head. The Bigfoot
thought so, too. He put his big arms around her and
squeezed. Suddenly, the fat lady had a waist. Then he lifted
her up. Ernie saw the pipes that ran up from the top of the
tank squish like cooked spaghetti against the ceiling. He
wasn't sure exactly where the pipes came out upstairs,
but . . . then he noticed the pool that was forming around
their feet. "You better put it down now," he advised.

The creature gave Ernie a look that said "Why?"

"It's the water heater," Ernie explained. "No hot water,
no baths. I wouldn't mind, but my mom would probably get
real mad."

The creature dropped the heater. Ernie could hear his mom screaming. "Ernie! Oh my god!"

He called up to her. "Yo! It's okay. Everything's okay."

They'd just finished explaining to Irene that Ernie had his science project in the basement when water started to pour out of the kitchen taps. It poured full blast, hit the dishes in the sink and shot up like fountains. George worked the faucets, trying to shut them off.

"So, when are we going to play cards?" Irene asked.

"Saturday, I suppose," Nancy said. She tried to sound casual. It sure was hard to sound casual with a flood in the kitchen. "Same as always," she said.

Ernie dumped a whole laundry basket full of dirty towels over on top of the place where the water was coming in, to slow down the flood. By the time he'd done that, Bigfoot had discovered the furnace. He especially liked those big round metal tubes that carried the heat around the house, so much so he decided it would be fun to swing from them. Ernie could hardly blame him—he'd always wanted to try it himself. But the creature outweighed Ernie by a good three hundred pounds. The duct gave like it was made of cardboard, leaving a big hole gaping in the ceiling. Curious as ever, the Bigfoot stuck his hairy hand inside.

Ernie looked around the basement. It looked almost as bad as the kitchen. And his mother said *he* was a slob. "Oh, brother," he said to the creature. "I hope they don't blame me for this."

Nancy almost had Irene backed out the kitchen door when the door came flying off the laundry chute beside it. A low growl echoed up from the depths of the basement. From the laundry chute emerged a large, hairy hand.

Nancy flung open a cabinet door to block Irene's view, then collected every dishtowel in grabbing distance and stuffed them, and the hand, down the chute.

"What was that all about?" Irene wanted to know.

Nancy was at a loss, but George came through. "Ernie's project. The one we were telling you about. He's got one of those, uh, gerbils."

"Oh, yes!" Nancy joined in. "It's such a cute little thing. Kind of like a . . ."

George contributed "Hamster." Nancy saw the hand emerge again. Inconspicuously as possible, she corned the last of her African violets and put it in the Bigfoot's hand. The hand withdrew. "But bigger than your average gerbil," Nancy said. "And always hungry."

"Nothing more than rats getting a lucky shake from society, if you ask me," Irene said. She looked appraisingly at George and Nancy, then smiled. "I know where you are if I need you." Grasping the peanut butter, she left at last.

Ernie figured Mrs. Moffitt must have finally gone home. Just in the nick of time, too, while they still had some basement left. He went to where the stairs used to be and found his father looking down at him. His mother appeared beside him. "What was all that racket?" she wanted to know.

"Well, uh, I was trying to teach him to play pool. Only I guess he got curious about where the little balls went, you know. I think he thought they went up."

Ernie's father lay down on the floor and reached his hands down to Ernie. "Grab my arms, son, and I'll pull you up."

Ernie tried to grab, but something was too short—either Ernie or his father's arms. Ernie turned to the Bigfoot. "Hey, fella, how about a lift?" The Bigfoot's hands closed gently around Ernie's waist. Seconds later, he was flying up toward his dad. When he got level with the door frame, his mom grabbed him and pulled him into the kitchen. "Thanks," Ernie hollered down.

His dad was still lying on his belly when the Bigfoot chinned himself on the kitchen floor. For a minute, they were eyeball to eyeball. Ernie thought he saw the creature smile.

11

"Sooooup is good fooooood," a syrupy voice crooned, six times louder than anybody should be allowed to sing, except in the shower. George winced. That meant it was 6:45, the time he normally hit the kitchen to make the morning coffee. It also meant that nobody had remembered to turn the timer off before they went on vacation. The TV had been playing to an empty house all week.

"Turn that thing off," George begged. He never could understand why they advertised things like soup in the morning, when all you wanted was a cup of coffee. It made him sick to think of soup so early.

Nancy turned off the TV and George settled back to enjoy the silence. No telling how long it would last. Not long. He remembered it was Monday. "Oh, my God. What am I going to do about work?"

"That's easy," Nancy said. "You're going to call in sick."

"Can I be sick too?" Ernie asked.

"I think you and Sarah would be safer at school."

"Awww." Then Ernie brightened. "At least I can tell all the kids my dad creamed a Bigfoot."

That was all George needed. "You're both sick," he said. "We're all sick. Nobody's going anywhere until we figure out what to do." He looked toward the basement, where the creature had retreated after his peep into the kitchen. Except for the distant sound of water dripping, all was quiet. He called it quiet. What was a little water. "Well, at least for now, it seems to be trapped down there."

But George was wrong. The creature picked that moment to untrap itself. Must have been lonely. It chinned itself on the threshold as easily as Ernie might have on the playground bars. Little Bob sped across the linoleum at full tilt, barking his head off at the invader. The mutt was braver than he was smart. He raced right up to the creature's giant jaws, proclaiming his territory. When the creature roared back, Little Bob went into a backward skid that sent him smack into the dishwasher. The creature stood up and surveyed the scene.

Sarah came racing into the kitchen, apologizing for losing Little Bob. "It's okay," George said. "She's gone." He turned to find the creature looking expectantly at him. "How you doing?" George asked.

The creature cocked his head and looked at George. He answered the question with a low, throaty sound, that seemed pleasant enough.

Just then, Little Bob attacked again. He made for the creature, yipping like mad, jumping higher than George had ever seen him leap, even for treats. The creature looked annoyed. He extended his hand and plucked Little Bob right out of the air. "George," Nancy whispered, but George shook his head. The creature's grip was gentle as he held the squirming, yapping dog in front of him. He was equally gentle when he closed his other hand around Little Bob's muzzle. Bob was persistent, even if he was a nuisance. He kept on barking inside the creature's palm.

The creature looked directly at George. Plain as day, his look said, "How do you stand it? Is he always like this?"

George shrugged. Beats me.

Suddenly it struck him that he was communicating with

the creature. They'd just exchanged two sentences, clearly as if they'd spoken. The Bigfoot *was* intelligent. George looked to the rest of his family, to see if they'd noticed. They had. They were all looking at George as if he were crazy, all except for Ernie, who was grinning.

Nancy stepped toward the creature then, locked eyes with him, reached out and took Little Bob in her own hands. She stroked and murmured reassurances to the dog until he quieted down and settled peacefully into the crook of her arm. The Bigfoot watched closely. When Little Bob was quiet at last, he reached out and gently patted the dog's head. Safe with Nancy, Little Bob didn't even growl.

Nancy shifted Little Bob and reached out to take the creature's hand. "Look, George, he's hurt himself."

"Musta been when he tried to chin himself on the heating pipes," Ernie said.

The Bigfoot tried to pull his hand away, but Nancy held on tight. "Ernie, get the first-aid kit, would you?" To the Bigfoot she spoke in a lower voice. "It's okay, fella, we'll have you fixed up in no time." The creature surrendered himself to Nancy's care. George smiled. If he was crazy, at least he wasn't alone.

Nancy looked around for a place for Bigfoot to sit while she worked on his injured hand. The chairs were too fragile, and she didn't want to risk the counters. Finally, she settled him on the kitchen floor, with his back against the refrigerator for support. Nancy was glad to see his cuts weren't too deep. He was patient while she washed them out with soap and water.

Ernie returned with the first-aid kit. After a week's camping, it was hopelessly disorganized. The only antiseptic Nancy could find was iodine. "Are you sure we don't have anything that doesn't sting?"

"Sarah used up all the Bactine on her mosquito bites," Ernie said. He handed his mother the iodine. "This is it."

Nancy spoke soft and low to the Bigfoot, a kind of singing. She recognized the voice as one she hadn't used much since her kids got older. "Now this might hurt, just a little."

The creature was nearly hypnotized into trust when Ernie piped up. "What I do is just close my eyes real tight, like this." He demonstrated the technique.

Nancy smiled. Ernie *did* do that when he was the patient. He had since he was a toddler. She soaked a gauze pad with iodine and took the creature's hand. He looked at her sheepishly, then squeezed his eyes shut tight. "It's okay, it's okay," Nancy crooned. Still, she felt the creature's hand wince when the iodine stung his cuts. "Okay, it's okay, easy boy. It's okay."

"Does this mean we can keep him?" Ernie asked, in a voice that was unusually quiet for Ernie.

"Grow up!" Sarah said.

George said, "Maybe . . . I don't know." He said it with the hint of a question mark at the end.

Nancy looked up from her doctoring. "You don't know? The answer's no. Now you know."

"It was just so different when he was dead," George mused.

Nancy looked sharply at him. "No, George. *You* were different. And I'm convinced it wasn't dead."

Sarah spoke up. "I thought we were going to sell it and get rich."

"Let's *keep* it and get rich," Ernie suggested.

"I can't *believe* this family," Nancy said. What she couldn't believe was their insensitivity. Oh, sure, she was always the bleeding heart, always the soft one, but somebody had to be. Enough was enough. The Bigfoot growled, and Nancy realized she'd been playing too rough with the iodine. "I'm sorry," she told him. She stopped dabbing and let her family have it. "We're talking about a living, breathing being here. It might even be some kind of person."

"It's a Bigfoot person," Ernie said. He seemed eager to redeem himself. Nancy smiled faintly to herself. Maybe there was hope for her son yet. Just a glimmer.

"We don't know what it is," George said. "We don't even know if it's male or female."

"It's definitely male," Sarah said.

"How could you tell?" Nancy asked. Immediately, she regretted the question. "Never mind," she said. "I don't want to know."

As she rose, Nancy raised an eyebrow at George, as if to say, Did you catch that? His face told her he hadn't; his mind was a million miles away. Slowly, he spoke. "Nan, I don't know how, but we've got to find a way to keep this thing. It's worth big bucks. Don't you see? This is a ticket to a better life."

What Nancy saw was trouble, for everyone involved. What *was* George thinking of? Sometimes, big as he was, he was as much a little kid as Ernie. She spoke to her husband as she might have to her son. "A better life for whom? What about his life?"

Her plea for common sense was lost on George. He was still building castles in the clouds. "I'm thinking about us, Nan. I just need time to figure a way . . ." His voice trailed off. For a moment, he was silent, figuring. Then he looked speculatively at the creature. "At least he's safe here," George said, and Nancy sighed.

12

LaFleur was pleased at the screech of his tires as he pulled into the parking lot of the Bigfoot Museum. He liked to make an entrance. The place was a dump—in even worse need of paint than the last time he'd stopped. Well, that might be changing soon. LaFleur patted the pocket of his hunting vest and climbed out of the cab.

Old Doc Wrightwood pretended he hadn't heard Jacques coming. He too looked shabbier than last time, if that were possible, tired and tattered. Jacques thought he was even wearing the same clothes, an ancient flannel shirt and pants that bagged around his thin legs. "It's an ill wind," Doc greeted him.

"Bonjour to you. You won't find the wind so ill when you see what it's brought you." With that, Jacques pulled the baggie out of his vest pocket and waved it at the old man.

"You taken to selling dope?" Wrightwood asked him.

"What would you say to Sasquatch hairs?" With a flourish, Jacques handed the bag to Wrightwood. "The real thing. You shouldn't have given up, Doc."

"We may be old, Jocko, but we still aren't friends." Doc examined the contents of the baggie for a moment, then turned to one of the tacky bear-fur Bigfoot statues he sold for souvenirs and snatched out a few hairs. "And the only difference between these and those is that I get a buck a strand for mine."

LaFleur snatched back his baggie and waved it under the old man's nose. "These are real, Doc! I chased a set of tracks that ran for two, three miles."

Wrightwood's canny old eyes narrowed. "Okay, Jock. If you've got castings, I'll buy 'em. But let's keep the price on the ground."

Doc wandered off among the claptrap. Jacques followed. "For Pete's sake! I almost had him. I was that close." He handed the baggie back to LaFleur. LaFleur shook it under Doc's nose. "These are real. I almost had him. I was that close."

"Yeah? And then what happened? Your gun jam? Or maybe a change of heart. You had him in your sights and you couldn't do it? What's the story this time?"

"I think he was hit by a car," Jacques said.

"Well, then. That should have made it easy."

"I know," Jacques mused. "But there was no trace, no tracks. Nothing. It just vanished."

Doc Wrightwood snorted. "Well, Jocko, it's like I tell my customers—Bigfoot eat their dead."

"I don't know why the hell I bother." LaFleur spat out the words.

"Because you figure I'm the only one who deep-down wants to believe you." Wrightwood set his jaw and looked Jacques in the eye. "But I don't. Not anymore."

LaFleur headed for the door. He was angry with himself for coming at all. Wrightwood always made him mad, and this time was no exception. "You know the difference between you and me, old man?"

"Where shall I start?" Doc shot him a sour grin. "With your famous quote: 'If the only way to prove an endangered species exists is by killing one, I would not hesitate to pull the trigger.' The difference, Jocko, is philosophy. That's with a 'P.' "

Pompous old goat. Jacques seethed with aggravation. "You can throw around all the two-dollar words you want, but the answer is simple. Guts. We both spent our whole lives chasing after that beast, and we both had to stare at ourselves in the mirror every morning and say, 'I'm not a fool.' The difference between us is—you blinked."

"Or finally opened my eyes."

Smug old fool. Jacques was going to enjoy showing him. He was going to enjoy it a *lot*. "We'll find out soon enough," he said. It was both a promise and a threat.

"Go for it, Jock," Doc said. "Raise a ruckus. God knows, I could use the business." He turned away from Jacques.

The sight of his stooped shoulders inside the faded flannel shirt made Jacques even more exasperated. How many years was it now they had been baiting each other? Decades. And yet, there was no respect between them, no admiration. All they shared was an obsession. It was enough to keep them bickering for thirty years. Jacques smiled grimly to himself. Soon the long argument would be over. And he was going to win.

He looked at his watch. Just time to make it to Seattle, provided he didn't get snarled up in traffic. "I have to go now," he said to Doc. "Au revoir."

"Same to you, Jocko," the old man said.

Traffic was good to him. No breakdowns on the freeway. No accidents. Downtown Jacques wasted no time looking for a parking meter. This time he treated himself to a lot. It was ten minutes to five when he arrived, panting, in the Washington State License Bureau.

The clerk in her bureaucrat's cage was about twenty-five, with fingernails too long to be real and a look of limited intelligence. Jacques spilled out the story he'd been practicing. "I was driving along the freeway, and all of a sudden, I see an old Army buddy in the fast lane. I haven't seen my friend in thirty, forty years. Not since Okinawa. I honked my horn, I waved my arms, but he didn't see me. Then the idea came to me. His license plate!"

"You got the number?"

Jacques handed her a neatly folded piece of paper. "Here it is."

The clerk took it, then began to type something on her computer terminal. Jacques couldn't believe it was going to be so easy. He was afraid that only policemen and insurance companies were allowed to trace parties through their license plates. That and maybe bill collectors. The clerk hadn't even listened to his elaborate lie.

Only a few seconds after the clerk punched in the numbers, the computer responded with a rapid rat-a-tat-tat. When it fell silent, the clerk ripped off the print out and handed it to Jacques. "That'll be ten bucks," she said.

LaFleur handed over the cash and looked down at the paper she'd given him. The car was a 1971 four-door station wagon, registered to George F. Henderson. LaFleur couldn't believe his luck. Henderson lived right here in Seattle. Jacques chuckled under his breath as he left the License Bureau. "*Bon soir, M. Henderson,*" he said. "*Comment ça va?*"

13

George stood by the phone and tried to think sick for a few minutes before he dialed. He was calling early, in hopes his father hadn't arrived yet, but it was the old man himself who answered. George wasn't sure his dad bought his story about "a touch of the flu—or maybe it was something we ate."

"Well, take care of yourself," his father said. "Casting rods go on sale tomorrow. I need you here."

"I'm headed back to bed right now," George assured him. "I'm sure this will blow over soon."

"It better," his dad said. He hung up.

"So how's old Rough and Ready?" Nancy asked.

"Let's put it this way," George said. "I'm glad he couldn't see my face. I never could put anything over on him, you know. That guy can make me feel like I'm still ten years old."

Nancy smiled sympathetically. "So, are you feeling better, dear?"

George looked around the kitchen and sighed. "Nothing a couple thousand bucks' worth of carpentry wouldn't cure."

"Cheer up," Nancy said. "You've got all day to work on it."

"Actually," George told her, "I really was thinking about going back to bed. You know how I hate to lie."

Nancy let fly with the dishrag she'd been using to mop out the refrigerator. "Don't even consider it," she said. "Not when there's no hot water."

"No what?"

"Read my lips," Nancy said. She spoke slowly and loudly, as she would to a small child or a dumb animal. "*No. Hot. Water.*"

George groaned. Nancy continued in her dog trainer mode. "*We. Need. Hot. Water.*"

"I'll have a look downstairs," George told her. "As soon as I figure out how to *get* downstairs. By the way, where's our house guest?"

"With Ernie," Nancy said. She consulted the kitchen clock. "I think they're watching *Sesame Street*. Ernie thought Bigfoot might get a kick out of seeing Big Bird."

George wished he'd worn his waders into the basement. Already his Nikes were wet and squishy inside. The hot water heater had been totally uprooted. It was pinched in at the middle and lying on its side. In the basement gloom, it closely resembled a headless corpse. "Sorry about that, old girl," George mumbled. "No showers for a while."

Cautiously, he moved the mound of soggy bath towels and uncovered the source of the underground spring. George was a pretty good handyman—he'd installed the storm windows by himself and built Nancy's greenhouse—but this job was beyond him. It called for a professional. The best he could do was shut the water off until the plumber came. As he battled the rusty valves with his wrench, George tried to remember what their homeowner's policy said about natural disasters.

When he'd done what he could to restore order in the basement, George sat up his painter's ladder and climbed into the kitchen. "I've got good news and bad news," he told Nancy.

"Tell me the good news first," she said.

"Okay. We've still got a basement."

"And the bad news?"

"We've got a pool."

Sarah stormed into the kitchen. She was still wearing her bathrobe, and her hair looked like a Caesar salad, tossed and oiled, "Daddy," she wailed. "What's wrong with the shower? When I tried to turn the water on, nothing happened."

"That's a relief," George said. "I guess I found the shutoff valve."

"The shutoff valve! Daddy, I just put Damage Pak Twenty-Minute Conditioning Treatment on my hair. What am I going to do?"

"Have very well-conditioned hair, I guess," George said.

Sarah turned to her mother. Nancy turned to George. "You could have warned us first," she said.

George counted to ten, then twenty, before he spoke. "I'm sorry," he said.

"You should be," Sarah said. "How am I ever going to get this gunk out of my hair?"

"You could turn on the sprinklers," George suggested. "I think we've still got water outside."

Sarah glowered at her father and marched out the back door.

George had just finished patching the wall between the living and dining rooms when Nancy called the family to lunch. Bigfoot followed Ernie into the kitchen, sniffing the air. When Ernie and George pulled out their chairs, the Bigfoot mimicked them. He was about to sit down when Nancy caught him. "No," she shrieked, then lowered her voice. "I mean, you sit over there." She pointed to a spot on the floor.

The Bigfoot looked offended. Ernie patted his arm. "I'll sit by you," he said. "That's okay, isn't it, Mom?"

"As long as it keeps him happy," Nancy sighed. Ernie and Bigfoot sat on the floor. Nancy put steaming bowls before them. "Alphabet soup," she said. "Don't worry. It's vegetarian."

Nancy had put the creature's lunch in a serving bowl, but it still looked absurdly dainty in his hands. He lifted the bowl to drink, but the rising steam tickled his nose. "It fogs up *my* glasses," Ernie told him. "You've got to wait for it to cool down."

Sarah came late to lunch, a towel wrapped around her head. "Mom, does he have to eat in the kitchen?"

"I thought about taking him to McDonald's," Nancy said, "but I was afraid he'd try to climb the golden arches."

"That's not funny, Mom," Sarah said.

"Thanks, Sarah," Nancy said. "I won't use it on the Carson show."

"First, you slurp it in like this," Ernie instructed. "Then when all the soup's gone, you can play with the letters." Ernie slurped energetically, they began to fish out the pasta alphabet. He arranged the limp letters on his napkin. "Look, I've almost got your name." He addressed the rest of the family. "Who's got an extra 'O'?"

"Sorry, son," George said. "I just ate all my vowels."

"Sarah?" Ernie asked.

"Forget it, Ernie," Sarah said.

The Bigfoot raised his bowl and drank his soup in one great gurgle. Then he scooped up all the noodles in the bottom and offered them to Ernie. "Thanks," Ernie said. "But you squished them."

The fact that Ernie and the Bigfoot were communicating wasn't lost on George. The creature was obviously intelligent. He learned fast. As George spooned his soup, an idea began to take shape. By the time he swallowed his last consonant, it was a full-blown scheme. Now all he had to do was find a way to spend some time alone with Bigfoot.

Luck was on his side. The phone rang. "Look, Irene," Nancy said, "why don't I come over there? George isn't feeling well, and things are still a little crazy around here . . ." When she hung up, she looked apologetically at George. "You don't mind, do you? I figured it was better to head her off at the pass."

"Good thinking," George said. "You go ahead. And don't worry about a thing, Nan. I'll hold down the fort."

"You're looking kind of stressed out, Nan," Irene said. "Why don't you try some of this?" She pointed to the frothy light-brown stuff in the blender. "It'll make you feel like a million bucks."

"Thanks," Nancy said, "but I just ate."

"What?" Irene asked.

"What what?"

"What did you eat?"

"Alphabet soup."

"Nancy, Nancy. I can't believe you feed your family that junk. It's full of chemicals."

"George is allergic to brewer's yeast," Nancy said. "I'll just have a cup of coffee, if you don't mind."

They settled at the kitchen table. Irene was full of questions: What was wrong with George? (Just a touch of indigestion.) How was their vacation? (Great, just great.) You kids didn't have a fight or anything, did you? (Who us? We never fight.) Nancy finally found a way to stop the interrogation. She asked Irene to fill her in on all the latest developments on *General Hospital*. It was a stroke of genius.

Irene was off and running.

Two hours later, Nancy managed to escape. Safe inside the kitchen, she leaned against the door and let out a long sigh. George was hard at work, trying to repair the doorway to the dining room. He flashed her an eager grin. "Ready to see something?"

"Give me a minute. Irene just ran two weeks of soaps by me. You'd think they were her relatives, the way she carries on. But I asked for it. It was better than the third degree. Oh, and she invited us out tonight. Dinner and bowling." Nancy smiled hopefully at George. "I said no. Told her you had something to drop off. Don't you?"

George gave her the cat-digesting-canary grin that reminded her of Ernie. "Don't be so sure. You just might change your mind when you see this."

"Where *is* our guest?" Nancy asked.

"Ernie's showing him the bathroom."

Nancy was sorry she asked. She used to like their bathroom. George motioned her to follow him into the living room. Sarah was engaged in a meaningful relationship with the telephone receiver. When she saw Nancy, she covered the mouthpiece. "I feel like a prisoner, Mom. Can I go out?"

George shook his head. "No. You're home sick. Besides, I don't want you to miss this."

"Sasha? My dad's being Attila the Hun. I can't go."

Ernie and the creature emerged from the bathroom. Ernie shut the door carefully behind them. Nancy took it for a bad sign. Ernie never remembered to shut a door.

"How'd he do?" George asked.

Ernie's expression was not encouraging. "C-minus, D-plus. I'd recommend using the upstairs john for the next couple of years."

Nancy wanted to assess the damage. She headed for the bathroom, but Ernie stepped in front of the door. "Trust me, Mom. You've got your whole life ahead of you."

Nancy was not so sure. She wanted to know the worst, but George was bouncing up and down like a carnival barker. "Okay, okay, everybody. Your attention, please. We"—he pointed to the creature—"have something to show you. But first, I want you to think about this for a moment. Us. Life. Time."

For a moment, Nancy worried about George. It wasn't like him to turn philosophical in the middle of a family crisis. Sarah and Ernie stared blankly at their father. They weren't prepared to contemplate life's mysteries right then, either.

George gaped back at them. "Magazines? You know? Cover stories. I mean you could be looking at old Dad here on the Carson show, for heaven's sakes. Okay, you'll see. Just watch." With that, he reached in his pocket, brought out a sugar cube, and held it up in front of Bigfoot. The creature went for it. George raised his hand, palm out, like a schoolboy patrol. The creature stopped dead.

George beamed at the family. "We started with something simple, but I think you'll see there's no stopping him." Again, George raised the sugar cube.

Tilt. Mistake. All Nancy's warning lights were flashing. Still, when George looked at her to see if she was watching, he seemed so proud of himself, so eager to please, that Nancy tried to smile.

"Sit!" George commanded. "Sit!"

The creature thought about it for a second or two. Then he sat. His method of sitting consisted of kicking his legs straight out in front and letting his butt fall where it would. In this case, it landed on the sofa. The sofa would never be the same.

"That's great, Dad!" Ernie was impressed. Sarah dropped the telephone. She looked as appalled as Nancy felt. George shrugged. The creature stood up and looked at the sagging couch.

"You taught him to sit!" Ernie enthused.

He'd said the magic word. The creature sat. He sat on the coffee table this time. The coffee table wasn't quite up to the excitement. It splintered like kindling into a sorry heap.

George raced into the kitchen and returned with a whole box of sugar cubes. He offered them all to Bigfoot. "Enough! Here! Don't sit."

Either the creature wasn't quite fluent in English yet, or he didn't hear the "don't." He sat on the lamp. It was Nancy's favorite lamp. She used to like the end table it sat on, too. Now both were pulverized. George looked like he knew just how Frankenstein felt when his monster got out of hand. He raced up to the Bigfoot, begging, "Stay! Stay!"

The Bigfoot stayed. Nancy thought he looked proud of himself. She might have laughed at the "yes, master" look he gave George, if only she hadn't been so tempted to cry about her furniture.

Ernie was enthralled by the performance. "That was outstanding, Dad!" George winced at his son's praise.

Nancy turned to George. "If I could have a word with you before the Carson show calls?" She motioned him toward the kitchen. George looked a little hangdog as he followed her. Behind them, in the living room, she could hear Sarah returning to her phone, while Ernie invited Bigfoot to catch some cable TV. "Might be something R-rated on," he told the creature. Under the circumstances, Nancy couldn't decide which would be safer, sex or violence.

When they were alone in the kitchen, Nancy counted to ten but it didn't help. She was still mad. George should have been glad she didn't yell at him in front of the kids. They'd agreed a long time ago to present a united front. Well, she'd kept her part of the bargain but now, by God, she was going to let him have it.

"George Henderson! What on earth's the matter with

you? This is our home! Our stuff. George! You're acting like a crazy person."

George seemed to know he had it coming. He took it well and answered quietly. "That wasn't supposed to happen."

Nancy was beyond apologies. She wanted action. "This whole thing wasn't supposed to happen, but it did. And now we have to do the right thing."

The right thing was totally obvious to her, but it seemed to elude George. "I know it seems bad," he said, "but just give me a week."

"George! We don't have enough house for two days. It doesn't fit here. And it doesn't fit in our lives. Now do the right thing. Think about *him*." Nancy was just hitting her stride, about to get eloquent about the right thing. George would have to listen. She *was* right, and he must know it. No matter what crazy illusions of fame and fortune had temporarily misguided him, her husband was not a fool. Nancy hoped he was not a fool.

Ernie came sailing in, in mid-lecture. "Mom! Dad! Hurry! This is great."

Nancy looked at George. He looked at her. In the face of impending disaster, they were back on the same team. Warily, they followed Ernie into the living room.

In kingly fashion, the Bigfoot reclined in George's La-Z-Boy. His big feet hung over the end and rested on the ottoman. His eyes were glued to the television screen. There, in living color, a younger version of the President of the United States was conversing with a chimpanzee.

"It's called *Bedtime for Bonzo*," Ernie said. "He really likes the monkey."

"He has good taste, then," Nancy said. "The monkey is the better actor."

"Now watch this," Ernie said. He dipped a Doritos into the plastic tub of clam dip and popped it in his mouth. The Bigfoot plucked a yellow leaf from Nancy's ficus tree, dipped it and ate. "Cool, huh?" Ernie said. "He didn't care for the blue cheese."

Ernie pointed to the living room wall, where the contents of a pint of blue cheese dip were slowly sliding down. As they watched the Roquefort ooze onto the carpet, Bigfoot leaned forward to cop another snack. The chair collapsed under him. Not quickly, not even noisily, but in a kind of graceful slow motion, George's recliner, his favorite chair, the chair from which he'd watched something like two million televised sporting events, gave up the ghost. For a moment, the Bigfoot lay spraddled on his back like a giant furry beetle, then, rolling to his knees, he freed himself and settled cross-legged in front of the TV.

George's face looked as decimated as the recliner. Now that her point was made, Nancy felt sorry for him. She was sure his head had been full of beautiful dreams. With a surge of real affection, she put her arm around the big lug and kissed him. Poor dear George.

"Okay, you're right," he said. "I'll take him back. But this might not be so easy."

Just then the Bigfoot laughed out loud. Nancy looked to the television in time to see Bonzo making a monkey out of the future President.

"I think he likes it here," George said.

14

Ernie promised himself he would never be a grown-up. Grown-ups were stupid. They did bad things. His grown-up mother and grown-up father were going to take the Bigfoot back to the woods. He tried and tried to talk some sense into them, but they hardly listened. All they did was give him those dumb grown-up smiles and pat his head. Ernie couldn't stand it. And his jerk of a sister was on their side. Of course, she was half grown-up herself. Much as he hated to admit it.

Ernie tried to keep the creature happy while they waited around for dark. They watched some more TV. They listened to records. Ernie showed the Bigfoot how to dance. Mom wouldn't let them go outside, or they could have shot some hoop in the driveway. With a little practice, the creature would have an awesome slam dunk. After it was dark, they had to wait some more, for Mrs. Moffitt to leave for the bowling alley. Finally, he heard her car start up.

His mom turned from the window. "All clear. It's time, Ernie."

Ernie gave it one last shot. "How about if he stays in my room? I don't mind this kind of destruction."

His mom's look told him she wasn't willing to negotiate. Ernie took the Bigfoot's big warm hand in his and led him out through the kitchen onto the back proch. The car was ready and waiting.

Mom turned to the Bigfoot. "You remember this, don't you? Your favorite station wagon. It's nicer inside."

Her voice was all syrupy and reassuring, the same voice she used in the doctor's office just before the nurse would sink her shot needle in Ernie's arm. The Bigfoot was suspicious. He wasn't going near the car.

Ernie's dad was crouched in front, trying to tie the bumper back on with baling wire. A mountain of junk food, the kind they usually didn't get to eat, sat on the hood. Mom nudged Ernie. He nudged the Bigfoot. Together they moved toward the car. As soon as the neighborhood dog pack caught wind of the creature, they gathered at the fence. Dad looked up and gave the Bigfoot a phony smile. "Hungry?" he said. "We're . . . uh . . . we're going to have a little party."

"Yeah," Ernie said. "A goodbye party."

Now his dad gave him a phony smile. Ernie wasn't buying it.

The creature studied his dad's repair job. He leaned down and shook the bumper, then ripped it off the car. His dad gritted his teeth and smiled again. "Ah, plan B. No problem," Dad said. Ernie wished his face would crack. It ought to be illegal to smile when you didn't really mean it.

The Bigfoot lifted up the bumper as if it was light as a chopstick, which to him, it probably was, and sent it flying over the hedge. A few seconds later they heard the *splash*. Without even looking, he'd hit the Moffitt's pool. "See what we're going to be missing?" Ernie said.

His dad wiped his hands on his pants. "Well, let's eat. Nancy? Ern?" He turned to the Bigfoot. "How about a burger?"

Ernie grabbed a fish sandwich from the pile on the car and passed a burger to his mom. Food always made him feel better. Dad unwrapped a burger and held it out to the Bigfoot. The Bigfoot took it, smelled it, then peeled off the top bun. Underneath the lettuce and tomato he found the hamburger. It didn't look too appetizing when he held it up between two of his big fingers—almost but not quite enough to spoil Ernie's appetite. Bigfoot's nose wrinkled like he smelled something dead. He roared at the hamburger patty, then threw it to the pack of the dogs outside the fence. They dove for it.

"Right!" Dad said. "Yours was the fish."

He snatched the fishwich Ernie'd just opened and handed it to the creature. "These are for him," Dad said. "The burgers are for you."

There were a honking lot of burgers on the hood. Ernie felt his stomach lurch, especially after the burger autopsy the creature had just performed. Bigfoot liked fish better, too. He finished off Ernie's sandwich in one swallow. Dad offered him another. Just as the Bigfoot reached out to take it, Dad started to back away, around the side of the car. He opened the door and put the fishwich on the back seat. "Come on," he muttered, "a tasty catch, smothered in tartar sauce . . ."

The creature started to follow, then wised up. Dad went for the fries. "And french fries. Larges! Two orders!" The french fries appealed to the Bigfoot's vegetarian appetite. He inched toward the car.

"And how about a chocolate shake to wash those down, huh?"

That did it. Bigfoot followed Dad. Dad opened up the whole food bag and let him peek inside. Then he tossed it into the back seat. Then Bigfoot climbed in after it. Maybe he thought it was another trick. As soon as he was inside the wagon, Dad climbed in front. Ernie heard the door locks click. Through the window, Ernie could see the Bigfoot try to sit up. The ceiling was a little low.

"Comfortable?" Dad asked.

The Bigfoot sat up. A huge metal blister rose from the

roof of the station wagon as the creature customized it with his head. Now he could sit up straight. He grinned at Ernie.

"That's the thing about these old beauties," Dad said. "Plenty of head room."

It wasn't funny. Not at all. Ernie wasn't sure he would have felt worse if his dad was taking his mom to live in the woods. If it were Sarah, he wouldn't shed a tear. But it tore him apart to see the Bigfoot in the back seat and know he'd never see him again. Ernie ran into the house so the Bigfoot wouldn't see him crying. He heard Mom come in after him. Sarah was still talking on the telephone to her dumb friend Sasha. Girls had no feelings at all.

Ernie was taking it hard. George sighed. No way he could drive off with his son in tears. George climbed out of the car and locked the doors. To the Bigfoot, looking puzzled in the back seat, he said, "Just—" He caught himself before he uttered sit. "You just stay right here."

Sarah and her pet telephone were in the doorway. When Geoge hurried past her, she dropped the receiver long enough to say, "You're not changing your mind, are you?"

George didn't stop to answer. In the kitchen, Nancy had her arm around Ernie. She was doing her best to explain why an eight-foot Sasquatch wouldn't flourish in the suburbs. Her arguments were sound and sensible, but they didn't seem to be having much impact on their son. Ernie's shoulders were rounded sadly, and George could hear him sniffing back his tears. George put his hands on his son's shoulders and turned him round. Ernie's eyes were red and disappointed. George knelt beside him, hoping he could find the right words to explain, to comfort.

"Mom's right, Ernie. I know this is hard. It's hard for me, too, but it's the right thing to do. I was wrong to think we could just claim him to be ours, like some kind of stray dog. He's a man. You were the first to see it. He deserves to be free. So what do you say we go out there like a couple of men and say, 'Goodbye, hairy . . .'"

George meant to say "hairy friend," but before he got the last word out, a bone shattering thud sounded in the driveway. Ernie looked quizzical. "Harry? Since when does he have a name?"

"Since now," George said.

They all, even Sarah, went outside to see what made the noise. The door lay on the ground and the car was empty. As the family stared at the car, they could hear two dozen dogs running off into the night, yipping, their toenails clicking against the pavement.

A moment later, above the canine howls, there rose a long and mournful wail that could only have come from Harry.

"That's him!" Ernie said what they all were thinking. "He doesn't sound too happy."

George put his hand on Ernie's shoulder. "No, son, he doesn't."

"Why did he run away, Dad?"

"I'm not sure, son. But I think he understands more than we realized. I think he didn't want to cause us trouble."

"What now?" Nancy said. "We can't just let him go wandering around the city streets. He's innocent as a baby, George. And there are lots of creeps out there."

Slowly George nodded. He looked at the remains of his recently classic car, then fished for the keys in his pocket. "I better go look for him," he said.

"Can I come, too, Dad?" Ernie asked.

"No, son," George said. He watched Ernie's face fall, and he thought as fast as he could. "I need you to wait here with Mom and Sarah. In case he comes back."

That seemed to satisfy Ernie. George climbed into his disintegrating station wagon and set off in search of Bigfoot.

15

It had taken Harry a while to understand that the male was full-grown, he was so small. But the other members of his group treated him with respect. The female with the shining hair was full-grown, too. She was the mate of the male, the mother of the others. The young male who played with him and the young female who growled at him were immature. Together they made a family. There were no elders.

Harry wondered when he would see his mate again. He missed his children.

Still, these creatures were kind to him. The female nursed his hand and gave him food. The young male shared his tools and toys. These creatures had wonderful toys. The male played with him, too—the Food Game. The male offered Harry food and asked him to do something. When Harry did it, the male gave him the food. Harry did not understand why the male wanted him to sit down, it was so simple, but he liked the little pieces of sweet white food the male gave him when he sat. He knew of nothing quite so sweet in the forest.

None of his kind had ever left the forest. Legend told of other two-legged creatures on the earth, but few had ever seen them. The young ones were warned to keep hidden from them. The elders said they were cruel. They killed and ate other animals. They ate their own dead.

Perhaps the elders were wrong. True, these creatures
hung parts of dead animals on the walls of their cave, but
Harry did not believe they ate their own kind. The female
grew many kinds of plants. He liked the taste of her flowers.
When he returned to the forest, Harry would tell the elders
about these creatures and their ways. He wondered if they
would believe him. Already Harry had seen many winters.
One day he would be an elder himself. It made him smile to
think he would be called "The One Who Left the Forest."

Harry did not understand why he had been chosen for this
adventure. He was not sure how he would get back to the
forest. But it encouraged him that the creatures seemed to
be intelligent. More and more, he was able to communicate
with them. When the time was right, when he had learned
more of their language, or they had learned more of his, he
would ask them to help him return to his home.

Darkness came. The creatures lighted their cave. Harry
was hungry and wondered when they would give him food.
The young male took his hand and led him outside the cave.
The male knelt beside the thing they called car. Inside it, the
creatures could move as fast as Harry could run. The car
was broken. Harry helped the male fix it.

The male offered him food. The food did not smell good.
Harry threw it away. The male gave him better food. Harry
understood they were playing a game. The male put the
food in the car. Harry got into the car. He ate the food. The
male got in the car.

Through the hole in the side of the car, Harry saw the
young male begin to cry. He saw sadness on the face of the
female. The child and the female returned to the cave. The
male made an unhappy sound. He got out of the car but told
Harry to stay inside it.

Through the entrance to their cave, Harry watched the
creatures and saw they were unhappy. He did not know how,

but he knew it was he who had made them unhappy. This made him unhappy, too. He did not wish to hurt them.

If he went away, perhaps they would be happy again. He did not want to go away. This place was strange to him. He had no way of knowing if all the creatures were as kind as these. He did not know how he would find his way home. But he knew he must leave.

Harry tried to open the door as he had seen the male do, but it would not open. Inside the cave, the female held the young male while he wept. Harry pushed against the door until it gave way and climbed out of the car. He stepped into the shadows. A pack of four-legged animals that reminded him of wolves, or of coyotes, came yapping after him. Fast as he could, Harry ran into the night.

Soon Harry had outrun the yapping creatures. He ran on and on for a long time. The stars came out. As the night wore on, the place became quieter. There were fewer people and fewer cars. Harry ran for a long time. When he stopped to get his bearings, he did not believe he was any closer to the forest than he had been before. And he was hungry. The food the creatures gave him did not fill him up for long.

Around him there were many caves. He picked one that reminded him of the cave of his friends. He watched and listened. The creatures who lived there must be gone, or sleeping. He crept closer and looked inside. There was a food box like the one in the cave of his friends. Quietly as he could, Harry let himself into the cave and crept up to the food box. He opened it and began to explore inside. He sampled the food. Some of the food fell out on the floor. By accident, he broke the light inside the food box. In the darkness, he found more food.

Harry was so hungry and so busy eating, he did not hear footsteps or see the light until it shone on his foot. He stepped backward, out of the light and tried to hide himself. He was afraid. The light went out. Harry waited.

All of a sudden, the light flashed on again. A female creature sprang at him. She hit his foot. It scared more than hurt him. Harry growled at the female. The female closed her eyes and fell at Harry's feet. She did not move.

Harry reached down and poked at the female. Still she did not move. She was dead. He had not touched the creature, but he had killed her. It was forbidden among his kind to kill another living animal. He had meant the creature no harm. Harry knelt beside her and wept.

Among his own kind, it was important to honor the dead. Harry wished to honor the dead creature, but he was not sure how. His kind buried their dead deep in the earth. He thought about burying the female. Then he remembered the male deer he had found on the wall of his friends' cave. Was that their way? He studied the dead creature.

Then he remembered. When the creatures thought he was dead, they had laid him on top of their car. The more he thought about it, the more it made sense. The creatures were very fond of their cars. He did not doubt they had some legend to explain it. Harry smiled, pleased that he understood their custom.

Through the door to the cave, he saw a car outside. Gently, he lifted the dead creature in his arms and carried her out of the cave. Carefully, he laid her body on top of the car. He folded her arms across her chest. The creature looked as if she were asleep. Harry was sorry she was dead. He honored her.

16

When Ernie woke up, Little Bob was snuggled warmly against his back. Obnoxious music from the local early morning TV show blared up the stairs. The TV in the kitchen was like the family alarm clock. At night, his mom set the timer and turned the volume up full blast. Ernie shook Little Bob awake, then rough-housed with him.

"We were going to take Harry back to the woods last night," Ernie told the dog, "but he ran away. That's what Dad named him—Harry. It kind of fits, don't you think?"

Little Bob climbed on Ernie's chest and licked his face. Mrs. Moffitt probably hadn't given him enough attention while they were gone. Ernie wouldn't have been surprised if she'd forgotten to feed him, too. He closed both hands around Little Bob's ribcage and lifted him high above the bed. "Zoom. It's Super Dog." Bob clawed at the air, and Ernie let him down. The dog settled back down in his nest in Ernie's blankets.

"Say, Bob," Ernie said, "you're an animal. Do you think you'd rather live in the woods than in a house?"

With a contented growl, Little Bob snuggled deeper in the covers.

"I mean, you're a wild thing, too, aren't you? Just think, you could spend your time catching rabbits and squirrels instead of waiting around for us to give you your Kibbles and Bits." The more he thought about it, the more that sounded right to Ernie. Civilization wasn't good for animals. It was unnatural. When Ernie's third grade class had won the paper drive, the reward was a movie, *Born Free*, about a lioness. It made a deep impression on Ernie, so deep he could still whistle the theme music from memory. The more he thought about it, the clearer it became to him. Ernie climbed out of bed and snatched up Little Bob.

Luckily, the rest of the family was in the kitchen when he got downstairs. Ernie opened the front door as quietly as he could and put Little Bob out on the welcome mat. "You're free, Little Bob," he told the dog. "Go back to the wild. Run free."

Little Bob looked up at Ernie. He was used to company on his morning walk. "Go on, Bob," Ernie said. He shooed the dog toward the street and tried to feel as sad as his dad looked last night, when they let the Bigfoot go. Little Bob trotted off, and Ernie shut the door. With the sleeve of his pajamas, he wiped away the one tear he'd managed to squeeze out, before he went into the kitchen to see what was for breakfast.

The Alaska Airlines commercial was just ending. The morning show came on. "And now, your host, the toast of the Olympic coast, Jerry Seville!" The kitchen filled up with the sound of fake clapping. Ernie's mom was making everybody's lunch. His dad came in from the downstairs bathroom, shaved and dressed for work. Even over the coffee, Ernie could smell his aftershave. Old Spice. Ernie was going to wear the same kind when he was old enough to shave. Ernie's mom handed his dad a cup of coffee.

"God, I hate this guy," his dad said.

His mom said, "I'll change it."

"No, let me hate him. It'll keep me awake until the coffee kicks in."

Ernie looked closely at his dad. His eyes were kind of red and puffy. Dad had spent half the night driving around, looking for Harry. Mom made Ernie go to bed before he got home. She promised to wake him up if Dad found Harry.

The guy his dad hated on TV was saying how glad he was it was already Tuesday. "Up yours, Jerry," Ernie's dad said back. Ernie laughed, but not too loud. He didn't want to discourage his father from saying what he really felt.

Ernie opened the refrigerator door, looking for some juice, or maybe milk. Pickles, ketchup, mustard, a couple cans of beer. The icebox was as empty as Ernie ever remembered seeing it. "Hey, Mom, what are we supposed to eat for breakfast around here?" he asked.

His mother shushed him. "Listen."

Ernie stared at the television. The announcer guy, the one his dad hated, was reading from the newspaper.

"Last night, a Hawthorne Hills man reported that he found his wife lying unconscious on the roof of their car . . ." The announcer looked up from the paper and snickered. "When the woman was revived by paramedics, she said she must have been put there by the huge, hairy, manlike creature resembling the legendary Bigfoot that she had earlier mistaken for a mouse." The announcer laughed his head off.

Dad sat back down at the table. "Harry!"

"He went to the Hills?" Mom said.

"Come on," the announcer guy said. "Bigfoot? We go through this every couple of years, for crying out loud!"

Dad stood up. He started to take off his tie. "I can't go to work. I've got to find him."

"George," Mom said, "he wouldn't have left if he didn't want to. Let him go. Go to work!"

It was pretty clear to Ernie that the announcer didn't believe there was such a thing as Bigfoot. Ernie could understand why his dad couldn't stand the guy. Dad was staring at the television with a glazed look. Her mom waved her hand in front of his face. "Earth to George. It's time to go to work. Now. Mush."

Slowly, Ernie's dad snugged up the knot on his tie and kissed his mom goodbye. Ernie looked away. He hated kissing. His dad left. The television cycled on to another commercial. His mother turned to him and Sarah. "All right, guys, let's get a move on. What'll it be? Cereal? Eggs? Juice?"

"Uh, mom? Have you looked in the refrigerator lately?" Ernie asked.

"Oh, right," his mom said. "How about some toast and a nice glass of water? Specialty of the house."

Just then Ernie heard a familiar scratching sound at the back door. When he opened the door, Little Bob came bouncing in. Ernie was glad to see him, he had to admit. He crouched down and held out his arms. Little Bob jumped in. Ernie gave him a welcome home squeeze. "You came back, Little Bob. Hey, Mom, he came back."

His mother gave him one of her that's-nice-dear smiles. She probably thought Little Bob had just been outside to take a dump. Ernie shrugged and sat down to his toast and water. It wasn't much of a way to start a school day. His mom noticed him gagging down the dry toast and grinned at him. "Don't worry, Ernie, I'll make it to Safeway before supper time."

All the time he was getting dressed and walking to school, Ernie debated whether or not to say anything to the other kids about the Bigfoot. Everybody was going to want to know why he was a day late. For now, he decided , he'd tell them they'd had an accident on the way home from camping. Then, if the picture he took turned out maybe he'd come across with the whole story. Meanwhile, he swore himself to secrecy. He didn't want to get laughed at this early in the year.

• • •

Sarah was worried about her hair. Nancy assured her it looked fine. Sarah studied herself in the glass front of the microwave. "No it doesn't, Mom. It looks like I washed it in the sprinkler."

Nancy gave her daughter a hug. "No one will ever know. You better get going or you'll miss the bus."

With one last glance at her reflection, Sarah grabbed her notebooks and headed out. Nancy cleared the table, turned off the television set and sat down to enjoy her second cup of coffee. It was still too early to call the plumber or the contractor to come repair the damage. She kicked off her slippers and put her feet up on the empty chair across the way. Peace. She deserved it.

No sooner had Nancy turned her attention to the crossword puzzle in the morning paper than she heard a sharp knock on the kitchen door. No mistaking that sound. Irene had arrived.

So much for peace. If anything ever drove Nancy back into the work force, it would be Irene. Nancy felt sorry for her, but that didn't make her daily visits any easier to take. Nancy sometimes wondered what it must be like at Irene's house to make the Hendersons' so appealing.

Irene let herself in, as usual. "Morning, neighbor. Gee, I'm glad you guys are back. Not that Lil Bob's bad company. He just doesn't talk much, you know."

Nancy nodded while Irene helped herself to coffee and sat down at the kitchen table. "Say, you read the paper yet? Seems Bigfoot's back in the news. Jeez, when are people going to grow up?"

"I'm a grown-up and I like Bigfoot stories," Nancy said.

"Yeah, he's right up there with Santa and the Easter Bunny." Irene blew on her coffee. "You know, there's supposed to be some old hunter out there who's spent his whole life trying to catch one. Isn't that the silliest thing you ever heard?"

Nancy nodded agreement. Just then, the phone rang. Nancy went to answer it. As soon as she picked up the receiver, a sharp knock sounded on the door. Irene heaved herself up from the table and went to answer it.

The man on the front stoop didn't look like he lived in the neighborhood. Actually, he looked kind of like an over-the-hill Marlboro Man, all tan and weathered. He wasn't exactly dressed for downtown. Irene stopped staring and remembered her manners. "Can I help you?" she asked.

The man opened a leather bag and pulled out a license plate. "Quite possibly," he said, "we can help each other. I believe this is yours."

Irene knew very well the license plate was not hers. She shoved it back at the stranger. "What are you selling, buster?"

Nancy hung up the phone—it was a wrong number—and joined Irene at the door. The man outside was well past middle age and looked like he belonged in the woods. When he spoke, Nancy thought she heard the trace of an accent in his gruff voice. "Mrs. Henderson?"

Nancy was surprised the stranger knew her name. She was even more surprised when he handed her a battered license plate. She recognized the number. It was theirs. The man's look questioned her. She turned to Irene. "Say, would you go turn off the kettle? I left it on high."

"I'm Richard Smith, U.S. Forestry Service. We're investigating a possible road kill . . . an animal killed or maimed in an auto accident."

Nancy wished George were at home. They hadn't discussed what to do if anyone found out. She decided to play dumb.

"You did hit something on Route A-4? A small fire road?" Even as he spoke, the man tried to see around her, into the house. Nancy had the uneasy feeling that he was sniffing the air. Had the air freshener done its work?

"Yes, we did hit something."

"What was it, Mrs. Henderson?"

"I don't know," Nancy said. "I mean, it was fat, we couldn't really see."

"Where is it now?"

The man hammered away, just like a TV detective. His persistence rattled Nancy. "Now? It . . . whatever it was ran away." She had the feeling the Forest Service man knew she wasn't exactly telling the whole truth. His voice was stern. "Mrs. Henderson. Our main concerns are for the safety of your family. To be sure no one was injured."

"Oh, no. No one was injured."

"But we're also deeply concerned for the well-being of the animal. If it's out there suffering, well, surely you'd want to help us find it and take care of it."

"Surely," Nancy said. "But it's okay. It just walked into the woods. Didn't even limp."

The stranger raised his eyebrows. "It walked?"

"Ah, you know . . . ran. Ah, waddled. Scurried. Scrambled. Crawled. Like animals do. But we're okay and I'm sure it's okay."

This time she was sure the visitor was sniffing the air. Nancy took a deep sniff herself. Maybe the house still did smell a little weird. "Oh, jeez, I almost forgot. I've got a sink backed up in here. The toilet, too. Gotta go now. Bye." She slammed the door shut and leaned against it. Irene appeared. She carried a steaming mug. "I made you a cup of tea."

"Oh, thanks, Irene."

"License plates. The guy's probably a convict. What you don't need right now is somebody bothering you. Just sit down and try to relax."

For once, Nancy kind of appreciated Irene's company.

She took her tea mug and looked for a place to sit down and enjoy it. The living room was out of the question. It looked like a vicious and very localized tornado had just blown through. Irene surveyed the rubble, then gave Nancy a sympathetic smile. "I remember Herb's and my first fight," she said.

Nancy curbed the impulse to say she and George never fought. She smiled weakly at Irene. "Why don't you come in the kitchen and tell me all about it?" She settled back to hear the gory details. It wasn't like she was prying. Irene was going to tell her whether she wanted to hear or not. Irene was like that.

17

All the way to work, George worried about Harry. The car was still full of his pungent scent. It also looked like hell. George wasn't ready for any smart remarks about his missing bumper or the homemade sunroof. He pulled into the very last slot in the employees-only section of the parking lot.

Inside, the store was depressingly the same as when he'd left for his vacation, two Fridays before. Billers, from fishing, and Stuart, from fitness, were gathered around the Bunn Automatic Coffeemaker in the backroom. George looked around for his favorite cup. There was a week's worth of dust inside. He wiped it out with the end of his tie.

"How about you, Henderson?" Stuart said. "You see any Bigfoot?"

George couldn't hide his surprise. "What?"

"Bigfoot," Stuart said. "You know, on your vacation."

Whew. Safe. George managed a smile. Gone a week and he'd forgotten how to kid with kidders. He shook his head no. He didn't really want more coffee, but he poured it anyway. It was hard enough being the boss's son. Sometimes it was even harder to be one of the boys.

Billers picked up the Bigfoot stuff. "I read that the things weigh over four hundred pounds and have a real bad smell."

Stuart, the store funny man, lifted up his nose and started sniffing the air. "Well, gee. Looks like we got one right here. What's your shoe size, Billers?"

"Very funny!" Billers said. Maybe he thought it was, though, because he started laughing. George figured he should laugh, too, but he didn't think it was funny at all. He nodded to the guys and wandered off for his department. On his way, he sniffed his shoulders, his shirtsleeves, then his hands. If the car still smelled of Bigfoot, maybe he did too.

George had just taken up his post in the hunting department when they unlocked the front door. Two seconds later, a short, stocky guy strode in. He was bald as a billiard ball and deeply tanned. Briefly, he scanned the store, then drew a bead on George in hunting.

"Can I help you?" George inquired.

"Probably not. You carry .458 Magnum rounds?"

George turned to the boxes of ammunition on the shelves behind him. "We don't get much call for these monsters. Ah, here we are." He put the box of cartridges on the counter.

Instead of being happy George had them, the customer was angry. "Criminy! This is the fourth place I've been to. Got anymore?"

Just to be sure, George looked again. "Sorry. That's it. You going on safari?"

"Son," the guy told him, "the really big game is American grown."

As far as George knew, there were no elephants native to North America. The Ice Age was supposed to have wiped out the mastadons. But, like his father insisted, the customer is always right. He nodded. "That will be ten-ninety-five."

The big game hunter didn't wait for his nickel back, and apparently he didn't need a bag. He shoved the ammo in his coat pocket and hightailed it out of the store. As soon as he was gone, George's dad appeared on the floor. He looked tall, lean, tough, like a real sportsman. George was always impressed when he hadn't seen his father for a while. The old man really looked the part. He came over and leaned on the hunting counter. "Jacques LaFleur. Like clockwork."

George, who was never very talkative in his father's presence, said, "Uhm?"

"He's always the first to show whenever these crazy sightings start up."

"He bought some pretty serious ammo—.458s," George said.

His father shook his head. "Before this Sasquatch thing got under his skin, he was a class A hunter. Where do you think Claws came from?"

Claws was the biggest grizzly bear George had ever seen. For years, stuffed, it had stood guard at the entrance of his father's store. It was a nice touch, George had to admit. It scared little kids and women and made the male customers feel real macho. Beyond Claws, George saw the hunter climbing into a powerwagon, parked in front of the store. "That guy shot Claws? Why would he part with a trophy like that?"

His dad said, "Probably because it was the smallest one."

George tightened his grip on the counter. What if he'd just sold the bullets that would kill Harry?

With admiration, George's father watched the hunter depart. Then he looked back to George. "He may be crazy, but he's real man."

"I bet," George said.

On his lunch hour, George hotfooted it to the downtown library. He hadn't actually been inside it since he graduated from high school. To save himself time, he consulted the bespectacled librarian at the information desk. "Hi. I'm on my lunch break and I'm in kind of a hurry. Could you please point me to some books on the Sasquatch? Bigfoot. You know."

Without looking up from her computer terminal, the librarian said, "Fantasy, Folk Lore, Myths and Legends. Fourth floor, at the very back of the library."

George nodded thanks. "You can also try Children's Books," the librarian called after him. George bolted up the stairs. The library was bigger than he remembered, with reading rooms fanning out north, south, east and west from a central lobby on each floor. On four, he circled the compass, then decided on east for anthropology. Students bent over books at the long tables; and in the easy chairs, sometimes with books for props, sometimes without them, old men dozed. When he found his section, George looked around for the card catalogue, only to find that since his school years, they'd put the whole thing on microfiche. When he finally figured out how to use the viewer and found his categories, he copied down the numbers and headed for the shelves. Seventeen minutes of his lunch hour was already gone.

The selection wasn't the best. All of the books had a small-time, unofficial look to them, like they'd been published by Crackpot press in somebody's basement. George scanned indexes—B for Bigfoot, S for Sasquatch— and filled his arms with everything that looked like it might possibly be useful.

The librarian who checked out his stack gave George a gentle smile. "Nobody's checked these out since last time there was a sighting. See?" She pointed to the stamped date on the card. "Nineteen eighty-one. I think that's the time the *National Enquirer* ran a front page story called "I was Bigfoot's Love Slave." We had to put the books on reserve for a while there."

"Yeah, right," George said. "Actually, these are for my

son. He's doing a term paper." George thought the librarian knew he was lying. He grabbed the books and ran.

That night, after supper, George and Ernie settled in to study the Bigfoot books. The first one they picked up featured pictures of Sasquatch looking meaner and weirder than Frankenstein's pet monster. Over George's shoulder, Ernie exclaimed, "This book sucks."

Nancy automatically protested her son's choice of words.

"These pictures don't look at all like Harry," Ernie said.

George looked up. "He's right, Nan. No wonder people want to kill them. The accounts in here, the pictures, they make them out to be killers." Nancy sat down beside him to check out the pictures as he flipped through. Near the back, he hit upon a picture of Jacques LaFleur. Nancy pointed at the page. "Hey, that's him."

"That's LaFleur. The hunter who bagged Claws."

"It can't be."

"Yeah. He was in the store today."

"No," Nancy insisted. "His name is Smith, the forestry guy I told you about. He was here at the house."

A terrible look crossed Nancy's face just as a terrible thought crossed George's mind. "That lying slime!" she said.

Both kids turned to stare at their mother. She never talked like that. It got them sent to bed. When they were up the stairs, Nancy put her hand on George's shoulder. "Come on to bed now, George. You need some rest."

George put his hand over Nan's and squeezed. "I'll be up in a minute. I just want to finish this first. It's the only one that's halfway accurate."

Nancy said goodnight and went upstairs. George flipped through the pages. He found another picture of Jacques LaFleur, grinning beside some plaster castings of Bigfoot prints. LaFleur looked a lot younger in the picture. He had more hair. George turned to the copyright page. 1956. No wonder. The guy had been hunting Bigfoot for more than thirty years. George prayed LaFleur's dedication was greater than his luck.

"Take care of yourself, Harry," he said out loud.

18

As long as it was dark, Harry kept moving. Just past dawn, the streets began to fill with cars. Harry remembered the warnings of the elders. Even if the creatures were not dangerous to him, he might be dangerous to them. Harry did not want to cause more deaths.

He found a small green place that reminded him of the forest, helped himself to a meal of leaves and flowers, hid carefully in the bushes and settled down to sleep.

When Harry woke, it was near dark. No creatures were about. His stomach was empty. Again he fed on the edible plants, then set out on his journey. The creatures lighted their streets. Harry moved in and out of shadows.

Soon, his instincts told him he was being hunted. Harry was not afraid. The creatures were poor hunters. Their noses and their ears were weak compared to his, and he had learned from childhood how to avoid them. All night they searched and Harry stayed ahead of them. It was as easy as a children's game.

Once, in the spirit of play, he let them catch a glimpse of him. He heard their voices rise, calling to one another. He heard their footsteps, running to where they thought he was. But Harry was not there anymore. He was an expert at the hiding game.

19

Nancy pulled on her favorite flannel nightgown and sat down on the edge of the bed. She was looking forward to a good night's sleep. Just as she was about to crawl under the covers, there was a soft knock on the door. Sarah stuck her head into the bedroom.

"Mom, could I talk to you for a minute?"

"Sure." Nancy patted the bed beside her.

"Mom, I know you're awful busy, trying to repair the house and everything, but you did promise you'd take me shopping. I was wondering if we could make it tomorrow after school."

Nancy sighed. She used to enjoy shopping with her daughter. That was back in the days when Sarah could still make up her mind. Now it took her forty-five minutes just to pick out a pair of panty hose. "What's so important it won't wait until the weekend?" she asked.

"I'm the only girl in the sophomore class without a pink big shirt," Sarah said.

Nancy said, "Great. Who wants to look like everybody else?"

"I do," Sarah said.

"Look, honey, you've only been back to school one day. What if tomorrow everybody's wearing yellow?"

"They won't be. Pink is definitely big this year. I've talked it all over with Sasha."

"Is that what took you an hour and a half on the phone tonight? I thought you were doing your homework."

"We did some homework, too. But, Mom, there's more to high school than studying. These are supposed to be the best years of my life, and I intend to make the most of them."

"I thought college was supposed to be the best years of your life."

"I'm not taking any chances," Sarah said. "There might be a nuclear war before I get to college. Will you take me to Southcenter tomorrow, Mom?"

Nancy put her arm around Sarah's shoulders. "The way things have been going around here lately, I'm not planning anything more than five minutes in advance."

"Does that mean yes?"

"It means we'll see. You get on to bed now. It's after ten o'clock."

Sarah stood up and headed for the door.

"And don't forget to brush your teeth."

"Mom, I'm not a baby anymore."

"I noticed," Nancy said. "Goodnight."

"Night, Mom."

Nancy climbed under the covers. To lie down felt delicious. She punched her pillow into the right shape for sleeping and leaned over to turn off the light. George padded into the room in his stocking feet. "Finish your research?" Nancy asked.

"It isn't really research," George told her. "Most of those things are comic books. Godzilla meets Jane Fonda in the western woods." He sat down on the edge of the bed and pulled off his shoes. "I did find one lead, though. There's somebody called Wallace Wrightwood, Ph.D., who seems like he might know what he's talking about. He's got an anthropological institute or something, not too far from the National Forest. I might drive up there after work tomorrow afternoon and check him out."

"Oh, do," Nancy said. "Then I won't have to take Sarah to Southcenter."

"I thought you took her shopping before we went on vacation."

"I did," Nancy said. "I did. But it seems everyone in high school is wearing this one particular kind of shirt. Sarah isn't going to rest until she has one, too."

"I thought she was saving for college," George said.

"That was last week. This week it's live for today. Seems she's afraid the world might blow up before she gets to college."

George unbuttoned his shirt. "Kids," he said. "Were we ever that silly, Nan?"

Nancy smiled at him. "Yes, George. We were." She lay back down on her prepunched pillow. George stood up to take off his pants. He hung them over the back of a chair, then went to the dresser for clean pajamas. When he opened the drawer, he let out an "eeek."

"There's an animal in here, Nan, and it isn't Little Bob."

Alarmed, Nancy sat up again. Then she remembered. "Relax, George. It's just mother's stole. I hid it."

George pulled the furs out of his pajama drawer and held them up. "I never did like this thing." Wiggling the furs, he turned to Nancy. "I mean, come on. Does this look like one of the finer things in life?"

It was an old joke, but Nancy laughed. Mother thought her only daughter should have married a doctor, or at least an orthodontist, not a sporting goods salesman. "Well," she said, "Mother would never forgive me if her precious little critters ended up six feet deep."

"Do me a favor and keep 'em on your side." George laid the stole on top of the dresser. Suited up for sleep, he crawled in bed. "I'm exhausted. What a day. I'm going to sleep like a log tonight for sure."

"Be sure to stay away from chain saws, then," Nancy said. "Goodnight."

But George couldn't sleep. He lay on his back and watched the patterns of moonlight on the ceiling. Beside him, Nan turned over every thirty seconds or so. Finally, he said, "Honey, can't you sleep?"

"Uh-uh."

"What are you thinking about?"

"Nothing," Nancy told him. "Garden of Eden. Mr. Darwin, stuff like that."

George stared at the ceiling. "Harry. He's amazing. If he's hungry, he eats. If he's thirsty, he drinks. Don't worry about him. He can take care of himself."

"If he's curious, he takes out a wall." Nancy was silent for a moment, watching the light show on the ceiling. "George, we're so lucky. We have each other. And Sarah and Ernie. And Harry, he's out there all alone."

"He's all right," George said. "He's survived all these years."

Nancy turned to her side so she could see George in the darkness. "People have seen him. They are going to go hunt him down and try to kill him."

George had no answer for that, too. "There've been a zillion sightings and nobody has ever killed one. Besides, all the people who say they've seen one are usually kooks or crazies. Except for our family, of course."

Nancy couldn't tell if George was trying to reassure her or himself. "Oh, George, do you think Harry's a family man?"

"Thing, sweetheart," George corrected.

"What if he's a family thing? What if there's a cave somewhere full of little Bigfoots?"

"Little Bigfeet."

"Little Bigfeet, waiting for Big Bigfoot to come home. Only he might not make it."

"Well, I'm sure Mrs. Bigfoot will take care of them, sweetheart."

The very thought brought tears to Nancy's eyes. "Oh, George! Mrs. Bigfoot!"

George put his arm around her and held her while she cried.

In his bedroom down the hall, Ernie shared his pillow with Little Bob. "What do you think, boy?" he said. "Do you think that Bigfoot will make it back home?"

Little Bob didn't answer. Instead, he licked Ernie's chin. Ernie wiped the dog slobber from his chin. "Jeez, Bob, I wish you'd learn to brush your teeth," he said.

20

Work. George was starting to hate going to work. It was just five minutes till opening when he arrived. Fortunately, his father didn't see him come in late. A bunch of the guys were lounging on the display cases in the hunting department while Stuart read out loud from the morning paper. George found the keys in his pocket and knelt down to unlock the gun displays.

"One said . . ." Stuart stopped to chuckle to himself. "Now get this: 'It must have been the large, hairy giant he saw running from the scene.'"

The guys joined Stuart in a big guffaw. George kept his face averted. He straightened the row of silencers inside the case and looked toward the doors. Not open yet, but a crowd was growing fast outside. Waiting customers spilled off the sidewalk, into the street. When George's father approached the gun counter, doing his best Teddy Roosevelt stride, the rest of the guys scattered to their stations.

"Look at that, would you, son?" George's dad said. "It's starting already?"

"We having a sale?"

"No." His dad chuckled. "It's these Bigfoot sightings. Brings 'em out of the woodwork. Everybody and his brother wants to load up and get into the act. Real shot in the arm for shoot 'n' stuff." His dad turned a greedy grin on the horde of customers outside. They might be fools, but he was more than willing to take their money. Then he turned to George. "Say, do you still fool around with that painting stuff?"

It was the first time his father had mentioned George's hobby since he refused to pay for art school. Maybe the old boy was coming around. "Yeah," George said. "In fact, I've just been . . ."

"Good." His father never had been one to let somebody else finish a sentence. "Maybe you could save your old man a few bucks. How about you draw up a big, full-size Bigfoot? We'll put it in the window next to the gun section. Make him look real big and scary, you know, how they're supposed to look, George? Hands in the air, claws out? Big fangs, a lot of drool . . ."

He should have known better, George told himself. he should have known.

"Let's put up a map of the area," his dad went on, "and we'll mark all the spots where people say they've seen this thing." His dad stared into space, envisioning the glory of it all. "This'll become kind of a Bigfoot Central. A BHQ."

The old man might have gone even further—sweatshirts? rewards?—except George interrupted him. "Don't you think we might be encouraging a lot of unqualified people to go out running around with loaded weapons?"

His father gave him one of his best grow-up-and-get-with-the-program looks. "Come on. You know as well as I do there's nothing out there to shoot at." The old man glanced down again at the crowd of would-be killers outside. "We're going to do more business today than Christmas eve. And George. I want to keep an eye on the stock. If we start running low on anything, get on that phone and reorder. Tell 'em to put a rush on it."

"Right," George said.

His father looked at his watch, the super sport model that

came with a built-in compass and barometer and was water-resistant up to four hundred feet. "Nine-oh-five, son. Let's not keep the good people waiting any more. Get out there and *sell guns*."

It was one of those mornings George regretted being manager. Keys in hand, he headed for the front door. The crazies on the pavement watched him closely. When he opened up the store, they nearly trampled him.

George wondered now why he'd spent all that time teaching Harry to sit, when a few lessons in urban guerilla tactics would have been more useful.

21

George had come looking for science. What he found was schlock. The North American Anthropological Institute had rip-off written all over it. It was the kind of building that just sort of grows over the years—a hunk of plywood here, a sheet of tarpaper there, with some long-gone relative's house trailer incorporated into the overall design. The only thing missing was the fleet of dead cars in the yard. In their place, there were signs, big loud tacky signs, proclaiming THE TRUTH ABOUT BIGFOOT—AUTHENTIC SOUVENIRS. Harvard it wasn't. George's heart sank to his knees.

Still, he was there. He might as well get out and stretch his legs. The entrance to the "museum" was tall enough for Bigfoot. On the doormat were painted two Bigfoot prints. Inside them, George's size thirteens looked small. He straightened his shoulders and entered the building.

It was even worse inside than out. The walls were papered with tattered clippings about Bigfoot mementos— three or four sizes of Bigfoot statues, plastic baggies full of genuine Bigfoot hairs and toenail clippings, rubber Bigfeet (amaze your friends) and plaster castings of "authentic" Bigfoot prints. A layer of dust encased it all.

George wondered what Harry would make of the "museum." The place gave him the creeps. He was about to leave when a voice spoke. "I can tell by the look on your mug you think it's a load, doncha?"

Startled, George turned toward the voice. An old guy in a New York Giants baseball cap stepped into view around a moth-eaten diorama of BIGFOOT IN THE WILD. He was wiping plaster off his arms.

"Well . . ." George said.

"Everybody asks, Has anybody ever seen one? Well, let me ask you—being from the city, as you obviously are—you've seen hundreds, thousands of pigeons, right?"

George nodded yes to pigeons.

"Ever seen a baby pigeon?"

George thought about it.

"Well, neither have I," the old guy said. "But I got a real strong hunch they exist." He grinned at George. "Am I losing you yet?"

"No, not at all," George said. "Are you Dr. Wrightwood? I'm George Henderson."

The old guy looked George up and down, then turned to straighten some merchandise. "Wrightwood ain't here," he said.

"Will he be back?"

"Might. How do you know Wrightwood?"

"His books," George said. "His research. He really believes in"—George's gesture took in all the Bigfoot paraphernalia—"all this. I just need some answers."

The old guy turned back to George. His voice was crusty. "The doctor's old, and tired. Spent the better part of his life chasing a dream. By the time he woke up, it was too late."

George ripped a deposit slip out of his checkbook and wrote a note. He handed the slip to the old man. "Well, I'd love to talk to him. My phone number's on this. If you could possibly get it to Dr. Wrightwood."

The old guy unfolded the note and read out loud. ". . . vital facts that could prevent an unnecessary and tragic end for . . ." He paused to laugh at George's wording. "For the big fellow?"

George looked for a way to make himself clear. "I have a friend, a man called, ah, Jack. And say there was this giant . . ."

The old guy cocked his head. "Is there a beanstalk involved in this, Mr. Henderson?"

"A beanstalk?" For a minute, George thought the old fellow had lost it. Then he realized he'd started to put Jack and giants together in the same story. "Oh, I get it. Nope, no beanstalk. What I meant was, with all these Bigfoot sightings, what if Jack and his family opened their home and their lives to this, ah, thing. I mean, what if it was more human than animal? And they just said, we'll take him in. We'll accept the responsibility, until there's a safe place for him to be. Not a zoo or anything like that."

George hoped that made sense. It made perfect sense to him.

The old man looked at him quizzically. "So, what you're saying is that you—excuse me—that *Jack* is willing to take the creature in and care for it and love it like a pet?"

George nodded. "Like a member of the family," he said, with conviction.

The old man shook his head. "Noble gesture, but impossible. Sasquatch is a primitive ancestor of modern man. If you ever came face to face with one, you'd see that they are still very much animals."

"Only on the outside," George insisted. "I know what I'm talking about!"

The old guy's face closed down. His voice turned gruff. "And I know it's closing time. So it you want to talk shop, then shop."

George shopped. At random, he picked junk off the dusty shelves until his arms were full and his wallet was empty. The old goat might not have known much about Bigfoot,

but he did know about fleecing customers. George left the
North American Anthropological Institute with a car full of
kitsch and no answers. Once again, he had the strong and
desolate feeling that he was on his own.

Doc Wrightwood watched Henderson toss his Bigfoot
souvenirs into his station wagon. He felt almost guilty about
not coming clean with the guy. There was something about
him. Still, you couldn't be too careful. Every time there was
a rash of sightings, crazies flocked to the museum like bees
to a hive. Most of them wanted Sasquatch for a rug, though,
not for a pet. This Henderson had a new angle.

As Henderson climbed into his car, Wrightwood could
see the trouble on his face. He was pretty sure he hadn't
come clean, either. Something was eating him. Doc read the
address on Henderson's deposit slip. Seattle. Then he folded
up the paper and stuck it in the pocket of his faded flannel
shirt. Just in case.

22

Nancy was relieved to see George pull into the driveway. She was less than delighted with the load of Bigfoot claptrap he carried into the house. There was nothing she'd consider giving her worst enemy, even for a joke. The foot lamp was, she thought, perhaps the tackiest piece of junk she'd ever seen. The way George explained it, it was the price of conversation. To Nancy, it sounded like extortion.

"For a salesman, George, you've got low sales resistance."

As soon as she said it, she was sorry. In all their years together, she'd never seen George so troubled for so long. And now his jerk of a father expected him to draw a life-size cartoon Bigfoot to help sell guns. Overnight, no less. That rated right up there with, "Why would any red-blooded male want to be an *artist,* for crying out loud?" and "You want to marry *her*?" Nancy disliked George's father even more than George disliked her mother. One of these days, she was going to tell the old Tartar just what she thought of him.

They dumped the Bigfoot souvenirs in the living room. George settled in at his drawing board. Nancy brought him a snack and hovered to watch him draw. The kids wandered into the living room and discovered the Bigfoot junk.

"This lamp is outstanding!" Ernie cried. "Can it go in my room?"

"You won't have to fight me for it," Sarah told him.

"It's yours, Ernie. Take it. Please," Nancy told him. "Don't you two have homework?"

"No," Sarah said.

"No," Ernie said.

Nancy sighed. No rest for the wicked. The kids had been driving her nuts ever since they got home from school that afternoon. Now they gathered around George's drawing table, while he told her about his visit to the Bigfoot Museum. The story got a little confusing in places.

"Jack and the Beanstalk, George?" she asked.

"It just came out that way. I didn't know what I was saying."

"Sounds to me like you knew exactly what you were saying," Sarah said. "Face it, Dad. You want him back."

George laid down his pencil and looked up at his daughter. "Sarah, I want to *take* him back where he belongs, but that means I've got to find him first. He's an . . . an innocent. I was wrong, treating him like an animal. Maybe we somehow managed to hurt his feelings."

"You really believe that big, dumb animal has feelings?" Sarah was incredulous.

Nancy had to smile. If Sarah hadn't been spending so much time on the telephone, she might have paid more attention to what was going on around the house.

"Yeah," George told her. "I believe he does. In many ways, he was one of us. Maybe even a little better, you know? Did what our kind aren't good at . . ."

"Ran around naked without getting busted," Ernie chirped.

"I'm serious here, Ern!" George said. "Anyhow . . ."

Sarah had taken Ernie's interruption as an opportunity to sneak away. Now that she was fifteen, she believed if an adult said more than two consecutive sentences to her, she was being lectured. Sarah hated to be lectured. George, turning back to continue his "lecture," was surprised to find her gone.

Ernie, too, had reached his upper limit for serious conversation. He scooped up Little Bob and headed off for parts unknown. Peace at last. Nancy put her arms around George's neck and kissed his ear. The snarling Bigfoot on his sketchpad glared up at her. George rubbed his cheek against hers for a moment, then took up his pencil again, adding drool to the Bigfoot's pointed fangs.

Nancy rifled through the stack of sketches on the corner of the drawing board. Among the monsters, she found a portrait of the smart, gentle creature they had known. She slid it out of the pile to take a better look. "George, this is really Harry." She looked back to the drooling villain on the sketchpad. "Did you draw this?"

Claiming his work, George gave her a sheepish grin.

"*This* is beautiful," Nancy said.

Modestly, George shrugged. "It's the subject, Nan. I mean, Harry's kind of beautiful, don't you think? For a Bigfoot."

Nancy squeezed George's shoulder. "Prettiest one *I* ever saw," she said.

23

It was night again and most creatures were inside their caves. Light shone out through the holes cut in their walls. A male creature came into view. There was a small animal with him, like the one his friends called Bob. While Harry watched, the dog squatted and left a steaming pile of droppings on the grass. The male squatted and picked up the droppings with some kind of tool. Harry was puzzled by such strange behavior. What could it mean?

The creature and his dog went inside the cave. Harry continued his search. He moved close to a hole in the wall of another cave. A female was inside. She put leaves and roots into a large container. She put in the carcass of a small bird. Steam rose from the pot.

A sound caught Harry's attention and he turned toward its source. A male and a female creature stepped into a big bubbling pool. They had almost no hair on their bodies. Harry felt sorry for them. They must be cold.

Harry looked back to see the female in the cave pick up a small tool. She dipped it into her pot, then lifted it to her lips. When she had blown the steam away, she drank the liquid. It was food.

He looked back to the creatures in their steaming pool. Harry's stomach lurched as he understood the truth. They too were food. So the elders had been right, after all.

Sounds caught his attention. They were loud and persistent but not unpleasant. He followed the sounds and peered into a house. There were many male and female creatures inside. They jumped and swayed together, in pairs, in a way that made Harry remember the mating dance of his own kind. Somehow the loud sounds seemed to match their movements.

One of the males stopped dancing. He stopped the sounds. He took one of the females by the hand and led her to a doorway. When he opened the door, an even stranger creature stood behind it. This creature was covered head to foot with thick dark hair, yet it stood on two legs. It was the size and shape of Bigfoot, except its face was cruder and more animal than the faces of Harry's kind. The creature danced forward and handed something to the female. Then the male closed the door and the creature was gone.

Slowly, Harry moved around the house. The creature was outside. As Harry watched, the creature reached up, lifted off its own head and tucked it under its arm. Beneath the first, the creature had another. It was a female. The creature walked away from Harry and climbed into a car. The car drove away.

A male came out of the house. He said words to Harry. Hey, wait a minute. The male moved close to Harry and held out a large green leaf. He said more words. Sorry. Too much excitement. Almost forgot your tip.

Harry stared at the leaf. Come on, the male said. Take it. He took Harry's hand and pressed the leaf into his palm. You were a big hit.

The creature went back inside. Harry ate the leaf. It was unlike any leaf he'd ever eaten, but he liked the taste.

24

All night George drew. All night, his drawing style and his feelings seesawed back and forth. They were always at odds. The tireder he got, the clearer some things became. He had spent most of his life trying to please his father. And hard as he tried, he never quite succeeded. The old man should have had Dirty Harry for a son. That would have made him proud.

For years, George had wanted his father to show some interest in his paintings. He didn't have to like them, just acknowledge them somehow. George remembered back in fifth grade, when his father went to Open House at school and George's teacher told him his son had artistic talent. At first, the old man looked embarrassed. Then he laughed. "Thanks for the warning," he said. "I'll take away his color crayons."

Mrs. Entwhistle had looked confused. "Mr. Henderson, I don't understand. Your son shows an unusual aptitude for design. He has a fine imagination. You should be very proud."

"Proud?" the old man thundered. "I'll be proud when he pitches a no-hitter. I'll be proud when he climbs Mount Rainier, or shoots a grizzly bear. Don't ask me to be proud because he watercolors well." He gave young George, standing there beside him, a hearty slap on the back. "And don't you worry. I'll straighten him out."

Mrs. Entwhistle started to protest. "But Mr. Henderson . . ."

George watched his father glare at his teacher. "Whose son is he anyway?"

"Yours, of course," Mrs. Entwhistle said.

"That's right." His father nodded curtly. "Don't you forget it." With that, he whisked his son away, muttering, "Artist, indeed."

Nan always encouraged him to stand up to the old man. When they were first married, she used to say, "You want to be an artist, we'll find a way," but first George had to prove to his father that he could provide for his family. He could just hear what the old man would have to say if Nancy went to work to help support his dreams. "Who cares what he says, anyway?" Nan used to say. But George did. He cared deeply.

That night, sitting at his drawing table, it occurred to George that maybe he didn't care quite so much anymore. The house was almost paid for. The kids were healthy and happy. He and Nan had been married for a lot of years and still loved each other. That was more than a lot of people could say. So what exactly did he have to prove?

That night, as his pencil moved across page after page, George practiced not caring what his father thought. He silently practiced saying, "Stuff it." Once or twice, in the privacy of his den, he even said it out loud. Then he waited for something bad to happen. When nothing did, he smiled. "*Stuff it,*" he said, louder still.

Stuffing was fine for turkeys, of course, but Thanksgiving was still months away, and all the stuffing in the world wasn't going to produce a life-size Bigfoot by nine a.m. George studied the current version. It looked something like Walt Disney's Goofy wearing Halloween vampire fangs, a bad compromise between mean and just plain silly. He crumpled it up and started again.

Around 2:30, Nan padded in, wearing the Japanese silk kimono George had given her for their last anniversary. He liked to see her in it. "George, come to bed."

George pointed to his drawing. "I've sort of got a problem, Nan. If I make him look mean and vicious, people will shoot first and then worry about the consequences. It's like drawing the wanted poster of a friend. If I make him peaceful, like Harry is . . . that's not what my father is looking for."

Nancy responded to his dilemma with an affectionate smile. "George, I'm so happy," she said.

"Huh?"

"I'm so proud of you," Nancy said. "You don't know what to do."

At the same time he understood what Nan meant, he also knew exactly what to do. He almost laughed out loud, it was suddenly so clear to him. His problem with the Bigfoot drawing was exactly the same as the problem with his life. Only now he had a solution.

"You go to bed," he told Nancy. "I'll be up in a minute."

Now George's pencil flew across the page. He felt like his drawings hadn't come so easily or been so good since he was in the fifth grade.

Next morning, George was at work early. Whistling, he spread glue in the big cardboard cutout, then carefully unfurled his Bigfoot and laid him in place. Upright, he looked terrific, George waltzed him into the hunting department and put him in place in the display window, next to the sighting map.

There. George was pleased. His Bigfoot looked just like Harry. When it came right down to it, making the fur look three-dimensional had been the hardest part. He'd even managed that funny kind of half-smile Harry had. George poured himself a cup of coffee from the Bunn Automatic and joked around with the guys until his dad showed up.

There was no mistaking it when he did. "*George!*" the old man roared.

"Yes, Dad?"

"Front and center. Forward march. *Now.*" When his father used military jargon, it meant that he was really mad. George's fellow employees shot him sympathetic looks as his father marched him toward the front of the store. George smiled benignly back at them.

"Outside!" the old man ordered.

George held the door for him. "I take it you've already seen my drawing. What do you think?"

The old man exploded. "I wanted a King Kong and you bring me a gosh darned giant gerbil. I told you exactly what to do and you didn't even come close."

George felt his stomach start to knot up the way it always had when his father yelled at him. Lucky he'd rehearsed his response. He said it without the slightest stammer. "Well, maybe it's right on the nose. What if he's not vicious? What if he's some kind of man? Maybe he's gentle . . . has feelings . . ."

George didn't get to finish his speech. "Where did you dream up that garbage? Go stick a pin on Queen Anne Hill. We just got another sighting."

George moved off to do his father's bidding. It beat a fight. Behind him, he heard his father mumble, "I shoulda got a real artist."

George shook his head. There was no winning with the old man.

From inside the window, George's Bigfoot flashed his friendly smile at George's father. The old man growled.

25

LaFleur cruised through streets lined with middle-class split-levels until the congregation of news vans, police cars and rubberneckers told him he'd found the right place. He parked the powerwagon, climbed out and hurried into the crowd. These tracks would be fresh, if the clods hadn't trampled them already. His eyes scanned for prints on the well-kept lawn.

"Morning, Jocko." A familiar voice spoke near his ear. LaFleur looked up to see Doc Wrightwood. It was the last place he would have expected to meet him. In the woods, maybe. "What are you doing here, Wally?"

Hands in his pockets, Doc shrugged. "Curiosity. Trying to figure out why anybody would go to such extremes to fake these ridiculous sightings. I'm not surprised to find you here."

Jacques hated the old man's riddles. "What the hell's that supposed to mean?" he asked.

Doc gave him one of his cynical smiles. "You're not trying to raise money for a new expedition, are you, Jocko?"

No one could make Jacques angrier. "Listen, old man. You believe what you want. But he's real and he's here. I don't know why or how. But he's here. Out of his element, and very vulnerable."

Doc grinned at him. "You're scratchin' at straws, Jock. Give it up, why don't you? Life's too short."

"Jacques LaFleur does not give up. In a short while, I'll have your 'baby pigeon.' I'll stake my reputation on it."

Wrightwood took his hands out of his pockets. In his right, he held a crumpled bill. "I'll do better than that, Jock. I'll bet you five bucks." Laughing, he waved the five under LaFleur's nose.

LaFleur was too angry to speak. He sputtered instead. He'd make the old cretin eat his five. Jacques comforted himself with thoughts of the glory to come.

26

The night before Christmas had never seen the store so crowded. Everyone—young, old, housewives and businessmen, city slickers and sportsmen—all knew exactly what they wanted. They wanted guns.

Every salesman in the place was working the hunting department, and still the lines were six deep. George found it hard to sell and worry at the same time. Every gun he sold might be the one that nailed his friend. George dawdled, he developed a speech impediment, he parted with the merchandise reluctantly. Around him, his fellow employees passed out weapons as efficiently and unfeelingly as if they were bricks of government cheese.

Between customers, Stuart elbowed George. "What's the matter, Henderson? You sick or something?"

"Now that you mention it, I do feel sort of funny," George said.

A would-be marksman collared Stuart. Someone tugged at George's sleeve. He looked down into the wild eyes of a tiny blue-haired lady. "What kind of gun do I need to protect myself against a Bigfoot?" she demanded.

The old girl should have been home knitting booties for the great-grandkids. George didn't want to take her money any more than he wanted to give her a weapon. He leaned down and spoke in a low voice. "Believe me, you don't need protection. They're harmless. They eat sugar cubes."

Just then a very wild-eyed, very excited man came panting up. He pushed the old lady aside. "I need a gun. I need a big, big gun. Maybe one of those Dirty Harry Magnums. Or an M-16. Will those go fully automatic?"

"Full autos are illegal," George took pleasure in informing him, "and handguns take seven days to clear. I'm afraid if you want a gun right now, it will have to be a rifle or a shotgun."

"Give me the biggest one you've got. Anything with a night scope?"

George was wondering how he could look himself in the mirror the next morning if he actually sold a gun to this bozo. He stalled. "Well, we've got some big guns, and we've got some big, big guns, but I think we're out of big, big ammo."

The customer stared at George as if he'd lost his marbles. So, George noticed, did Stuart and Billers.

"Look, pal." The customer leaned across the counter to speak confidentially to George. "They just spotted that thing, not three blocks from my house. Now I got a family to protect. I need a gun *now!*"

"Where do you live?" George pulled out his receipt book to make the question seem more reasonable. "It's for the gun. Just a few questions."

"One-one-four-eight-four Devon Drive," the man told George.

Quickly, George wrote it down. "And where was the sighting?"

"At the corner of Maple and Overview. Hey, what's that got to do with it?"

George tossed the receipt book on the counter and headed for the door. He knew where he belonged. It wasn't here.

He was on his way out the door when he ran smack into the old man, jockeying the eight-foot Bigfoot cutout. "See?" his dad said. "You're not the only artist in the family."

George saw. The old man had taken a magic marker to George's masterpiece. He had drawn on Harry's teeth. He had made his eyebrows frown. He had done it badly. What's more, he was proud of himself.

"Not bad for an arthritic old shooter, huh?"

For the first time in his life, George yelled at his old man. "What the heck did you do? The way I did it was right. You shouldn't have changed it."

His dad looked around. He backpedaled. "Okay, George, cool down. It's just a piece of cardboard."

"Not to me," George informed his father. "It means something to me. *He* means something to me."

As George spoke, the old man's expression changed from blank to bewildered. "What the heck are you talking about?"

George showed him before he told him. He ripped the assistant manager badge off his sport coat and stuffed it in his father's pocket. To make sure the old man got the message, he said, "I quit!"

Marching out of the store, George felt ten years younger and ten pounds lighter. Amazing how much that badge had weighed.

His father called after him. "Over this? You can't quit. We've never been so busy. What the hell's the matter with you?" The farther away George got, the louder his father yelled. "*Why are you doing this?*"

A smile just tickled the corners of George's lips. He didn't turn back. Old man Ronan called after him, but that didn't stop George. If he didn't have a job tomorrow—well, he'd worry about that tomorrow. Right now, he had more important things on his mind.

As he started the station wagon, George pulled his city

map out of the glove compartment, got it folded the right
way and looked for Overview. He didn't know the south
part of the city very well. The freeway entrance he needed
was closed for repairs, and the detour to the next one
snarled him up in downtown traffic. A real scenic tour.
Finally, he was on his way.

Around the intersection of Maple and Overview, it looked
like a carnival or— George remembered the police sergeant's words—a war zone. Cops, reporters, paramedics
everywhere. George elbowed his way through a tangle of
onlookers and found a couple of fire department EMTs
plastering a bandage on a small bald man in an expensive
jogging suit. Beside him a cop crouched down, notebook in
hand. George approached the policeman.

"Excuse me. How long ago did this happen?"

The policeman shot him an exasperated look. "Do you
mind? I'm taking a statement here."

George backed off and looked around. A badly mangled
bicycle lay in the street. George deduced it belonged to the
guy with the bandages. The guy was waving his hands as he
talked to the cop. George tuned in.

". . . huge, gigantic. A monster. A rabid ape, but
bigger than a regular rabid ape. I mean uh . . ."

Beside the witness, the policeman gritted his teeth. "Just
calm down and tell me exactly what happened."

"Okay. I'm okay. I brought my poor ten-speed Roadmaster to a complete stop, like I always do at stop signs . . ."

"It's okay, fella," the policeman said. "I'm not here to
pass out tickets."

By now, a gaggle of reporters, TV and print, had found
the action. A bouquet of microphones blossomed around
cop and witness. All the attention went to the little guy's
head. George figured he wanted to make the five o'clock
news.

". . . when out of nowhere, this humongous hairy thing

is standing right in front of me, growling with these enormous fangs, and giant hands . . . and he grabs me and, uh, he picks me up, bike and all, over his head, and then he smashes me down on the cement." It didn't sound like Harry to George. He got the feeling the guy was making all this up as he went along.

"And now he's all over me. Snarling. His pointed teeth dripping with saliva, so I . . . I grabbed my mace and . . ."

That's when George lost it. The thought of this little lying creep macing Harry was more than George could stand. "You what? Mace! You idiot."

The little creep cringed as George advanced. The policeman stepped between them. "Hold on. Stay back."

The creep spoke to the cop. "I didn't really mace him. But, but I was about to be eaten."

"Eaten?" George roared. "By a vegetarian? You, you . . ." George took a deep breath. "I don't doubt that you saw him, but what *really* happened is that when you saw him, you got so scared . . . out of your mind, that you crashed your, your dumb Roadmaster into the stop sign, bumped your head on the curb here and probably scared him half to death in the process."

The policeman started to ask a question, but George wasn't through. "I'm right, aren't I? That's what *really* happened, isn't it?"

The little creep cracked. "Yes! Yes! That's what happened."

There. Harry was cleared. George had never heard such a ridiculous story in his life. No wonder things got out of hand, with people running around making up tales like that. For a moment, George felt like Captain America. Suddenly, the press were thrusting their microphones in *his* face. The questions came thick and fast.

"How did you know this?"

"Did you see it happen?"

"What's your name, sir?"

"My name is George Henn . . ." George came to his senses in time to swallow the last two syllables of his name. Harry was out there somewhere, in danger. Harry needed him, a whole lot worse than George needed publicity. He waved the microphone aside. "Uh, I have to leave now. Sorry. Goodbye."

"But Mr. Hen! Mr. Hen! Just a few quick questions, sir," the press called after him.

George hurried back to the station wagon. The most intrepid of the reporters dogged him all the way, but George Hen didn't say another word.

27

Nancy kept the TV on all morning, listening for Bigfoot news. She wasn't disappointed. There was a major sighting. A man on a bicycle claimed to have been accosted by a monster.

"And now a report from Phil Cheever and our mobile news unit at the scene . . ."

There was a brief knock at the back door. Irene let herself in. "Morning, Nan. Everything okay here?"

Finger to her lips, Nancy nodded. "Shhh. I'm watching the news. Bigfoot."

"Ah, that's all a lot of hooey." Irene helped herself to coffee in her favorite mug.

"Let's see if we can't pick this up," Phil Cheever said. His microphone joined half a dozen others in front of a bald man patched with bandages.

Irene sat down at the kitchen table. "What happened to him?"

". . . and he picks me up, bike and all, over his head and then smashes me down on the cement. And now he's all over me. Snarling . . ."

"Bigfoot?" Irene said. "That sounds more like Jack the Ripper."

". . . so I grab my mace and . . ."

"That's a good idea," Irene said. "Maybe I ought to carry mace."

Nancy heard a familiar voice. She turned around, expecting to see George in the doorway. George wasn't there.

"Eaten! By a vegetarian? You, you . . ." George's voice.

Irene craned forward, toward the screen. "Say, isn't that . . ."

Nancy switched off the set.

"That guy sure looked like George. Sounded like him, too," Irene said.

"Don't be silly," Nancy told her neighbor. "It couldn't be George. George is at work."

"Must be his double then," Irene said. "People have them, you know. I read this article in the *Star*—"

"Tell me all about it," Nancy said.

Recess. Ernie popped a leaf in his mouth and pretended to chew. "Oh, boy, is this ever good," he growled.

Frankie McDowell lowered the baseball bat rifle he'd been pointing at Ernie's heart. "Come on, Ernie. If you can't do it right, let somebody else be Bigfoot."

"Oh, I suppose you know everything about Bigfoot," Ernie said.

"I know he's big and mean and wild. He doesn't go around munching on leaves, for cripe's sake," Frankie said.

"Oh yeah?"

"Yeah."

"Well, watch this," Ernie said. He filled his lungs and let out his biggest, best imitation of Harry's roar. Then he knocked the baseball bat out of Frankie's hands and ran like crazy.

"Get him, men," Frankie hollered. "Get the Bigfoot!"

The chase was on.

• • •

Bigfoot. Bigfoot. That's all anybody could talk about. Sarah was sick of it. She'd had enough of Bigfoot to last a lifetime. In biology, fourth period, someone asked the teacher, Mr. Krebs, if there was such a thing.

"There is absolutely no scientific evidence to suggest that Bigfoot exists," Krebs told the class.

"Then what's everybody so excited about?" someone in the third row asked.

"Well," Mr. Krebs said, "if there were such a thing as Bigfoot, and if somebody caught one, it could be very scientifically important. Those are several big ifs. But *if* all those ifs were true, we would probably have found the missing link between animal and man."

Sarah's new lab partner, Jamie Conway, leaned over the dissecting pan and whispered, "What do you think of all this Bigfoot business, anyway?"

"Personally, I think it's highly overrated," Sarah whispered back.

"May I be excused now?" Sarah asked when she finished her supper.

She was already out of her chair when George said no. "Sit down, honey. I have an important announcement to make."

"You found Harry!" Ernie guessed.

Nancy held her breath.

"No, Ern. I didn't find him," George said. "But I did quit my job."

For a moment, Nancy was too surprised to say a thing. The whole family greeted the news with silence.

George looked at each of them in turn. "Well?"

Nancy spoke first. "George, that's wonderful!"

Sarah looked at her in disbelief. "What's so wonderful about it?"

"Was Grandpa mad?" Ernie asked.

George grinned. "Very."

Nancy clapped her hands in delight. "Oh, George. I wish I could have seen his face."

"Yeah," George said. "The old man was pretty upset."

"How did it happen?" Nancy asked. "What drove you to it? I want to know everything."

"Well," George said, "it's kind of a long story. But when I saw what he'd done to my Bigfoot, I just saw red. Yelled at him. I think I told him off pretty good."

"I suppose this means I won't be getting my allowance on Saturday," Sarah said. "I suppose this means I'll have to go back to work at Burger King."

Nancy shot her a calming look. "We're not sure what it means yet, honey. Give us time to think it through."

"You know what I think?" Sarah said. "I think you think more of that smelly Bigfoot than you do of your own family."

"Harry. Right," George said. "That's the other thing. I have to find Harry."

Ernie jumped up from his chair. "What are we waiting for? I'll go with you, Dad. Sarah, you go with Mom."

"Calm down, son," George said. "Nobody's going anywhere. It's not safe out there. I know. I spent half the day arming idiots. This is something I better try alone."

"Great!" Sarah said. "First he tells us we're going on welfare. Now he says I'm going to be an orphan."

"Sarah, don't overdramatize," Nancy said, in her most no-nonsense voice. She looked to George. He looked . . . different. Good. Nancy thought she'd never loved him so much. "Do you have a plan, George?"

"Yep," George said. "I do. I'm going to stop by the store first, and then I'm going to hit the streets."

"How come you're going to the store, Dad?" Ernie asked. "I thought you quit."

George smiled at Ernie. "Let's put it this way, son. If you think Grandpa's mad tonight, just wait until tomorrow."

"Wow," Ernie said.

"Please be careful, George," Nancy said.

"I will," George promised. "Don't worry about me."

28

George left home after dark. Downtown rose up eerily between the freeway and the bay, its nocturnal glow made hazy by a light fog. The full moon topped the tallest of the city's towers, shrinking and paling as it rose. George had lived in Seattle all his life. Just an hour before, he would have said he knew it like the back of his hand. Now he was struck by its size, by its complexity, by how much he did not know. Tonight, as he took his accustomed freeway exit and followed familiar streets to the store where he had worked for more than twenty years, he noticed things that he had never seen before.

He imagined he was Harry, trying to find his way safely through the urban maze. Suddenly, George felt lost in his hometown.

At the store, George punched in the code to disarm the security system and let himself in the back way. The tall shelves of the stockroom were spooky in the darkness, and huge shipping cartons, delivered but not yet unpacked, loomed like monsters. Since he had quit, George felt like an intruder.

He went out front and confronted the giant stuffed grizzly with its stiff-jawed snarl. "Well, buddy," he said. "It's you and me. Take it easy, now, big boy. This won't hurt a bit." George took out the big rasp he'd brought from home and set to work. The job wasn't as hard as he'd imagined it might be. With a good manicure and his fangs filed flat, *Claws* didn't look so ferocious anymore. In fact, he almost seemed to be smiling.

George studied his handiwork. A new thought struck him, and he laughed out loud. It was really the old man he wanted to defang. Like father, like bear. With his teeth blunted, the old man's bark was probably a whole lot worse than his bite. It was just that George had never dared put it to the test before. He considered the possibility that if he stood up straight and looked the old curmudgeon in the eye, he might actually come to *like* his dad. He considered a possibility his dad might like him better if he did. It was a long shot, but George was willing to give it a try.

He scribbled a note on the back of a store receipt and pinned it to the grizzly's chest. It said simply, "Dad, I love you. G." How could anybody argue with that?

That done, George climbed into the display window for a last look at the Bigfoot sighting map. The pattern of the pushpins seemed to confirm his hunch. Harry was downtown tonight.

George reset the alarm system, locked up the store and hit the streets.

29

Harry moved cautiously inside the forest of tall caves. Here his feet left no prints on the hard pathways. All the smells of this place were strange to him, all of its sounds. Here and there, small trees and shrubs grew in little containers full of earth, and Harry helped himself to what leaves he could pick in passing. Still, his stomach felt empty. He did not know if he would ever find his home.

He moved close to the fronts of buildings, trying to stay out of the light. The holes in the buildings were filled with something clear and hard and shiny. Sometimes he saw himself reflected in it. At first he thought it was another Bigfoot, not himself, but when he reached out to touch the other, all he could feel was the coldness of the glass. Slowly, he came to realize it was himself he saw. Harry moved on.

He came to a lighted window with many picture boxes arrayed inside it. They were like the picture box in the home of his friend. He had watched it with the young male. Now, as he looked at the boxes, the face of his friend, the male creature, appeared on them. Harry roared greetings. On the faces of the different boxes, there were many pictures of his friend. A metal fence separated Harry from the boxes. Until he removed it, his friend would not be able to see or hear him. He shook the metal fence until it gave way. When it did, a loud bell began to shrill. Harry did not like the sound of it. He smashed through the clear shiny stuff and reached out for the box with the picture of the male. Harry lifted the box to his lips and licked his friend's face. Harry knew it was not skin he touched, but he was happy. He would take the box with him on his journey.

The box was on some kind of leash. When Harry stepped away from the building, the surface of the picture box grew dark. His friend disappeared. Harry threw the picture box away and went to get another. The same thing happened again. As he moved away, the box went dark. His friend died. When he looked back to the lighted boxes, his friend was gone.

A car came screaming around the corner and fixed its lights on him. Harry sensed he was in danger. He lifted the picture box high above his head and flung it at the approaching car. The box exploded in the street. The car swerved and smashed into the face of a building across the street. Creatures, all males, jumped from the car and pointed guns at him.

Harry made for the safety of a nearby alley.

30

For a while, George cruised. Uptown, around the posh department stores and slick boutiques, the streets were all but empty. Heading west, he peered into the shadows of the Pike Place Market, closed for the night. South, toward Pioneer Square, there was more nightlife. Strains of jukebox music wafted out of open tavern doors. Drunks staggered up the street or took rest in the doorways of the older office buildings where lawyers plied their trade by day. On top of the dark courthouse, he could see the lighted windows of the county jail.

George decided to concentrate his search between First and Third, south of Pike Street and north of King. It was a long stretch of three main avenues, stitched together by a maze of alleys. There were lots of recessed doorways, places to hide. A wary creature could easily stay out of sight.

When George reached the area, a swelling crowd of freelance Rambos and city police confirmed his intuition. The blue lights of police cars tore the sky. Sirens rose around him. As George was about to turn onto First, a police car squealed into his path, laying rubber. When it stopped, officers climbed out and sealed the street. George backed up and drove away from the excitement. On a street that seemed safely deserted, George nosed the station wagon into a hillside parking place and set out on foot. He looked around. There was no one to see him slip into the alley.

With his trigger finger, Jacques traced the thick black line that connected sightings on his map. Bigfoot was in downtown Seattle. Now. Tonight. If Jacques LaFleur could help it, the Sasquatch would never leave. A lifetime of tracking and a box of cartridges said so. In the darkness of his powerwagon, LaFleur threw back his head and laughed out loud.

He headed down Pine Street toward what his calculations told him was prime hunting ground. As he prepared to turn left on Third, a policeman flagged him down. A small battalion of gendarmes were setting up barricades. LaFleur rolled down his window.

"Area's closed, buddy," the officer said. "Third to First, from here down past the Kingdome. No civilians allowed in the area."

"Why's that? You chasing terrorists? Bank robbers, maybe?"

"We have reason to believe that Bigfoot is in the area."

"What reasons?" LaFleur asked, but the cop said, "Look, fella. I've got work to do here. Now move along. You'll have to find yourself a detour. Try going north a few blocks, then cut down to Alaskan."

For a moment, LaFleur considered offering his services to the police. "Excuse me, officer, but I am a seasoned hunter. I have been tracking Bigfoot for years." He thought better of it. If he helped the police find Bigfoot, they would take credit for it. They would keep the hide. No, he was going to have to outwit the police.

LaFleur nodded to the officer and backed into Pine Street, then turned right, in case the cop was paying attention. Out of their sight, he circled back to the midpoint of the cordoned area and parked his wagon. Rifle under his arm, he slipped past the barricades. What was meant to keep him out would also contain his prey. How nice of the police to isolate the area for him. Now all he had to do was beat them to Bigfoot.

Noise spilled into the alley from the intersection. From the sound of it, there was quite a crowd out there. Flattened against the side of a building, George crept toward the alley's mouth and peered out at the scene. A cop car, its top light spinning, blocked the street. Uniformed officers surrounded the car and held back the growing crowd, while the boss cop studied a city map spread on the hood.

The boss cop looked up and barked at his men. "I want this quadrant airtight. Nothing gets out. Nothing! And no force, except in self-defense. I don't need some prankster in a monkey suit bleeding all over the streets. Now move!"

The clump of officers dispersed in all directions. Swinging their nightsticks, a pair made for George's alley. He inched deeper into shadow and held his breath as they passed him.

Jacques moved soundlessly through the city alleys. He could hear distant voices, but here it was quiet. He rounded a corner and was almost startled by the bulk of a dump truck parked in the alley. A Dumpster was mounted on the front of the truck, but its drivers were gone. LaFleur resumed his tracking. It was a hard job on cement, but when he looked down, he was rewarded. In a half-dried puddle, he found what he was looking for—a perfect big foot imprinted in the mud. Its toes pointed toward the garbage truck. LaFleur followed.

Deer hunting had never been like this. George's heart pounded. Despite the fall chill, he was sweating freely. The pavement showed no trail. And George felt hunted. He'd never been in competition with the cops before. His progress was slow. Too slow. He wished there were a way to cover more ground faster.

There was. It was risky, but his voice could go farther faster than his legs could. He slipped around a corner, determined to try. A low rumble startled him, until he realized it was only the sound of an engine idling. George took a few deep breaths, then whispered Harry's name a few times before he realized that Harry didn't know his name.

George rose up to his full height and filled his lungs with air. Then he threw back his head and let loose with his best imitation of Harry's thunderous howl. His voice grew even bigger as it bounced off walls.

Only twice before in all his years of tracking Sasquatch had Jacques heard the huge, full-bodied howl that echoed through the alley now, but there was no mistaking it. His quarry was nearby. Jacques hid himself in the darkness of a doorway and looked out, his hunter's senses on full alert. A huge shadow loomed against the wall opposite his hiding place. LaFleur took off the safety and readied his rifle for action.

George walked slowly and deliberately, defying the light that shone behind him. He almost felt like Sasquatch when he summoned up another ear-splitting howl. George stopped and waited for an answer from his friend.

When Sasquatch howled again, adrenaline surged through LaFleur's body, sharpening his every reflex. He shouldered his rifle and moved toward the intersection. A third call thundered, filling the alley with its echoes. Jacques whipped around, his weapon ready. A shadow twice as big as the first one loomed against the wall. He turned back to the smaller shadow. It was running now. Jacques turned again, to the place where the shadows should intersect.

A dark, hairy mass filled his vision, just as a strong musk stench filled his nostrils. After more than thirty years of searching, Jacques found himself just inches from his prey. The sheer animal mass of Bigfoot numbed him. His only reflex, for the moment, was awe.

The Bigfoot seized Jacques' rifle. Jacques let go. The rifle fell. When it hit the ground, it fired. The explosion annoyed the creature. His massive hands closed on Jacques and lifted him high in the air. In a long arc, LaFleur flew through the night. He landed painfully. Then everything went dark.

At the sound of a nearby rifle shot, George nearly jumped out of his skin. When his brain kicked in again, it was full of fear for Harry. It sounded like the cops, or one of the crazies, had found him first. Well, maybe there was still something he could do for his friend. George advanced slowly. With apprehension, he rounded the corner.

Harry. Unharmed. Unscathed. George's heart expanded in his chest. Breathing thanks, he raced toward the Bigfoot, arms wide, and found himself enfolded in a powerful embrace.

The sound of running footsteps dispersed their joy. George could hear the clatter of hardware he did not doubt was weapons. Even as they listened, the sounds drew nearer. A metallic clunk rang from the Dumpster. Harry responded with a low growl.

George turned toward the idling garbage truck. "Get in!" he told Harry. Come on, hop in. They'll never look for you up there!"

George headed for the cab, expecting Harry to climb in beside him. There was a small glitch in communication.

Harry climbed into the Dumpster instead. At least he was out of sight. In the sideview mirror, George saw the shadows of running men. He ground the truck into gear and started down the alley. Behind them, the intersection filled up with cops.

Harry did as his friend told him. He climbed in the back of the truck. The smell was terrible. Worse yet, there was a creature there, the same male Harry had disarmed and thrown aside before. Instinctively, Harry knew the creature meant him harm. As he watched, the male's eyes opened. Harry growled at him. He stared at Harry, then reached behind him and drew a small gun from his coat.

All of a sudden, the truck lurched to a stop. Harry and the male slammed against the metal side of the Dumpster. The creature dropped his gun. Harry picked it up and examined it. The truck moved forward. Harry could feel the creature's fear.

The police were hot on his trail. George examined the dashboard of the garbage truck. He slammed on the brake and released one of the levers. The back end of the truck dropped off, spewing garbage, but the Dumpster held fast in front. It would take the cops a while to dig themselves out. George threw the truck in gear and gunned it.

When the truck stopped for a second time, the Bigfoot dropped Jacques' pistol. It planted itself butt up in a mess of rotting cantaloupe. Without taking his eyes from the creature, LaFleur bellied forward and reached for his gun. There. He had it. He cleared the soft, stinking mess from the barrel and aimed the pistol.

With the police slowed down behind, it looked like they were home free. Thirty yards and they'd be out of the alley, back on city streets. With any luck, they'd be in the station wagon and on their way home before the cops knew what had hit them. George kept the accelerator flat to the floorboards.

Suddenly, a man staggered into the alley. The headlights illumined him as the truck zoomed forward. He was dressed in tatters, red-faced and very drunk. A wino. And George was about to blow the guy to kingdom come.

This was it, the moment he'd waited most of a lifetime for. His pistol was in his hand, his finger curled around the trigger. He aimed at the creature's heart. Whenever he imagined killing Sasquatch, it was in the woods, but LaFleur was not about to argue with fate. A dumpster would have to do. His finger teased the trigger.

George hit the brakes. The wino squatted in front of the garbage truck and shielded his head with crossed arms.

Jacques cocked the hammer back. Slowly, steadily, his trigger finger squeezed.

The brakes grabbed just in time. The truck shuddered to a stop so violently the Dumpster flew off the front. It sailed through the air, hit ground and skidded, shooting sparks.

Before he could fire, the truck lurched and a slimy, stinking wall of garbage crashed down on Jacques. Damp coffee grounds rained into his eyes. The Dumpster was airborne. With a bone-rattling crash, it hit the ground and skidded, flattening LaFleur against a mound of soggy trash. Dripping slime, Bigfoot rose above him. LaFleur had never imagined the creature would kill *him*. He closed his eyes and waited to die.

• • •

Blinking and looking dazed, Harry peered out of the Dumpster.

"We did it!" George hollered. "Come on, boy!"

Harry climbed out. His fur was covered with garbage. Even from a distance, he reeked. George didn't care. The station wagon was right around the corner. He grabbed Harry's hand and tugged him toward it. They both climbed in. As George started the engine, Harry modified the design. He sat up straight and made himself another skydome. They sped away.

31

Jacques waited, but nothing happened. Cautiously, he opened one eye in time to see the monster clambering out of the Dumpster. Jacques rose up on one elbow and wiped his face with his shirtsleeve. His body ached all over, but nothing seemed to be broken. Bigfoot had let him live. His mistake.

LaFleur rose to his knees, then to his feet and struggled to the side of the dumpster. He arrived in time to see a very peculiar station wagon, with two large welts rising from its metal roof, drive past the intersection before him. Sasquatch sat in the passenger seat. Jacques just had time to read the rear license plate before the station wagon disappeared. It matched the number on the plate he'd found beside the highway. George Henderson was Bigfoot's chauffeur.

Footsteps sounded in the alley, growing louder. LaFleur dug in the garbage to retrieve his pistol. Just as he grabbed the handle, he lost his footing to an overripe avocado and fell hard into the garbage. He scrambled to his feet, pistol ready, and peered over the side of the Dumpster. A forest of guns blossomed around his head.

"Hold it right there, fella," a policeman ordered.

Jacques froze.

The police took his pistol. They handcuffed him. They laughed at the way he looked and smelled. Then the officer in charge, Sergeant Schwarz, held up his rifle, lost in the alley. "Ever see this before? It's got your initials on it, just like this pistol here."

Jacques said nothing. The officer flashed him a wicked grin. "Well, well. I'm sure you have a concealed weapon permit. I'd like to see it."

"You can't do this," Jacques said. "A man's got a right to protect himself. I want to talk to my lawyer."

Schwarz laughed. "Yeah, sure. Maybe you and your pals can chip in for one. Save yourself some dough." He turned to an underling. "Okay, take him away."

The officer swung open the door of a large police van. It was already full of handcuffed men. Some wore hunting jackets. The rest were dressed from movies—Road Warrior, Rambo. There was even a cowboy hat or two. "Welcome to the Bigfoot Brigade," the cop said. He prodded Jacques from behind with his nightstick. "Come on. Climb in there with your buddies."

Jacques turned to Sergeant Schwarz. "Wait. You're making a big mistake. Do you know who I am? I am Jacques LaFleur, world's foremost Bigfoot hunter. Surely you recognize my name. I can help you."

"You can help me by climbing in the paddy wagon, Mr. La Flour."

"I know where Bigfoot is," Jacques told them. "I can take you to him."

"Sure," Schwarz said. "While you're at it, maybe you can help us find Judge Crater and Jimmy Hoffa."

"This is no laughing matter," Jacques said.

"Who's laughing?" Schwarz said. "Bunch of crazies like you guys almost makes you want to vote for gun control."

"You . . . you communist!" Jacques shouted, as the paddy wagon doors slammed shut behind him. "You won't get by with this."

32

Ernie hovered around the kitchen television. He used to hate it when they interrupted his favorite shows with news—news bulletins were *boring*—but tonight he wanted more updates and fewer laughs. How was he supposed to care about the dumb problems of some fake family when his own dad was out there in the mean streets and the cops were after Harry?

"Is your homework done?" his mom asked.

"How am I supposed to concentrate on spelling words at a time like this?"

"Get your book," his mother said. "I'll quiz you."

"Mom . . ."

"Get it."

Ernie got his spelling book. They settled at the kitchen table and his mom turned the TV volume down. "We'll keep the picture on," she promised. "We can turn the sound up if something happens." She opened the book. "Lesson One. Spell danger."

Ernie thought about it. "D-A-I-N-J-E-R."

"Wrong," his mom said. "Try again."

"Look, Mom." Ernie pointed to the TV screen. The news announcer was talking. His mother turned the volume up, just as the picture switched to the mobile news van downtown. The TV reporter in his trenchcoat was standing

in front of a police barricade. "In response to Bigfoot
sightings in downtown Seattle, police have closed streets to
civilian traffic. Earlier this evening, a Third Avenue
television and stereo dealership was broken into and
vandalized. Police now believe that the culprit was"—the
announcer couldn't help smiling—"get this, Bigfoot. We'll
keep you posted on events as they develop. Meanwhile,
back to you, Dave."

Dave appeared at his news desk. "Thanks, Phil. I wonder
what Bigfoot wants with a stereo? Well, more later. Now
back to our regularly scheduled programming."

His mother turned the sound off. "So far, so good," she
said.

"What's good about it?" Ernie asked.

"They haven't shot Harry and they haven't arrested your
father," his mom said. "That's good. Spell friend."

"Jeez, Mom, give me a break."

"Spell it."

"H-A-R-R-Y," Ernie said. For a minute, he thought his
mother was going to get mad, but then she smiled at him.

Sarah came in and browsed in the refrigerator. "There's
nothing to eat," she complained.

"Are you finally off the phone?" Mom asked.

"For now," Sarah said. "I promised I'd call Sasha back
after I read the English assignment."

"What are you reading?" Mom asked.

"*The Call of the Wild*," Sarah said. "It's boring."

"Sarah, I want you to stay off the phone for the rest of the
night," Mom said. "Your father might need to reach us."

"Mom," Sarah said. "I promised Sasha. Besides, we've
got call waiting. I don't see what's the big deal."

"Well, I don't want your father waiting," Mom said.
"You can explain to Sasha in the morning."

"Yo, Mom," Ernie said. He turned to Sarah. "You gotta
zip your lip, motor mouth."

"Zip your face," Sarah said. "Besides, if you're not nice to me, I won't tell you the Bigfoot joke Sasha told me."

"A Bigfoot joke," Ernie said. "Wow."

"Go on," Mom said. "The suspense is killing me."

"Well, okay. What do you call one-tenth of a Bigfoot?" Ernie loved riddles. He thought about it. "How about 'sir'?"

"Wrong," Sarah said. "Mom?"

Mom shook her head. "I have no idea."

Sarah grinned, delivering the punch line. "A big toe. Get it?"

Mom groaned. Ernie said, "That's dumb."

"It's better than your stupid jokes, Ernie. Like, why did the chicken cross the road—to get a peanut butter and jelly sandwich."

"That's a very funny joke," Ernie said. "You just don't have any sense of humor."

"Kids," Mom said. It was her cool-it voice.

"Well, back to the books," Sarah said. She grabbed a bag of potato chips from the cupboard and headed upstairs.

Ernie turned to his mother. "Mom, do you think Dad's all right?"

"I hope so, Ernie," Mom said. "I'm believing both he and Harry are just fine until we hear otherwise. You know what they say—no news is good news."

Ernie thought about that. "What's that supposed to mean?"

"I'm not quite sure," his mother said.

At nine o'clock, Nancy told Ernie to go to bed. He didn't want to go. At 9:30, she told Ernie to go to bed. "Please, Mom, just let me stay up a little longer." At ten o'clock, Nancy said, "Come on, Ern. Come sit with me. We'll wait for Dad together." By 10:15, Ernie was sound asleep beside her on the sofa. Gently, she took off his glasses and put them on the coffee table. He was a good kid, especially sleeping. Nancy stroked Ernie's hair back off his forehead and tried to imagine what was happening to George.

At 10:30, the phone rang. Nancy answered before it woke Ernie. "Are you all right? Where are you?"

"I'm in the kitchen," Irene said, "and I'm fine, except we're all out of prune juice. I wondered if you guys had some."

"Not a prune in the house," Nancy said.

"I was just wondering," Irene said. "Well, I guess I'll go to bed now."

"Good idea," Nancy said. "Goodnight, Irene."

At eleven o'clock, Nancy watched the news. The only new information was that police were arresting all the armed maniacs who'd run downtown to shoot Bigfoot. The ones they showed all looked like criminals and crazies. George didn't have a gun. Nancy wasn't sure if that was good or bad. She started to doze off, wondering.

The telephone woke her up. "Is Betty there?"

"No Betty here. Wrong number."

At midnight, Nancy dozed off.

Around one in the morning, something woke them. It was the living room light. Slowly, Nancy opened her eyes. George was home. He was safe.

"Harry!" Ernie exclaimed.

"George. Where the hell have you been?" Nancy said. "We've been worried." She saw the Sasquatch beside her husband. "Harry. Welcome home."

Sarah came trotting down the stairs. "I knew it was him." She turned to Harry. "I could smell you all the way upstairs."

"Rrrrfff." Little Bob raced down the stairs, skidding on the hardwood floors, and leapt up on the back of the couch. He took a flying leap. Harry palmed him like a basketball.

"Looks like it's unanimous," George said.

Nancy bounced up off the sofa. "Let's celebrate."

Sarah groaned. "Let's move."

George held up his hand to catch the family's attention. When everyone was quiet, he turned to Harry. "You may not understand a word of this, Harry, but I'm going to say it anyway. When we found you, when we ran you over with the car, I should have seen right away how special you were."

Puzzled but attentive, Harry kept his eyes on George. George went on. "I have no excuse for not realizing that your feelings could be hurt a lot more easily than the rest of you. But I'm a human, and sometimes we make mistakes." He paused, then said, "I mean, bacon bits. Why? But there is a lot we've learned from you, even if it might just be things we've forgotten."

Harry looked serious for a moment, like he was going to make a speech back, but then Little Bob yipped at him and they started playing instead.

"Let's get a picture!" Ernie said. Before George could stop him, Ernie was in the den, opening the closet door. All of George's stuffed hunting trophies came tumbling out. Harry was surrounded by glassy-eyed, disembodied animals. He looked sadly down upon them, then raised his eyes to meet George's.

"This he understands," George said. The funny thing was, he no longer understood himself. The trophies used to make him proud. Now they embarrassed him. Harry growled, a soft growl that sounded disappointed. George was disappointed in himself. "Nancy? Ern? You too, Sarah."

The family lined up and George filled their arms with dead animals. He carried the ten-point buck himself. To Harry he handed the wolf head. Solemnly, Harry took it.

George dug the grave himself. It was the least he could

do. After so much tension, the exercise felt good. When the pit was deep enough, the family laid the trophies one by one inside it. George covered them with dirt and packed it down.

"Hey, Dad, aren't you supposed to say something at a funeral?" Ernie asked.

"Like what?" Sarah demanded.

"Uh, I don't know," Ernie said. "How about, goodnight, sleep tight, don't let the bedbugs bite?"

"That's disgusting," Sarah said.

Ernie shrugged. George looked at the grave. "How about, uh, I'm sorry?" he said. "Will that do it?" He looked to Harry. Harry responded by gathering the entire family into a giant Bigfoot hug. His scent, garbage and musk, almost knocked them out.

Nancy gripped her nose shut with her fingers. "Arggh. George, what are we going to do?"

"I think," George said, "that Harry needs to take a bath."

"Oh, no," Sarah said. "Not in my bathtub, he's not. Think of the stink. Think of the ring." She turned to Harry. "Besides, you're too big."

"You got any better ideas, Sarah?" George asked.

"I do!" Ernie said. "How about the Moffitt's swimming pool?"

33

Ernie wore his swimming trunks under his bathrobe. He was not only the best swimmer in the family, but also he had the least sensitive nose. It only made sense for him to be named designated bather. Holding Harry's hand, he crept through the low wall of shrubbery that separated the Hendersons' backyard from the Moffitts'. With soap, shampoo and a stack of towels, his mom and Sarah followed.

The yard was dark, but the full moon lit the yard. Its reflection floated like a silver coin on the dark surface of the swimming pool. Ernie peeled off his bathrobe and grinned at Harry. "Let's go swimming," Ernie said.

For a moment, Harry studied Ernie's small hairless body. "Okay, so I'm not Arnold Schwarzenegger," Ernie said. "But just wait till my next growing spurt." Then he grabbed his nose and jumped into the pool. When he surfaced, he saw Harry crouched by the edge, watching closely. He seemed relieved when Ernie reappeared. "Come on in," Ernie urged. "The water's fine."

Harry stuck his big toe on the water and withdrew it. He seemed to frown.

"Okay, so it's a little cold," Ernie, treading water, said. "But you can't tell me they have heated pools where you come from."

Harry stuck one whole foot in the water, then pulled it out and delicately shook the water from his fur. Nancy joined him at poolside. "I don't like cold water either," she said. "But you have to take a bath. Come on, Harry. Won't it feel good to be clean?"

"Sissy, sissy. Harry is a sissy," Ernie taunted from the middle of the pool.

That did it. Imitating Ernie, Harry held his nose and jumped. A huge geyser rose up when he hit the water. The enormous splash showered Nancy with spray and bits of garbage.

"Yo! A cannonball," Ernie exclaimed.

His mother shushed him. "We don't want to wake Irene."

Cautiously, Sarah stepped to the edge of the pool. "Mother, he's been down an awfully long time."

"Sarah's right. Ernie, is Harry all right?"

"I'll check it out." Ernie dove down underwater, searching for Harry. It was too dark to see. He swam near the bottom, feeling for his friend. Suddenly, arms closed around him and Ernie felt himself flying upward. Locked in a bear hug, Ernie and Harry came zooming out of the water. Harry lifted Ernie high above his head. Ernie put his feet on Harry's shoulders and dove back into the water. Harry submerged, too. Ernie grabbed his ankle, and Harry gave him a free ride.

When they came up for air, Ernie's mom said, "Come on, you guys. Stop horsing around. Ernie, you've got work to do." She held out a family-size bottle of baby shampoo, a giant-size bar of Ivory soap and a toilet brush.

"Aw, Mom, do I have to? We were having fun. Besides, the garbage has already come off." Ernie swatted the water's surface. It was coated with a greasy scum.

"I want him clean, Ernie. And I mean clean."

Ernie padded to the edge of the pool. "Come on, Harry. Fun's over. You've got to have your bath."

Harry still wanted to play. He stood in the middle of the pool, grinning his Bigfoot grin at Ernie. When Ernie didn't come, Harry used his big hands as scoops. When he splashed, it was like a sudden downpour.

Ernie's mom got soaked. She stood up to her full height, stamped her foot and read the riot act. "Harry, you come here. Now!"

Harry looked at her for a minute, then obediently dog-paddled to the edge of the pool.

Ernie held up the shampoo. "Look, no more tears." He opened the bottle and started pouring the contents on Harry. One bottle covered his head, shoulders and chest. Ernie bobbed around Harry, massaging in the shampoo, until he worked up a lather that turned Harry's dark fur white. "You look like the abominable snowman," Ernie told him. "Okay, it's time to rinse. You just duck down, like this."

He demonstrated. Harry thought it was playtime again. He ducked and kept swimming. "Ernie," Ernie's mother said, in her sternest voice. Ernie swam after Harry, caught his hand and towed him back to the shallow end. After a few tries, he persuaded Harry to sit on the side of the pool. His mom handed him the Ivory soap. "Scrub," she said.

Ernie scrubbed. His mom handed him the toilet brush, and Ernie used it to work the soap through Harry's fur. Harry's nose twitched at the unfamiliar smell. He didn't look too happy. When Ernie had lathered all of Harry, he handed him the bar of soap and pointed at his private parts. "You do that yourself," he said.

Harry studied the soap. Then licked it. He made a face and spat the bubbles out. "Go ahead," Ernie said. "Wash yourself." He patted his lower belly. "Down there." Harry watched Ernie, then imitated him. "Good boy," Ernie said.

Sarah was getting impatient. "Come on, Ernie, we haven't got all night. What if Mrs. Moffitt wakes up and sees us?"

"She'll think we're a bad dream, Sarah," Ernie said. "Relax."

"I can't relax," Sarah said. "Hurry up."

Ernie studied Harry and decided he was well-scrubbed. "Okay, boy. Rinse time." He plunged into the water and Harry followed. They bobbed and fooled around until Ernie's mom made him get out. She handed him a towel, then held another open for Harry. "Time to get dry," she said. "You don't want to catch a cold."

"Mom," Ernie protested, "Bigfoots don't catch colds."

"How do you know?" Sarah asked. "They probably get terrible colds. Can you imagine? One sneeze would blow the house down. Ugh. How disgusting."

Harry crawled out of the pool. Ernie's mom tried to wrap a towel around his waist, but it wouldn't reach. "Maybe you could just shake yourself off," she suggested. "That's what Little Bob does." Mom imitated Little Bob. Harry imitated her. The water flew. Sarah jumped back. "Yuck."

"Okay, everybody. Back to the house. It's starting to get light," Ernie's mom ordered. She took Harry by the hand and marched him toward the hedge. Following in formation, Ernie looked back over his shoulder at the Moffitts' pool. "Yo! The world's biggest bathtub," he said.

In the kitchen, Harry sniffed his fur, the way Little Bob did after a bath, as if he missed his animal smell. Nancy made cocoa for the kids and fed Harry a head of lettuce and a bunch of bananas. He didn't bother to skin them before he wolfed them down.

"Good stuff, huh?" Ernie asked.

Harry replied with a satisfied belch. Nancy surveyed the scene. "Ernie, you're a mess. Run upstairs and take a quick shower."

"Mom, I just had a bath."

"In dirty water. You run along now."

Ernie headed for the stairs. Harry tried to follow him. "Oh, no you don't," Nancy said. "You wait down here. Let's see what we can find in the refrigerator. I think there's a whole head of cauliflower. Yum." she led him back to the kitchen.

Harry liked cauliflower. George got up from his nap on the sofa. "Harry, you look like a new man," he said. "Whoops. A new Bigfoot."

Ernie took the world's shortest shower. In no time, he was back, Sarah's blow-dryer in hand. "Hey, Harry. I bet you'd love the dry look."

Ernie sat Harry on the kitchen floor and Ernie plugged in the dryer. When he turned it on, Harry looked puzzled by the warm wind flowing from it. Ernie blew it on him. Harry flinched. "It's okay, big guy," Ernie said. "Watch." He directed the airstream at his own head. "See? It doesn't hurt a bit." He turned it on Harry. Harry leaned back and closed his eyes.

Nancy picked the matted hair out of Little Bob's brush and handed it to Sarah. "You give him a good brushing. And I"—she held up the toenail clippers—"am going to do your nails." She knelt down and started on his feet. Harry opened his eyes for a minute, then decided it didn't hurt and relaxed again. Sarah stopped brushing to get a baggie from the drawer. She held it out to her mother. "Save the clippings," she advised. "They're probably worth a lot of money." Nancy laughed, but she collected the toenail clippings and put them in the bag.

"Look at this," Ernie said. "He's a punk rocker."

Nancy looked. Ernie was drying Harry's hair so that it stood straight up. "He looks like he just stuck his big toe into an electric socket."

The phone rang. Nancy looked to George. He nodded. "It's okay."

Nancy picked up the phone. "You're not going to believe this," Irene said. "I don't believe it."

"Believe what?" Nancy asked, sounding as innocent as she could.

"The pool," Irene said. "The pool man came this morning to clean it out and change the filter, like he does every other month. I just told him to go about his business, but pretty soon he's at the back door. 'Mrs. Moffitt, there's something I think you should see,' so I went out with him and do you know what?"

"What, Irene?" Nancy asked.

"Well, the water looked like a sewer, I mean an absolute sewer, but that's not the half of it. The pool man picked up the net he uses to scoop out leaves and stuff, and it's full of this disgusting big hairy *glop*. So the guy says, 'Mrs. Moffitt, do you have a cat?' I told him no. 'Good,' he says, 'then it's just a hair ball.'"

"Amazing," Nancy said. "How do you suppose it got in your pool?"

"Beats me," Irene said. "The pool man said, 'It looks like that big monster that's been running around loose—you know, that Bigfoot thing—had himself a little dip in your pool.' What do you think of that?"

"I think it's nice your pool man has a sense of humor," Nancy said. "If you ask me, it was kids."

"Yeah, maybe," Irene said. "I wonder."

"Not my kids, of course," Nancy said. "Oop. Kettle's whistling. I've got to turn it off."

"I think I'm going back to bed," Irene said. "Catch you later."

Nancy waited until Irene hung up to laugh.

34

The police told their prisoners they could make one phone call. They would be called in alphabetical order. Jacques groaned. That put him near the middle of the list. He moved around the holding pen, looking for an Anderson or a Baker he could trade places with. The best he could do was Gordon, and that cost him ten bucks. It was early morning when he got his shot at the telephone.

Luckily, he kept his lawyer's phone numbers, work and home, with him at all times. Jerome was home but not awake. It took him a while to grasp the situation.

"I'll see what I can do," Jerome said. "I should be able to have you released by sometime tomorrow morning."

Jacques growled into the phone. "You got an ear? I said, get me out of here *now*. Tomorrow's too late."

His lawyer started to mumble some excuse. The guard was standing there, nonchalant, pretending like he wasn't listening, but Jacques knew he was. He cupped his hand over the mouthpiece. "I know where he is," he said.

"You know where who is?"

"For goodness sake, Jerome. What have I been doing for the last twenty-five years? *Him*."

"I'm afraid I don't quite understand," his lawyer said.

Jacques looked at the guard, then whispered into the phone, "Sasquatch. I know where he is."

"It seems to me I've heard that one before," Jerome said.

"This time is different. I've got his address."

"Jacques, you're talking crazy."

LaFleur exploded. He didn't care who heard. "Crazy? You want to see crazed? Just let me sit here one more hour and I'll show you crazy. Make something happen. *Now!*"

The guard looked at his watch. "Time's running out."

"*Do it, Jerome!*" LaFleur bellowed, before he hung up the phone.

35

Ernie was a good teacher and Harry a fast learner. Harry had a gift for mimicry, and even though most human toys and tools were too small for him, his big hands mastered most of them after a few tries. By midmorning, he'd learned how to use faucets, how to turn the television on and off, how to vacuum and how to imitate King Kong. Ernie dug out one of Sarah's outgrown Barbie dolls to be Fay Wray and showed Harry how to beat his chest with his fists while yodeling.

Watching them play, George had mixed feelings. He was moved by Harry's innocence and enthusiasm, and the gentleness he showed Ernie. It also troubled him to see a wild creature so easily seduced by the gadgetry of so-called civilized life. George suspected God had not intended Sasquatch to play Atari. He was not all surprised when Ernie asked if they could keep him. George had been wondering the same thing himself.

"He's a lot more fun than Little Bob, Dad, and I can teach him to be a big help around the house. You know how Mom's always wishing we had a maid."

Nan turned from the stove, where she was grilling cheese sandwiches. "Oh, Ernie. That's just talk. What do I need a maid for when I've got you and Sarah."

Ernie fixed pleading eyes on George. "Come on, Dad.

He's happy here. He likes me. He likes all of us. Even Sarah."

"I know he does, Ern. And I like him. I really do, but . . ."

"But what?"

Nan said. "We can't *afford* to keep him, Ernie. Harry needs to live in the forest, where food is free. We'd have to give Safeway a second mortgage on the house."

"I'll get a paper route," Ernie said.

Sarah said, "He's an *animal,* Ernie. He isn't even housebroken."

"I can train him just like *that!*" Ernie snapped his fingers.

"Lunch," Nancy called out. "Time to eat, everybody."

The family sat down at the table. Harry served himself straight from the refrigerator—a little of this, a little of that—whatever caught his eye. In the family silence, his crunching and slurping was loud. "Besides," Sarah said, "he has terrible manners."

"He does not."

"Next to yours, Ernie, I'll admit his look good. But I wouldn't want to take him to a restaurant," Sarah said.

Ernie said, "He could have his own room in the basement. We could put in some rocks and Astro Turf and stuff so he'd feel right at home."

George ate his sandwich slowly. He almost wished that Ernie could convince him. When he was finished eating, George turned to his son. "I know how you feel, but it's impossible. Harry needs to be in a safe place, and that isn't here."

Sarah flashed Ernie one of her I-told-you-so looks. "Dad's right."

George knew he was only half right. "I just wish I knew where a safe place was," he said.

After lunch, Nancy took her wounded plants out on the

back deck to see what she could do for them. She'd only been outside a few seconds when Irene called to her over the hedge. "Yoo-hoo, Nancy. Do you have a second?"

Nancy looked behind her. No Harry in sight. "Sure, Irene."

Her neighbor stepped through the hedge. "I just need somebody to talk to," she said. "This hasn't been easy, with the pool and all. Herb's no help. His latest theory is that a condor flew over and did his business in it."

Yipping wildly, the neighborhood dog pack came racing around the house and disappeared around the other side. Nancy had almost gotten used to them. Faithfully, they followed Harry's movements inside the house.

Irene looked after them. "Unless it's those crazy dogs. What's wrong with them, anyway?"

"Ah, it's just Little Bob," Nancy said. "He's quite the ladies' man."

Inside the kitchen, Nancy could hear the ringing of the telephone. "Oops. There's the phone," she told Irene. "I gotta go now."

George ran through a mental list of all the people he didn't want to talk to. At the moment, this included his father, the media and the entire Seattle Police Department. He'd decided not to be home when Harry picked up the receiver and handed it to him. "Hello?"

"I saw you on television last night, Mr. Hen, and I think we should talk. I'm sorry about the . . ."

"Who is this?" George asked.

"Do the words 'vital facts that could prevent a tragic and unnecessary end for the big fellow' ring a bell?"

The bell rang loudly. "Yes! Yes, Dr. Wrightwood?"

"I think we need to talk as soon as possible. You name the time and place."

"Fine. How about our house? Great. This afternoon. How about dinner?"

Dr. Wrightwood accepted the invitation. George hung up and told Nan they were having company.

36

When Nancy got home from shopping, the house was a mess again. At least Harry was a help. He carried all her grocery sacks from garage to kitchen in just one trip. When Nancy got inside, she threw back her head and bellowed, loudly enough to make Harry stare at her in admiration. *"Er-nie! Sa-rah! George! On the double!"*

When the family assembled, she gave them their marching orders. Everything, including themselves, was to be clean, shiny and on its best behavior no later than five o'clock. Ernie made a face. Nancy grabbed his shirt collar. "This means you."

Nancy laid her purchases out on the kitchen counter: five extra-long loaves of French bread, two pounds of fresh spinach, three different kinds of lettuce, a couple of pounds of fresh mushrooms, collard greens, half a pound of unsalted sunflower seeds, four avocados, half a dozen tomatoes, six bunches of celery, eight baking potatoes, a pound of bean sprouts, and for the humans, an eight-pound sirlion-tip roast. It added up to the family food budget for an entire week.

If she got the roast in the oven now, it would be ready in time. As she knelt and felt for the roasting pan, she heard Harry come into the kitchen. Why not? It was his favorite room. Even the television couldn't hold a candle to the refrigerator. When Nancy stood up, Harry was helping himself to a very big handful of bean sprouts. She swatted his hand. "No snacking. I don't want you to spoil your supper."

Looking just a little bit ashamed of himself, Harry moved back and watched intently while she unwrapped the roast. The butcher paper was red with beef blood. Harry sniffed, then wrinkled up his nose in distaste. "Oh, this," Nancy said. "Don't worry. You don't have to eat any." She went to the cabinet to get salt, pepper and garlic. When she turned back, Harry was holding the roast in his hands. "Roast," Nancy said. "Dinner."

Harry shook his head from side to side.

"What do you mean, no? You know what that thing cost per pound?"

Quick as he was to learn most things, Harry hadn't quite grasped the concept of money. He obviously didn't care about the price of beef. Palming the roast, he marched out the kitchen door. Nancy followed in time to see Harry solemnly inter her entree. He returned to the kitchen, gave her a disapproving look and helped himself to a bunch of celery before he went off to find Ernie. Nancy checked her salad dressing supply.

By six o'clock, the house looked good. The kids looked good. Nancy had found time to shower and put on a pretty dress. George was proud of his family. Now he had to coach Harry. He led him into the den. "You stay. Stay. Sorry. I mean, you just hang out here, okay? Until I call you." He turned to his son. "Ernie, see if you can find something for Harry to do." The bell rang. "Good boy," George said, as he shut them in the den.

Whomever he expected, it was not whom he found on the front stoop. "You," George stuttered. Better dressed, cleaner shaven, but unmistakably the same, the old man from the museum stood on the porch. He was carrying a large bouquet of flowers.

The old man took off his hat and extended his hand to George. "Hello, Mr. Henderson. I'm Wallace Wrightwood."

"You're *Doctor* Wrightwood?"

The old doctor gave George a pleasant if slightly guilty smile. "May I come in?"

George stepped back to let him pass. Nancy appeared. George introduced her. With a flourish, the old man presented his bouquet to Nancy. "Very pleased to meet you, Mrs. Henderson."

"Likewise. These are beautiful. Thanks. Oh, and this is Sarah and . . ." Nan looked around. "Where's Ernie?"

Ernie knew better than to tell Harry to sit. Instead, he pointed at the armchair. Harry got the idea. He sat down carefully. Ernie flipped through the tape case. "What do you want to hear?" He picked out a tape. "How about this? Randy Newman. You're gonna love *Short People*."

Ernie loaded the tape and put the earphones on Harry. His head was so big they almost broke. Ernie punched forward. Harry looked amazed when he heard the music playing in both ears.

"Pretty neat, huh?" Ernie said. "I gotta go. Company. That's why I'm in this monkey suit." Maybe that was the wrong thing to say. "Dress-up clothes," he corrected. As he turned toward the door, Ernie saw Harry smile. He was starting to move in time to the music.

George ushered their guest into the living room. "By the way," Dr. Wrightwood said, "I'd be more than happy to buy back the lamp and all the other articles you . . ."

"Don't be silly. Besides, they're buried somewhere and . . ." Ernie appeared in the living room. "Ah, here's our Ernie," George said. "Meet Dr. Wrightwood, son. He's . . ." George stopped talking when he noticed Wrightwood sniffing the air. He'd caught the Bigfoot scent. Ernie grinned so wide George thought his face would break.

"Something sure smells"—the doctor paused, looking for the right word and finished lamely—"good."

Nancy clapped her hands. "Dinner! It's almost ready. Why don't we all sit down? George, you settle people in. I want to get these flowers in some water."

Harry got up. He discovered he could pick up the Walkman and take it with him. He began to explore. Hanging on the wall, he saw a leaf like the one the male creature had given him to eat. It was in some kind of container, but that was easily broken. Carefully, Harry extracted a twenty-dollar bill and popped it in his mouth.

Best dishes, good silver. The table was nicely set. The children sat up straight and kept their hands off the food. George poured wine for the grown-ups. Nancy set Wrightwood's bouquet, prettily arranged, on the table. She nodded graciously to their guest. "Please, Dr. Wrightwood, help yourself."

Ernie eyed the table. "Uh, Mom, where's the roast?"

George bounced up from his chair. "Oh, the roast. I'll get it, hon'."

Nancy motioned him to sit. "The roast is resting in a shallow unmarked grave in the backyard."

"Too bad he doesn't hate broccoli," Ernie said.

George passed the French bread to Dr. Wrightwood. "Here. Take lots." He watched Wrightwood taking stock of their meatless meal. The old man smiled tolerantly.

"Are you folks vegetarians?" he asked.

George smiled back. "Sometimes," he told him. "It depends on the guest." He piled his own plate high with bread and greenery. For a meat and potatoes man, it looked a little bleak. George raised his fork and saluted their guest, then began to eat.

Doc Wrightwood crunched his vegetables. George hoped they wouldn't hurt his dentures. "Ummm, delicious," Wrightwood said. His lie was obvious but polite. Nancy acknowledged the compliment with a skeptical nod. Then Wrightwood turned to the kids. "As you probably know, your dad paid me a visit the other day, at my museum," he said. "I didn't let him know who I was, because to tell you the truth, I've had it up to here with people who think they've discovered Bigfoot and want to share the secret with me. I used to listen even if I didn't believe them, because I believed in *him*."

Ernie grinned broadly, barely able to stay in his chair. George frowned him a warning. "Are you saying you don't anymore?" he asked.

Through with the rabbit food, Wrightwood laid his folded napkin beside his plate. "Will you allow an old man to tell a story? It just might save your lives."

Nancy nodded encouragement. "If you put it that way," she said.

"When I was younger," Doc said, "I used to have a good job working as a lab scientist. Life was great. I was in love with a set of curves named Lee Ann." He looked at Nancy. "I thought of her about half an hour ago when I met a certain somebody."

Nancy blushed prettily.

Doc went on. "Anyway, we were going to get hitched, have us a couple little tax exemptions . . ." Now he looked at Sarah and Ernie. "A boy and a girl, if we had any say in it." His eyes got a faraway look. "But something happened on a hunting trip darned near fifty years ago that let the air out of everything."

Poor old guy. George wanted to show his sympathy. "She was killed?" he asked.

Wrightwood shot George a sharp glance. "Hell, no, she wasn't killed. She married a Buick dealer from Portland, and now she's got more money than God."

Nancy spoke for them all when she said, "I'm afraid I'm lost."

"Yeah. I don't get it," Ernie echoed.

"Listen up," Wrightwood said. "Here's what happened. I went out for a walk in the woods, alone. It was late afternoon, just before sunset. I heard a rustle behind me, loud—like a bear or a man would make. Then I smelled something that made my eyes water and my lungs smoke."

"Tell me about it," Sarah said.

The den door opened quietly behind Wrightwood. Just as quietly, Harry entered the room. George willed himself to keep a poker face. It was hard.

"What do you think it was?" Ernie asked Wrightwood. Good boy, George thought.

"The honest truth, is I don't know. By the time I turned around, all I saw was a flash of fur. On the ground, there was a footprint—a big footprint, just like a man's, only three times the size." Wrightwood paused.

"Please, Doctor," Nancy said. "Finish your story."

"Well . . . I was hooked from that moment on."

Harry was on his way across the living room, but something in Wrightwood's voice caught his attention. He stopped moving and stared at the old man.

"Well, I started spending all the time I could spare

searching for the beast. Then I spent time I couldn't spare. That's how I lost Lee Ann, then my job, then my friends."

"That's the saddest story I ever heard," Sarah said. There were real tears in her eyes. George smiled fondly. There was more to his daughter than Michael Jackson and styling gel after all.

"Well, I didn't tell it so you could cry in your bean sprouts, or whatever this is, darlin'," Doc Wrightwood said gruffly. "I told it so your father here wouldn't make the same mistake." He looked at George. "You're holding good cards here. Don't fold 'em."

George said, "I appreciate that, Doctor. But there's a big difference between you and me."

The old man shook his head. "Not as big as you think."

Harry wandered into the dining room, in search of food. He stood right behind Dr. Wrightwood, eyeing the spinach. George tried to contain his smile. "Maybe even bigger," he said.

"Don't kid yourself, Mister Hen. I saw you on the boob tube last night and I remember what you said when you came into my shop. 'Bigfoot can come live with us. We'll accept responsibility.' " Wrightwood rasped a cynical laugh. "Can you imagine what a Bigfoot would do to your home?"

Fighting giggles, the family looked around at the fresh plaster, the patched furniture. Nancy opened her eyes wide, all innocence, and nodded no.

"Well, I can," Dr. Wrightwood said. "You're good people. I'm going to say this once, and I'm going to say it simple, and I hope to God for your sakes that you all listen." Wrightwood's voice rose and his face grew red. *"There are no abominable snowmen. There are no Sasquatches, and there are no Bigfoots."*

The jig was up. Harry stood behind the doctor, about to

snatch the salad. The family's faces melted into smiles. Ernie giggled. The doctor looked confused. "Am I missing something?"

George looked up at Harry. "Yes, Doc. For too long."

The old man swiveled in his chair, following the direction of George's gaze. He found himself staring at Harry's lower abdomen. George watched the double take, how Doc's eyes traveled, up, up, up, until they reached Harry's. The doctor's amazement met Harry's gentle curiosity. They stared at each other for a long moment.

The doctor stood up, small beside the Sasquatch, whose existence he had just denied. "Lordy . . . Lord . . . God!"

"Dr. Wrightwood, say hello to Harry."

The old man could barely speak. His words came slowly as a two-year-old's. "Hello, Harry." Wrightwood looked Harry up and down, down and up, his smile rising like the sun on a clear morning. Then he opened up his mouth and yelped. "*Yah . . . hooooo!*"

Harry was interested in the old man who stood below him, watching his every move. Harry looked Wrightwood in the eye with compassion in his curiosity.

Nancy leaned close to the old man and whispered. "He's pretty smart. *George* even taught him to sit."

Wrightwood looked astonished. "*Sit?*" he repeated.

Harry sat. The chair couldn't take it. He sat on the floor. It made him just the right height for the dining room table.

"We're still perfecting it," George said.

Nancy filled a salad plate for Harry. "What kind of dressing do you want?" she asked, then set the salad plate aside and took Wrightwood's bouquet from the center of the table. She set it in front of Harry. "What the heck. Enjoy."

Harry was on his best behavior. Instead of stuffing the whole arrangment in his mouth at once, he delicately plucked the blossoms off, one by one, and savored them. He even chewed with his mouth closed.

"And he lives here with you?" Doc Wrightwood asked.

"It's only temporary," Sarah said.

37

It was night before that yo-yo Jerome showed up at the jail. All day, Jacques had been pacing like a caged animal, which was exactly what he was. After a while, he became accustomed to his own ripe garbage smell, but his fellow prisoners continued to give him a wide berth.

Jerome was turned out like the sissy Jacques always suspected he was—three-piece suit, dark tie and shiny shoes. He gave his disgruntled client a slick professional smile. "How are you?"

"How do you think I am?" Jacques growled. "Am I free to go?"

"Afraid not, LaFleur." Jerome deliberated. "If I call in a favor, I might be able to get you out sometime tonight."

It was all Jacques could do not to rip the bars off the holding pen. "Sometime tonight! It might be too late already—"

"But I'm going to need a darn good reason," Jerome informed him.

The man's head was made of wood. He had straw between his ears. It was probably a requirement to get into law school these days. Jacques roared at his lawyer. "*Sacré bleu*! I'm talking about bagging a Sasquatch!"

"Great," Jerome said. "Terrific, LaFleur. That ought to cut a lot of ice with the judge."

Jacques reached between the bars and grabbed his attorney's necktie. *"Get me out of here . . ."* He dropped his voice. "Or we'll see what I can cut besides ice." Jacques let go of the lawyer's tie.

Jerome looked flustered. "You're a wild man, LaFleur. But I'll see what I can do." The lawyer straightened his tie. "You do understand that there's an extra charge for night work?"

"Extortionist!" Jacques spat. Then he said, "I don't care what it costs. Just get me out."

38

"Hey! Watch this." Ernie tugged at Doc Wrightwood's sleeve. "Harry wants to show you how he can play Space Invaders."

"Ernie," his dad warned. "The doctor and I have important things to talk about."

"Please, Dad . . ."

Doc came through. He put his hand on Ernie's shoulder. "Show me. This I've got to see." He turned to Ernie's dad. "We've got all night, don't we?"

What could Dad say? Ernie took Wrightwood by the hand and led him to the living room, where Harry was waiting for them in front of the TV. Ernie turned on the game and installed the joystick in Harry's giant hand. Animated blips of spaceships cruised across the television screen. "Blast 'em, Harry!" Ernie urged. "You can do it, boy."

With grave concentration, Harry peered at the screen, his whole head following the moving graphics.

"Shoot! Now!"

Blam! Harry exploded an alien rocket.

"All right!" Ernie hugged him. They watched as Harry bagged two more invaders. "He's got great reflexes," Ernie told Doc. "It took him a while to figure out what you're supposed to do, but once he caught on, *Pow!*"

"'Bigfoot Shoots Spacemen,'" Doc said. "Now there's a headline for you."

"I wish he could join my soccer team," Ernie said. "Harry would make a great goalie. I bet nothing would get by him." Ernie liked the old guy his dad had invited home for dinner. He sort of wished they could keep him, too. Grandpa Henderson was too busy to spend any time with Ernie, and their other grandparents lived in Arizona now. They'd moved there for the sunshine, and Ernie hardly ever got to see them. Maybe the family could adopt Doc Wrightwood.

"Ernie, Harry, come over here. Now! It's time for dessert. Your dad's built a fire in the fireplace." Mom was on the warpath again.

Ernie was torn between wanting to finish the game and keep Doc to himself, and his mother's chocolate pie. She'd made one and hidden it in the dishwasher so Harry wouldn't find it in one of his refrigerator raids.

"Ernie!" his dad called.

Doc Wrightwood put his hand on Ernie's shoulder. "What do you say we see what's for dessert?" His voice dropped to a whisper. "It's got to be better than dinner."

"Yo. Come on, Harry. I think you're really gonna like this."

They joined the family at the coffee table in front of the fireplace. Ernie counted only three slices of chocolate pie. "Where's ours?" he asked.

"In the kitchen," Mom said. "Your dad and Doctor Wrightwood need to talk, Ernie. You kids take Harry out of the way and eat your dessert. Then I want you to get on with your homework."

"The kitchen?" Ernie couldn't believe they were sending him to the kitchen, just when things were getting interesting.

"Be glad I'm not making you do the dishes," Mom said.

Doc Wrightwood gave his mother a winning smile. "With all due respect, Mrs. Henderson—Nancy—why not let the boy stay? He might learn something."

"All right!" Ernie hollered.

The doctor turned to him. "And you, Ernie, you have to promise to be quiet and not interrupt." His voice was stern.

"I promise," Ernie said.

Both he and Doc looked at his mom. She nodded. "Okay, you can stay. As long as you're quiet."

Doc settled on the sofa and patted the cushion beside him. "You sit by me, where I can keep an eye on you." Ernie plopped down. Harry sat with his back against the wall. Sarah helped Mom serve pie and coffee. Harry gulped his pie and held out his plate for more. Mom said, "You wait until everyone else is done, Harry." The Bigfoot licked the last crumbs off his finger fur and sighed.

"How can I help you, George?" Doc asked Dad.

"I want to do the right thing," Dad said, "but it's not always easy to figure out just what that is."

Doc nodded. "That's the human condition, George. If we all agreed on what was right, well . . . we'd never disagree with each other. No fights. No wars." The old man looked at Harry. "I can't help wondering what *he* knows."

"He knows how to vacuum," Ernie said. "I taught him how this afternoon."

"Ernie, you promised," Sarah said.

"I know, but . . ."

Doc's glare shut Ernie up. "What he knows about living," Doc went on. "Think about it. Sasquatch is much bigger and more powerful than man. He may well be equally intelligent. But you haven't seen him building any bombs or starting any wars. In fact, he's lived peacefully in the forest for centuries, keeping out of sight while we've brought *our* race, and his, to the brink of disaster."

Suddenly, Doc turned to Sarah. "Why do you think that is?"

Sarah looked flustered. She played with her napkin. "Uh, maybe because he doesn't eat meat? Or watch television?"

Doc smiled at her. "Very good, Sarah." Ernie was glad Doc hadn't put him on the spot. "The fact is, we don't know why. It would sure be interesting to find out. It might even be important."

"That's what I've been thinking, Doc. There's so much Harry could teach us about . . . well, a lot of things. But I'm not exactly sure who's willing to learn," Dad said.

"Just so," Doc said.

Mom spoke up. "All this stuff you read about what they do to laboratory animals," she said. "It makes my blood run cold. What if they thought of Harry as just another dumb animal? We did, at first."

"On the other hand," Dad said, "what if Harry could help humans discover something they need to know, like a cure for cancer, or where we all came from?"

Doc nodded. "Even scientists, in their enthusiasm, sometimes overlook the obvious. And don't forget, Harry is a very *valuable* find. Imagine how much Ringling Brothers would pay to put him in the circus. Imagine what collectors would pay to own the only known stuffed Bigfoot."

Ernie looked at Harry. His big brow was wrinkled, as if he had a headache. He followed the conversation, keeping his eyes on the person who spoke. Ernie wondered if he understood. If he did, he had every reason to feel bad. Quietly, he got up from the sofa and slipped into the kitchen. There was about a third of the chocolate pie left. Ernie looked longingly at it, then took it in to Harry. "Here. This is for you." Harry stuck one big finger into the chocolate filling and offered it to Ernie. Ernie licked the chocolate off. "Thanks, Harry. Don't you worry. You can trust these guys." He nodded at his dad and Doc Wrightwood. "They'll figure out what's best." Ernie sat back down beside the doctor and tried to follow the conversation. His eyes were getting heavy. Ernie yawned.

George poured his heart out to Dr. Wrightwood. He told him all the thoughts and questions that had been running around his head for days. One by one, the kids conked out, Ernie first, then Sarah. Harry in his corner was starting to look drowsy. His yawns were big as caves.

"Poor Harry," Nan said. "You've had a big day. The trouble is, I don't know quite where to put you to bed." She got up from her armchair and stood beside Harry, patting his head.

"Harry's a woodland creature, you know," Doc said. "If you could build him some kind of nest, he'd probably feel right at home."

George thought a minute. "Say, Nan, how about those branches we trimmed from the tree in the yard? I haven't had a chance to take them to the dump yet." He looked at Doc. "We've gotten a little behind in household maintenance lately."

"They're behind the garage," Nan said. She took Harry's hand. "Come on, buddy. Let's make your bed."

"You want help, Nan?" George offered.

"No, you two talk. Harry and I can manage," she said. A few minues later, they were back, their arms full of branches. Harry looked questioningly at Nancy. She pointed to a corner near the fireplace. "How about over there?" Harry carried his branches to the corner and started to build his nest. Nancy laid her armload beside him.

"I don't know," George told the doctor, "after people caught on that Bigfoot was in town, they sort of went crazy. And when I saw all those bozos, armed to the teeth and eager to kill, well . . ." George shook his head. "Not ten days ago, I was just like them. Now, that's a sobering thought."

Doc nodded thoughtfully.

"The point is, Doc, if I thought everybody, I mean like, well, mankind in general, would learn what I have in the last week just from having Harry around, I wouldn't hesitate . . . but the way I see it, even the scientific community is gonna poke and prod him until he hates every man he sees, including you and me."

Doc looked at Harry peacefully reclined in his bed of boughs. "It's gonna be harder letting him go than it was finding him."

Nancy nodded. "We know."

"A safe place is the only answer," George said.

Doc Wrightwood stroked his chin. "I might just know one. But we'll never be able to find it at night."

George leaned forward. "Then you'll help us?"

"In every way I possibly can."

"Thank you," George said. "We'll head out first thing in the morning." Stretching his arms, he stood up. Gently, Nan roused the kids and sent them off to bed. Harry curled up in his bed of branches. George was about to offer their visitor the guest room when Wrightwood got up, stretched and headed out the front door without so much as a goodbye.

Nancy looked as confused as George felt. "What an odd man. No goodbyes, nothing."

"God," George said, "I don't even know what time he's coming back."

A few minutes later, they heard the doorknob rattle. A knock. "What the . . ." George opened the door. Wright-wood stood there with his camping gear, knapsack in one hand, a battered sleeping bag under his arm. The old man nodded to George and Nancy, then proceeded to unfurl his bedroll in the corner, right next to Harry's nest. Fully dressed, he climbed inside. "Time to catch some z's. Goodnight, all," Wrightwood said.

"Goodnight, Doctor. Goodnight, Harry." George switched off the living room light and followed his wife upstairs. With Harry safe and Wrightwood by his side, George was sure he would sleep soundly.

39

"Okay, you creeps! Wake up. It's time to go."

The voice of the police guard interrupted LaFleur's dreams of revenge. He woke on the hard floor of the holding pen. Around him, his cellmates sat up, cursing.

"You've been bailed out, all of you," the cop hollered. "Get a move on."

Jacques rose slowly to his feet, stiff from two nights of confinement. His fellow prisoners, most of them much younger then he was, beat him through the narrow door. Riffraff, all of them. Thirty-six hours in their company had only confirmed LaFleur's disdain for them. He elbowed his way through their ranks, into the lobby of the police station. His lawyer, Jerome, was flattened against the far wall to avoid being trampled in the stampede to freedom.

LaFleur confronted Jerome. "Some lawyer you are. Where have you been?"

His lawyer shrugged. "Nothing I could do. They weren't releasing anybody till they processed all the guns. There were a *lot* of guns." Jerome reeled backward, away from his client. "Whew! You stink. You sure could use a bath."

LaFleur had never had much use for lawyers, including

205

his own, or for the stupid games they played. "What? And blow my cover?" he said. He left his attorney gaping after him, to figure out just what *that* meant, and strode into the street.

40

The family learned something about Harry that night. He snored. *Harry snored big snores*. The house reverberated with them.

Doc Wrightwood, who slept like the dead, slept through them.

Sarah went to the bathroom and stuffed wads of surgical cotton in her ears.

George and Nancy put their pillows over their heads.

Ernie took direct action. When his dad snored, his mom just poked him until he rolled over on his side and stopped. Ernie figured the same might work with Harry. He grabbed his teddy bear, Max, and padded downstairs.

Sure enough, Harry was sleeping on his back. Carefully, Ernie stepped over Doc Wrightwood in his sleeping bag and lay down next to Harry. The bed was kind of itchy, with all those leaves. Ernie stuck his elbow in Harry's ribs. The rhythm in his snoring changed a little, but it didn't stop. Ernie poked again. Harry was out like a light. Ernie got to his knees and tried to roll Harry over, but he didn't budge. Finally, he found the solution. He dug his fingers into the thick hair over Harry's rib cage and tickled for all he was worth. It worked. Harry wrapped his arms around himself, turned over on his side and curled up in a ball. No more snoring. Ernie snuggled in beside him and fell asleep.

Screams shattered the early morning quiet.

Ernie sat up. Doc Wrightwood opened his eyes and peered at the unfamiliar surroundings. Harry did nothing. He wasn't there. "My God, he's gone," Doc said.

George and Nancy woke face to startled face. In unison, they jumped out of bed and ran to the bedroom window. Irene. She was waving her arms and hollering at her Oriental gardener. George opened the bedroom window. They both leaned out to listen, which wasn't hard. Irene was yelling at the top of her lungs.

"You killed them!" She was pointing at her prize rose bushes. Yesterday they had been covered wtih lush blooms. Now they were naked.

"No, no," the gardener protested. "Not me. Maybe it was Pig Foot."

"What's Pig Foot? Oh, my precious babies! What kind of Japanese gardener can't even take care of roses? That should be one of the first things you learn in Japan."

"I am Korean," Mr. Kimchee said.

"Don't try to worm your way out of this by changing your nationality, you . . . you . . ."

The little gardener stood right up to Irene. "I quit," he announced. He turned on his heel and marched toward his truck, parked in the alley.

Irene screamed after him. "Come back here, you Third World rose killer!"

Mr. Kimchee did not turn back. Shaking his head, he climbed into the cab of his pickup.

"You blew it, mister," Irene yelled at his exhaust. "I gave you a chance to be Japanese."

Chuckling softly, George closed the window.

Mrs. Moffitt's screams penetrated the cotton Sarah had stuffed in her ears. She pulled it out and listened to their neighbor. Sarah wondered what had her so upset this time.

Pale sunshine crept through the curtains. Sarah sat up on her elbows. Her bedside clock said it was a few minutes before six.

Without a sound, her bedroom door swung open. Harry crept in. On his arm he carried Mom's wicker basket. It overflowed with roses, beautiful roses, all in full bloom. Walking softly, Harry approached Sarah's bed. He took a red rose from his basket and held it out to her.

Sarah took the rose and buried her nose in its soft petals, enjoying the perfume. "It's beautiful," she said. "Thank you." Sarah looked up from the rose blossom. "I'm sorry I yelled at you . . . Harry."

Harry seemed to have forgiven her for her lecture and all the remarks about his smell. He took another rose, a yellow one, from the basket, smelled it briefly, then ate the flower.

"Don't swallow the thorns," Sarah warned him.

41

Having been bailed out himself, Jacques found he had to bail out his powerwagon, too. The cops had impounded it. It took his last dime to get his car back. Once he did, he headed one more time for the home of the mysterious George Henderson. There would be no mistakes this time.

Well, not many. It was a mistake to take the freeway. The entire first shift at Boeing was on its way to work. LaFleur was stuck in the procession turtling its way toward factories and engineering offices. Lying on his horn didn't make traffic move faster, but it did relieve some of his frustration. Soon other drivers were honking back at him. A loud wail rose from the freeway.

At last he arrived in the Hendersons' neighborhood. LaFleur parked across the street and took his rifle, also ransomed from the city authorities, from its rack in the rear window. No, better not show all his cards right off. He covered the rifle with a blanket and climbed out of the cab.

Darn! Wally Wrightwood's battered panel van sat in the Hendersons' driveway. The old fool had gotten here before him. As LaFleur stood there, a motley pack of dogs ran full speed around the side of the Hendersons' house. They almost knocked him over. Seconds later, they were gone. Stealthily, Jacques approached the house.

The back was safest. No sense in letting neighbors spot

him snooping and call the cops. Jacques had had more than enough of the police recently. He flattened himself against the house and moved cautiously toward the rear. Something colorful, perhaps significant, caught his eye. He stooped and picked up a broken rose blossom. Another lay beside it, and another. LaFleur examined them, then tossed them, all but one, away.

Irene returned from her early morning foray to the all-night grocery. She wasn't really going to start overeating again—she'd only bought enough goodies to soothe her frayed nerves. She deserved a sugar fix. It wasn't every day some villain stole your whole crop of prize roses, after all. Her prune juice and squid cocktail stood on the counter. Irene dumped it in the sink and began to stuff her purchases into the blender. Twinkies, a Sara Lee cheesecake, a bag of M&Ms, a couple of Ding Dongs and two packages of Nerds. She hit the whizzer and turned it all into one giant sucrose cocktail. Straight out of the shaker, she took a long swallow and immediately felt the welcome rush. AAAAAHHHHH!!

Irene was about to take another pull when the flicker of something past the window caught her eye. She pulled back the curtain in time to see the same ruffian who'd turned up on Nancy's doorstep a few days ago sneaking past with a handful of roses. *Her roses*.

So it wasn't Mr. Kimchee, after all. Poor man. She'd have to call him later to apologize. Now she was going to catch a thief. In the utensil drawer, she found the battery-operated carving knife she'd given Herb two Christmases ago, took another long swig of straight vodka, and prepared to confront the vicious brutalizer of her roses.

Between them, the family and their guests put away a dozen eggs and a whole loaf of raisin bread, toasted, while

Doc and George discussed a safe place for Harry. Wright-wood pushed his empty plate aside. "Sure would be a dream come true if we could keep him."

"You know what they say . . . the best things in life are supposed to be free."

"You make that up?" Doc asked.

George realized he was being teased. Profundity had never been his strong suit. He smiled. "No. But I'm starting to believe it." Harry picked up the discarded breakfast plates and one by one licked them clean with his tongue, then passed them to Nancy at the dishwasher. Suddenly, something outside the window caught his attention. Beside it, he tensed.

LaFleur crept up to what he guessed must be the kitchen window. The window was covered, but a thin pencil of space showed between the curtains. Jacques moved closer and pressed one eye against the glass.

"Hold it right there, mister," a female voice behind him said.

LaFleur spun around to find a wild-eyed woman in curlers and wearing a flowered housecoat. She waved a knife at him.

"One false move and I'll prune your plant, fella. And I am talking *nip it in the bud*."

LaFleur was an experienced tracker, he had encountered many dangers in the woods, but this crazed housewife struck fear into his heart.

Conversation stopped when they heard Irene's voice. It sounded like it came from just outside the kitchen window. Harry stood by the sink, his head cocked, listening. Then he growled, a low grumble deep in his throat, and reached out his long arm to part the curtains. Pressing his face against the window, Harry bared his teeth and roared.

• • •

Irene was relieved when she saw her neighbors' curtains
open. They would see she needed help. She raised her face
to the window, expecting to see George or Nancy there. A
snarling monster stared back at her. Irene threw back her
head and screamed. The neighborhood dog pack gathered,
leaping, at her ankles and bayed at the Hendersons'
window.

George pulled Harry aside and looked out the window.
He drew the curtains closed. "LaFleur!" he said.

Doc Wrightwood peeked out the window at his old
colleague. Harry strained toward the window, teeth bared,
growling. George held his arm, talking softly. "Easy now,
Harry, it's okay, boy." He could feel the power tensed in the
big arm.

Doc Wrightwood headed for the kitchen door. "I'll go
out and talk to Jock. You keep our friend in here. He'll be
perfectly safe as long as he's inside."

With one swift thrust, Harry pulled away from George.
Without stopping to open it, he smashed through the kitchen
door and into the yard. The door splintered with a
thunderous crash.

Irene jumped at the sound of a terrible commotion. Her
adversary took advantage of her surprise and reached out to
take the knife away from her. No way, Jose. Irene felt for
the switch and turned her weapon on. She brandished it at
the rose-killer.

Then the monster appeared again. No doubt about it—a
genuine gigantic snarling growling *angry* monster appeared
in the Hendersons' backyard. Paralyzed by fear, Irene
watched as the monster stilled the yapping dogs with one
stern glance, then sicced them on the rose thief. Teeth

bared, they rushed to do his bidding. The creep was trapped.

Doc couldn't help smiling when he found his old antagonist surrounded by the pooch patrol.

"It's not fair!" LaFleur shouted. "You gave up the search. He should be *mine*."

To LeFleur, Doc said, "He should be *free*." To George, he said, "What do you say we hit the road? We'll take my van."

"Sounds good," George said. "Come on, everybody. Let's go!" Wrightwood, the Hendersons and Harry all ran for the van. The family scrambled in, and Doc raced the engine while Harry's canine disciples held LaFleur at bay on the lawn. Little Bob leapt through Nancy's open window onto her lap. Harry sat up and customized Doc Wrightwood's van with a Bigfoot dome. Squealing the tires, Doc backed out of the driveway.

"All right!" Ernie said.

Doc stopped the van directly across the street. He opened his door and hopped out. "You drive, George."

"What's he doing?" Nancy asked. "Isn't he coming with us?"

Ernie stared wide-eyed out the window. "Look at that," he said. The family looked. Doc was plunging his pocket knife deep into the tires of LaFleur's pickup. They deflated on the spot. When LaFleur's truck was effectively crippled, Doc hopped in back with Harry, and George sped away.

LaFleur watched his tires melt slowly into the street. There was nothing he could do until the pack of dogs took off after Wrightwood's van. "Damn you, Wally! This isn't over yet," LaFleur shouted after them. He looked wildly around. To change his tires would take an hour. Besides, he only had one spare. Then his eyes lit on the Hendersons' station wagon in the garage. It looked like a wreck, but it if ran, Jacques was prepared to borrow it. He grabbed his rifle from the pickup, then climbed into the station wagon. Someone had obligingly left the keys in the ignition.

Jacques roared away.

Irene watched him go. So the rose thief was a car thief, too. She regretted not carving him up like a leg of lamb. Irene raised her fist and shook it at the retreating station wagon. "You won't get by with this, you creep!" she yelled. "I've got your license number!"

42

Doc's panel van did fine at thirty, but once George put it in the third, the whole rig shuddered. "Uh, what year did you say this thing was, Doc?" George called over his shoulder.

"Tell the truth, I don't quite remember. Let's see . . . I think I bought her back in '48. Or was it '50?"

"Jeez," Ernie said. "Your van is three times older than me."

"Something like that," Doc said. "Don't worry, George. There's life in the old girl yet."

George hoped so. They were hitting Highway 99, bound for the interstate. Once they hit a fast road, the dogs thought better of following. In the mirror, George watched them one by one give up the chase. A ragged file of panting dogs lined the emergency lane behind them. "Well, we lost the mutts," he told them. "Hope they can find their way home."

Earnie looked back as the van sped on. He spotted a station wagon with two major head wounds, gaining on them from behind. "Uh-oh. Don't look now, but I think we're being followed by our own car."

A glance in the side mirror confirmed it. The station wagon zipped lane to lane, barely escaping collisions on all sides. From the rear, Harry growled at it. George wasn't sure whether he was reacting to the wagon or to LaFleur.

Traffic slowed in front of him and George checked to see if it was safe to maneuver left. As he pulled parallel to the car in the next lane, a small boy in the passenger seat spotted Harry in the van. His mother, driving, turned her head for a quick look and almost broadsided them. George wrestled the steering wheel, the van escaped with a scratch.

"All right, Dad!" Ernie cheered. "You're driving like an escaped psycho."

The I-5 South entrance appeared on their right, and George took it before he realized the freeway was having one of its bad days. Too many cars, too little road. Traffic was moving at about 40 and slowing steadily. He was no sooner installed in the slow lane then a police siren wailed behind him. Its red and blue lights flashed and spun, growing larger in the rearview. Obediently, the cars in George's lane pulled over to yield the right of way.

"Is he after us, Dad?" Sarah asked.

"I'm not sure."

They waited in silence as the police car came even and sped by. "Whew!" Ernie said. "That was a close one." The impromptu lane the cop car traveled closed up again. They were even more stuck than before. Behind them, their station wagon bounced out of the slow lane onto the shoulder and picked up speed.

"Hey! What's he doing to my car?"

Everyone in the van turned to watch Lafleur and the station wagon jolt closer. Traffic moved at a snail's pace. There was no escape. That is, until Harry stuck his head out the window and let fly with an ear-splitting roar.

"Wow, Dad," Ernie said, "he sounds just like a cop car." Ernie was right. Their fellow motorist were convinced. Again, they pulled aside, creating a temporary fast lane for the police. "Keep it up, Harry," George yelled as he pulled into the opening and floored it. The van stalled for an instant, then farted out a massive backfire that left most of the exhaust system lying in the road. A trail of blue-white smoke poured from the rear end as they raced up the freeway. "Eat that, Jocko," Doc called out his window as traffic filled in behind them.

South of the city, traffic eased and the van picked up speed. There was no sign of the station wagon behind them when they hit the Mount Rainier turnoff just north of Tacoma. "We did it!" George exclaimed. "That sucker's history."

"Don't kid yourself," Doc said. "This is the part he's good at."

LaFleur had still not caught up by the time Doc directed them off the main highway onto a logging road. "Home-free, Doc," George said hopefully. "Aren't we?"

"Don't count on it," Wrightwood said. "Remember, I've known Jock for thirty years, more or less. There are lots of things you can call him, but quitter's not one of them."

"Step on it, Dad," Ernie advised.

"I am," George said. He was almost used to the shudder by now.

Nancy started the family singing "Ninety-nine Bottles of Beer on the Wall," to ease the tension. Harry growled along, keeping time. He seemed to enjoy the song.

When they got down to fifty-one bottles of beer on the wall, Doc hollered "Stop! Stop! We just passed it." George slammed on the brakes and backed up.

"I always miss the turnoff. It's real hard to spot," Doc said.

George said. "That's a good sign."

Doc peered out the window. "Here it is," he said. The van bounced into the forest. Ernie pointed out the window. "Look at that! It's already snowed up here."

"Yeah, it's freezing," Sarah said.

George turned on the heater, which, amazingly enough, still worked.

"Forty-six bottles of beer on the wall," the family chorus chirped.

"Thirty-nine bottles of beer."

At twenty-eight, Doc told them they were there. The family piled out of the van. "How you wanna handle this, George?" Doc asked.

George signed. "We've got to get Harry off in the woods, away from LaFleur. And us." He turned to Harry. The Bigfoot's face was sad. George moved closer. "You understand, Harry? You've got to go back to where you belong. You're in danger here."

Abruptly, Harry's eyes, which had been fixed on George's, rose. Seconds later, the humans, too, picked up the sound. It was the station wagon. The family converged on Harry, urging him to run, shoo, scat, blow this popstand now. George looked over his shoulder, then turned back to Harry. "Go, Harry! Run!" He pointed back down the road. "Danger! LaFleur! Hunter!"

Harry understood danger. He wanted to protect them from it. He stood his ground and growled. Then he started down the road himself. George planted a restraining hand on Harry's chest. "No. Please."

It was hopeless. Not only was Harry huge, he was hugely loyal. George hardened his heart and his expression. "Get out of here. Can't you see we don't want you anymore," he yelled at Harry. "Go back to where you came from."

Slowly, Harry looked at the faces of the family, one by one.

"Leave us alone!" George hollered. Then he slapped Harry squarely across the face. Harry's immediate response was anger. George watched as it melted into a deep sadness. George's heart ached inside him. "Go! Go!" he screamed at his friend.

Harry stepped back from George, then turned and walked toward the woods. After a few steps, he turned back to George. His face was sad and hopeful.

George turned his back on Harry. Under his breath, his voice breaking, he whispered, "Goodbye, my friend."

In silence, the family watched Harry disappear among the trees. Ernie sniffed loudly. Nancy looked down and saw his tears. Her own were fighting to come out. "Ernie, stop that right now." Neither she nor Ernie could stop. They cried. George hugged them both.

Sarah was dry-eyed but her face was sad. She said what everyone else was thinking. "We'll never see him again, will we?"

Ernie pulled out of his father's embrace. His face brightened. "Sure we will. We can just follow his footprints." He pointed at the snow around them.

"Oh, my God," George said.

"The footprints," Doc said.

Ernie said, "Yeah, right there. See? They're clear as a bell."

And so they were.

43

LaFleur never doubted he would find them, not with the engine-spoor, that blue-white smoke, to guide him. Even when it faded from sight, its stench lingered in the air. Jacques had an educated nose. He saluted the decrepitude of Wally Wrightwood's ancient van.

In the station wagon, he followed them off I-5, at the Mount Rainer turnoff, then onto a smaller logging road, the same one where he'd first found evidence of the accident. They were returning to the scene of the crime. Time to be alert. His eyes combed the dense forest on either side of the road. Windows down, he sniffed the air as he drove.

Just as expected, the smoke showed him the way. He switched back onto a turnoff he'd never seen before. Here tire marks on the wet ground collaborated with the smoke. He followed until he found the place they'd stopped.

Grabbing his rifle, Jacques climbed out of the car. A confusion of human tracks and—yes, a set of Bigfoot prints in the snow. Clear as a map, they led him into the forest. He cocked his gun.

About a hundred yards into the trees, LaFleur detected something curious—another set of Bigfoot prints crossed those he followed. A meeting? A welcome home? The thought of more than one Sasquatch exhilarated him. He followed the second set of tracks until they deadended in a dry patch.

Looking around, he spotted a third set of giant footprints. Could there be three? He followed closely. Another hundred yards, and one set of tracks branched into two. Two multiplied to four. They came and went in all directions.

LaFleur took off his hat and scratched his head. His brain was reeling. Bigfoot musk teased his nose.

"It's a darn herd," the tracker said. He was so intent on mayhem he never thought to be afraid.

Harry reclined in the top of a tall cedar. It was good to be home. When he stretched out his arms, the forest birds came to roost on them. The birds tittered in his ears. They seemed glad to have him back.

From his treetop, Harry could just see his friends in the distance, still playing their strange game. With peculiar, heavy tools tied to their feet, they were wandering this way and that through the woods. Harry picked a place to rest where he could keep an eye on them.

The tracks were everywhere. Usually, Jacques could read animal prints like a book, but this tale had no plot. No sooner did he run one way, thinking he'd made sense of it at last, than the tracks stopped, or separated, or simply disappeared. His grip on reality was beginning to slip. Would Bigfoot drive him mad?

Wait! Something white that wasn't snow lay on the ground. LaFleur crouched to study it. When he examined it, the object in his palm turned out to be a giant plaster toe. Suddenly the mystery made sense. Jacques muttered every oath in his vocabulary of curses.

Behind him, a crow cawed and clattered into flight. Startled, Jacques turned toward the sound. There, in the bushes, a giant figure loomed. Bigfoot had been watching, mocking him. LaFleur raised the rifle to his shoulder and fired, point-blank, at the giant form.

LaFleur edged closer to examine his handiwork, close enough to discover his target was two-dimensional, a mere cartoon. With a hole through the middle of his silly grin, a plywood moose advised Jacques to MAKE A FRIEND IN THE FOREST.

Jacques kicked the figure over and stomped on it. As he did, a small dog ran out of the forest and attacked his pants leg. LaFleur aimed his rifle at the pest but couldn't get a clear shot that didn't have his own foot in it. He set his rifle aside and pried the wretched creature from his leg.

When Little Bob appeared and attacked his enemy, Harry decided it was time to intervene. Silently he slid down the tree trunk and dropped to the ground. The creature was too busy fighting Little Bob to see him. When he threw Little Bob into the air, Harry slammed his foot down and felt the rifle break. The male reached for the small gun on his belt. Harry seized him by the pants and hoisted him into the air. He dropped his pistol and cried out in pain.

A shot boomed, not far away. "Harry!" George struggled toward the sound. Wrightwood struggled after him. The heavy, awkward castings made speed impossible. George tripped over a tree root and toppled over. When he got up, he smashed his plaster feet against a tree. Wrightwood did the same. They ran.

Little Bob's frenzied barking guided them to a small clearing. The station wagon was parked there. Harry stood on its roof, while LaFleur lay unmoving beneath him. George ran toward them. "Oh, no! Harry! Oh, God, no!"

Harry looked at George with a proud smile. While Harry wasn't looking, LaFleur slid off the car. He approached the family, begging, "Help me. Please don't let it kill me."

"Listen to me," George said. "Please. You're wrong. I was like you. I almost killed him. But it would have been murder. He's not an animal."

Nancy said simply, "He's our friend, Mr. LaFleur."

Doc said, "For heaven's sake, Jock. Open your eyes!"

LaFleur said, "You people are crazy. This is an animal. It could turn on you without warning."

Without warning, all the excitement, the confusion and frustration of the past week boiled up inside George and exploded. He turned on the tracker. Seizing him by the shirt front, he slammed LaFleur into the car again and again. "We won't let you harm him," George yelled. "You don't understand. We can't let you go!"

For a moment, the rest of the family stared numbly at George. Harry looked shocked. "George stop!" Nancy pleaded. Then she turned to the Bigfoot. "Harry, please?"

Harry sprang into action. He put one huge hand behind LaFleur's head, to buffer it from bashing. With the other, he pushed George away. Sternly, he shook his head. No, George.

LaFleur was half mad with fear. "Stop him! Don't let him kill me! Please. Stop him."

Gently, Harry stroked LaFleur's head, as he had seen Nancy do with Little Bob. LaFleur gazed into Harry's face. His voice grew quiet, almost meek. "Please don't let him kill me?"

Harry snuggled LaFleur against his massive chest. Slowly, the tracker relaxed in his embrace. His expression grew tranquil. Watching them, the family began to breathe easier.

When LaFleur was calm, Harry released him. Backing away, LaFleur reached out a timid hand and touched Harry. He turned to the family.

"I'm so sorry. I had no idea. I feel like such a . . . !"

The Frenchman's accent deleted the "h" from his last word. It sounded just like "sit."

Eager to please, Harry sat. He sat on the station wagon. What was left of the body crumpled. George heard his axles crack.

"He's got it down now, Dad!" Ernie exclaimed.

44

Jacques stood by while Wally Wrightwood took a picture of Bigfoot with his friends, the Hendersons. This was hardly how Jacques had expected Sasquatch to be shot. After the shutter clicked, the family portrait dissolved into a group hug.

"Well, Doc," Jacques said, "I guess it's over."

"Over?" Wally said. "Jocko, I haven't felt the old ticker thump like this in years. It's like going to heaven with your feet still on the ground." Doc looked at Harry, then back to Jacques. "And we get to share it with one of our oldest friends. What are you going to do, Jock?"

The fact is, Jacques had no idea what to do. His life's mission had just evaporated. Funny thing, though. It didn't really bother him. He shrugged and shot Doc something like a smile. "Well, there's always Loch Ness." He even liked it when Wally laughed.

Even more than he hated kissing, Ernie hated goodbyes. He could tell from the heavy, sort-of-damaged way he felt inside that this was really going to be one. Harry was going back to the forest. Before he went, Dad made a little speech. "I guess this really is goodbye, Harry. I never really got to thank you. You'll never know . . . of course you know what you've meant to us."

Ernie could hear his Dad's voice crack. He was glad it wasn't him talking. He would have been bawling by now.

"You take care of yourself now, okay?" Dad said.

Harry reached out and pulled Dad up close. He patted him on the back. Then Harry said, "Okay!"

Old Doc Wrightwood almost fell over. "I can't believe it. They have a language!"

Dad nodded at Harry and Harry nodded back. With a smile, he turned toward the woods. Ernie moved close enough to put his arm around his dad. His mom put her arm around him. "We're the luckiest people on the planet," his dad whispered, in a voice that sounded all choked up. The whole family watched Harry walk away.

Except he didn't really walk away. He just went a little bit into the woods, and then something they thought was a tree moved up to him, and then another tree moved, and they were really Bigfoots and Harry had a family. He led his wife and his kid back to meet the Hendersons. For a little bit, the two families just stood there, staring at each other, with the dads out front. Then Harry started to walk toward Dad, and Dad walked toward Harry and then, when they met in the middle, they hugged each other tight.

EPILOGUE
AND THEN WHAT HAPPENED?

Well, ladies and gentlemen, boys and girls, what happened then is everybody changed.

The biggest change was that Wally Wrightwood and Jacques LaFleur buried the hatchet and became friends. The Bigfoot mania brought so much business to Doc's museum that Jacques agreed to help him out for a while. He moved into one of the old housetrailers and eventually fixed it up so it was habitable. What the two old bachelors found was that they had more in common with each other than anybody else. They enjoyed each other's company. They liked each other's cooking. They gave each other the courage to go to Grange Hall on Saturday night and dance with pretty widows. Both of them were too single-minded, and too shy, to go before.

With the profits from the Bigfoot bonanza, they built themselves a little cabin in the woods, close to the place they left off Harry, near where the Hendersons built theirs. When things are slow at the store, they take to the woods. Harry and his family visit them. So do George and his.

Obsession dies hard, of course, but now the two old dream-chasers have a new cause. Having discovered that Bigfoot really does exist, they're fighting to have him added to the endangered species list. Any day now, they expect a

Congressional delegation to visit the Mount Rainier National Forest to meet Harry for themselves.

After her encounter with Harry and Jacques LaFleur, Irene Moffitt swore off junk food for good. She made Herb build her a greenhouse to protect her roses, took up exercise and gave up diets. She is now a fully licensed instructor of aquatic aerobics. Being busy, she no longer haunts the Hendersons' kitchen. When they get together for lunch or to play cards, George and Nancy are actually glad to see her.

The story of how George Henderson finessed his midlife crisis and became a celebrated painter of Northwest wildlife is a little bit less simple. It didn't happen overnight.

First, Nancy got a part-time job for the Seattle Horticultural Society, tending the rare plants in the Conservatory at Volunteer Park. That brought in enough money for George to go part-time at the sporting goods store. Yes, his father took him back. Despite George's eccentricities, George was the best salesman he had.

The half days he spent at home, George painted. He painted like a man obsessed.

His first one-man show, held at the Northwest Anthropological Institute and Bigfoot Museum, coincided with the publication of the last installment of Jacques LaFleur's Bigfoot memoirs. It was a huge success. Every one of his paintings sold. Critics compared George's sensitive portraits of Bigfoot favorably with Albert Bierstadt's buffalo. He began to get commissions. The Washington State Arts Commission gave him a grant. George quit his job. His father professes interest in his career.

The change in Sarah was dramatic. Her interest in Michael Jackson waned. She replaced posters of her former idol with wildlife posters. She got an after-school job at the office of the neighborhood veterinarian, to gain a little firsthand experience in her chosen field. She joined the Animal Protection League and got arrested picketing the

Animal Experimentation Laboratory at the University of Washington. While picketing she met a high school senior with similar interests and began her first real relationship with a member of the opposite sex. The Hendersons were proud to bail their daughter out of the city jail.

And Ernie? Well, boys will be boys. He's in the fifth grade. He still plays baseball. He still torments his older sister. He still sleeps with Max, the teddy bear. He's still fiercely proud of his father. He proved it by getting a black eye in a fight with Frankie McDowell because Frankie said something about artists being wimps and Ernie insisted that he take it back. Ernie won the fight. Frankie went home with two black eyes and a fat lip. His dad got mad at him for fighting.

Ernie's very favorite thing of all are the vacations when the family packs up their new mini-van and heads for the forest to visit their friends Doc and Jacques and Harry. The last time they stayed for three weeks. Ernie taught Harry how to say "awesome." Harry taught Ernie how to catch fish with his hands. Doc and Jacques have invited Ernie to spend all of the next summer in the woods with them. Ernie is already trying to get his parents to agree. In part, he does this by being annoying around the house.

Harry is known among his kind as The One Who Left the Forest. He is glad to have gone, and glad to be back home. Now he has the best of both worlds. Except perhaps for eating, there is nothing Harry enjoys more than watching his mate and his friend's mate gather flowers in the meadows, or his son and his friend's son running together through the woods, or of an evening sitting with his friend beside the lake.

POIGNANT AND UNFORGETTABLE
NOVELS BY TODAY'S FOREMOST
* WOMEN WRITERS *
OF QUALITY FICTION!

168